SACRED READING

The 2018 Guide to
Daily Prayer

"*Sacred Reading* offers a superb introduction to Ignatian prayer that anyone can use. Too often Ignatian prayer is seen as something reserved only for Jesuits, for people trained in the Spiritual Exercises, or for those who have time for a directed retreat. But this book, created by experts in the traditions of Ignatian prayer, helps the reader to encounter Jesus through short scripture passages, inviting questions, and accessible reflections. It's an innovative way to be invited, with gentle wisdom, into meeting Jesus in your prayer."

Rev. James Martin, S.J.
Author of *Jesus: A Pilgrimage*

"I encourage anyone looking to deepen their prayer life to spend time learning this ancient practice, and to come to know a God who dances freely in our imaginations if we will but go there with him."

Tim Muldoon
Author of *The Discerning Parent*

"Communion with God increases dramatically as we grow in knowledge of God's Word. For most people the problem is simply getting started: determining where to begin. A most ancient and venerable practice is lectio divina, scripture reading that is meditation and contemplation but also application. *Sacred Reading* is an uncommonly useful tool in really getting into scripture in just this way."

Rev. Michael White and Tom Corcoran
Authors of *Rebuilt*

"In just six simple steps, *Sacred Reading* opens our minds and hearts to scripture in refreshing and profound ways. The daily meditations are clear and concise and yet filled with wisdom and promise. Reading scripture daily is good; reading scripture daily with *Sacred Reading* as your guide is awesome."

Marge Fenelon
Author of *Imitating Mary*

"This guide through the gospel texts of the daily lectionary offers a fully-embodied experience that includes the mind, heart, imagination, desire, and behavior. This way of prayerfully reading the gospels as the Spirit-empowered Word of God shows us how to open our lives to be continually formed in Christ."

Stephen J. Binz
Speaker and author of *Transformed by God's Word*

"In his apostolic exhortation *The Joy of the Gospel,* Pope Francis invites us to be people of prayer. *Sacred Reading* is an excellent aid in responding to that invitation. This book offers a clear, helpful, and inspirational guide to deepen our love for scripture as we ponder God's Word and live it out in our daily lives."

Most Rev. Robert F. Morneau
Auxiliary Bishop Emeritus of Green Bay

"*Sacred Reading* is the perfect companion for the lectio journey."

Sonja Corbitt
Author of *Unleashed*

"*Sacred Reading* has become a friend in prayer. I find the format particularly engaging as it inspires me to reflect on the Word of God in a prayerful, practical, and personal way."

Hilda Walter
Administrative assistant at Gesu Parish
University Heights, Ohio

"*Sacred Reading* is an invaluable companion that helps you cultivate the daily habit of praying with scripture. Learn about God, talk to him, listen to his special message for you, and rest in his presence using the engaging lectio divina format."

Lillian Moore
High school and adult faith formation catechist
St. Joseph Catholic Church
Honey Creek, Texas

"*Sacred Reading* is an indispensable resource in deepening your prayer and devotional life. Lectio divina will change how you see your relationships—with the Lord, with others, and with yourself. Highly recommended!"

Most Rev. David L. Ricken
Bishop of Green Bay

SACRED READING

The 2018 Guide to Daily Prayer

Apostleship of Prayer
The Pope's Worldwide Prayer Network

Douglas Leonard

Ave Maria Press Notre Dame, Indiana

Founded in 1865, Ave Maria Press is a ministry of the United States Province of Holy Cross.

www.avemariapress.com

Paperback: ISBN-13 978-1-59471-773-4

E-book: ISBN-13 978-1-59471-774-1

Cover design by Katherine J. Ross.

Text design by David Scholtes.

Printed and bound in the United States of America.

CONTENTS

INTRODUCTION

Christians throughout the world are rediscovering a powerful, ancient form of prayer known as *sacred reading*, also called "lectio divina," which invites communion with God through scripture reading and contemplation. What better way to deepen one's friendship with Jesus Christ, the Word of God, than by prayerfully encountering him in the daily gospel reading? This book will set you on a personal prayer journey with Jesus from the start of Advent in December 2017 through the end of Ordinary Time in December 2018: the entire Church year.

Sacred reading is a spiritual practice that, guided by the Holy Spirit, invites you to interact with the words of the daily gospel. As you read and pray this way, you may find—as many others have—that the Lord speaks to you in intimate and surprising ways. The reason for this is simple: as we open our hearts to Jesus, he opens his heart to us.

St. Paul prays beautifully for his readers:

> For this reason I kneel before the Father, from whom every family in heaven and on earth is named, that he may grant you in accord with the riches of his glory to be strengthened with power through his Spirit in the inner self, and that Christ may dwell in your hearts through faith; that you, rooted and grounded in love, may have strength to comprehend with all the holy ones what is the breadth and length and height and depth, and to know the love of Christ that surpasses knowledge, so that you may be filled with all the fullness of God. (Eph 3:14–19)

This book moves you through each day's gospel by prompting you at each step of lectio divina, getting you started with reading, observing, praying, listening, and resolving to act. But most important is your own response to the Word and to the Spirit, for that is how you will grow in your relationship with Jesus. If you are sincerely seeking God, the Holy Spirit will lead you in this process.

How to Use This Book

The *Sacred Reading* prayer book is intended to guide your prayerful reading during the entire Church year. (Small booklets, suitable for use in parish groups, are also available for Advent and Lent.) Each weekday reflection begins with the date, and some include a reference to the solemnity or feast on that day for which there is a special lectionary gospel reading. When these are indicated, the regular lectionary gospel reading for that day has been replaced with the gospel reading used to celebrate the solemnity or feast. Sunday reflections include both the date and its place in the liturgical calendar; any Sunday reading that includes a reference to a feast day rather than its place in the liturgical calendar uses the gospel reading for the feast day. For the sake of simplicity, other feast days are not cited when their gospel reading has not been used. Due to the length of the gospel readings during Lent, some have been shortened. The citation for shortened readings will first show the reading that is included in the book and will then show the citation for the day's complete reading in parentheses.

In prayerful reading of the daily gospels throughout the year—including feast days, days during the high seasons, and days in Ordinary Time—you join your prayers with those of believers all over the world. Each day you will be invited to reflect on the gospel text for the day in six simple but profound steps:

1. Know that God is present with you and ready to converse.

At all times God is everywhere, including where you are in this very moment. The human mind is incapable of fully grasping the mystery of God, but we do know some things about God from scripture. God is the transcendent ground of all being: invisible, eternal, and infinite in power. God is Love, with infinite love for you and me. God is one with and revealed through the Word, Jesus Christ, who became flesh. Through him all things were made, and by him and for him all things subsist. Jesus is the Way, the Truth, and the Life. He says that those who know him also know his Father. Through the Passion, Death, and Resurrection of Jesus, we are reconciled with God. If we believe in Jesus Christ, we become the sons and daughters of Almighty God.

God gives us the Holy Spirit to lead us to truth and understanding. The Holy Spirit also gives us power to live in obedience to the teachings of Jesus. The Holy Spirit draws us to prayer, and works in us as we pray. No wonder we come into God's presence with gladness! All God's ways are good and beautiful. We can get to know God better by encountering God in the Word, which is Jesus himself.

The prayer prompt at the beginning of each day's reading is just that: a prompt, something to get you started. In fact, all the elements in the process of sacred reading are meant to prompt you to your own conversations with God. After reading the prompt, feel free to continue to pray in your own words: respond in your own way, pray in your own way, and hear God speaking to you personally. The goal is to make sacred reading your own prayer time each day.

2. Read the gospel.

The entire Bible is the Word of God, but the gospels (Matthew, Mark, Luke, and John) contain the story of Jesus' life, his teachings, his works, his Passion and Death on the cross, his Resurrection on the third day, and his Ascension into heaven. Because of this, the Sacred Reading series (the prayer books as well as the seasonal booklets for Advent / Christmas and Lent / Easter) concentrates on praying with the daily gospel readings.

The gospels interpret Jesus' ministry for us. Much more, by the Holy Spirit, we can find in the gospels the very person of Jesus Christ. Prayerful reading of the daily gospel is an opportunity to draw close to the Lord: Father, Son, and Holy Spirit. As we pray with the gospels, we can be transformed by the grace of God, enlightened, strengthened, and moved. Seek to read each day's gospel passage with a complete openness to what God is saying to you. Many who pray with the daily gospel recommend rereading the gospel passage several times.

3. Notice what you think and feel as you read the gospel.

Sacred reading can involve every faculty—mind, heart, emotions, soul, spirit, sensations, imagination, and much more—though usually not all at once. Different passages touch different keys in us. Sometimes we may laugh. Sometimes we may need to stop and worship before we continue. Sometimes we will be puzzled, amazed, stung, abashed, reminded of something lovely, or reminded of something we had wanted to forget.

Seek to feel all of your emotions as you read. Apply your intellect, too. You will confront problems of context and exegesis on a daily basis. That's okay. Sometimes you may experience very little. That's okay, too. God is always at work. Give yourself to the gospel reading and take from it what is there for you each day.

Most important, notice what in particular jumps out at you: it may be a word, a phrase, a character, an image, a pattern, an emotion, a sensation—some arrow to your heart. Whatever it is, pay attention to it, because the Holy Spirit is using it to accomplish something in you.

Sometimes a particular gospel passage repeats during the liturgical year of the Church. To pray through the same gospel passage even on successive days presents no problem whatsoever to your sacred reading. St. Ignatius of Loyola, founder of the Jesuits and author of *The Spiritual Exercises,* actually recommends repeated meditation on passages of scripture. Read in the Spirit, gospel passages have unlimited potential to reveal to us the truths we are ready to receive. The Word of God has boundless power to illuminate and transform the prayerful believer.

4. Pray as you are led for yourself and others.

Praying is simply talking with God. Believe God hears you. Believe God will answer you. Believe God knows what you need even before you ask. Jesus says so in Matthew 6:8. Your conversation with God can go far beyond asking for things, though. You may thank, praise, worship, rejoice, mourn, explain, or question, revealing your fears, seeking understanding, or asking forgiveness. Your conversation with God has no limits. God is the ideal conversationalist, and God wants to spend time with you.

Being human, we can't help being self-absorbed, but praying is not just about our own needs. We are often moved by the gospel to pray for others. We will regularly remember our loved ones in prayer. Sometimes we will be led to pray for someone who has hurt us. At other times we will be moved to pray for a class of people in need wherever they are in the world, such as persecuted Christians, refugees, the mentally ill, teachers, the unborn, or the lonely.

We may also pray with the universal Church by praying for the pope's prayer intentions. Those intentions are entrusted to the Apostleship of Prayer and are available through its website and its annual and monthly leaflets. You may get your own copy of this year's papal prayer intentions by contacting the Apostleship of Prayer. The Apostleship is the pope's prayer group and has more than thirty-five million members worldwide. Jesus asked us to unite in prayer, promising that the Father would grant us whatever we ask in his name, and it is during this time of sacred reading that we take advantage of this invitation to speak with God for ourselves and others.

5. Listen to Jesus.

Jesus, the Good Shepherd, speaks to his own sheep, who hear his voice (see Jn 10:27). This listening is a most wonderful time in your prayer experience. The italicized words in this passage are the words I felt impressed upon my heart as I prayed with these readings. I included them in order to help you listen more actively for whatever it is the Lord might be saying to you.

Jesus speaks to all in the gospels, but in *Sacred Reading,* he can now speak exclusively to you. If you wish, write down what he says to you and reread his words during the day. Put all of Jesus' words to you in a folder or keep a spiritual notebook. Believers through the ages have recorded the words of Jesus to them, holy mystics and ordinary believers alike.

It takes faith to hear the voice of Jesus. This faith will grow as you practice listening. Ideally, we will learn to hear what Jesus is saying to us all day long, as we face difficult situations perhaps. Listening to the voice of Jesus is practicing the presence of God. As St. Paul said, "In him we live and move and have our being" (Acts 17:28).

St. Ignatius of Loyola called this conversation with Jesus *colloquy*. That word simply means that two or more people are talking. St. Ignatius even urges us to include the saints in our prayer conversations. We believe in the communion of saints. If you have a patron saint, don't be afraid to talk to him or her. In her autobiography, St. Thérèse of Lisieux, a member of the Apostleship of Prayer, describes how she spoke often with Mary and Joseph, as well as with Jesus.

6. *Ask God to show you how to live today.*

Pope Benedict XVI commented that sacred reading is not complete without a call to action; something in our praying leads us to do something in our day. Perhaps we find an opportunity to serve, to love, to give, to lead, or to do something good for someone else. Perhaps we find occasion to repent, to forgive, to ask forgiveness, to make amends. Open your heart to anything God might want you to do. Try to keep the conversation with God going all day long.

Asking God to show you how to live is the last step of the *Sacred Reading* prayer time, but that doesn't mean you need to end it here. Keep it going. You may drift off in the presence of God, lose attention, or even fall asleep, but you can come back. God is always present, seeking to love you and to be loved. God is always seeking to lead us to the green pastures. God is our strength, our rock, our ever-present help in time of trouble. God is full of mercy, ready to forgive us again and again. God sees us through very difficult times. God heals us. God gives his life to us constantly. God is our Maker, Father, Mother, Lover, Servant, Savior, and Friend. We know that from the Gospel. He is an inexhaustible spring of blessing and holiness in our innermost selves. The sanctification of our souls is God's work, not our own.

As you read, ask the Holy Spirit to lead you in this process. With genuine faith, open yourself to respond to the Word and the Spirit, and your relationship with Jesus will continue to deepen and grow just as the infant Jesus grew within the womb of the Blessed Mother. This in turn will lead you to share the love of Christ with all those you encounter, just as the Blessed Mother draws all those who encounter her directly to her Son.

Other Resources to Help You

These *Sacred Reading* resources, both the seasonal books and this annual prayer book, are enriched by the spirituality of the Apostleship of Prayer. Since 1844 our mission has been to encourage Catholics to pray each day for the good of the world, the Church, and the prayer intentions of the Holy Father. In particular, we encourage Christians to respond to the loving gift of Jesus Christ by making a daily offering of themselves. As we give the Lord our hearts, we ask him to make them like his own heart, full of love, mercy, and peace.

These prayer books are intended to guide you to a prayer experience that you will find personally helpful and spiritually enriching. In addition to the daily prayers in the book, you can also adapt your prayer time in ways that are best suited to your particular needs. For example, some choose to continue to reflect upon each day's reading in writing, either in the book or in a separate journal or notebook, to create a record of their spiritual journey for the entire year. Others supplement their daily reading from the book with online resources, such as those available through the Apostleship of Prayer website.

For more information about the Apostleship of Prayer (The Pope's Worldwide Prayer Network) and about the other resources we have developed to help men and women cultivate habits of daily prayer, visit our website at apostleshipofprayer.org.

I pray that this experience may help you walk closely with God every day.

Douglas Leonard, PhD
Apostleship of Prayer

The Advent and Christmas Seasons

INTRODUCTION

Advent is all about waiting for Jesus Christ. The gospel readings of Advent make us mindful of three ways we await Jesus: past, present, and future. First, we remember and accompany Mary, Joseph, and the newborn Jesus. Second, we prepare for the celebration of his birth this Christmas so that the day doesn't pass us by with just meaningless words and worthless presents. Third, we anticipate the second coming of Jesus Christ, who will come in power and glory for everyone to see and will establish his kingdom of peace and justice upon the earth.

Christ is born, and we follow him in exile and in those joyful early years with the Holy Family. We are blessed, but we are challenged, too, to understand the ways of God and how we personally may respond to them now.

Sunday, December 3, 2017
First Sunday of Advent

Know that God is present and ready to converse.

The Church has waited many centuries for the Lord to return in power and glory. Anticipating that, Jesus exhorts us not to grow discouraged or slacken in our duties. We are to expect his return at all times, staying awake, and serving him in the people of our lives.

"Lord God of Abraham, Father of Jesus, you are Love, and you are with me now. Teach me by your Word."

Read the gospel: Mark 13:33–37.

Jesus said, "Beware, keep alert; for you do not know when the time will come. It is like a man going on a journey, when he leaves home and puts his slaves in charge, each with his work, and commands the doorkeeper to be on the watch. Therefore, keep awake—for you do not know when the master of the house will come, in the evening, or at midnight, or at cockcrow, or at dawn, or else he may find you asleep when he comes suddenly. And what I say to you I say to all: Keep awake."

Notice what you think and feel as you read the gospel.

Jesus understands how hard it is to wait for him, yet he demands it. And even so, he will return unexpectedly—unexpectedly, at least, for those who are not watching and waiting.

Pray as you are led for yourself and others.

"Lord, throughout history, until John the Baptist, Jews waited for your coming. You came as a baby. Thank you. Help me to stay awake until you come again. Let those you have given me be ready, too . . ." (Continue in your own words.)

Listen to Jesus.

I am the Alpha and the Omega, my beloved child. I am your beginning and your end. Rest in me. What else is Jesus saying to you?

Ask God to show you how to live today.

"Open my eyes, Lord; awaken me to your presence. Amen."

Monday, December 4, 2017

Know that God is present and ready to converse.

"Lord, in your greatness you condescend to give me life, and life more abundantly, through your Son, Jesus, the Word of God."

Read the gospel: Matthew 8:5–11.

When Jesus entered Capernaum, a centurion came to him, appealing to him and saying, "Lord, my servant is lying at home paralyzed, in terrible distress." And he said to him, "I will come and cure him." The centurion answered, "Lord, I am not worthy to have you come under my roof; but only speak the word, and my servant will be healed. For I also am a man under authority, with soldiers under me; and I say to one, 'Go,' and he goes, and to another, 'Come,' and he comes, and to my slave, 'Do this,' and the slave does it." When Jesus heard him, he was amazed and said to those who followed him, "Truly I tell you, in no one in Israel have I found such faith. I tell you, many will come from east and west and will eat with Abraham and Isaac and Jacob in the kingdom of heaven."

Notice what you think and feel as you read the gospel.

Jesus responds to the centurion's humility, but, even more, he is "amazed" by his faith. Faith is the key to the kingdom of heaven.

Pray as you are led for yourself and others.

"Lord, humility and faith are virtues, and all virtues flow from God as gifts to us. I pray for the virtues of faith, hope, and love, not just for myself, but also for . . ." (Continue in your own words.)

Listen to Jesus.

You know my mind; you speak my heart, beloved disciple. I long for the salvation of all those you love. What else is Jesus saying to you?

Ask God to show you how to live today.

"Give me the faith to be obedient to you, Lord, that my actions may bring others your love and healing. I glorify you, Jesus. Amen."

Tuesday, December 5, 2017

Know that God is present and ready to converse.

"You know me, Father; how may I know you? I will listen to your Word."

Read the gospel: Luke 10:21–24.

At that same hour Jesus rejoiced in the Holy Spirit and said, "I thank you, Father, Lord of heaven and earth, because you have hidden these things from the wise and the intelligent and have revealed them to infants; yes, Father, for such was your gracious will. All things have been handed over to me by my Father; and no one knows who the Son is except the Father, or who the Father is except the Son and anyone to whom the Son chooses to reveal him."

Then turning to the disciples, Jesus said to them privately, "Blessed are the eyes that see what you see! For I tell you that many prophets and kings desired to see what you see, but did not see it, and to hear what you hear, but did not hear it."

Notice what you think and feel as you read the gospel.

Jesus thanks his Father that he has hidden divine truths from intelligent people and revealed them to children. Only the Son can reveal God to us. And the Son is willing to bless us. Then he speaks to his disciples privately about their privilege.

Pray as you are led for yourself and others.

"I am sorry for thinking I understand things, Lord. I know nothing apart from what you teach me. Help my heart receive your Spirit. Help others . . ." (Continue in your own words.)

Listen to Jesus.

The world waited for me but did not know me when I came. I am among you now, and the world still does not know me. Join the saints in heaven in praying for those who do not know me. What else is Jesus saying to you?

Ask God to show you how to live today.

"You are right that I don't know how to show you to those who do not know you. Give me opportunity, words, action, and courage to show love to one of those today. Amen."

Wednesday, December 6, 2017

Know that God is present and ready to converse.

"Jesus, Bread of Life, let your Word be the bread of my life today."

Read the gospel: Matthew 15:29–37.

After Jesus had left that place, he passed along the Sea of Galilee, and he went up the mountain, where he sat down. Great crowds came to him, bringing with them the lame, the maimed, the blind, the mute, and many others. They put them at his feet, and he cured them, so that the crowd was amazed when they saw the mute speaking, the maimed whole, the lame walking, and the blind seeing. And they praised the God of Israel.

Then Jesus called his disciples to him and said, "I have compassion for the crowd, because they have been with me now for three days and have nothing to eat; and I do not want to send them away hungry, for they might faint on the way." The disciples said to him, "Where are we to get enough bread in the desert to feed so great a crowd?" Jesus asked them, "How many loaves have you?" They said, "Seven, and a few small fish." Then ordering the crowd to sit down on the ground, he took the seven loaves and the fish; and after giving thanks he broke them and gave them to the disciples, and the disciples gave them to the crowds. And all of them ate and were filled; and they took up the broken pieces left over, seven baskets full.

Notice what you think and feel as you read the gospel.

In compassion for the crowd in the deserted place, Jesus feeds them all, multiplying the loaves and fish. Strangely, no one seems surprised that it is happening. Did they not realize?

Pray as you are led for yourself and others.

"Lord, how much do I not realize how you work among us. Forgive me for not seeing and trusting your compassion for me and for all you have given me . . ." (Continue in your own words.)

Listen to Jesus.

I am feeding you, beloved. Come to me every day, and I will give you secret bread I have reserved for only you. What else is Jesus saying to you?

Ask God to show you how to live today.

"Let my heart, mind, words, and actions be full of you today, gracious Lord, loving Jesus. Amen."

Thursday, December 7, 2017

Know that God is present and ready to converse.

"Lord, show me how to please you and remain in you."

Read the gospel: Matthew 7:21, 24–27.

Jesus said, "Not everyone who says to me, 'Lord, Lord,' will enter the kingdom of heaven, but only one who does the will of my Father in heaven. . . .

"Everyone then who hears these words of mine and acts on them will be like a wise man who built his house on rock. The rain fell, the floods came, and the winds blew and beat on that house, but it did not fall, because it had been founded on rock. And everyone who hears these words of mine and does not act on them will be like a foolish man who built his house on sand. The rain fell, and the floods came, and the winds blew and beat against that house, and it fell—and great was its fall!"

Notice what you think and feel as you read the gospel.

Jesus tells us how to get to heaven: do the will of his Father—hear the word of God and act upon it. This takes daily effort, faith, and commitment. This is how we build our house on the Rock of Jesus.

Pray as you are led for yourself and others.

"Jesus, you are very clear in this teaching. Forgive me for the times I sought my own will, would not listen to you, would not act upon your words. I offer myself to you now for conversion . . ." (Continue in your own words.)

Listen to Jesus.

My beloved, you are mine and I care for you. I set you on solid ground and build you up. What else is Jesus saying to you?

Ask God to show you how to live today.

"Show me the will of the Father, Jesus, and give me the strength to carry it out. Amen."

Friday, December 8, 2017
Immaculate Conception of the Blessed Virgin Mary

Know that God is present and ready to converse.

"Here I am, mighty Spirit of Holiness. Be it done to me according to your Word."

Read the gospel: Luke 1:26–38.

In the sixth month the angel Gabriel was sent by God to a town in Galilee called Nazareth, to a virgin engaged to a man whose name was Joseph, of the house of David. The virgin's name was Mary. And he came to her and said, "Greetings, favored one! The Lord is with you." But she was much perplexed by his words and pondered what sort of greeting this might be. The angel said to her, "Do not be afraid, Mary, for you have found favor with God. And now, you will conceive in your womb and bear a son, and you will name him Jesus. He will be great, and will be called the Son of the Most High, and the Lord God will give to him the throne of his ancestor David. He will reign over the house of Jacob forever, and of his kingdom there will be no end." Mary said to the angel, "How can this be, since I am a virgin?" The angel said to her, "The Holy Spirit will come upon you, and the power of the Most High will overshadow you; therefore the child to be born will be holy; he will be called Son of God. And now, your relative Elizabeth in her old age has also conceived a son; and this is the sixth month for her who was said to be barren. For nothing will be impossible with God." Then Mary said, "Here am I, the servant of the Lord; let it be with me according to your word." Then the angel departed from her.

Notice what you think and feel as you read the gospel.

In a single moment, Mary's plan for her life is demolished by an angel's perplexing message. How can this be? But she soon understands it doesn't matter what she understands—she makes herself absolutely available to God for whatever God wills, even if it is "impossible."

Pray as you are led for yourself and others.

"Thy will be done, Lord, in earth as in heaven, and in me as in Mary. I surrender, and with your grace I will be able to give myself more fully each day. I am also giving to you today those you have given me, that you may do your will in them . . ." (Continue in your own words.)

Listen to Jesus.

God is good, beloved servant, God knows what you need before you ask, and God has granted your prayers today. What else is Jesus saying to you?

Ask God to show you how to live today.

"Help me be aware of moments when I need to stop wondering and just bow to your will with grateful acceptance. Give me grace to trust you in my circumstances. Thank you. Amen."

Saturday, December 9, 2017

Know that God is present and ready to converse.

"Lord, may your Word move my heart to love you and my will to action—action that serves others as you would have me serve."

Read the gospel: Matthew 9:35–10:1, 5a, 6–8.

Then Jesus went about all the cities and villages, teaching in their synagogues, and proclaiming the good news of the kingdom, and curing every disease and every sickness. When he saw the crowds, he had compassion for them, because they were harassed and helpless, like sheep without a shepherd. Then he said to his disciples, "The harvest is plentiful, but the laborers are few; therefore ask the Lord of the harvest to send out laborers into his harvest."

Then Jesus summoned his twelve disciples and gave them authority over unclean spirits, to cast them out, and to cure every disease and every sickness. . . .

These twelve Jesus sent out with the following instructions: ". . . Go rather to the lost sheep of the house of Israel. As you go, proclaim the good news, 'The kingdom of heaven has come near.' Cure the sick, raise the dead, cleanse the lepers, cast out demons. You received without payment; give without payment."

Notice what you think and feel as you read the gospel.

The people are "harassed and helpless," Jesus says, and he wishes to provide them shepherds. He gives the twelve power and sends them out to preach and do wonders not for personal gain, but only to show the love of God and the truth of the kingdom.

Pray as you are led for yourself and others.

"So many now are harassed and helpless, in poverty, sickness, war, persecution, violence, abuse, addiction, prison. Lord, send laborers to bring them relief and knowledge of you . . ." (Continue in your own words.)

Listen to Jesus.

You see how nothing has changed, my child? This world needs redemption that comes only through God. When will people turn to me? What else is Jesus saying to you?

Ask God to show you how to live today.

"Lord, how can I help? Send me. Amen."

Sunday, December 10, 2017
Second Sunday of Advent

Know that God is present and ready to converse.

John the Baptist is a fascinating figure in the unfolding of God's plan to visit his people in Person. For all his charisma, he has a limited role that requires great humility and incredible courage. His preaching of repentance led to his martyrdom.

"Lord, by your Spirit and your Word, you raise up holy men and women to serve you. I am ready to hear you now because I know you can do all things, even in me."

Read the gospel: Mark 1:1–8.

The beginning of the good news of Jesus Christ, the Son of God.
As it is written in the prophet Isaiah,

"See, I am sending my messenger ahead of you,
who will prepare your way;
the voice of one crying out in the wilderness:
'Prepare the way of the Lord,
make his paths straight.'"

John the baptizer appeared in the wilderness, proclaiming a baptism of repentance for the forgiveness of sins. And people from the whole Judean countryside and all the people of Jerusalem were going out to him, and were baptized by him in the river Jordan, confessing their sins. Now John was clothed with camel's hair, with a leather belt around his waist, and he ate locusts and wild honey. He proclaimed, "The one who is more powerful than I is coming after me; I am not worthy to stoop down and untie the thong of his sandals. I have baptized you with water; but he will baptize you with the Holy Spirit."

Notice what you think and feel as you read the gospel.

This is the beginning of the Good News of the Kingdom of God. John must have appeared as a wild man, yet people flocked to him in the wilderness, repented, and were baptized. John told them about the greater, more powerful One who was to follow.

Pray as you are led for yourself and others.

"Lord, let repentance be the first step for me, too, so I will be ready for your baptism with the Holy Spirit. I pray that all sinners see their need to repent and then do so. I think of . . ." (Continue in your own words.)

Listen to Jesus.

I long to open the eyes of the blind, to soften the hearts of the hard-hearted. I invite whoever will hear to come to me and be baptized into the kingdom. Pray with me for sinners. What else is Jesus saying to you?

Ask God to show you how to live today.

"Remind me and I will pray for sinners many times today, saying 'Have mercy upon us, Lord.' Remind me, Jesus. Thank you for asking me to serve. Amen."

Monday, December 11, 2017

Know that God is present and ready to converse.

"Jesus Christ, let me spare no effort to come to you every day. I need your healing touch."

Read the gospel: Luke 5:17–26.

One day, while Jesus was teaching, Pharisees and teachers of the law were sitting nearby (they had come from every village of Galilee and Judea and from Jerusalem); and the power of the Lord was with him to heal. Just then some men came, carrying a paralyzed man on a bed. They were trying to bring him in and lay him before Jesus; but finding no way to bring him in because of the crowd, they went up on the roof and let him down with his bed through the tiles into the middle of the crowd in front of Jesus. When he saw their faith, he said, "Friend, your sins are forgiven you." Then the scribes and the Pharisees began to question, "Who is this who is speaking blasphemies? Who can forgive sins but God alone?" When Jesus perceived their questionings, he answered them, "Why do you raise such questions in your hearts? Which is easier, to say, 'Your sins are forgiven you,' or to say, 'Stand up and walk'? But so that you may know that the Son of Man has authority on earth to forgive sins"—he said to the one who was paralyzed— "I say to you, stand up and take your bed and go to your home." Immediately he stood up before them, took what he had been lying on, and went to his home, glorifying God. Amazement seized all of them, and they glorified God and were filled with awe, saying, "We have seen strange things today."

Notice what you think and feel as you read the gospel.

Because Jesus is Emmanuel, God with us, he can both heal infirmities of the body and forgive sins of the soul. The scribes and Pharisees do not understand that, and Jesus makes his identity clear to them, even though they may not receive it. Yet all present are filled with awe and glorify God.

Pray as you are led for yourself and others.

"Lord, let me be lowered down before you, so you can heal me and forgive my sins. I need you. Others need you, too, so I pray . . ." (Continue in your own words.)

Listen to Jesus.

Servant, I am always here to heal you and wash you clean. I love you. Our love is the most important thing. I am happy when you show your love to me. What else is Jesus saying to you?

Ask God to show you how to live today.

"I am awed that you love me—and grateful, for I am but sinful flesh and blood. Be with me, loving Savior, and I will do your will today. Amen."

Tuesday, December 12, 2017
Our Lady of Guadalupe

Know that God is present and ready to converse.

"Lord God of Hosts, Master of the Universe, you stoop to live among the humble of the earth. Let me be one of them."

Read the gospel: Luke 1:26–38.

In the sixth month the angel Gabriel was sent by God to a town in Galilee called Nazareth, to a virgin engaged to a man whose name was Joseph, of the house of David. The virgin's name was Mary. And he came to her and said, "Greetings, favored one! The Lord is with you." But she was much perplexed by his words and pondered what sort of greeting this might be. The angel said to her, "Do not be afraid, Mary, for you have found favor with God. And now, you will conceive in your womb and bear a son, and you will name him Jesus. He will be great, and will be called the Son of the Most High, and the Lord God will give to him the throne of his ancestor David. He will reign over the house of Jacob forever, and of his kingdom there will be no end." Mary said to the angel, "How can this be, since I am a virgin?" The angel said to her, "The Holy Spirit will come upon you, and the power of the Most High will overshadow you; therefore the child to be born will be holy; he will be called Son of God. And now, your relative Elizabeth in her old age has also conceived a son; and this is the sixth month for her who was said to be barren. For nothing will be impossible with God." Then Mary said, "Here am I, the servant of the Lord; let it be with me according to your word." Then the angel departed from her.

Notice what you think and feel as you read the gospel.

The angel tells Mary she is favored by God, but what a world of woe lies in store for her! Yet through her comes Emmanuel, the Messiah, the Savior of the World, the King of Glory. Thus she is the Mother of God.

Pray as you are led for yourself and others.

"Lord, like Mary, I am sometimes perplexed by events in my life, all of which come from your hand. Help me to accept them, and let it be done unto me according to your will . . ." (Continue in your own words.)

Listen to Jesus.

Your role, my dear follower, is to make my will your own. You can accomplish this through prayer. I will bless you beyond what you can imagine. What else is Jesus saying to you?

Ask God to show you how to live today.

"Help me seek your will for me, Lord, and let my suffering be used to bring your kingdom into the world. Amen."

Wednesday, December 13, 2017

Know that God is present and ready to converse.

"I come to you, Lord. Give me both rest and the power to take your yoke upon myself."

Read the gospel: Matthew 11:28–30.

Jesus said, "Come to me, all you that are weary and are carrying heavy burdens, and I will give you rest. Take my yoke upon you, and learn from me; for I am gentle and humble in heart, and you will find rest for your souls. For my yoke is easy, and my burden is light."

Notice what you think and feel as you read the gospel.

Jesus says he is gentle and humble of heart. Why? So the weary and over-burdened will not be afraid to come to him for rest.

Pray as you are led for yourself and others.

"Gentle Jesus, I know you value humility. Strike down all my pride and give me humility like yours. I certainly cannot manufacture it in myself. Then let me take on the burdens of others . . ." (Continue in your own words.)

Listen to Jesus.

My heart is my love for you and for all humanity. I am willing to give you my heart, friend, so that you may give it to others. This is the only hope for the world. What else is Jesus saying to you?

Ask God to show you how to live today.

"Jesus, I am willing to receive your heart, and with your grace I will give it to others. Glory to you, O Lord. Amen."

Thursday, December 14, 2017

Know that God is present and ready to converse.

"Lord, let me receive and accept your Word."

Read the gospel: Matthew 11:11–15.

Jesus said, "Truly I tell you, among those born of women no one has arisen greater than John the Baptist; yet the least in the kingdom of heaven is greater than he. From the days of John the Baptist until now the kingdom of heaven has suffered violence, and the violent take it by force. For all the prophets and the law prophesied until John came; and if you are willing to accept it, he is Elijah who is to come. Let anyone with ears listen!"

Notice what you think and feel as you read the gospel.

I do not understand how the kingdom of heaven has suffered violence, and the violent take it by force. Yet Jesus implies that things have changed now, for he has opened the kingdom to all who heed the words of repentance and grace.

Pray as you are led for yourself and others.

"Lord, I aspire to be greater than John only in humility. Mold me to your will . . ." (Continue in your own words.)

Listen to Jesus.

Dear one, can you imagine my task of teaching men and women the power and glory of God? They accused me of speaking in riddles. Let me speak to you plainly now. I love you. I hear your prayers. Follow me. What else is Jesus saying to you?

Ask God to show you how to live today.

"Lord, I need your Holy Spirit even to receive your message of love. Help me apply your love in all I do. Amen."

Friday, December 15, 2017

Know that God is present and ready to converse.

"Open my mind to your Word, Lord, for without your grace I will not understand it."

Read the gospel: Matthew 11:16–19.

Jesus said, "But to what will I compare this generation? It is like children sitting in the market-places and calling to one another,

> 'We played the flute for you, and you did not dance;
> we wailed, and you did not mourn.'

For John came neither eating nor drinking, and they say, 'He has a demon'; the Son of Man came eating and drinking, and they say, 'Look, a glutton and a drunkard, a friend of tax-collectors and sinners!' Yet wisdom is vindicated by her deeds."

Notice what you think and feel as you read the gospel.

Jesus complains that people won't receive God's message no matter how it's presented. They constantly find fault with the messenger. But, he concludes, after all is said and done, one's wisdom is proven by one's actions and deeds.

Pray as you are led for yourself and others.

"Move me to right action, Lord. Be a lamp to my feet. Strengthen my hands and heart for the labors of love you give me. Let me help . . ." (Continue in your own words.)

Listen to Jesus.

Blessed and wise is the one who does the will of God. Seek, beloved, to know and to do the will of God in your own life. What else is Jesus saying to you?

Ask God to show you how to live today.

"Then increase my desire for you, Jesus, and to do the Father's will. Help me act in your love. Amen."

Saturday, December 16, 2017

Know that God is present and ready to converse.

"Jesus, beloved Son, let me listen to you and be filled with awe."

Read the gospel: Matthew 17:9a, 10–13.

As they were coming down the mountain, Jesus ordered them, "Tell no one about the vision until after the Son of Man has been raised from the dead." . . . And the disciples asked him, "Why, then, do the scribes say that Elijah must come first?" He replied, "Elijah is indeed coming and will restore all things; but I tell you that Elijah has already come, and they did not recognize him, but they did to him whatever they pleased. So also the Son of Man is about to suffer at their hands." Then the disciples understood that he was speaking to them about John the Baptist.

Notice what you think and feel as you read the gospel.

The disciples understand he is speaking about John, but they seem deaf to his mention about being raised from the dead, and deaf again at his mention of his own suffering. They would not fully understand until after it had happened, after they had seen it for themselves, and after the Holy Spirit fully informed them.

Pray as you are led for yourself and others.

"Jesus, I don't want to be deaf or in denial of truth. Open my understanding to what you deem I need to know, for I want to please you, not myself. I offer myself today for the good of those you have given me . . ." (Continue in your own words.)

Listen to Jesus.

I am ready to give every person the knowledge he or she needs, but the person must seek it with an open heart and mind. Some refuse to open to me. Pray for them, beloved. Thank you. What else is Jesus saying to you?

Ask God to show you how to live today.

"So I will spend many moments of my day praying for those who refuse to open to your truth and grace. Remind me to do so often, Lord. Praise God Almighty! Amen."

Sunday, December 17, 2017
Third Sunday of Advent

Know that God is present and ready to converse.

"Light of the world, light of my life, let me see you in your Word."

As the candles in the Advent wreath continue to burn during this time of hopeful anticipation, our longing for the Lord grows. We love the infant Jesus. We love the triumphant Messiah who is to come. But, best of all, for now and for eternity, we love the coming and abiding of Jesus Christ in our hearts. The kingdom of heaven is already within us.

"I welcome you into my day, Lord, though you are always with me. I am here with you."

Read the gospel: John 1:6–8, 19–28.

There was a man sent from God, whose name was John. He came as a witness to testify to the light, so that all might believe through him. He himself was not the light, but he came to testify to the light. . . .

This is the testimony given by John when the Jews sent priests and Levites from Jerusalem to ask him, "Who are you?" He confessed and did not deny it, but confessed, "I am not the Messiah." And they asked him, "What then? Are you Elijah?" He said, "I am not." "Are you the prophet?" He answered, "No." Then they said to him, "Who are you? Let us have an answer for those who sent us. What do you say about yourself?" He said,

> "I am the voice of one crying out in the wilderness,
> 'Make straight the way of the Lord,'"

as the prophet Isaiah said.

Now they had been sent from the Pharisees. They asked him, "Why then are you baptizing if you are neither the Messiah, nor Elijah, nor the prophet?" John answered them, "I baptize with water. Among you stands one whom you do not know, the one who is coming after me; I am not worthy to untie the thong of his sandal." This took place in Bethany across the Jordan where John was baptizing.

Notice what you think and feel as you read the gospel.

John has a positive message, for he proclaims the imminent coming of the Lord. Those who hear him press him for more, so he has to declare plainly that he is not the Messiah, Elijah, or the prophet. He declares also that he is not worthy to untie the thong of the sandal of the one who is to come after him.

Pray as you are led for yourself and others.

"How human we are, Lord, as we dispute about your words. Let me avoid dispute and with simple heart and mind receive you. I pray others do as well . . ." (Continue in your own words.)

Listen to Jesus.

You see why I have said that intelligent people cannot understand, while children can. Study to be a child, for you are my child. Love and trust your Lord and God. All shall be well with you and yours. What else is Jesus saying to you?

Ask God to show you how to live today.

"By your grace, let me learn and practice simplicity, love, and trust today. Let it bring honor to you, Lord. Amen."

Monday, December 18, 2017

Know that God is present and ready to converse.

"Father in heaven, you sent your son out of love for us. You made yourself present in history and in the flesh. Thank you."

Read the gospel: Matthew 1:18–25.

Now the birth of Jesus the Messiah took place in this way. When his mother Mary had been engaged to Joseph, but before they lived together, she was found to be with child from the Holy Spirit. Her husband Joseph, being a righteous man and unwilling to expose her to public disgrace, planned to dismiss her quietly. But just when he had resolved to do this, an angel of the Lord appeared to him in a dream and said, "Joseph, son of David, do not be afraid to take Mary as your wife, for the child conceived in her is from the Holy Spirit. She will bear a son, and you are to name him Jesus, for he will save his people from their sins." All this took place to fulfill what had been spoken by the Lord through the prophet: "Look, the virgin shall conceive and bear a son, and they shall name him Emmanuel," which means, "God is with us." When Joseph awoke from sleep, he did as the angel of the Lord commanded him; he took her as his wife, but had no marital relations with her until she had borne a son; and he named him Jesus.

Notice what you think and feel as you read the gospel.

More than half of the words of this gospel passage concern Joseph's dream. He went to sleep facing a personal crisis and a social crisis, too, with Mary's pregnancy. He awakens to follow not his own plans but what the angel commanded him. He married Mary, and they named the child Jesus.

Pray as you are led for yourself and others.

"Human predicaments sometimes seem impossible, but you can untangle the knots, Lord. I place before you my greatest knot today. Command me what to do, and give me grace to do it . . ." (Continue in your own words.)

Listen to Jesus.

You are right to seek me when you are in trouble of any kind. I love you, and I am willing and able to save you, and also those you pray for. Cast your cares upon me! What else is Jesus saying to you?

Ask God to show you how to live today.

"Let me return in prayer often today, Lord, as I turn my cares over to you. Thank you for your daily love and guidance. Amen."

Tuesday, December 19, 2017

Know that God is present and ready to converse.

"How marvelous are your ways and works, Lord. Open my eyes to adore you."

Read the gospel: Luke 1:5–25.

In the days of King Herod of Judea, there was a priest named Zechariah, who belonged to the priestly order of Abijah. His wife was a descendant of Aaron, and her name was Elizabeth. Both of them were righteous before God, living blamelessly according to all the commandments and regulations of the Lord. But they had no children, because Elizabeth was barren, and both were getting on in years.

Once when he was serving as priest before God and his section was on duty, he was chosen by lot, according to the custom of the priesthood, to enter the sanctuary of the Lord and offer incense. Now at the time of the incense-offering, the whole assembly of the people was praying outside. Then there appeared to him an angel of the Lord, standing at the right side of the altar of incense. When Zechariah saw him, he was terrified; and fear overwhelmed him. But the angel said to him, "Do not be afraid, Zechariah, for your prayer has been heard. Your wife Elizabeth will bear you a son, and you will name him John. You will have joy and gladness, and many will rejoice at his birth, for he will be great in the sight of the Lord. He must never drink wine or strong drink; even before his birth he will be filled with the Holy Spirit. He will turn many of the people of Israel to the Lord their God. With the spirit and power of Elijah he will go before him, to turn the hearts of parents to their children, and the disobedient to the wisdom of the righteous, to make ready a people prepared for the Lord." Zechariah said to the angel, "How will I know that this is so? For I am an old man, and my wife is getting on in years." The angel replied, "I am Gabriel. I stand in the presence of God, and I have been sent to speak to you and to bring you this good news. But now, because you did not believe my words, which will be fulfilled in their time, you will become mute, unable to speak, until the day these things occur."

Meanwhile, the people were waiting for Zechariah, and wondered at his delay in the sanctuary. When he did come out, he could not speak to them, and they realized that he had seen a vision in the sanctuary. He kept motioning to them and remained unable to speak. When his time of service was ended, he went to his home.

After those days his wife Elizabeth conceived, and for five months she remained in seclusion. She said, "This is what the Lord has done for me when he looked favorably on me and took away the disgrace I have endured among my people."

Notice what you think and feel as you read the gospel.

Zechariah hears the prophecy from the angel and is struck dumb for not believing. Despite his opinion that his aged wife cannot conceive, she does—just as the angel had said—and Elizabeth is joyful.

Pray as you are led for yourself and others.

"Lord, forgive me for being slow to believe your promises. They are so wonderful. I pray that you increase my faith in you and your Word. Let hearts around the world be opened to your Word, especially . . ." (Continue in your own words.)

Listen to Jesus.

Faith in my promises pleases me. I grant you what you seek, dear friend. Meditate upon my promises to you. What else is Jesus saying to you?

Ask God to show you how to live today.

"Throughout the day, Lord, bring to my mind one of your promises, that I may thank you for it and trust in you with all my heart. Thank you, precious Lord. Amen."

Wednesday, December 20, 2017

Know that God is present and ready to converse.

"Lord, let me not fear your presence in my life, especially now as I seek you in your Word."

Read the gospel: Luke 1:26–38.

In the sixth month the angel Gabriel was sent by God to a town in Galilee called Nazareth, to a virgin engaged to a man whose name was Joseph, of the house of David. The virgin's name was Mary. And he came to her and said, "Greetings, favored one! The Lord is with you." But she was much perplexed by his words and pondered what sort of greeting this might be. The angel said to her, "Do not be afraid, Mary, for you have found favor with God. And now, you will conceive in your womb and bear a son, and you will name him Jesus. He will be great, and will be called the Son of the Most High, and the Lord God will give to him the throne of his ancestor David. He will reign over the house of Jacob forever, and of his kingdom there will be no end." Mary said to the angel, "How can this be, since I am a virgin?" The angel said to her, "The Holy Spirit will come upon you, and the power of the Most High will overshadow you; therefore the child to be born will be holy; he will be called Son of God. And now, your relative Elizabeth in her old age has also conceived a son; and this is the sixth month for her who was said to be barren. For nothing will be impossible with God." Then Mary said, "Here am I, the servant of the Lord; let it be with me according to your word." Then the angel departed from her.

Notice what you think and feel as you read the gospel.

The angel Gabriel tells Mary not to be afraid, and then announces how Mary will serve God in a way no other has or ever will. She will conceive by the Holy Spirit and bear a human son who would also be the Son of God. Mary must have been overwhelmed by the mystery and by the love of God. She must have been overwhelmed the rest of her life as she pondered these things in her heart.

Pray as you are led for yourself and others.

"Mary, thank you. Intercede for me with Jesus that I may be as humble and willing to serve as you were. Pray, too, for all those God has given me, especially . . ." (Continue in your own words.)

Listen to Jesus.

You love my mother, and she is easy to love. I love you, too, beloved disciple. I hear your prayer today. Trust in me. What else is Jesus saying to you?

Ask God to show you how to live today.

"Keep me in your presence today, Lord, for I am prone to stray. Make your will clear to me. Praise to you, Lord Jesus Christ. Amen."

Thursday, December 21, 2017

Know that God is present and ready to converse.

"Bless me with faith, Lord, as I encounter you in your Word."

Read the gospel: Luke 1:39–45.

In those days Mary set out and went with haste to a Judean town in the hill country, where she entered the house of Zechariah and greeted Elizabeth. When Elizabeth heard Mary's greeting, the child leapt in her womb. And Elizabeth was filled with the Holy Spirit and exclaimed with a loud cry, "Blessed are you among women, and blessed is the fruit of your womb. And why has this happened to me, that the mother of my Lord comes to me? For as soon as I heard the sound of your greeting, the child in my womb leapt for joy. And blessed is she who believed that there would be a fulfillment of what was spoken to her by the Lord."

Notice what you think and feel as you read the gospel.

Elizabeth blesses Mary for believing God's message to her. Both are pregnant with sons who would change the world forever. God is with these women, working out his great plans through them. They don't know what's happening, but they rejoice in God.

Pray as you are led for yourself and others.

"Lord, I rejoice in your working in my life, even though I cannot know the future. All I need to know is that you are true and you are good. Let me please you by believing. I pray for these people I love . . ." (Continue in your own words.)

Listen to Jesus.

It is so simple to love me, child. If you love me, I will abide in you. When you are in the dark or hurting in any way, know that I am with you. I am all you need. What else is Jesus saying to you?

Ask God to show you how to live today.

"Let me leap for joy in your presence, Lord. Thank you. Amen."

Friday, December 22, 2017

Know that God is present and ready to converse.

"Let the Word of the Lord speak to my heart and change me into the person God wants me to be."

Read the gospel: Luke 1:46–56.

And Mary said,

"My soul magnifies the Lord,
    and my spirit rejoices in God my Savior,
for he has looked with favor on the lowliness of his servant.
    Surely, from now on all generations will call me blessed;
for the Mighty One has done great things for me,
    and holy is his name.
His mercy is for those who fear him
    from generation to generation.
He has shown strength with his arm;
    he has scattered the proud in the thoughts of their hearts.
He has brought down the powerful from their thrones,
    and lifted up the lowly;
he has filled the hungry with good things,
    and sent the rich away empty.
He has helped his servant Israel,
    in remembrance of his mercy,
according to the promise he made to our ancestors,
    to Abraham and to his descendants forever."

And Mary remained with her for about three months and then returned to her home.

Notice what you think and feel as you read the gospel.

Mary is very confident that God favors those who are weak, poor, and humble but scatters those who are strong, rich, and proud. She rejoices in God's mercy and faithfulness.

Pray as you are led for yourself and others.

"Oh, for the gift of prayer such as Mary had, Lord. Inspire me as you inspired her, that I may please you, know you, and love you as never before. Let others be drawn to holy prayer as well, namely . . ." (Continue in your own words.)

Listen to Jesus.

I like the time we spend together, dear one. The only agenda I have for you is loving me. When you love me, you become what I want you to be: a child of God. What else is Jesus saying to you?

Ask God to show you how to live today.

"Let me love and praise you in every moment of the day, Lord, and humbly serve you in the poor and the weak, whom you love. Amen."

Saturday, December 23, 2017

Know that God is present and ready to converse.

"Grant me silence to hear your Word, and then free my tongue to praise you, Lord."

Read the gospel: Luke 1:57–66.

Now the time came for Elizabeth to give birth, and she bore a son. Her neighbors and relatives heard that the Lord had shown his great mercy to her, and they rejoiced with her.

On the eighth day they came to circumcise the child, and they were going to name him Zechariah after his father. But his mother said, "No; he is to be called John." They said to her, "None of your relatives has this name." Then they began motioning to his father to find out what name he wanted to give him. He asked for a writing-tablet and wrote, "His name is John." And all of them were amazed. Immediately his mouth was opened and his tongue freed, and he began to speak, praising God. Fear came over all their neighbors, and all these things were talked about throughout the entire hill country of Judea. All who heard them pondered them and said, "What then will this child become?" For, indeed, the hand of the Lord was with him.

Notice what you think and feel as you read the gospel.

Zechariah and Elizabeth name their new baby boy John, despite the neighbors' and relatives' protests. When Zechariah regains his speech, they know God is working a plan. They had no idea.

Pray as you are led for yourself and others.

"Lord, I have no idea what you are doing in my life and in the lives of those you have given me. Let me praise you in faith and hope for future blessings for all of us, including . . ." (Continue in your own words.)

Listen to Jesus.

You tend to lose the big picture in the day-to-day events of your life. Dearly beloved, grasp that the kingdom of heaven is within you and that with God all things are possible. Now and forever. What else is Jesus telling you?

Ask God to show you how to live today.

"All right, Jesus. Today is enough for me. Stay with me and help me do what you would have me do. Amen."

Sunday, December 24, 2017
Fourth Sunday of Advent

Know that God is present and ready to converse.

"How can it be that you are here with me today, Lord? I am not worthy. I offer myself to you that I may learn to know you and love you through your Word."

Read the gospel: Luke 1:26–38.

In the sixth month the angel Gabriel was sent by God to a town in Galilee called Nazareth, to a virgin engaged to a man whose name was Joseph, of the house of David. The virgin's name was Mary. And he came to her and said, "Greetings, favored one! The Lord is with you." But she was much perplexed by his words and pondered what sort of greeting this might be. The angel said to her, "Do not be afraid, Mary, for you have found favor with God. And now, you will conceive in your womb and bear a son, and you will name him Jesus. He will be great, and will be called the Son of the Most High, and the Lord God will give to him the throne of his ancestor David. He will reign over the house of Jacob forever, and of his kingdom there will be no end." Mary said to the angel, "How can this be, since I am a virgin?" The angel said to her, "The Holy Spirit will come upon you, and the power of the Most High will overshadow you; therefore the child to be born will be holy; he will be called Son of God. And now, your relative Elizabeth in her old age has also conceived a son; and this is the sixth month for her who was said to be barren. For nothing will be impossible with God." Then Mary said, "Here am I, the servant of the Lord; let it be with me according to your word." Then the angel departed from her.

Notice what you think and feel as you read the gospel.

Mary was "much perplexed" by the message of the angel, and she hadn't yet even heard the amazing announcement that she would be overshadowed by the Most High and conceive a child who would be the Son of God. As she listened to the angel's amazing announcement, she must have felt the peace of God, for she answers so beautifully, so humbly, so trustingly as she gives herself to the Lord's will.

Pray as you are led for yourself and others.

"Lord, let your peace descend upon me this day, as I wait to celebrate again your birth. Let your peace fill the world tonight, that all may sense that the Messiah has come . . ." (Continue in your own words.)

Listen to Jesus.

I give you my peace, beloved. Let yourself become a child as you contemplate the mysterious, loving ways of my Father. What else is Jesus saying to you?

Ask God to show you how to live today.

"Let me shine with your peace, grace, and joy today, Lord. Be with me in all I do. Amen."

Monday, December 25, 2017
The Nativity of the Lord

Know that God is present and ready to converse.

"Emmanuel, you have come. You are here. Praise to the Infant Jesus."

Read the gospel: John 1:1–18.

In the beginning was the Word, and the Word was with God, and the Word was God. He was in the beginning with God. All things came into being through him, and without him not one thing came into being. What has come into being in him was life, and the life was the light of all people. The light shines in the darkness, and the darkness did not overcome it.

There was a man sent from God, whose name was John. He came as a witness to testify to the light, so that all might believe through him. He himself was not the light, but he came to testify to the light. The true light, which enlightens everyone, was coming into the world.

He was in the world, and the world came into being through him; yet the world did not know him. He came to what was his own, and his own people did not accept him. But to all who received him, who believed in his name, he gave power to become children of God, who were born, not of blood or of the will of the flesh or of the will of man, but of God.

And the Word became flesh and lived among us, and we have seen his glory, the glory as of a father's only son, full of grace and truth. (John testified to him and cried out, "This was he of whom I said, 'He who comes after me ranks ahead of me because he was before me.'") From his fullness we have all received, grace upon grace. The law indeed was given through Moses; grace and truth came through Jesus Christ. No one has ever seen God. It is God the only Son, who is close to the Father's heart, who has made him known.

Notice what you think and feel as you read the gospel.

This passage reveals the cosmic, theological Jesus Christ in his mysterious relationship with God and humanity. He is the eternal Word, God's own self, Life, and Light, sent into a world of sin and darkness to gather a people for God the Father. Christ has made the Father known to us.

Pray as you are led for yourself and others.

"You have given me grace upon grace. Thank you. I pray that many hearts of those you have given me may be open to your graces . . ." (Continue in your own words.)

Listen to Jesus.

You are right to love and to care for others. That pleases me, beloved. If you love them, consider how much God loves them. Entrust them to God. What else is Jesus saying to you?

Ask God to show you how to live today.

"Let my heart and mind remain in awareness of your birth, glorious in its humility. Praise to you, Savior. Amen."

Tuesday, December 26, 2017
Saint Stephen, First Martyr

Know that God is present and ready to converse.

"Lord God of Hosts, you dwell on high, yet you are here with me now in my struggles and sufferings. Let me hear your holy Word, Father."

Read the gospel: Matthew 10:17–22.

Jesus said, "Beware of them, for they will hand you over to councils and flog you in their synagogues; and you will be dragged before governors and kings because of me, as a testimony to them and the Gentiles. When they hand you over, do not worry about how you are to speak or what you are to say; for what you are to say will be given to you at that time; for it is not you who speak, but the Spirit of your Father speaking through you. Brother will betray brother to death, and a father his child, and children will rise against parents and have them put to death; and you will be hated by all because of my name. But the one who endures to the end will be saved."

Notice what you think and feel as you read the gospel.

Persecution, betrayal, and hatred are part of witnessing to the Messiah, the Lord, Jesus Christ. Under duress, we are to not worry but trust the Holy Spirit to speak through us. The goal is to endure in faithfulness to the end, even unto death.

Pray as you are led for yourself and others.

"Lord, we have experienced rejection by the world for speaking of you. I pray we may be strengthened and informed by your Spirit, to endure to the end. I think of . . ." (Continue in your own words.)

Listen to Jesus.

When I chose you for my own, child, I ordained you to suffering that the world may know that you are mine. This is your glory, as it was mine. Know that in your dying body, my life grows, and beyond the end is eternal life. What else is Jesus saying to you?

Ask God to show you how to live today.

"Help me to view all persecution and rejection from your perspective, Lord. Let my suffering testify to you and give you glory. Your kingdom come! Amen."

Wednesday, December 27, 2017
Saint John, Apostle and Evangelist

Know that God is present and ready to converse.

"You ask me to seek you, Lord, and so I do, and I find you here already. Glory to God."

Read the gospel: John 20:1a, 2–8.

Early on the first day of the week . . . Mary Magdalene came to the tomb and saw that the stone had been removed from the tomb. So she ran and went to Simon Peter and the other disciple, the one whom Jesus loved, and said to them, "They have taken the Lord out of the tomb, and we do not know where they have laid him." Then Peter and the other disciple set out and went towards the tomb. The two were running together, but the other disciple outran Peter and reached the tomb first. He bent down to look in and saw the linen wrappings lying there, but he did not go in. Then Simon Peter came, following him, and went into the tomb. He saw the linen wrappings lying there, and the cloth that had been on Jesus' head, not lying with the linen wrappings but rolled up in a place by itself. Then the other disciple, who reached the tomb first, also went in, and he saw and believed.

Notice what you think and feel as you read the gospel.

John, who wrote this passage, describes himself as the other disciple, which seems like modesty, yet he also refers to himself as the "one whom Jesus loved," which almost seems like vanity. He's also the faster runner, yet he defers to Peter, who enters the tomb immediately. John is human, but he is right to center his identity on Jesus' love for him.

Pray as you are led for yourself and others.

"Lord, let me be myself, the person you love, at all times. Let those you have given me recognize their own standing as beloved children of God . . ." (Continue in your own words.)

Listen to Jesus.

You are my beloved disciple; I promise you that. I love all uniquely and infinitely. I proved it on the Cross. What else is Jesus saying to you?

Ask God to show you how to live today.

"Lord, make me aware every moment that I am the disciple Jesus loves. Amen."

Thursday, December 28, 2017
Holy Innocents

Know that God is present and ready to converse.

"God, you give us your Word, Jesus, your Son. Let it be sharper than a two-edged sword in me today, transforming me as you will."

Read the gospel: Matthew 2:13–18.

Now after they had left, an angel of the Lord appeared to Joseph in a dream and said, "Get up, take the child and his mother, and flee to Egypt, and remain there until I tell you; for Herod is about to search for the child, to destroy him." Then Joseph got up, took the child and his mother by night, and went to Egypt, and remained there until the death of Herod. This was to fulfill what had been spoken by the Lord through the prophet, "Out of Egypt I have called my son."

When Herod saw that he had been tricked by the wise men, he was infuriated, and he sent and killed all the children in and around Bethlehem who were two years old or under, according to the time that he had learned from the wise men. Then was fulfilled what had been spoken through the prophet Jeremiah:

"A voice was heard in Ramah,
wailing and loud lamentation,
Rachel weeping for her children;
she refused to be consoled, because they are no more."

Notice what you think and feel as you read the gospel.

I feel violence in the clash between good people and evil people and horror at the death of the innocent infants. God allows evil, with all its tragedy, as he moves forward his unstoppable plan of salvation. He will keep his promise, however mysterious his ways.

Pray as you are led for yourself and others.

"Lord, let me embrace your will, though it takes me through the valley of the shadow of death, for you are with me. Be also with those I remember now . . ." (Continue in your words.)

Listen to Jesus.

Give yourself entirely to me, and you have life no one can take from you—no person, no devil, no circumstance. I am the Way, the Truth, and the Life. Enter into the joy of the Lord, my child. What else is Jesus saying to you?

Ask God to show you how to live today.

"Help me to keep your hope foremost, relying upon your promises, not succumbing to my fears. Thank you, Mighty God. Amen."

Friday, December 29, 2017

Know that God is present and ready to converse.

"Lord, by your Word, by Jesus, you shed your light on me. I open myself to your light."

Read the gospel: Luke 2:22–35.

When the time came for their purification according to the law of Moses, they brought him up to Jerusalem to present him to the Lord (as it is written in the law of the Lord, "Every firstborn male shall be designated as holy to the Lord"), and they offered a sacrifice according to what is stated in the law of the Lord, "a pair of turtledoves or two young pigeons."

Now there was a man in Jerusalem whose name was Simeon; this man was righteous and devout, looking forward to the consolation of Israel, and the Holy Spirit rested on him. It had been revealed to him by the Holy Spirit that he would not see death before he had seen the Lord's Messiah. Guided by the Spirit, Simeon came into the temple; and when the parents brought in the child Jesus, to do for him what was customary under the law, Simeon took him in his arms and praised God, saying,

"Master, now you are dismissing your servant in peace,
according to your word;
for my eyes have seen your salvation,
which you have prepared in the presence of all peoples,
a light for revelation to the Gentiles
and for glory to your people Israel."

And the child's father and mother were amazed at what was being said about him. Then Simeon blessed them and said to his mother Mary, "This child is destined for the falling and the rising of many in Israel, and to be a sign that will be opposed so that the inner thoughts of many will be revealed—and a sword will pierce your own soul too."

Notice what you think and feel as you read the gospel.

Simeon is close to God, and he perceives through the Spirit and prophesies about the child Jesus and his mother: he will disrupt the world, and she too will be pierced.

Pray as you are led for yourself and others.

"Let me walk with you faithfully in the Spirit without fear, as Simeon and Mary did. Let your peace fall upon all those you have given me . . ." (Continue in your own words.)

Listen to Jesus.

In the world you too will have trouble, but don't be afraid because I have overcome the world. Walk with me, beloved. What else is Jesus saying to you?

Ask God to show you how to live today.

"Help me to walk step-by-step with you all day, doing what pleases you most. Thank you for your faithfulness to me, Jesus. Amen."

Saturday, December 30, 2017

Know that God is present and ready to converse.

"Lord, you make yourself known to your servants. Please number me among them."

Read the gospel: Luke 2:36–40.

There was also a prophet, Anna the daughter of Phanuel, of the tribe of Asher. She was of a great age, having lived with her husband for seven years after her marriage, then as a widow to the age of eighty-four. She never left the temple but worshipped there with fasting and prayer night and day. At that moment she came, and began to praise God and to speak about the child to all who were looking for the redemption of Jerusalem. When they had finished everything required by the law of the Lord, they returned to Galilee, to their own town of Nazareth. The child grew and became strong, filled with wisdom; and the favor of God was upon him.

Notice what you think and feel as you read the gospel.

Like Simeon, Anna is a prophet because of her closeness with God. She learned to love being with God, night and day, and God rewarded her with a glimpse of the Redeemer.

Pray as you are led for yourself and others.

"God, give me Anna's love for you and teach me to fast and pray in a way that pleases you. I want to pray well because I want you to bless the ones I pray for now . . ." (Continue in your own words.)

Listen to Jesus.

I look upon the heart, child. Do you seek me with all your heart? Do you pray for others with a heart full of love? Do you persist in prayer? Ask me for what you need, and you shall have it. What else is Jesus saying to you?

Ask God to show you how to live today.

"Lord, help me to see where I fall short, so that I may seek from you the power to pray effectively. Amen."

Sunday, December 31, 2017
Holy Family of Jesus, Mary, and Joseph

Know that God is present and ready to converse.

"Lord, I thank you for including me in your family. I sit at your feet to know you better."

Read the gospel: Luke 2:22–40.

When the time came for their purification according to the law of Moses, they brought Jesus up to Jerusalem to present him to the Lord (as it is written in the law of the Lord, "Every firstborn male shall be designated as holy to the Lord"), and they offered a sacrifice according to what is stated in the law of the Lord, "a pair of turtledoves or two young pigeons."

Now there was a man in Jerusalem whose name was Simeon; this man was righteous and devout, looking forward to the consolation of Israel, and the Holy Spirit rested on him. It had been revealed to him by the Holy Spirit that he would not see death before he had seen the Lord's Messiah. Guided by the Spirit, Simeon came into the temple; and when the parents brought in the child Jesus, to do for him what was customary under the law, Simeon took him in his arms and praised God, saying,

"Master, now you are dismissing your servant in peace,
according to your word;
for my eyes have seen your salvation,
which you have prepared in the presence of all peoples,
a light for revelation to the Gentiles
and for glory to your people Israel."

And the child's father and mother were amazed at what was being said about him. Then Simeon blessed them and said to his mother Mary, "This child is destined for the falling and the rising of many in Israel, and to be a sign that will be opposed so that the inner thoughts of many will be revealed—and a sword will pierce your own soul too."

There was also a prophet, Anna the daughter of Phanuel, of the tribe of Asher. She was of a great age, having lived with her husband for seven years after her marriage, then as a widow to the age of eighty-four. She never left the temple but worshipped there with fasting and prayer night and day. At that moment she came, and began to praise God and to speak about the child to all who were looking for the redemption of Jerusalem. When they had finished everything required by the law of the Lord, they returned to Galilee, to their own town of Nazareth. The child grew and became strong, filled with wisdom; and the favor of God was upon him.

Notice what you think and feel as you read the gospel.

Seeking merely to present the infant Jesus according to the law, Mary and Joseph witness marvelous things in the Temple and hear surprising prophesies from two ancient servants of God. Afterward, the Holy Family returns to Nazareth. In the midst of God's mysterious workings, they simply raised their boy day by day. God was with their son.

Pray as you are led for yourself and others.

"Be with me and mine, Lord, as we seek to meet our responsibilities every day. Bless our efforts, especially . . ." (Continue in your own words.)

Listen to Jesus.

Seek me first, beloved, and we will live every day in love. Every day will be new for us. You will grow in strength, wisdom, and the favor of God. What else is Jesus saying to you?

Ask God to show you how to live today.

"What you want is what I want, Lord. And when I resist, bend my will to your own. Amen."

Monday, January 1, 2018
Solemnity of the Blessed Virgin Mary, Mother of God

Know that God is present and ready to converse.

"Lord God Almighty, you humble yourself to be with us and to speak with us because you love us. Let me receive your Word now and return your love."

Read the gospel: Luke 2:16–21.

So the shepherds went with haste and found Mary and Joseph, and the child lying in the manger. When they saw this, they made known what had been told them about this child; and all who heard it were amazed at what the shepherds told them. But Mary treasured all these words and pondered them in her heart. The shepherds returned, glorifying and praising God for all they had heard and seen, as it had been told them. After eight days had passed, it was time to circumcise the child; and he was called Jesus, the name given by the angel before he was conceived in the womb.

Notice what you think and feel as you read the gospel.

God sent his angels to tell the shepherds about the birth of Jesus. He chose the shepherds to be witnesses to the amazing event—God chooses the humble, the poor, the simple to do his will.

Pray as you are led for yourself and others.

"Let me encounter Jesus as humbly as the poor shepherds, Lord, and send me out to spread your love and serve those you have given me . . ." (Continue in your own words.)

Listen to Jesus.

You may learn the ways of God, dear disciple, by meditating on the words of God. I will show you everything you need to know, but you must look to me faithfully. Turn to me in your great need. What else is Jesus saying to you?

Ask God to show you how to live today.

"Teach me, Lord; let me be your student attentive to all you say in all the people and events of my life, starting today. Amen."

Tuesday, January 2, 2018

Know that God is present and ready to converse.

"Let me learn from you, Holy Spirit, that I may have an answer to any who are trying to trap me. Glory to you, O Lord."

Read the gospel: John 1:19–28.

This is the testimony given by John when the Jews sent priests and Levites from Jerusalem to ask him, "Who are you?" He confessed and did not deny it, but confessed, "I am not the Messiah." And they asked him, "What then? Are you Elijah?" He said, "I am not." "Are you the prophet?" He answered, "No." Then they said to him, "Who are you? Let us have an answer for those who sent us. What do you say about yourself?" He said,

> "I am the voice of one crying out in the wilderness,
> 'Make straight the way of the Lord,'"

as the prophet Isaiah said.

Now they had been sent from the Pharisees. They asked him, "Why then are you baptizing if you are neither the Messiah, nor Elijah, nor the prophet?" John answered them, "I baptize with water. Among you stands one whom you do not know, the one who is coming after me; I am not worthy to untie the thong of his sandal." This took place in Bethany across the Jordan where John was baptizing.

Notice what you think and feel as you read the gospel.

Except for the middle paragraph quoting scripture, each paragraph in this passage contains four negatives as the priests try to trap John in his words. He simply says, no, I am not the Messiah, and quotes Isaiah, "I am the voice of one crying in the wilderness." In the final paragraph, John speaks the most powerful negative of all: "I am *not* worthy to untie the thong of his sandal."

Pray as you are led for yourself and others.

"Lord, I am not worthy either, yet you have called me to follow you and love others. As I follow, Lord, I pray with all my heart for the needs of others, including . . ." (Continue in your own words.)

Listen to Jesus.

Sometimes the simple truth is "no." Try to speak the simple truth in all your affairs, child. Know that all God's promises are "yes" in me. What else is Jesus saying to you?

Ask God to show you how to live today.

"I want to be a more honest, simple, straightforward person, Lord, to please you. Give me opportunities and teach me to do it. Amen."

Wednesday, January 3, 2018

Know that God is present and ready to converse.

"You are always with me, Lord. Thank you. Let me turn to you now with my heart, mind, soul, and spirit so that I may hear and be converted."

Read the gospel: John 1:29–34.

The next day John the Baptist saw Jesus coming towards him and declared, "Here is the Lamb of God who takes away the sin of the world! This is he of whom I said, 'After me comes a man who ranks ahead of me because he was before me.' I myself did not know him; but I came baptizing with water for this reason, that he might be revealed to Israel." And John testified, "I saw the Spirit descending from heaven like a dove, and it remained on him. I myself did not know him, but the one who sent me to baptize with water said to me, 'He on whom you see the Spirit descend and remain is the one who baptizes with the Holy Spirit.' And I myself have seen and have testified that this is the Son of God."

Notice what you think and feel as you read the gospel.

John recognizes Jesus even as he approaches, calling him the Lamb of God. John says he saw the Spirit descending upon Jesus, a sign to him that Jesus is the Son of God.

Pray as you are led for yourself and others.

"John's ministry of water baptism gave way to Jesus' ministry of baptism with the Holy Spirit. Baptize me and all those you have given me in your Spirit, Lord! . . ." (Continue in your own words.)

Listen to Jesus.

Those who walk by the Spirit do not always know where they are going, but you may know that I always go with you. You ask me for the Holy Spirit. I grant your prayer. Receive the Holy Spirit. What else is Jesus saying to you?

Ask God to show you how to live today.

"Guide me with your Spirit today. Make me free to abandon habit, to do inspired acts of love for God and for others. Amen."

Thursday, January 4, 2018

Know that God is present and ready to converse.

"Jesus, I have found you as my Savior, but you have known me all along."

Read the gospel: John 1:35–42.

The next day John again was standing with two of his disciples, and as he watched Jesus walk by, he exclaimed, "Look, here is the Lamb of God!" The two disciples heard him say this, and they followed Jesus. When Jesus turned and saw them following, he said to them, "What are you looking for?" They said to him, "Rabbi" (which translated means Teacher), "where are you staying?" He said to them, "Come and see." They came and saw where he was staying, and they remained with him that day. It was about four o'clock in the afternoon. One of the two who heard John speak and followed him was Andrew, Simon Peter's brother. He first found his brother Simon and said to him, "We have found the Messiah" (which is translated Anointed). He brought Simon to Jesus, who looked at him and said, "You are Simon son of John. You are to be called Cephas" (which is translated Peter).

Notice what you think and feel as you read the gospel.

John calls Jesus the Lamb of God, and immediately John's disciples follow Jesus, who invites them over for a visit. When Andrew tells his brother Simon that they have found the Messiah, he brings him to Jesus, who already knows him. Jesus tells Simon he will be called Cephas, Peter, the rock.

Pray as you are led for yourself and others.

"Lord, you know everything about me. Give me what I need. Just draw me, and all those you have given me, to yourself . . ." (Continue in your own words.)

Listen to Jesus.

Everyone in the kingdom of God has a new name already inscribed, ready to be revealed, for you have been known and loved by God for eternity, my child. What else is Jesus saying to you?

Ask God to show you how to live today.

"Help me to follow you closely. Help me get to know you as you know me, Lord. Thank you. Amen."

Friday, January 5, 2018

Know that God is present and ready to converse.

"Jesus, King of Kings, Lord of Lords, you allow me to be with you now. Someday I will see the angels ascending and descending upon the Son of Man."

Read the gospel: John 1:43–51.

The next day Jesus decided to go to Galilee. He found Philip and said to him, "Follow me." Now Philip was from Bethsaida, the city of Andrew and Peter. Philip found Nathanael and said to him, "We have found him about whom Moses in the law and also the prophets wrote, Jesus son of Joseph from Nazareth." Nathanael said to him, "Can anything good come out of Nazareth?" Philip said to him, "Come and see." When Jesus saw Nathanael coming towards him, he said of him, "Here is truly an Israelite in whom there is no deceit!" Nathanael asked him, "Where did you come to know me?" Jesus answered, "I saw you under the fig tree before Philip called you." Nathanael replied, "Rabbi, you are the Son of God! You are the King of Israel!" Jesus answered, "Do you believe because I told you that I saw you under the fig tree? You will see greater things than these." And he said to him, "Very truly, I tell you, you will see heaven opened and the angels of God ascending and descending upon the Son of Man."

Notice what you think and feel as you read the gospel.

Nathanael is skeptical when Philip tells him that they have found the one foretold in Moses and the prophets. "Out of Nazareth?" Nathanael asks. Yet he, like Philip, Andrew, and Peter, is from Bethsaida, hardly a major city. Jesus pays Nathanael a wonderful compliment, again showing that he knows the heart of everyone. Nathanael believes.

Pray as you are led for yourself and others.

"Take all guile from my heart, Lord, so that I can please you and follow you closely. In your love, let me serve others by prayer and service. I think of . . ." (Continue in your own words.)

Listen to Jesus.

I will give you the opportunity to show love today, dear disciple. The love you show will be our love, not yours alone and not mine alone. This is how I work in the hearts of people. What else is Jesus saying to you?

Ask God to show you how to live today.

"Give me the love that is both yours and mine, Lord, and help me to apply it generously today. Amen."

Saturday, January 6, 2018

Know that God is present and ready to converse.

"Holy Spirit, Creator God, author of the Word of God, Spouse of Mary, the Mother of God, open my eyes and my heart to God right now."

Read the gospel: Mark 1:7–11.

John proclaimed, "The one who is more powerful than I is coming after me; I am not worthy to stoop down and untie the thong of his sandals.

I have baptized you with water; but he will baptize you with the Holy Spirit."

In those days Jesus came from Nazareth of Galilee and was baptized by John in the Jordan. And just as he was coming up out of the water, he saw the heavens torn apart and the Spirit descending like a dove on him. And a voice came from heaven, "You are my Son, the Beloved; with you I am well pleased."

Notice what you think and feel as you read the gospel.

Through Jesus, God is performing the most loving act possible—he is saving the human race from sin and death. Jesus brings mercy, forgiveness, atonement, and eternal life for whomever will receive him. The Father, Son, and Holy Spirit are united in this endeavor. Praise God.

Pray as you are led for yourself and others.

"Father, Son, and Holy Spirit, I long to join your circle of love. Let that be the goal of my day and my lifetime, never faltering. With you, that is possible. I pray the same for all those you have given me and think particularly of . . ." (Continue in your own words.)

Listen to Jesus.

I rejoice that you desire my love, my friend. What you desire you shall have, for you are asking for what is of supreme good. Through love and love alone you enter into fellowship with God. What else is Jesus saying to you?

Ask God to show you how to live today.

"Let my love and desire for you grow today, so that I will see you in anyone who needs some help, and I will act in love. Amen."

Sunday, January 7, 2018
Epiphany of the Lord

Know that God is present and ready to converse.

"Lord above, you have come down to earth, and you stop here with me as I read and pray. I praise you."

Read the gospel: Matthew 2:1–12.

In the time of King Herod, after Jesus was born in Bethlehem of Judea, wise men from the East came to Jerusalem, asking, "Where is the child who has been born king of the Jews? For we observed his star at its rising, and have come to pay him homage." When King Herod heard this, he was frightened, and all Jerusalem with him; and calling together all the chief priests and scribes of the people, he inquired of them where the Messiah was to be born. They told him, "In Bethlehem of Judea; for so it has been written by the prophet:

'And you, Bethlehem, in the land of Judah,
are by no means least among the rulers of Judah;
for from you shall come a ruler
who is to shepherd my people Israel.'"

Then Herod secretly called for the wise men and learned from them the exact time when the star had appeared. Then he sent them to Bethlehem, saying, "Go and search diligently for the child; and when you have found him, bring me word so that I may also go and pay him homage." When they had heard the king, they set out; and there, ahead of them, went the star that they had seen at its rising, until it stopped over the place where the child was. When they saw that the star had stopped, they were overwhelmed with joy. On entering the house, they saw the child with Mary his mother; and they knelt down and paid him homage. Then, opening their treasure chests, they offered him gifts of gold, frankincense, and myrrh. And having been warned in a dream not to return to Herod, they left for their own country by another road.

Notice what you think and feel as you read the gospel.

When the star stops, the wise men are filled with joy. How mysterious their foreknowledge of this event, their collaboration, their journey! They seem to have understood what was happening. They even respond to the warning in a dream and do not return to Herod.

Pray as you are led for yourself and others.

"Lord, lead me to you and let me worship you with joy. I pray that all those you have given me learn the joy of worshipping God, incarnate in Jesus, the child born in Bethlehem . . ." (Continue in your own words.)

Listen to Jesus.

If you love me, child, you will seek me. If you seek me, you will find me. When you do, you will be filled with joy that transcends all your struggles and suffering. Find me in your heart, my love. What else is Jesus saying to you?

Ask God to show you how to live today.

"Lord, I am overwhelmed by the mystery of worship, this prayer relationship we have. Please keep me going steadily toward you. What gift may I give you today? Amen."

Ordinary Time

INTRODUCTION

Ordinary Time is the time of the year in which Christ walks among us, calling us, teaching us, transforming us. Advent, Lent, and the Christmas and Easter seasons are special periods excluded from Ordinary Time. Ordinary Time begins on the Monday following the first Sunday after the Feast of the Epiphany and runs until Ash Wednesday; it then continues on the Monday after Pentecost Sunday and runs until the First Sunday of Advent, which is when the new liturgical year begins.

Ordinary Time is called "ordinary" simply because the weeks are numbered. Like the word *ordinal*, the word *ordinary* comes from a Latin word for numbers. Ordinary Time refers to the ordered life of the Church; the gospels of Ordinary Time treat all aspects of Jesus' ministry and sayings more or less in sequence.

Monday, January 8, 2018

Know that God is present and ready to converse.

"Holy Spirit, you are the Lord. Touch me, teach me, bring me to Jesus."

Read the gospel: Mathew 4:12–17, 23–25.

Now when Jesus heard that John had been arrested, he withdrew to Galilee. He left Nazareth and made his home in Capernaum by the sea, in the territory of Zebulun and Naphtali, so that what had been spoken through the prophet Isaiah might be fulfilled:

"Land of Zebulun, land of Naphtali,
  on the road by the sea, across the Jordan, Galilee of the
    Gentiles—
the people who sat in darkness
  have seen a great light
and for those who sat in the region and shadow of death
  light has dawned."

From that time Jesus began to proclaim, "Repent, for the kingdom of heaven has come near." . . .

Jesus went throughout Galilee, teaching in their synagogues and proclaiming the good news of the kingdom and curing every disease and every sickness among the people. So his fame spread throughout all Syria, and they brought to him all the sick, those who were afflicted with various diseases and pains, demoniacs, epileptics, and paralytics, and he cured them. And great crowds followed him from Galilee, the Decapolis, Jerusalem, Judea, and from beyond the Jordan.

Notice what you think and feel as you read the gospel.

Jesus begins his ministry as John the Baptist is arrested. He is the great light prophesied by Isaiah. Like John, he urges repentance, the ticket into the kingdom he proclaims. He proves his goodness and his divinity by healing the sick.

Pray as you are led for yourself and others.

"Lord, give me your Spirit, that I may be freshly baptized and clean. I pray for the goodness and holiness that comes only by your Spirit, not by my own proud striving . . ." (Continue in your own words.)

Listen to Jesus.

My beloved, you are precious to me. Continue to throw yourself upon me. Give me all that you are, and I will form you into the person you should be. Come to me. What else is Jesus saying to you?

Ask God to show you how to live today.

"Help me repent, Lord. I tend to be slow to respond to you, slow to obey, but you will be with me all day. Amen."

Tuesday, January 9, 2018

Know that God is present and ready to converse.

"Mysterious Lord of goodness and mercy, you triumph over evil. Be with me now in power."

Read the gospel: Mark 1:21–28.

They went to Capernaum; and when the sabbath came, he entered the synagogue and taught. They were astounded at his teaching, for he taught them as one having authority, and not as the scribes. Just then there was in their synagogue a man with an unclean spirit, and he cried out, "What have you to do with us, Jesus of Nazareth? Have you come to destroy us? I know who you are, the Holy One of God." But Jesus rebuked him, saying, "Be silent, and come out of him!" And the unclean spirit, throwing him into convulsions and crying with a loud voice, came out of him. They were all amazed, and they kept on asking one another, "What is this? A new teaching—with authority! He commands even the unclean spirits, and they obey him." At once his fame began to spread throughout the surrounding region of Galilee.

Notice what you think and feel as you read the gospel.

Jesus amazes people with his power and authority. He changes the lives of all who come to him.

Pray as you are led for yourself and others.

"Lord, change my life. Align me with your goodness. Make me new, pleasing to you. Let me serve others as you served. I give to you these people I love . . ." (Continue in your own words.)

Listen to Jesus.

I look at your heart, dear one. To love me is to find me and to understand me. Let us journey together. What else is Jesus saying to you?

Ask God to show you how to live today.

"Lord, my only desire is to follow you and be your own. I want to accept your authority: teach me, cleanse me, keep my will for you strong and pure today. Thank you. Amen."

Wednesday, January 10, 2018

Know that God is present and ready to converse.

"Lord, I come to you, searching for you. And here you are. Lead me to true worship, Lord."

Read the gospel: Mark 1:29–39.

As soon as Jesus and his disciples left the synagogue, they entered the house of Simon and Andrew, with James and John. Now Simon's mother-in-law was in bed with a fever, and they told him about her at once. He came and took her by the hand and lifted her up. Then the fever left her, and she began to serve them.

That evening, at sunset, they brought to him all who were sick or possessed with demons. And the whole city was gathered around the door. And he cured many who were sick with various diseases, and cast out many demons; and he would not permit the demons to speak, because they knew him.

In the morning, while it was still very dark, he got up and went out to a deserted place, and there he prayed. And Simon and his companions hunted for him. When they found him, they said to him, "Everyone is searching for you." He answered, "Let us go on to the neighboring towns, so that I may proclaim the message there also; for that is what I came out to do." And he went throughout Galilee, proclaiming the message in their synagogues and casting out demons.

Notice what you think and feel as you read the gospel.

Jesus works for, prays for, and commissions those who follow him. The work is to spread the message that the Messiah has come, offering salvation from sin and death.

Pray as you are led for yourself and others.

"Lord, give me simple faith in you. Let me take you at face value. I need you, search for you, love you, and thank you. I thank you, too, for the work you have given me. I pray now for . . ." (Continue in your own words.)

Listen to Jesus.

Beloved, I love your simplicity, for that is childlike. No one and nothing can shake your faith as long as you remain in me. Visit me often. What else is Jesus saying to you?

Ask God to show you how to live today.

"I have much to do, many distractions, Lord. Let me seek only you today; you will send me forth to serve you and others in peace. I am yours. Amen."

Thursday, January 11, 2018

Know that God is present and ready to converse.

"Invisible God, around me and in me now, to seek you is to find you. I open myself to your teaching, your precious Word, Jesus."

Read the gospel: Mark 1:40–45.

A leper came to Jesus begging him, and kneeling he said to him, "If you choose, you can make me clean." Moved with pity, Jesus stretched out his hand and touched him, and said to him, "I do choose. Be made clean!" Immediately the leprosy left him, and he was made clean. After sternly warning him he sent him away at once, saying to him, "See that you say nothing to anyone; but go, show yourself to the priest, and offer for your cleansing what Moses commanded, as a testimony to them." But he went out and began to proclaim it freely, and to spread the word, so that Jesus could no longer go into a town openly, but stayed out in the country; and people came to him from every quarter.

Notice what you think and feel as you read the gospel.

Jesus chooses to cleanse the leper. God is good to all who come to him. No wonder people flocked to Jesus.

Pray as you are led for yourself and others.

"Lord, I know many who need your healing touch. I offer my prayers, my thoughts, words, and deeds today, my whole day for the good of those you have given me. I pray for . . ." (Continue in your own words.)

Listen to Jesus.

To offer one's self for others, child, is my way of loving. By losing your life this way, day by day, you save it for eternity. I will welcome you into my everlasting kingdom. What else is Jesus saying to you?

Ask God to show you how to live today.

"Lord, your goodness is so great that I cannot take it in. Help me to love others for love of you, serving however I can. Lead me, Lord. I praise you! Amen."

Friday, January 12, 2018

Know that God is present and ready to converse.

"Lord Jesus, what do you have for me today? Open my heart to you so that I can receive it."

Read the gospel: Mark 2:1–12.

When Jesus returned to Capernaum after some days, it was reported that he was at home. So many gathered around that there was no longer room for them, not even in front of the door; and he was speaking the word to them. Then some people came, bringing to him a paralyzed man, carried by four of them. And when they could not bring him to Jesus because of the crowd, they removed the roof above him; and after having dug through it, they let down the mat on which the paralytic lay. When Jesus saw their faith, he said to the paralytic, "Son, your sins are forgiven." Now some of the scribes were sitting there, questioning in their hearts, "Why does this fellow speak in this way? It is blasphemy! Who can forgive sins but God alone?" At once Jesus perceived in his spirit that they were discussing these questions among themselves; and he said to them, "Why do you raise such questions in your hearts? Which is easier, to say to the paralytic, 'Your sins are forgiven,' or to say, 'Stand up and take your mat and walk'? But so that you may know that the Son of Man has authority on earth to forgive sins"—he said to the paralytic—"I say to you, stand up, take your mat and go to your home." And he stood up, and immediately took the mat and went out before all of them; so that they were all amazed and glorified God, saying, "We have never seen anything like this!"

Notice what you think and feel as you read the gospel.

Jesus knows that forgiveness of sins is more important than healing of the body, so Jesus gives the paralytic what he most needs but doesn't ask for. In forgiving sins, Jesus reveals to all present that he is not an ordinary prophet. He is the Messiah, the Son of God. The people are still seeking to understand that. For now they are astounded and glorify God.

Pray as you are led for yourself and others.

"Lord, forgive my sins and keep me from sin today. I want to walk in the wholeness of your love. I want to share your love, peace, and truth with others. Help me do it, Jesus . . ." (Continue in your own words.)

Listen to Jesus.

I forgive you, dear friend. Don't you feel my healing grace within? There is no freedom like the freedom forgiveness confers. Walk in that freedom, and you will witness to my glory. You are pleasing to me. What else is Jesus saying to you?

Ask God to show you how to live today.

"Lord, I accept your freedom. I use it to choose you. I use it to serve others. Help me do so today. Thank you. Amen."

Saturday, January 13, 2018

Know that God is present and ready to converse.

"Jesus, you are a wonder-worker, the Lord here among us, showing us the truths of God. I long to learn from you today."

Read the gospel: Mark 2:13–17.

Jesus went out again beside the lake; the whole crowd gathered around him, and he taught them. As he was walking along, he saw Levi son of Alphaeus sitting at the tax booth, and he said to him, "Follow me." And he got up and followed him.

And as he sat at dinner in Levi's house, many tax collectors and sinners were also sitting with Jesus and his disciples—for there were many who followed him. When the scribes of the Pharisees saw that he was eating with sinners and tax collectors, they said to his disciples, "Why does he eat with tax collectors and sinners?" When Jesus heard this, he said to them, "Those who are well have no need of a physician, but those who are sick; I have come to call not the righteous but sinners."

Notice what you think and feel as you read the gospel.

Jesus must have had an incredibly attractive power, for when he says to someone, "Follow me," the person stops what he is doing and follows. Here he calls a despised tax collector. Of course the self-righteous Pharisees criticize him for it, especially because he goes to Levi's house for dinner. Jesus responds to them, "I have come to call not the righteous but sinners."

Pray as you are led for yourself and others.

"Jesus, the price of entry is to admit to being a sinner. I am a sinner. I thank you for calling me, for dining with me, for loving me. Help me love you as you deserve . . ." (Continue in your own words.)

Listen to Jesus.

My friend, I have called you out of your life to live my life. I have called you to love, to pray, to work for the good of others. The secret is to stay near me in your heart and mind. What else is Jesus saying to you?

Ask God to show you how to live today.

"Let me walk closely with you today, Lord, so I may do your will. I do not trust my own ways. I do trust yours. Lead me, Lord. Amen."

Sunday, January 14, 2018
Second Sunday in Ordinary Time

Know that God is present and ready to converse.

"Lamb of God, you take away the sins of the world, have mercy on me. God has anointed you and you are Lord of all. Teach me."

Read the gospel: John 1:35–42.

The next day John again was standing with two of his disciples, and as he watched Jesus walk by, he exclaimed, "Look, here is the Lamb of God!" The two disciples heard him say this, and they followed Jesus. When Jesus turned and saw them following, he said to them, "What are you looking for?" They said to him, "Rabbi" (which translated means Teacher), "where are you staying?" He said to them, "Come and see." They came and saw where he was staying, and they remained with him that day. It was about four o'clock in the afternoon. One of the two who heard John speak and followed him was Andrew, Simon Peter's brother. He first found his brother Simon and said to him, "We have found the Messiah" (which is translated Anointed). He brought Simon to Jesus, who looked at him and said, "You are Simon son of John. You are to be called Cephas" (which is translated Peter).

Notice what you think and feel as you read the gospel.

John points to Jesus as the Lamb of God. Disciples follow him, calling him "Teacher." Jesus invites them to the place he is staying, and he continues to show that he is master of every situation.

Pray as you are led for yourself and others.

"Lord, let my life be meaningful as your life was. Teach me, Teacher, and guide me into meaning that I may please God and do God's will. I know it is God's will that I pray for those you have given me, including . . ." (Continue in your own words.)

Listen to Jesus.

Nothing is small, my child. Loving me, obeying me, getting to know me better—that is what gives meaning to your life and fruitfulness to God's glory. Let yourself be mine. I love you. What else is Jesus saying to you?

Ask God to show you how to live today.

"Lord, you make it sound easy and simple. Give me the childlike faith to trust you and love you with all my heart today as I do your will. Praise you! Amen."

Monday, January 15, 2018

Know that God is present and ready to converse.

"Jesus, you make all things new. Thank you for this new day. I reach out to you for something that will make me new, closer to you."

Read the gospel: Mark 2:18–22.

Now John's disciples and the Pharisees were fasting; and people came and said to Jesus, "Why do John's disciples and the disciples of the Pharisees fast, but your disciples do not fast?" Jesus said to them, "The wedding guests cannot fast while the bridegroom is with them, can they? As long as they have the bridegroom with them, they cannot fast. The days will come when the bridegroom is taken away from them, and then they will fast on that day.

"No one sews a piece of unshrunk cloth on an old cloak; otherwise, the patch pulls away from it, the new from the old, and a worse tear is made. And no one puts new wine into old wineskins; otherwise, the wine will burst the skins, and the wine is lost, and so are the skins; but one puts new wine into fresh wineskins."

Notice what you think and feel as you read the gospel.

Jesus compares himself to a bridegroom—while he is with us, we rejoice; when he is not, we fast. This is the great opportunity to be renewed in him.

Pray as you are led for yourself and others.

"Jesus, you promised to be with me always, even to the end. Therefore I rejoice. If I need to draw closer to you, let me fast and pray. But let me always be ready to be made new, a vessel of your Spirit . . ." (Continue in your own words.)

Listen to Jesus.

You are my beloved. I rejoice in you. I made you for this love we have between us. There is no one like you. Your purpose is to love God, our Father, his Son, your Savior and Bridegroom, and the Holy Spirit, your mighty Sanctifier. Love God. What else is Jesus saying to you?

Ask God to show you how to live today.

"Lord, I don't love you enough. Give me a stronger sense of your presence with me to help me walk in love all day. Thank you. Amen."

Tuesday, January 16, 2018

Know that God is present and ready to converse.

"Lord, teach me your truth, that I may be free of all rules and limitations and human judgment."

Read the gospel: Mark 2:23–28.

One sabbath Jesus was going through the cornfields; and as they made their way his disciples began to pluck heads of grain. The Pharisees said to him, "Look, why are they doing what is not lawful on the sabbath?" And he said to them, "Have you never read what David did when he and his companions were hungry and in need of food? He entered the house of God, when Abiathar was high priest, and ate the bread of the Presence, which it is not lawful for any but the priests to eat, and he gave some to his companions." Then he said to them, "The sabbath was made for humankind, and not humankind for the sabbath; so the Son of Man is lord even of the sabbath."

Notice what you think and feel as you read the gospel.

Jesus, who fulfills the law and the prophets, is free of artificial human strictures. He is obedient to his Father in all things. His Father is Love; Jesus is Truth. In God, his followers are free to obey.

Pray as you are led for yourself and others.

"Lord, let me know your freedom as I should. If I do all for love of God and others, how can I go wrong? Let me show love through prayer and action to these people . . ." (Continue in your own words.)

Listen to Jesus.

These ideas are brittle in the mind but easy in the soul. I give you my peace. When you worry, come to me and love me. You have nothing to fear. What else is Jesus saying to you?

Ask God to show you how to live today.

"Lord, I have so much to learn, so far to go. I won't make progress in holiness, obedience, freedom, or love without your constant guidance. Be with me today. Amen."

Wednesday, January 17, 2018

Know that God is present and ready to converse.

"Lord, be with me now and soften my heart to hear your Word and grow in understanding and love."

Read the gospel: Mark 3:1–6.

Again Jesus entered the synagogue, and a man was there who had a withered hand. They watched him to see whether he would cure him on the sabbath, so that they might accuse him. And he said to the man who had the withered hand, "Come forward." Then he said to them, "Is it lawful to do good or to do harm on the sabbath, to save life or to kill?" But they were silent. He looked around at them with anger; he was grieved at their hardness of heart and said to the man, "Stretch out your hand." He stretched it out, and his hand was restored. The Pharisees went out and immediately conspired with the Herodians against him, how to destroy him.

Notice what you think and feel as you read the gospel.

The Pharisees continually attempt to catch Jesus violating some of the man-made laws of Judaism, and this occasion is no exception. As Jesus prepares to heal the man with the withered hand, he questions them about the Sabbath laws. They cannot answer him. They are more concerned with their own sense of self-importance than with the suffering of others. Jesus grieves at their hardness of heart, then heals the man's hand. For that, the Pharisees conspire with the Herodians to destroy Jesus.

Pray as you are led for yourself and others.

"Lord, have I envied the talents or success of others? Forgive me. You alone are my hope and my salvation. I pray for those with hardened hearts . . ." (Continue in your own words.)

Listen to Jesus.

I give you a new heart today, beloved—my own heart. Receive it and look out upon others with my eyes, loving and serving in every way you can. Then you will have joy in this life, eternal life hereafter. What else is Jesus saying to you?

Ask God to show you how to live today.

"Thank you for your heart, my Jesus. Let me stay in your grace today, doing all the things you want me to do. Amen."

Thursday, January 18, 2018

Know that God is present and ready to converse.

"Jesus, so many people look to you, yet you have time for me. You are the Lord of Hosts. All things were created by you, through you, and for you. Praise your name!"

Read the gospel: Mark 3:7–12.

Jesus departed with his disciples to the lake, and a great multitude from Galilee followed him; hearing all that he was doing, they came to him in great numbers from Judea, Jerusalem, Idumea, beyond the Jordan, and the region around Tyre and Sidon. He told his disciples to have a boat ready for him because of the crowd, so that they would not crush him; for he had cured many, so that all who had diseases pressed upon him to touch him. Whenever the unclean spirits saw him, they fell down before him and shouted, "You are the Son of God!" But he sternly ordered them not to make him known.

Notice what you think and feel as you read the gospel.

Growing in celebrity, Jesus is swarmed by people, even to the point of danger to himself and to them. Everyone wants to touch him and be healed. Even evil spirits recognize him as the Son of God. Jesus commands them not to make him known. His time is not yet come.

Pray as you are led for yourself and others.

"Lord, thank you for this blessing of time with you. I need your touch, too. Heal, forgive, and empower me, that I may be fruitful in serving you and these you have given me . . ." (Continue in your own words.)

Listen to Jesus.

I am with you always, dear child, every day and every hour of your life. You may turn to me in any moment. Let's stay close and grow in love for one another. What else is Jesus saying to you?

Ask God to show you how to live today.

"Keep me centered on you today, Lord, to keep you as my reason for living, for without you I can do nothing, and I am lost. Thank you for your faithfulness. Amen."

Friday, January 19, 2018

Know that God is present and ready to converse.

"Word of the Father, Jesus, you call me to yourself this day. I come to hear what you have to tell me."

Read the gospel: Mark 3:13–19.

Jesus went up the mountain and called to him those whom he wanted, and they came to him. And he appointed twelve, whom he also named apostles, to be with him, and to be sent out to proclaim the message, and to have authority to cast out demons. So he appointed the twelve: Simon (to whom he gave the name Peter); James son of Zebedee and John the brother of James (to whom he gave the name Boanerges, that is, Sons of Thunder); and Andrew, and Philip, and Bartholomew, and Matthew, and Thomas, and James son of Alphaeus, and Thaddaeus, and Simon the Cananaean, and Judas Iscariot, who betrayed him.

Then he went home.

Notice what you think and feel as you read the gospel.

Jesus calls to himself those he wants to appoint among his disciples as his apostles, and he gives them authority and power to preach and do mighty works as he does.

Pray as you are led for yourself and others.

"Lord, I hear you calling me. I want to obey you and do your will. Give me the power I need and keep me faithful in the service of those you have given me . . ." (Continue in your own words.)

Listen to Jesus.

My beloved disciple, I give you what you pray for, what you need. Give it away to others, and you will receive much more. That is the nature of my grace. I love you. What else is Jesus saying to you?

Ask God to show you how to live today.

"I am often slow of mind and heart, Lord. Make me aware of opportunities to give love and service to those I encounter in my day. Make me aware of my power to help. Amen."

Saturday, January 20, 2018

Know that God is present and ready to converse.

"Almighty God, you are all around me now. I rejoice in you, and I seek your wisdom in your Word. Speak to my heart, Lord."

Read the gospel: Mark 3:20–21.

And the crowd came together again, so that Jesus and his disciples could not even eat. When his family heard it, they went out to restrain him, for people were saying, "He has gone out of his mind."

Notice what you think and feel as you read the gospel.

Again we see that Jesus and his disciples are swarmed and imposed upon by the demands of the crowd. Hearing about it, the members of Jesus' family were naturally concerned about him. Why was he doing this? He was making enemies and putting himself in danger. Some people seriously thought he had gone out of his mind. Jesus' family wanted to protect him.

Pray as you are led for yourself and others.

"Jesus, I want to protect you too, for I know what is going to happen to you. Thank you for your willingness to suffer among us and then be killed. You are Love incarnate. I worship you, Lord . . ." (Continue in your own words.)

Listen to Jesus.

Your compassion for my sufferings pleases me. Thank you. In turn I give you my compassion for the suffering of others, including of those I have given you. What else is Jesus saying to you?

Ask God to show you how to live today.

"Let compassion be my watchword today, Jesus. Let it spring up from my heart whenever I see anyone suffering in any way. Let it move me to action. Amen."

Sunday, January 21, 2018
Third Sunday in Ordinary Time

Know that God is present and ready to converse.

"Lord of all, I will hear now the one you sent to do your will. What does he have to say to me?"

Read the gospel: Mark 1:14–20.

Now after John was arrested, Jesus came to Galilee, proclaiming the good news of God, and saying, "The time is fulfilled, and the kingdom of God has come near; repent, and believe in the good news."

As Jesus passed along the Sea of Galilee, he saw Simon and his brother Andrew casting a net into the lake—for they were fishermen. And Jesus said to them, "Follow me and I will make you fish for people." And immediately they left their nets and followed him. As he went a little farther, he saw James son of Zebedee and his brother John, who were in their boat mending the nets. Immediately he called them; and they left their father Zebedee in the boat with the hired men, and followed him.

Notice what you think and feel as you read the gospel.

Jesus' message goes one step further than John the Baptist's message. John said there was one who would come after him, one greater than he. Jesus says the kingdom has now come near. He exhorts the crowds to repent and believe the good news that the Messiah has come to establish his kingdom among them. Then he calls two pairs of brothers to leave their fathers and their fishing and follow him. They do.

Pray as you are led for yourself and others.

"Lord, let me obey with repentance and faith and follow you today. I renew my offering of self to God, and I pray for those you have given me . . ." (Continue in your own words.)

Listen to Jesus.

It is a daily journey, beloved. Your will is always free—free to give yourself to me or free to withdraw from me. Let me bless you and yours. Choose me every day. I have chosen you. What else is Jesus saying to you?

Ask God to show you how to live today.

"Help me to understand the operation of the freedom you give me, Lord. Teach me to discern and choose what glorifies God. Let me glorify your name! Amen."

Monday, January 22, 2018

Know that God is present and ready to converse.

"Holy Spirit, Author of scripture, Creator of the universe, open my eyes to your power moving in and through me, that I may be created anew by the power of the Word."

Read the gospel: Mark 3:22–30.

And the scribes who came down from Jerusalem said, "He has Beelzebul, and by the ruler of the demons he casts out demons." And Jesus called them to him, and spoke to them in parables, "How can Satan cast out Satan? If a kingdom is divided against itself, that kingdom cannot stand. And if a house is divided against itself, that house will not be able to stand. And if Satan has risen up against himself and is divided, he cannot stand, but his end has come. But no one can enter a strong man's house and plunder his property without first tying up the strong man; then indeed the house can be plundered.

"Truly I tell you, people will be forgiven for their sins and whatever blasphemies they utter; but whoever blasphemes against the Holy Spirit can never have forgiveness, but is guilty of an eternal sin"— for they had said, "He has an unclean spirit."

Notice what you think and feel as you read the gospel.

Jesus counters the accusation that Satan gives him power to cast out evil. Jesus is the strong man who binds Satan and plunders his property. Then he goes further to say that those who blaspheme will be forgiven, but those who blaspheme against the Holy Spirit will not be forgiven. Jesus works in the power of the Holy Spirit, constantly calling us, constantly saving and sanctifying us.

Pray as you are led for yourself and others.

"Lord, let me respect and love the Holy Spirit, one with the Trinity of the one Lord. What mystery! Let me and all those you have given me be open to the Holy Spirit working in and among us . . ." (Continue in your own words.)

Listen to Jesus.

The Holy Spirit is like the wind, present and working but invisibly. Yet you see the results of its actions, both within yourself and in others. Pray for the Spirit to renew the whole earth and bring peace to all humanity. Your prayers will be answered. What else is Jesus saying to you?

Ask God to show you how to live today.

"Blow in and through me, Spirit of God. Make me an instrument of your peace. Thank you. Amen."

Tuesday, January 23, 2018

Know that God is present and ready to converse.

"Lord, communion is the nature of your love. You dwell in loving communion as Father, Son, and Spirit. To that communion you add the Holy Family of Mary and Joseph. Then you invite all who follow Jesus."

Read the gospel: Mark 3:31–35.

Then his mother and his brothers came; and standing outside, they sent to him and called him. A crowd was sitting around him; and they said to him, "Your mother and your brothers and sisters are outside, asking for you." And he replied, "Who are my mother and my brothers?" And looking at those who sat around him, he said, "Here are my mother and my brothers! Whoever does the will of God is my brother and sister and mother."

Notice what you think and feel as you read the gospel.

Who has done the will of God in a greater way than the Blessed Virgin Mary? She surrendered her will to God at the annunciation. Of course Jesus is not repudiating his mother here but rather drawing others into his own family, his communion with God. We are all members of the Holy Family, one in the Lord.

Pray as you are led for yourself and others.

"Thank you for joining me to the Holy Family of God. What love! Let me look at all those who love God as equals in your great community, your kingdom. Let me not judge others but welcome them into our fellowship . . ." (Continue in your own words.)

Listen to Jesus.

People respond to God according to their light and circumstance. Do not judge or despair of any soul. I am at work, calling, teaching, and leading. All things are possible for God. What else is Jesus saying to you?

Ask God to show you how to live today.

"Lord, dear brother, let me invite someone into your family today. Our family. Praise be to you, Jesus Christ! Amen."

Wednesday, January 24, 2018

Know that God is present and ready to converse.

"Open my ears and my heart, O God, to your holy Word, that I may be saved."

Read the gospel: Mark 4:1–20.

Again Jesus began to teach beside the lake. Such a very large crowd gathered around him that he got into a boat on the lake and sat there, while the whole crowd was beside the lake on the land. He began to teach them many things in parables, and in his teaching he said to them: "Listen! A sower went out to sow. And as he sowed, some seed fell on the path, and the birds came and ate it up. Other seed fell on rocky ground, where it did not have much soil, and it sprang up quickly, since it had no depth of soil. And when the sun rose, it was scorched; and since it had no root, it withered away. Other seed fell among thorns, and the thorns grew up and choked it, and it yielded no grain. Other seed fell into good soil and brought forth grain, growing up and increasing and yielding thirty and sixty and a hundredfold." And he said, "Let anyone with ears to hear listen!"

When he was alone, those who were around him along with the twelve asked him about the parables. And he said to them, "To you has been given the secret of the kingdom of God, but for those outside, everything comes in parables; in order that

'they may indeed look, but not perceive,
  and may indeed listen, but not understand;
so that they may not turn again and be forgiven.'"

And he said to them, "Do you not understand this parable? Then how will you understand all the parables? The sower sows the word. These are the ones on the path where the word is sown: when they hear, Satan immediately comes and takes away the word that is sown in them. And these are the ones sown on rocky ground: when they hear the word, they immediately receive it with joy. But they have no root, and endure only for a while; then, when trouble or persecution arises on account of the word, immediately they fall away. And others are those sown among the thorns: these are the ones who hear the word, but the cares of the world, and the lure of wealth, and the desire for other things come in and choke the word, and it yields nothing. And these are the ones sown on the good soil: they hear the word and accept it and bear fruit, thirty and sixty and a hundredfold."

Notice what you think and feel as you read the gospel.

Why are those with eyes blind, those with ears deaf and unable to understand the Word of God? The parable shows that it is a matter of the heart, how we receive the Word and how seriously we take it. For it is easy to believe superficially until we face some adversity. We must let the Word fall deep within us; we must nurture it, grow with it, and love it as our own life, above all other things. Then we will bear abundant fruit, blessing ourselves and others and glorifying God.

Pray as you are led for yourself and others.

"Lord, I know those who see and hear and do not understand. I pray for them, especially . . ." (Continue in your own words.)

Listen to Jesus.

Do not stop praying for those who wander far from me. Love them with your deeds and speak a word to them in season as the Holy Spirit leads you. I will that all come to me for salvation from sin and death. What else is Jesus saying to you?

Ask God to show you how to live today.

"How long, Lord, will you extend your mercy? Plant your Word in me, that I may remain hopeful and faithful, today and until the end. Amen."

Thursday, January 25, 2018
Conversion of Saint Paul, Apostle

Know that God is present and ready to converse.

"Lord, by your Word you command your people. I will hear you and obey, if you give me the grace to do so."

Read the gospel: Mark 16:15–18.

And Jesus said to them, "Go into all the world and proclaim the good news to the whole creation. The one who believes and is baptized will be saved; but the one who does not believe will be condemned. And these signs will accompany those who believe: by using my name they will cast out demons; they will speak in new tongues; they will pick up snakes in their hands, and if they drink any deadly thing, it will not hurt them; they will lay their hands on the sick, and they will recover."

Notice what you think and feel as you read the gospel.

The stakes are high—salvation or condemnation. The way of salvation is simple—believe and be baptized. Those who do not believe will be condemned. God is a just judge. And God gives believers power to do wonderful things for good, testifying to him.

Pray as you are led for yourself and others.

"Lord, let me persevere in hope in this faithless age. I believe you are still at work saving souls. Give us power to bring in a mighty harvest of souls to the kingdom, for you work through us. Choose me, Lord, and show me what to do . . ." (Continue in your own words.)

Listen to Jesus.

Thank you for your willingness. I give you your work, beloved disciple. Pray and ask me how you may perfect it, that it may truly glorify God. The perfect way is love. What else is Jesus saying to you?

Ask God to show you how to live today.

"I do ask you how to perfect my work, how to do your will more lovingly. I need you today to show me and empower me. Thank you, Lord. Amen."

Friday, January 26, 2018

Know that God is present and ready to converse.

"Your Word penetrates all mysteries, Lord, if I have eyes and ears to understand. Teach me, Spirit of Jesus, as I read."

Read the gospel: Mark 4:26–34.

Jesus also said, "The kingdom of God is as if someone would scatter seed on the ground, and would sleep and rise night and day, and the seed would sprout and grow, he does not know how. The earth produces of itself, first the stalk, then the head, then the full grain in the head. But when the grain is ripe, at once he goes in with his sickle, because the harvest has come."

He also said, "With what can we compare the kingdom of God, or what parable will we use for it? It is like a mustard seed, which, when sown upon the ground, is the smallest of all the seeds on earth; yet when it is sown it grows up and becomes the greatest of all shrubs, and puts forth large branches, so that the birds of the air can make nests in its shade."

With many such parables he spoke the word to them, as they were able to hear it; he did not speak to them except in parables, but he explained everything in private to his disciples.

Notice what you think and feel as you read the gospel.

The growth of the kingdom is mysterious, much as nature mysteriously produces abundant harvests of grain from scattered seed. Similarly, the tiny mustard seed produces great shrubs for birds. There is no stopping the growth of the kingdom of God on earth. It is already in motion.

Pray as you are led for yourself and others.

"Lord, I long for the harvest, your return in glory to gather up your own into the everlasting kingdom. In the meantime, help me to keep the faith and scatter the seeds where I can . . ." (Continue in your own words.)

Listen to Jesus.

You live in the age of mercy, beloved. Rejoice in that. Extend my mercy to all you encounter. This is how the kingdom grows. What else is Jesus saying to you?

Ask God to show you how to live today.

"Thank you for letting me be a part of your growing kingdom, Lord. I am willing to do whatever you have for me today. What will you have me do? Amen."

Saturday, January 27, 2018

Know that God is present and ready to converse.

"Even when I am not aware of your presence, Lord, you are with me, mighty to save. Teacher, let me receive your Word."

Read the gospel: Mark 4:35–41.

On that day, when evening had come, Jesus said to them, "Let us go across to the other side." And leaving the crowd behind, they took him with them in the boat, just as he was. Other boats were with him. A great gale arose, and the waves beat into the boat, so that the boat was already being swamped. But he was in the stern, asleep on the cushion; and they woke him up and said to him, "Teacher, do you not care that we are perishing?" He woke up and rebuked the wind, and said to the sea, "Peace! Be still!" Then the wind ceased, and there was a dead calm. He said to them, "Why are you afraid? Have you still no faith?" And they were filled with great awe and said to one another, "Who then is this, that even the wind and the sea obey him?"

Notice what you think and feel as you read the gospel.

The disciples awaken the sleeping Jesus—how can he be undisturbed by the storm? The boat has already taken in water from the high waves. With a word he rebukes the wind and calms the sea, and they are struck with his power. They are still coming to believe that he is the Son of God. Who else can command the forces of nature?

Pray as you are led for yourself and others.

"Lord, calm the storms in me and in my life. Let me be brave and believe in your desire and power to save me and all those you have given me, including . . ." (Continue in your own words.)

Listen to Jesus.

You can trust me, dear friend. I know your limits. I don't expect you to do everything by yourself. But seek simply to do what I ask you to do, trusting me. When you feel fear, ask me, "Whom shall I love, Lord?" Love casts out fear. What else is Jesus saying to you?

Ask God to show you how to live today.

"As I face danger today, Lord, help me turn to you and trust your rescue. As I feel fears, let me love you and others. Amen."

Sunday, January 28, 2018
Fourth Sunday in Ordinary Time

Know that God is present and ready to converse.

"Jesus, God has given you all power in heaven and on earth. You do wondrous things to the glory of God. By your Word, Lord, do wondrous things in me. Thank you."

Read the gospel: Mark 1:21–28.

They went to Capernaum; and when the sabbath came, Jesus entered the synagogue and taught. They were astounded at his teaching, for he taught them as one having authority, and not as the scribes. Just then there was in their synagogue a man with an unclean spirit, and he cried out, "What have you to do with us, Jesus of Nazareth? Have you come to destroy us? I know who you are, the Holy One of God." But Jesus rebuked him, saying, "Be silent, and come out of him!" And the unclean spirit, throwing him into convulsions and crying with a loud voice, came out of him. They were all amazed, and they kept on asking one another, "What is this? A new teaching—with authority! He commands even the unclean spirits, and they obey him." At once his fame began to spread throughout the surrounding region of Galilee.

Notice what you think and feel as you read the gospel.

Jesus, unlike other religious teachers, shows his authority in his teaching. When an unclean spirit speaks out loudly in the synagogue, Jesus commands him to be silent and exorcises the unclean spirit from the possessed man. Just as he has authority to calm the wind and sea during the storm, he has authority in the spiritual realm, too.

Pray as you are led for yourself and others.

"I can do nothing unless you work in me, Lord. You have given me some authority in my own life. Let me use it according to your will, especially in serving those you have given me . . ." (Continue in your own words.)

Listen to Jesus.

As I came to serve, I ask you to serve, and I know you understand that. How can I help you serve more effectively? Ask me for what you need, disciple. What else is Jesus saying to you?

Ask God to show you how to live today.

"I need your Spirit to guide me and enable me to do your will. Please give me the gifts of wisdom, courage, and true devotion to you. Thank you for your blessings, Lord. Amen."

Monday, January 29, 2018

Know that God is present and ready to converse.

"Lord, drive away all distractions, that I may, in my right mind, turn to you."

Read the gospel: Mark 5:1–20.

They came to the other side of the lake, to the country of the Gerasenes. And when Jesus had stepped out of the boat, immediately a man out of the tombs with an unclean spirit met him. He lived among the tombs; and no one could restrain him anymore, even with a chain; for he had often been restrained with shackles and chains, but the chains he wrenched apart, and the shackles he broke in pieces; and no one had the strength to subdue him. Night and day among the tombs and on the mountains he was always howling and bruising himself with stones. When he saw Jesus from a distance, he ran and bowed down before him; and he shouted at the top of his voice, "What have you to do with me, Jesus, Son of the Most High God? I adjure you by God, do not torment me." For he had said to him, "Come out of the man, you unclean spirit!" Then Jesus asked him, "What is your name?" He replied, "My name is Legion; for we are many." He begged him earnestly not to send them out of the country. Now there on the hillside a great herd of swine was feeding; and the unclean spirits begged him, "Send us into the swine; let us enter them." So he gave them permission. And the unclean spirits came out and entered the swine; and the herd, numbering about two thousand, rushed down the steep bank into the lake, and were drowned in the lake.

The swineherds ran off and told it in the city and in the country. Then people came to see what it was that had happened. They came to Jesus and saw the demoniac sitting there, clothed and in his right mind, the very man who had had the legion; and they were afraid. Those who had seen what had happened to the demoniac and to the swine reported it. Then they began to beg Jesus to leave their neighborhood. As he was getting into the boat, the man who had been possessed by demons begged him that he might be with him. But Jesus refused, and said to him, "Go home to your friends, and tell them how much the Lord has done for you, and what mercy he has shown you." And he went away and began to proclaim in the Decapolis how much Jesus had done for him; and everyone was amazed.

Notice what you think and feel as you read the gospel.

This is a dramatic description of Jesus' encounter with a man who had superhuman strength and lived among the tombs because he was possessed by many evil spirits. The demons recognize Jesus as the Son of the Most High God and beg him not to torment them but send them into the huge herd of swine nearby. Jesus consents, and the swine rush down and are drowned in the lake. The man is restored to his right mind and wants to go with Jesus, but Jesus asks him to stay and tell others what mercy God has shown him.

Pray as you are led for yourself and others.

"Jesus, I see you have all power. Search me, Lord, and banish any evil within me. I ask for your peace and wisdom in my life, that I may fruitfully serve you and others. Thank you."

Listen to Jesus.

Mind your heart, my child, and root out sprouts of selfishness. I give you discernment to see it. Pray to me to remove it. I am Mercy. Forgiveness and healing I give you generously. I love you. What else is Jesus saying to you?

Ask God to show you how to live today.

"I love you, too, my Jesus. I have no one but you. Let me walk in your mercy all day long. Praise be to you, Lord Jesus Christ. Amen."

Tuesday, January 30, 2018

Know that God is present and ready to converse.

"Jesus, thank you for being present. I am one of many who love you and seek you. I need you now."

Read the gospel: Mark 5:21–43.

When Jesus had crossed again in the boat to the other side, a great crowd gathered round him; and he was by the lake. Then one of the leaders of the synagogue named Jairus came and, when he saw him, fell at his feet and begged him repeatedly, "My little daughter is at the point of death. Come and lay your hands on her, so that she may be made well, and live." So he went with him.

And a large crowd followed him and pressed in on him. Now there was a woman who had been suffering from hemorrhages for twelve years. She had endured much under many physicians, and had spent all that she had; and she was no better, but rather grew worse. She had heard about Jesus, and came up behind him in the crowd and touched his cloak, for she said, "If I but touch his clothes, I will be made well." Immediately her hemorrhage stopped; and she felt in her body that she was healed of her disease. Immediately aware that power had gone forth from him, Jesus turned about in the crowd and said, "Who touched my clothes?" And his disciples said to him, "You see the crowd pressing in on you; how can you say, 'Who touched me?'" He looked all round to see who had done it. But the woman, knowing what had happened to her, came in fear and trembling, fell down before him, and told him the whole truth. He said to her, "Daughter, your faith has made you well; go in peace, and be healed of your disease."

While he was still speaking, some people came from the leader's house to say, "Your daughter is dead. Why trouble the teacher any further?" But overhearing what they said, Jesus said to the leader of the synagogue, "Do not fear, only believe." He allowed no one to follow him except Peter, James, and John, the brother of James. When they came to the house of the leader of the synagogue, he saw a commotion, people weeping and wailing loudly. When he had entered, he said to them, "Why do you make a commotion and weep? The child is not dead but sleeping." And they laughed at him. Then he put them all outside, and took the child's father and mother and those who were with him, and went in where the child was. He took her by the hand and said to her, "Talitha cum," which means, "Little girl, get up!" And immediately the girl got up and began to walk about (she was twelve years of age). At this they were overcome with amazement. He strictly ordered them that no one should know this, and told them to give her something to eat.

Notice what you think and feel as you read the gospel.

Here is a miracle story wrapped in a miracle story. On his way to heal Jairus's daughter, Jesus heals a woman who had suffered from hemorrhages for many years. She touches his cloak and receives healing instantly. Jesus then speaks to her, telling her that her faith has healed her. Meanwhile, Jairus's daughter has died. People gathered at the house laugh at Jesus when he tells them the child is only sleeping, but he goes in and raises the little girl with a touch, and all are amazed.

Pray as you are led for yourself and others.

"Jesus, you spent your ministry performing interventions. You are the same today. I pray that you do intervene in the following cases . . ." (Continue in your own words.)

Listen to Jesus.

The power of God is active on the earth, dear servant. I hear your prayers and will do wonders, some greater than you have asked. Advance into the world with faith, even when the troubles of the world and the needs of others are daunting. What else is Jesus saying to you?

Ask God to show you how to live today.

"I sense that faith should be my spiritual weapon against suffering and need. Let me pray and work in faith today. Thank you. Amen."

Wednesday, January 31, 2018

Know that God is present and ready to converse.

"Lord Jesus, you do all things well! You are here to teach me and make me your own. Let it be so, Lord."

Read the gospel: Mark 6:1–6.

Jesus left that place and came to his home town, and his disciples followed him. On the sabbath he began to teach in the synagogue, and many who heard him were astounded. They said, "Where did this man get all this? What is this wisdom that has been given to him? What deeds of power are being done by his hands! Is not this the carpenter, the son of Mary and brother of James and Joses and Judas and Simon, and are not his sisters here with us?" And they took offence at him. Then Jesus said to them, "Prophets are not without honor, except in their home town, and among their own kin, and in their own house." And he could do no deed of power there, except that he laid his hands on a few sick people and cured them. And he was amazed at their unbelief.

Then he went about among the villages teaching.

Notice what you think and feel as you read the gospel.

Whether by his speaking or his mighty deeds, Jesus shows his divine authority. Unfortunately, the people of his home town cannot see him for what he is, the Messiah, the Son of God. Jesus is amazed by their unbelief, and their lack of faith limits his power to help them.

Pray as you are led for yourself and others.

"Lord, how often does my lack of faith limit your ability to aid me and those you have given me? How can I believe unless you give me faith? Give me faith in your power to do good in my life and in the lives of those you have given me . . ." (Continue in your own words.)

Listen to Jesus.

I grant you faith, beloved. I ask you to nurture it and act upon it, and you shall see good things happen. Do not take those things for granted. They are the fruit of your faith in me. Give me the honor and the glory. What else is Jesus saying to you?

Ask God to show you how to live today.

"I thank you and glorify you, Lord Jesus. By your grace I will walk in faith today, loving others and praying. Amen."

Thursday, February 1, 2018

Know that God is present and ready to converse.

"Master of the Universe, you give good gifts to people. Let me receive your Word out of gratitude to you."

Read the gospel: Mark 6:7–13.

Jesus called the twelve and began to send them out two by two, and gave them authority over the unclean spirits. He ordered them to take nothing for their journey except a staff; no bread, no bag, no money in their belts; but to wear sandals and not to put on two tunics. He said to them, "Wherever you enter a house, stay there until you leave the place. If any place will not welcome you and they refuse to hear you, as you leave, shake off the dust that is on your feet as a testimony against them." So they went out and proclaimed that all should repent. They cast out many demons, and anointed with oil many who were sick and cured them.

Notice what you think and feel as you read the gospel.

Jesus gives authority and power to the twelve and sends them out to preach the Good News with instructions. Instead of making elaborate preparations, they are simply to go and trust God to provide for them.

Pray as you are led for yourself and others.

"Jesus, I offer you myself for your service. Give me authority and power to pray and work for others as you will. I am particularly concerned about . . ." (Continue in your own words.)

Listen to Jesus.

My beloved disciple, I do have work for you, for we are partners on behalf of the coming kingdom of God. Pray earnestly each day and over time it will clearly emerge what I want you to do. You will know my will as you know me. What else is Jesus saying to you?

Ask God to show you how to live today.

"Let me make a first step in knowing and doing your will today, Lord. Lead me. Be with me. Amen."

Friday, February 2, 2018
Presentation of the Lord

Know that God is present and ready to converse.

"Holy Spirit, you are present in all the events of Jesus and the Holy Family. You are present with me now as I read the Word of God. Thank you."

Read the gospel: Luke 2:22–40.

When the time came for their purification according to the law of Moses, they brought him up to Jerusalem to present him to the Lord (as it is written in the law of the Lord, "Every firstborn male shall be designated as holy to the Lord"), and they offered a sacrifice according to what is stated in the law of the Lord, "a pair of turtledoves or two young pigeons."

Now there was a man in Jerusalem whose name was Simeon; this man was righteous and devout, looking forward to the consolation of Israel, and the Holy Spirit rested on him. It had been revealed to him by the Holy Spirit that he would not see death before he had seen the Lord's Messiah. Guided by the Spirit, Simeon came into the temple; and when the parents brought in the child Jesus, to do for him what was customary under the law, Simeon took him in his arms and praised God, saying,

> "Master, now you are dismissing your servant in peace,
> according to your word;
> for my eyes have seen your salvation,
> which you have prepared in the presence of all peoples,
> a light for revelation to the Gentiles
> and for glory to your people Israel."

And the child's father and mother were amazed at what was being said about him. Then Simeon blessed them and said to his mother Mary, "This child is destined for the falling and the rising of many in Israel, and to be a sign that will be opposed so that the inner thoughts of many will be revealed—and a sword will pierce your own soul too."

There was also a prophet, Anna the daughter of Phanuel, of the tribe of Asher. She was of a great age, having lived with her husband for seven years after her marriage, then as a widow to the age of eighty-four. She never left the temple but worshipped there with fasting and prayer night and day. At that moment she came, and began to praise God and to speak about the child to all who were looking for the redemption of Jerusalem. When they had finished everything required by the law of the Lord, they returned to Galilee, to their own town of Nazareth. The child grew and became strong, filled with wisdom; and the favor of God was upon him.

Notice what you think and feel as you read the gospel.

When the Holy Family enters the temple to present the infant Jesus to the priest, as prescribed by law, the Holy Spirit inspires two aged prophets to action. Through the Holy Spirit, Simeon recognizes Jesus as the Messiah, the Savior, but his prophecy over him and his mother is grim, foreshadowing conflict and suffering. The elderly woman Anna also recognizes Jesus and praises God, telling others who were also looking for a savior.

Pray as you are led for yourself and others.

"Holy Spirit, as you inspire scripture and the prophets, inspire my prayer, so that many good things may be accomplished in those I pray for, and thus God will receive glory. In you, I now pray for . . ." (Continue in your own words.)

Listen to Jesus.

To ask for my Spirit is to receive it, dear child. I breathe upon you. Pray and serve with authority. Stay very near to me. What else is Jesus saying to you?

Ask God to show you how to live today.

"Lord, I will try. I am feeble and vulnerable, so I need you to direct my steps. Give light to my eyes. I glorify you and worship you. Amen."

Saturday, February 3, 2018

Know that God is present and ready to converse.

"Good Shepherd, I need you today. Find me, carry me, and love me."

Read the gospel: Mark 6:30–34.

The apostles gathered around Jesus, and told him all that they had done and taught. He said to them, "Come away to a deserted place all by yourselves and rest a while." For many were coming and going, and they had no leisure even to eat. And they went away in the boat to a deserted place by themselves. Now many saw them going and recognized them, and they hurried there on foot from all the towns and arrived ahead of them. As he went ashore, he saw a great crowd; and he had compassion for them, because they were like sheep without a shepherd; and he began to teach them many things.

Notice what you think and feel as you read the gospel.

Jesus is such a celebrity he can't even stop to eat or to pray. But he has compassion for the crowd, and he teaches them.

Pray as you are led for yourself and others.

"Lord, will you teach me? And teach all those I love who are wandering far from you . . ." (Continue in your own words.)

Listen to Jesus.

I love you and those I have given you to pray for. Keep praying and trust in my plan. I know how to bring them home. What else is Jesus saying to you?

Ask God to show you how to live today.

"Lord, it's hard to remember that you and life everlasting are the most important things, the only important things. Keep my mind on that today. Amen."

Sunday, February 4, 2018
Fifth Sunday in Ordinary Time

Know that God is present and ready to converse.

"Lord, I live an ordinary life in an ordinary time. Give me what I need to serve you."

Read the gospel: Mark 1:29–39.

As soon Jesus and his disciples left the synagogue, they entered the house of Simon and Andrew, with James and John. Now Simon's mother-in-law was in bed with a fever, and they told him about her at once. He came and took her by the hand and lifted her up. Then the fever left her, and she began to serve them.

That evening, at sunset, they brought to him all who were sick or possessed with demons. And the whole city was gathered around the door. And he cured many who were sick with various diseases, and cast out many demons; and he would not permit the demons to speak, because they knew him.

In the morning, while it was still very dark, he got up and went out to a deserted place, and there he prayed. And Simon and his companions hunted for him. When they found him, they said to him, "Everyone is searching for you." He answered, "Let us go on to the neighboring towns, so that I may proclaim the message there also; for that is what I came out to do." And he went throughout Galilee, proclaiming the message in their synagogues and casting out demons.

Notice what you think and feel as you read the gospel.

Jesus comes into the life of ordinary people and transforms them with his healing and his power. He loves them. When he leaves them to pray before sunrise, they miss him, they find him, and without protest, he leads them throughout Galilee, delivering his message.

Pray as you are led for yourself and others.

"Lord, you come into ordinary families to bring good. I give you my family. How may I serve? . . ." (Continue in your own words.)

Listen to Jesus.

Your willingness to serve me and others touches me, beloved. You need not press or fret. Just love and trust me, and you will see things that bring you great joy. What else is Jesus saying to you?

Ask God to show you how to live today.

"Lord, with your grace I will be patient and trusting. You are pure love and infinite power. What have I to fear? Amen."

Monday, February 5, 2018

Know that God is present and ready to converse.

"Lord, I come into your presence, hoping to touch you, if only the fringe of your cloak."

Read the gospel: Mark 6:53–56.

When Jesus and his disciples had crossed over, they came to land at Gennesaret and moored the boat. When they got out of the boat, people at once recognized Jesus, and rushed about that whole region and began to bring the sick on mats to wherever they heard he was. And wherever he went, into villages or cities or farms, they laid the sick in the marketplaces, and begged him that they might touch even the fringe of his cloak; and all who touched it were healed.

Notice what you think and feel as you read the gospel.

The Lord suffers the crowds, the endless sick people needing his healing touch. He heals them all.

Pray as you are led for yourself and others.

"Lord, I too am in need of your touch. I have missed you. Give me what I need to please you today. Let me pray also for those you have given me . . ." (Continue in your own words.)

Listen to Jesus.

As long as you carry a burden of love for those I have given you, you are mine, for I too ache with love for those who need me the most. Help me bear the burden, friend. What else is Jesus saying to you?

Ask God to show you how to live today.

"Let me open my heart today to someone new who needs you. If I can help, let me help. If I can only pray, let me pray. Amen."

Tuesday, February 6, 2018

Know that God is present and ready to converse.

"Lord, I bask in your loving presence, I rejoice in the freedom you give me. I choose to love you now."

Read the gospel: Mark 7:1–13.

Now when the Pharisees and some of the scribes who had come from Jerusalem gathered around Jesus, they noticed that some of Jesus' disciples were eating with defiled hands, that is, without washing them. (For the Pharisees, and all the Jews, do not eat unless they thoroughly wash their hands, thus observing the tradition of the elders; and they do not eat anything from the market unless they wash it; and there are also many other traditions that they observe, the washing of cups, pots, and bronze kettles.) So the Pharisees and the scribes asked him, "Why do your disciples not live according to the tradition of the elders, but eat with defiled hands?" He said to them, "Isaiah prophesied rightly about you hypocrites, as it is written,

> 'This people honors me with their lips,
> but their hearts are far from me;
> in vain do they worship me,
> teaching human precepts as doctrines.'

You abandon the commandment of God and hold to human tradition." Then he said to them, "You have a fine way of rejecting the commandment of God in order to keep your tradition! For Moses said, 'Honor your father and your mother'; and, 'Whoever speaks evil of father or mother must surely die.' But you say that if anyone tells father or mother, 'Whatever support you might have had from me is Corban' (that is, an offering to God)—then you no longer permit doing anything for a father or mother, thus making void the word of God through your tradition that you have handed on. And you do many things like this."

Notice what you think and feel as you read the gospel.

Replying to their criticism about his disciples' not observing the traditions of the elders, Jesus tells the scribes and Pharisees that they are hypocrites, putting human doctrines before the law of God, including the commandment to honor father and mother.

Pray as you are led for yourself and others.

"Lord, let me escape legalism, that false righteousness, and be guided by your Spirit. Let me always recognize the good and pursue it, especially when I am dealing with people who do not know you . . ." (Continue in your own words.)

Listen to Jesus.

You will receive criticism, but nothing you cannot handle. Live to please me and no one else. I will never forsake you. What else is Jesus saying to you?

Ask God to show you how to live today.

"Lord, alert me to moments to act in love. Do not let me get so absorbed in my day that I am insensitive to those near me. Open my eyes to loving, Lord. Amen."

Wednesday, February 7, 2018

Know that God is present and ready to converse.

"Lord, I look to you with my heart, for it is my heart that needs radical transformation. I seek the purity of heart that comes only from you."

Read the gospel: Mark 7:14–23.

Then Jesus called the crowd again and said to them, "Listen to me, all of you, and understand: there is nothing outside a person that by going in can defile, but the things that come out are what defile."

When he had left the crowd and entered the house, his disciples asked him about the parable. He said to them, "Then do you also fail to understand? Do you not see that whatever goes into a person from outside cannot defile, since it enters, not the heart but the stomach, and goes out into the sewer?" (Thus he declared all foods clean.) And he said, "It is what comes out of a person that defiles. For it is from within, from the human heart, that evil intentions come: fornication, theft, murder, adultery, avarice, wickedness, deceit, licentiousness, envy, slander, pride, folly. All these evil things come from within, and they defile a person."

Notice what you think and feel as you read the gospel.

Jesus understands that evil comes from the evil intentions in the hearts of people. What we eat is irrelevant, but what we allow to fester in our hearts defiles us, and what we entertain in our hearts becomes sinful action.

Pray as you are led for yourself and others.

"Lord, protect me from the tendencies of my heart. Open my eyes to danger there, for I love to fool myself about my intentions. By your great power, cleanse my heart and fill it with grace, so that I may serve and please you . . ." (Continue in your own words.)

Listen to Jesus.

This is a process, beloved, this cleansing, this purification of the heart. But the process is supernatural, and you need to depend upon me every day. I love you. I am with you to wash your feet, to cleanse your heart each day. What else is Jesus saying to you?

Ask God to show you how to live today.

"Lord, let me stay humbly dependent upon your virtue, your cleansing, and never feel that I am good apart from you. Amen."

Thursday, February 8, 2018

Know that God is present and ready to converse.

"Jesus, I will persist in prayer for those you have given me. Teach me by your Word to pray."

Read the gospel: Mark 7:24–30.

From there Jesus set out and went away to the region of Tyre. He entered a house and did not want anyone to know he was there. Yet he could not escape notice, but a woman whose little daughter had an unclean spirit immediately heard about him, and she came and bowed down at his feet. Now the woman was a Gentile, of Syrophoenician origin. She begged him to cast the demon out of her daughter. He said to her, "Let the children be fed first, for it is not fair to take the children's food and throw it to the dogs." But she answered him, "Sir, even the dogs under the table eat the children's crumbs." Then he said to her, "For saying that, you may go—the demon has left your daughter." So she went home, found the child lying on the bed, and the demon gone.

Notice what you think and feel as you read the gospel.

Jesus challenges the Gentile woman as if he has no interest in her daughter. The woman persists in her request, and Jesus rewards her persistence by granting her prayer, healing her daughter.

Pray as you are led for yourself and others.

"Lord, I now persist in my frequent prayers for the good of these, the many you have given me for just this purpose. I pray for . . ." (Continue in your own words.)

Listen to Jesus.

Prayer is the way to exercise love in your heart. All love comes from God, so when you pray you involve yourself in my love for others, the love that caused me to come to the world, suffer, and die for all people. Join me in this love, my dear disciple. What else is Jesus saying to you?

Ask God to show you how to live today.

"Lord, how important is prayer! Let me humbly beg you to show your love for all people. Amen."

Friday, February 9, 2018

Know that God is present and ready to converse.

"Jesus, take me aside and touch me. Open my ears to your Word and let me speak of your goodness."

Read the gospel: Mark 7:31–37.

Then Jesus returned from the region of Tyre, and went by way of Sidon towards the Sea of Galilee, in the region of the Decapolis. They brought to him a deaf man who had an impediment in his speech; and they begged him to lay his hand on him. He took him aside in private, away from the crowd, and put his fingers into his ears, and he spat and touched his tongue. Then looking up to heaven, he sighed and said to him, "Ephphatha," that is, "Be opened." And immediately his ears were opened, his tongue was released, and he spoke plainly. Then Jesus ordered them to tell no one; but the more he ordered them, the more zealously they proclaimed it. They were astounded beyond measure, saying, "He has done everything well; he even makes the deaf to hear and the mute to speak."

Notice what you think and feel as you read the gospel.

Jesus continues to show his power to heal. Why does Jesus spit and touch the deaf man's tongue? Why does he sigh as he looks up to heaven? The evangelist never says, but this scene rings with truth. Jesus the man is also the Son of God, speaking and doing the Father's will.

Pray as you are led for yourself and others.

"Praise to you, Lord, for you use your power only for good, and all things you do in my life are good. Let me trust you for that. I pray that you also bring good out of the circumstances of others' lives. I think of . . ." (Continue in your own words.)

Listen to Jesus.

You hear my words, child. I am with you today, all day. Trust me in everything. I will not let you down. I grant you your prayers. What else is Jesus saying to you?

Ask God to show you how to live today.

"Lord, let the day's watchword be trust—complete trust in you, even when events frighten me. You are my rock. Amen."

Saturday, February 10, 2018

Know that God is present and ready to converse.

"Jesus, you know me to the depths of my soul. Nourish me by your Word."

Read the gospel: Mark 8:1–10.

In those days when there was again a great crowd without anything to eat, Jesus called his disciples and said to them, "I have compassion for the crowd, because they have been with me now for three days and have nothing to eat. If I send them away hungry to their homes, they will faint on the way—and some of them have come from a great distance." His disciples replied, "How can one feed these people with bread here in the desert?" He asked them, "How many loaves do you have?" They said, "Seven." Then he ordered the crowd to sit down on the ground; and he took the seven loaves, and after giving thanks he broke them and gave them to his disciples to distribute; and they distributed them to the crowd. They had also a few small fish; and after blessing them, he ordered that these too should be distributed. They ate and were filled; and they took up the broken pieces left over, seven baskets full. Now there were about four thousand people. And he sent them away. And immediately he got into the boat with his disciples and went to the district of Dalmanutha.

Notice what you think and feel as you read the gospel.

In his compassion, Jesus anticipates the hunger of the crowd and does not want them to become weak with hunger on their way home. So he multiplies loaves and fish and feeds four thousand people on the spot. Then he sends them away.

Pray as you are led for yourself and others.

"Jesus, you know my hunger. Be the Bread of Life to me today and every day. Feed those you have given me as well, for you have given me your love for them . . ." (Continue in your own words.)

Listen to Jesus.

I do love you, dear disciple. It is right for you to look to me and depend on me for all your needs and the needs of those you pray for. I am taking care of you and yours. What else is Jesus saying to you?

Ask God to show you how to live today.

"Thank you for your love for me, for us. I long for the day when we can all be together in your kingdom, Lord. Let all my hunger be for you today. Amen."

Sunday, February 11, 2018
Sixth Sunday in Ordinary Time

Know that God is present and ready to converse.

"Lord, here with me now, what is your will? Show me through your Word and your Spirit."

Read the gospel: Mark 1:40–45.

A leper came to Jesus begging him, and kneeling he said to him, "If you choose, you can make me clean." Moved with pity, Jesus stretched out his hand and touched him, and said to him, "I do choose. Be made clean!" Immediately the leprosy left him, and he was made clean. After sternly warning him he sent him away at once, saying to him, "See that you say nothing to anyone; but go, show yourself to the priest, and offer for your cleansing what Moses commanded, as a testimony to them." But he went out and began to proclaim it freely, and to spread the word, so that Jesus could no longer go into a town openly, but stayed out in the country; and people came to him from every quarter.

Notice what you think and feel as you read the gospel.

Jesus chooses to grant the request, the prayer, of the leper because he is moved with pity. After healing the leper, Jesus asks him not to tell anyone except the priest. But the healed leper goes out and tells everyone, so that Jesus could no longer go into town openly.

Pray as you are led for yourself and others.

"Jesus, I thank you for choosing to do the works of love that you did and still do. I place before you these people and their needs . . ." (Continue in your own words.)

Listen to Jesus.

I hear your prayers, beloved disciple. Prayer is our secret. By it we share everything. It is the conduit of our love for one another. Speak with me often. What else is Jesus saying to you?

Ask God to show you how to live today.

"Lord, give me the habit of instant prayer throughout the moments of my day. I long to stay close to you. Amen."

Monday, February 12, 2018

Know that God is present and ready to converse.

"Almighty God, creator and sustainer of all that is, I bow before you and worship, for you are Love."

Read the gospel: Mark 8:11–13.

The Pharisees came and began to argue with Jesus, asking him for a sign from heaven, to test him. And he sighed deeply in his spirit and said, "Why does this generation ask for a sign? Truly I tell you, no sign will be given to this generation." And he left them, and getting into the boat again, he went across to the other side.

Notice what you think and feel as you read the gospel.

The Pharisees argue with Jesus and demand a sign. Jesus sighs and does not comply. He departs by boat.

Pray as you are led for yourself and others.

"Lord, keep me from the arrogance of the Pharisees. Let me trust you to know my needs and satisfy them. Let me love and serve those you have given me as you love and serve me . . ." (Continue in your own words.)

Listen to Jesus.

You need no sign from heaven, for the kingdom of heaven is at hand, and I am the key. Trust in me, serve in love, and you will see heaven itself. What else is Jesus saying to you?

Ask God to show you how to live today.

"Lord, I long to do that today. Give me your own Spirit, and I will love others as you ask. Amen."

Tuesday, February 13, 2018

Know that God is present and ready to converse.

"Jesus, how much have you tried to teach me, yet I did not understand? Let me understand you fully as I read and pray with your Word."

Read the gospel: Mark 8:14–21.

Now the disciples had forgotten to bring any bread; and they had only one loaf with them in the boat. And Jesus cautioned them, saying, "Watch out—beware of the yeast of the Pharisees and the yeast of Herod." They said to one another, "It is because we have no bread." And becoming aware of it, Jesus said to them, "Why are you talking about having no bread? Do you still not perceive or understand? Are your hearts hardened? Do you have eyes, and fail to see? Do you have ears, and fail to hear? And do you not remember? When I broke the five loaves for the five thousand, how many baskets full of broken pieces did you collect?" They said to him, "Twelve." "And the seven for the four thousand, how many baskets full of broken pieces did you collect?" And they said to him, "Seven." Then he said to them, "Do you not yet understand?"

Notice what you think and feel as you read the gospel.

The disciples don't understand Jesus when he talks about the yeast of the Pharisees and of Herod. Do they think he is chastising them for forgetting to bring bread on the boat? He reminds them how he fed bread to the crowds of five thousand and four thousand, then adds, "Do you not yet understand?" He is asking them for their complete devotion and trust in him, without being distracted by religiosity or secularism.

Pray as you are led for yourself and others.

"Lord, often I am distracted from you by earthly things, and my devotion and trust in you weaken. Forgive me. Strengthen me and those you have given me in pure devotion to you . . ." (Continue in your own words.)

Listen to Jesus.

You have what you ask, dear friend. Seek to show love to others as I do. Remain in my presence and you will bear fruit. What else is Jesus saying to you?

Ask God to show you how to live today.

"Thank you for this chance, Lord, this day. I rejoice in you. Let me open my eyes and look around to see where I may be useful. Amen."

The Lenten Season

INTRODUCTION

In the gospel, Jesus says his disciples will fast when he, the Bridegroom, is taken from them. We know that Jesus is always with us, but during the season of Lent we honor him in a special way by entering a forty-day period of prayer, fasting, and almsgiving in preparation for the celebration of the Resurrection of the Lord, Easter Sunday. The forty days of Lent correspond to the forty days Jesus prayed and fasted in the desert before beginning his earthly ministry. Lent is a time to allow God to help us become holy, to help us look to the needs of others and minister to those needs, and, most of all, to grow in faith, hope, and love, for those virtues are of God, motivating and empowering us to live the gospel.

The season of Lent begins on Ash Wednesday, dividing the cycle of Ordinary Time in the Church year. Sundays in Lent are not counted as fast days. Lent officially ends on Holy Thursday, the beginning of the Easter Triduum. Fast days continue through Holy Saturday, the day before Easter.

Wednesday, February 14, 2018
Ash Wednesday

Know that God is present and ready to converse.

"Lord, Lent begins. I am so glad I can begin it with you and your Word."

Read the gospel: Matthew 6:1–6, 16–18.

Jesus said, "Beware of practicing your piety before others in order to be seen by them; for then you have no reward from your Father in heaven.

"So whenever you give alms, do not sound a trumpet before you, as the hypocrites do in the synagogues and in the streets, so that they may be praised by others. Truly I tell you, they have received their reward. But when you give alms, do not let your left hand know what your right hand is doing, so that your alms may be done in secret; and your Father who sees in secret will reward you.

"And whenever you pray, do not be like the hypocrites; for they love to stand and pray in the synagogues and at the street corners, so that they may be seen by others. Truly I tell you, they have received their reward. But whenever you pray, go into your room and shut the door and pray to your Father who is in secret; and your Father who sees in secret will reward you. . . .

"And whenever you fast, do not look dismal, like the hypocrites, for they disfigure their faces so as to show others that they are fasting. Truly I tell you, they have received their reward. But when you fast, put oil on your head and wash your face, so that your fasting may be seen not by others but by your Father who is in secret; and your Father who sees in secret will reward you."

Notice what you think and feel as you read the gospel.

Jesus gives some practical spiritual advice about penance, prayer, and fasting: Do it in secret, rather than for show before others. Pray, fast, and give alms to show your repentance and draw nearer to God, and he will reward you.

Pray as you are led for yourself and others.

"I have sinned, Lord, in my thoughts, words, and deeds. As I begin this season of repentance, reveal to me hidden faults and let them be washed away by your grace. I offer this season of Lent for all those you have given me . . ." (Continue in your own words.)

Listen to Jesus.

I will stay near you and wash you, enlighten you, and strengthen you as you seek me. Continue to seek me, for seeking is finding. I want us to draw nearer to one another, beloved. What else is Jesus saying to you?

Ask God to show you how to live today.

"Lord, I will to do as you ask. Use this season of prayer, fasting, and almsgiving to strengthen my resolve and keep me faithfully returning to you. Amen."

Thursday, February 15, 2018

Know that God is present and ready to converse.

"Lord, I want to follow you; I am listening to your Word."

Read the gospel: Luke 9:22–25.

Jesus said, "The Son of Man must undergo great suffering, and be rejected by the elders, chief priests, and scribes, and be killed, and on the third day be raised."

Then he said to them all, "If any want to become my followers, let them deny themselves and take up their cross daily and follow me. For those who want to save their life will lose it, and those who lose their life for my sake will save it. What does it profit them if they gain the whole world, but lose or forfeit themselves?"

Notice what you think and feel as you read the gospel.

Jesus prophesies his own suffering, death, and resurrection. Could they even hear it? But he goes on to exhort those who want to follow him to take up their cross every day, not seeking to save their lives but to lose their lives for his sake. You save your life by losing it.

Pray as you are led for yourself and others.

"My Jesus, I want to follow. Let me rejoice in my cross because you have given it to me. Let me rejoice in losing my life because I will be saved in you. Even in your hard way there is love and joy . . ." (Continue in your own words.)

Listen to Jesus.

You understand that suffering can be redemptive if you follow my way. Keep the good of others in mind and the suffering will seem less. Let suffering be an opportunity to minister to others. Learn from me. What else is Jesus saying to you?

Ask God to show you how to live today.

"Lord, help me. Help me use my own suffering to alleviate the suffering of others. Amen."

Friday, February 16, 2018

Know that God is present and ready to converse.

"Jesus, Bridegroom of all who love you, thank you for inviting me into your presence."

Read the gospel: Matthew 9:14–15.

Then the disciples of John came to Jesus, saying, "Why do we and the Pharisees fast often, but your disciples do not fast?" And Jesus said to them, "The wedding guests cannot mourn as long as the bridegroom is with them, can they? The days will come when the bridegroom is taken away from them, and then they will fast."

Notice what you think and feel as you read the gospel.

Jesus is answering the reasonable question of John's disciples with a reasonable answer. How can his disciples mourn when he, the Messiah, the Lord of Love, is among them? But they will fast when Jesus, the Bridegroom, is taken away from them.

Pray as you are led for yourself and others.

"Lord, I rejoice in your presence, but show me how to fast and pray when I do not feel your presence. Let that sense of distance be your signal to me that I ought to fast and pray and seek you earnestly . . ." (Continue in your own words.)

Listen to Jesus.

I understand you, beloved, and I am pleased to grant your prayer. Reach out to me in your suffering and in your abstinence, and I will draw near you and bless you. What else is Jesus saying to you?

Ask God to show you how to live today.

"With your help, Lord, I can do as you ask. Perfect in me the disciplines that please you. Glory to your holy name! Amen."

Saturday, February 17, 2018

Know that God is present and ready to converse.

"Jesus, I hear your call. You call me to repentance. I come."

Read the gospel: Luke 5:27–32.

After this Jesus went out and saw a tax collector named Levi, sitting at the tax booth; and he said to him, "Follow me." And he got up, left everything, and followed him.

Then Levi gave a great banquet for him in his house; and there was a large crowd of tax-collectors and others sitting at the table with them. The Pharisees and their scribes were complaining to his disciples, saying, "Why do you eat and drink with tax collectors and sinners?" Jesus answered, "Those who are well have no need of a physician, but those who are sick; I have come to call not the righteous but sinners to repentance."

Notice what you think and feel as you read the gospel.

The Pharisees and scribes judge Jesus for keeping company with those on the margins of society. In fact, they judge all those invited to the banquet. Jesus explains that just as healthy people don't need a doctor, he comes not for the righteous but for sinners.

Pray as you are led for yourself and others.

"Jesus, you speak so well, and you also demonstrate your mercy to sinners. You call and befriend sinners. You are my dear friend, merciful Lord. Let me show mercy to others . . ." (Continue in your own words.)

Listen to Jesus.

It is my joy to bring the lost into my kingdom. I am continuing to do this work of my Father. Invite others, dear disciple, and I will do my work within their hearts. What else is Jesus saying to you?

Ask God to show you how to live today.

"I wish to obey you, Lord. Give me opportunity and courage to do and say what is truly profitable for others. Amen."

Sunday, February 18, 2018
First Sunday of Lent

Know that God is present and ready to converse.

"Jesus, your message is consistent. As I read your Word, let me hear and obey."

Read the gospel: Mark 1:12–15.

And the Spirit immediately drove Jesus out into the wilderness. He was in the wilderness for forty days, tempted by Satan; and he was with the wild beasts; and the angels waited on him.

Now after John was arrested, Jesus came to Galilee, proclaiming the good news of God, and saying, "The time is fulfilled, and the kingdom of God has come near; repent, and believe in the good news."

Notice what you think and feel as you read the gospel.

Led by the Spirit, driven by the Spirit, Jesus goes into the wilderness for forty days. There he is tempted by Satan, but the angels wait on him. Afterward, he proclaims the good news of God: the time has come, the kingdom is near, repent, and believe the good news.

Pray as you are led for yourself and others.

"Jesus, I hearken to your simplicity and the simplicity in this passage from your Word. This is also your message to me: obey the Spirit with simplicity. Lord, I offer myself to you in obedience for the good of those you have given me . . ." (Continue in your own words.)

Listen to Jesus.

It is a grace to hear and respond to the Word of God, my beloved. I wish for all to hear and respond, but many do not. So it has always been. Pray for them. What else is Jesus saying to you?

Ask God to show you how to live today.

"Lord, let me join you in the wilderness; let me be driven by the Spirit to pray often for all those who need to hear your message of salvation."

Monday, February 19, 2018

Know that God is present and ready to converse.

"Glorious Lord, all your judgments are just. Let your goodness reign in my heart, so that I may do your will."

Read the gospel: Matthew 25:31–46.

Jesus said, "When the Son of Man comes in his glory, and all the angels with him, then he will sit on the throne of his glory. All the nations will be gathered before him, and he will separate people one from another as a shepherd separates the sheep from the goats, and he will put the sheep at his right hand and the goats at the left. Then the king will say to those at his right hand, 'Come, you that are blessed by my Father, inherit the kingdom prepared for you from the foundation of the world; for I was hungry and you gave me food, I was thirsty and you gave me something to drink, I was a stranger and you welcomed me, I was naked and you gave me clothing, I was sick and you took care of me, I was in prison and you visited me.' Then the righteous will answer him, 'Lord, when was it that we saw you hungry and gave you food, or thirsty and gave you something to drink? And when was it that we saw you a stranger and welcomed you, or naked and gave you clothing? And when was it that we saw you sick or in prison and visited you?' And the king will answer them, 'Truly I tell you, just as you did it to one of the least of these who are members of my family, you did it to me.' Then he will say to those at his left hand, 'You that are accursed, depart from me into the eternal fire prepared for the devil and his angels; for I was hungry and you gave me no food, I was thirsty and you gave me nothing to drink, I was a stranger and you did not welcome me, naked and you did not give me clothing, sick and in prison and you did not visit me.' Then they also will answer, 'Lord, when was it that we saw you hungry or thirsty or a stranger or naked or sick or in prison, and did not take care of you?' Then he will answer them, 'Truly I tell you, just as you did not do it to one of the least of these, you did not do it to me.' And these will go away into eternal punishment, but the righteous into eternal life."

Notice what you think and feel as you read the gospel.

Jesus speaks of the judgment of nations and of people. Who will be sent to eternal punishment? Those who ignore the poor, the hungry, thirsty, naked, sick, or imprisoned. But those who cared for the poor and suffering and welcomed strangers will be rewarded with eternal life, for they did it unto Jesus himself.

Pray as you are led for yourself and others.

"Jesus, give me your heart of solidarity with the poor and suffering of this world and of my own community. Show me what I can do for them, for you . . ." (Continue in your own words.)

Listen to Jesus.

I will show you, my dear disciple. Do not forget your resolution to minister to me. You will come to know me well through the faces of those who suffer. Thank you. What else is Jesus saying to you?

Ask God to show you how to live today.

"Lord, I thank you for your wisdom and your love. I praise you for the opportunities you give me to do your work. Keep me mindful, help me see you in all your family members, and give me courage to serve you. Amen."

Tuesday, February 20, 2018

Know that God is present and ready to converse.

"Heavenly Father, your Son opened the way to you and gave me the privilege to speak to you as a Father. I do so today as I read your Word."

Read the gospel: Matthew 6:7–15.

Jesus said, "When you are praying, do not heap up empty phrases as the Gentiles do; for they think that they will be heard because of their many words. Do not be like them, for your Father knows what you need before you ask him.

"Pray then in this way:

Our Father in heaven,
hallowed be your name.
Your kingdom come.
Your will be done,
on earth as it is in heaven.
Give us this day our daily bread.
And forgive us our debts,
as we also have forgiven our debtors.
And do not bring us to the time of trial,
but rescue us from the evil one.

For if you forgive others their trespasses, your heavenly Father will also forgive you; but if you do not forgive others, neither will your Father forgive your trespasses."

Notice what you think and feel as you read the gospel.

Jesus teaches his disciples to pray to his Father in this beautiful, profound prayer. There is much he could have said to explain every phrase, but he chooses to explain the words about forgiveness—that we are forgiven by God as we forgive others. He clearly wants to emphasize that.

Pray as you are led for yourself and others.

"Lord, whom have I not forgiven? Do I hold grudges in any relationship, old or new? Let me now forgive all those who have trespassed against me . . ." (Continue in your own words.)

Listen to Jesus.

And I forgive you, my child. Do not be afraid to face your sins and repent. That is pleasing to God. It lets you draw near to God's holy self. You are a beloved child of God. What else is Jesus saying to you?

Ask God to show you how to live today.

"Thank you for your grace, dear Lord. Let me be quick to forgive others today. Amen."

Wednesday, February 21, 2018

Know that God is present and ready to converse.

"Lord, I rejoice that you are here with me. Open me to understand your Word as you would have me understand it."

Read the gospel: Luke 11:29–32.

When the crowds were increasing, Jesus began to say, "This generation is an evil generation; it asks for a sign, but no sign will be given to it except the sign of Jonah. For just as Jonah became a sign to the people of Nineveh, so the Son of Man will be to this generation. The queen of the South will rise at the judgement with the people of this generation and condemn them, because she came from the ends of the earth to listen to the wisdom of Solomon, and see, something greater than Solomon is here! The people of Nineveh will rise up at the judgement with this generation and condemn it, because they repented at the proclamation of Jonah, and see, something greater than Jonah is here!"

Notice what you think and feel as you read the gospel.

Jesus does not curry favor or flatter his hearers. He speaks prophetically of judgment and lets them know he is greater than Jonah or Solomon. Yet, he says, they continue to seek a sign and will not repent.

Pray as you are led for yourself and others.

"Lord, I repent, I believe your words, and I pray with all my heart for those of this generation who refuse you . . ." (Continue in your own words.)

Listen to Jesus.

Many reject me, but many respond. I am glad you do not give up on those who resist my grace. Show them love and mercy, for I do not wish them to be lost. Your sincere love has power to draw them to me, my dearest one. What else is Jesus saying to you?

Ask God to show you how to live today.

"Lord, help me practice love and mercy today, that my actions may be a sign of your great love and salvation. Amen."

Thursday, February 22, 2018
Chair of Saint Peter, Apostle

Know that God is present and ready to converse.

"Father, you enlighten the minds of your people and give them power to do your will. Let me be enlightened and empowered by your holy Word."

Read the gospel: Matthew 16:13–19.

Now when Jesus came into the district of Caesarea Philippi, he asked his disciples, "Who do people say that the Son of Man is?" And they said, "Some say John the Baptist, but others Elijah, and still others Jeremiah or one of the prophets." He said to them, "But who do you say that I am?" Simon Peter answered, "You are the Messiah, the Son of the living God." And Jesus answered him, "Blessed are you, Simon son of Jonah! For flesh and blood has not revealed this to you, but my Father in heaven. And I tell you, you are Peter, and on this rock I will build my church, and the gates of Hades will not prevail against it. I will give you the keys of the kingdom of heaven, and whatever you bind on earth will be bound in heaven, and whatever you loose on earth will be loosed in heaven."

Notice what you think and feel as you read the gospel.

Jesus knows that many misunderstand his identity, so he questions his disciples. Peter answers, saying that Jesus is the Messiah, the Son of the living God. Jesus does not deny it but instead lets Peter and the other disciples know that Peter's answer was inspired by God and declares that he will build his church upon Peter and give him authority in heaven and on earth.

Pray as you are led for yourself and others.

"Jesus, Son of the living God, I give myself to you for any purpose or use whatsoever. I give myself for the good of all those you wish me to serve, including . . ." (Continue in your own words.)

Listen to Jesus.

The Spirit of God moves through the Church, and, though assaulted by people and by Satan, the Church will not fail. Do what you can to restore integrity among believers, for some grow cold and serve themselves, not others. What else is Jesus saying to you?

Ask God to show you how to live today.

"Lord, I would honor your presence in the Church and in myself. Let me speak of your goodness and faithfulness. Amen."

Friday, February 23, 2018

Know that God is present and ready to converse.

"Lord, I praise and worship you. Allow me to follow your teachings."

Read the gospel: Matthew 5:20–26.

Jesus said, "For I tell you, unless your righteousness exceeds that of the scribes and Pharisees, you will never enter the kingdom of heaven.

"You have heard that it was said to those of ancient times, 'You shall not murder'; and 'whoever murders shall be liable to judgement.' But I say to you that if you are angry with a brother or sister, you will be liable to judgement; and if you insult a brother or sister, you will be liable to the council; and if you say, 'You fool,' you will be liable to the hell of fire. So when you are offering your gift at the altar, if you remember that your brother or sister has something against you, leave your gift there before the altar and go; first be reconciled to your brother or sister, and then come and offer your gift. Come to terms quickly with your accuser while you are on the way to court with him, or your accuser may hand you over to the judge, and the judge to the guard, and you will be thrown into prison. Truly I tell you, you will never get out until you have paid the last penny."

Notice what you think and feel as you read the gospel.

Jesus insists on true righteousness among his followers, for without it, they will never enter the kingdom of heaven. He speaks of the commandment, "You shall not murder," explaining murder as any anger or insult against another. He urges us to apologize to those we have offended and to reconcile with our accusers, so that we may not be judged guilty of murder.

Pray as you are led for yourself and others.

"Lord, let me appreciate the seriousness of your words, so that I will take them to heart and obey them. To whom do I owe an apology? With whom do I need to seek reconciliation? . . ." (Continue in your own words.)

Listen to Jesus.

Let your righteousness be humility, and your only virtue, my mercy. Abide with me—talk with me, walk with me—and I will show you the way, I will teach you the truth, and I will give you life. What else is Jesus saying to you?

Ask God to show you how to live today.

"Lord, walk with me in every moment of the day; help me turn to you when I feel anger, and give me your grace, that I may respond to offenses with love and humility. Amen."

Saturday, February 24, 2018

Know that God is present and ready to converse.

"Merciful Father, send your Spirit into my heart as I contemplate your Word."

Read the gospel: Matthew 5:43–48.

Jesus said, "You have heard that it was said, 'You shall love your neighbor and hate your enemy.' But I say to you, Love your enemies and pray for those who persecute you, so that you may be children of your Father in heaven; for he makes his sun rise on the evil and on the good, and sends rain on the righteous and on the unrighteous. For if you love those who love you, what reward do you have? Do not even the tax collectors do the same? And if you greet only your brothers and sisters, what more are you doing than others? Do not even the Gentiles do the same? Be perfect, therefore, as your heavenly Father is perfect."

Notice what you think and feel as you read the gospel.

To love those who hate us is godly, says Jesus, even if they persecute and kill you. That is what it is to be perfect, like God our heavenly Father.

Pray as you are led for yourself and others.

"Lord, you make it so simple but so hard. I need your grace to love, truly love, those who hate me and hurt me. I offer myself to you. Conform me to your image, Jesus. . . ." (Continue in your own words.)

Listen to Jesus.

Child of our Father, you will find great power and peace in loving others, both those who love you and those who hate you. Lean on me, and you shall succeed. What else is Jesus saying to you?

Ask God to show you how to live today.

"Lord, let me encounter someone who hates me, dislikes me, or is rude to me, and let me truly love him or her. I seek to obey you, Master. Amen."

Sunday, February 25, 2018
Second Sunday of Lent

Know that God is present and ready to converse.

"Father of Light, speak to me today by your Word."

Read the gospel: Mark 9:2–10.

Six days later, Jesus took with him Peter and James and John, and led them up a high mountain apart, by themselves. And he was transfigured before them, and his clothes became dazzling white, such as no one on earth could bleach them. And there appeared to them Elijah with Moses, who were talking with Jesus. Then Peter said to Jesus, "Rabbi, it is good for us to be here; let us make three dwellings, one for you, one for Moses, and one for Elijah." He did not know what to say, for they were terrified. Then a cloud overshadowed them, and from the cloud there came a voice, "This is my Son, the Beloved; listen to him!" Suddenly when they looked around, they saw no one with them any more, but only Jesus.

As they were coming down the mountain, he ordered them to tell no one about what they had seen, until after the Son of Man had risen from the dead. So they kept the matter to themselves, questioning what this rising from the dead could mean.

Notice what you think and feel as you read the gospel.

Three of his disciples are present on the mountain when Jesus is transfigured. Even his clothes turn bright white. Elijah and Moses appear and talk with Jesus. Peter doesn't know what to do, and God himself provides Peter with the answer: "This is my Son, the Beloved; listen to him." Jesus tells them to keep this incident secret until after his has risen, and the disciples are left to wonder what that means.

Pray as you are led for yourself and others.

"Lord, I am sure that I am just as clueless as you move and work around me. Open my ears to listen to you, and open my eyes to your glory. Help me to pray for those you have given me . . ." (Continue in your own words.)

Listen to Jesus.

I love you as my Father loves me, and the Father's love is my glory. Make a dwelling for me in your heart, beloved; abide in this tremendous love and enfold others as you go. What else is Jesus saying to you?

Ask God to show you how to live today.

"School me in love, Lord—I am listening. Let me receive it, and let me give it—the pure love of God. Amen."

Monday, February 26, 2018

Know that God is present and ready to converse.

"Lord, teach me obedience to your law. Light my path with your holy Word."

Read the gospel: Luke 6:36–38.

Jesus said, "Be merciful, just as your Father is merciful.

"Do not judge, and you will not be judged; do not condemn, and you will not be condemned. Forgive, and you will be forgiven; give, and it will be given to you. A good measure, pressed down, shaken together, running over, will be put into your lap; for the measure you give will be the measure you get back."

Notice what you think and feel as you read the gospel.

Be merciful, don't judge, forgive, and give—that's what the Lord asks of us, and he will reward us proportionately to our generosity.

Pray as you are led for yourself and others.

"Sometimes I hold back mercy, forgiveness, generosity, Lord, because I am afraid and selfish. Breathe upon me with your Spirit, and blow away my fears and selfishness. Make me a worthy child of the Father, as you are. Do this not just for me but for those I pray for now. . ." (Continue in your own words.)

Listen to Jesus.

Holiness is simple, my child. It is what I will for you, for I wish you blessing and joy. I understand you need to die to yourself to become holy. Join yourself to the Crucified. What else is Jesus saying to you?

Ask God to show you how to live today.

"Lord, thank you for dying for me. Show me how to die to myself today. How can dying to myself become second nature for me? Amen."

Tuesday, February 27, 2018

Know that God is present and ready to converse.

"Lord, I rejoice in your presence here with me now. You must have something to tell me by your Word. I praise you!"

Read the gospel: Matthew 23:1–12.

Then Jesus said to the crowds and to his disciples, "The scribes and the Pharisees sit on Moses' seat; therefore, do whatever they teach you and follow it; but do not do as they do, for they do not practice what they teach. They tie up heavy burdens, hard to bear, and lay them on the shoulders of others; but they themselves are unwilling to lift a finger to move them. They do all their deeds to be seen by others; for they make their phylacteries broad and their fringes long. They love to have the place of honor at banquets and the best seats in the synagogues, and to be greeted with respect in the marketplaces, and to have people call them rabbi. But you are not to be called rabbi, for you have one teacher, and you are all students. And call no one your father on earth, for you have one Father—the one in heaven. Nor are you to be called instructors, for you have one instructor, the Messiah. The greatest among you will be your servant. All who exalt themselves will be humbled, and all who humble themselves will be exalted."

Notice what you think and feel as you read the gospel.

Jesus exhorts the crowds and his disciples not to live religiously to please or impress others. They are not our teachers; only God is. We are students, learning humility before others and before God.

Pray as you are led for yourself and others.

"Mighty Messiah, Son of the Father, instruct me in your ways, that I may draw my life from God alone, not from others. I give to you all those I love, that you may be their teacher, too . . ." (Continue in your own words.)

Listen to Jesus.

Beloved, return to me often; come as a student, as a child. Hold every circumstance up into my light, and I will guide you. What else is Jesus saying to you?

Ask God to show you how to live today.

"What a privilege to have constant access to God, my Jesus. Help me turn to the Father today, again and again, with joyful humility. Amen."

Wednesday, February 28, 2018

Know that God is present and ready to converse.

"Lord, I seek you, and here you are. Glory to your name, O Lord."

Read the gospel: Matthew 20:17–28.

While Jesus was going up to Jerusalem, he took the twelve disciples aside by themselves, and said to them on the way, "See, we are going up to Jerusalem, and the Son of Man will be handed over to the chief priests and scribes, and they will condemn him to death; then they will hand him over to the Gentiles to be mocked and flogged and crucified; and on the third day he will be raised."

Then the mother of the sons of Zebedee came to him with her sons, and kneeling before him, she asked a favor of him. And he said to her, "What do you want?" She said to him, "Declare that these two sons of mine will sit, one at your right hand and one at your left, in your kingdom." But Jesus answered, "You do not know what you are asking. Are you able to drink the cup that I am about to drink?" They said to him, "We are able." He said to them, "You will indeed drink my cup, but to sit at my right hand and at my left, this is not mine to grant, but it is for those for whom it has been prepared by my Father."

When the ten heard it, they were angry with the two brothers. But Jesus called them to him and said, "You know that the rulers of the Gentiles lord it over them, and their great ones are tyrants over them. It will not be so among you; but whoever wishes to be great among you must be your servant, and whoever wishes to be first among you must be your slave; just as the Son of Man came not to be served but to serve, and to give his life a ransom for many."

Notice what you think and feel as you read the gospel.

Jesus predicts his Passion, Death, and Resurrection, but the apostles don't seem to hear it. The mother of the sons of Zebedee, however, has great ambition for her sons, that they may be powerful and honored in the kingdom. Jesus tells them that they don't know what they are asking, for they must drink the cup he will drink. They say they can, and he says they will.

Pray as you are led for yourself and others.

"Lord, you give me your cup to drink, too. Because of you, I can and will drink it. Let me accompany you in the way of the Cross, truly understanding the meaning of it. I offer my suffering for others . . ." (Continue in your own words.)

Listen to Jesus.

The night passes. Hard times give way to joy. Shake off mourning and look to me, for you shall be like me, robed in glory. The night is short. What else is Jesus saying to you?

Ask God to show you how to live today.

"Lord, help me understand that the end of things gives meaning to the day by day proceedings of my life. Let me keep my eyes on the prize: you. Amen."

Thursday, March 1, 2018

Know that God is present and ready to converse.

"I am your student, Jesus, Messiah. What do you have to say to me?"

Read the gospel: Luke 16:19–31.

Jesus said, "There was a rich man who was dressed in purple and fine linen and who feasted sumptuously every day. And at his gate lay a poor man named Lazarus, covered with sores, who longed to satisfy his hunger with what fell from the rich man's table; even the dogs would come and lick his sores. The poor man died and was carried away by the angels to be with Abraham. The rich man also died and was buried. In Hades, where he was being tormented, he looked up and saw Abraham far away with Lazarus by his side. He called out, 'Father Abraham, have mercy on me, and send Lazarus to dip the tip of his finger in water and cool my tongue; for I am in agony in these flames.' But Abraham said, 'Child, remember that during your lifetime you received your good things, and Lazarus in like manner evil things; but now he is comforted here, and you are in agony. Besides all this, between you and us a great chasm has been fixed, so that those who might want to pass from here to you cannot do so, and no one can cross from there to us.' He said, 'Then, father, I beg you to send him to my father's house—for I have five brothers—that he may warn them, so that they will not also come into this place of torment.' Abraham replied, 'They have Moses and the prophets; they should listen to them.' He said, 'No, father Abraham; but if someone goes to them from the dead, they will repent.' He said to him, 'If they do not listen to Moses and the prophets, neither will they be convinced even if someone rises from the dead.'"

Notice what you think and feel as you read the gospel.

Circumstances in our lives do not necessarily correspond to what we deserve. But we all have opportunities to do good to those in need. The rich man does not do good to poor, sick Lazarus, who dies and goes to heaven. The rich man dies and is tormented in Hades where he begs for water, but Abraham says what he and Lazarus are receiving now is just. The rich man begs Abraham to send Lazarus back to his father's house to warn his brothers of the torment. Abraham says it would do no good: they won't believe it even if someone rises from the dead.

Pray as you are led for yourself and others.

"How true this parable is, my Jesus. People do not hear your words of truth nor believe you rose from the dead. I believe, Lord. I pray now for all those who do not believe. Open their hearts . . ." (Continue in your own words.)

Listen to Jesus.

Every day the glory of God is on display, my child. Attune your heart to God's glory. As you do that, others will see it and follow. What else is Jesus saying to you?

Ask God to show you how to live today.

"Lord, Creator of the universe, let me glimpse your glory today and worship you with my whole heart, mind, soul, and strength. Amen."

Friday, March 2, 2018

Know that God is present and ready to converse.

"Lord, your ways are high above our ways. I open my heart to the truth of your Word."

Read the gospel: Matthew 21:33–43, 45–46.

Jesus said, "Listen to another parable. There was a landowner who planted a vineyard, put a fence around it, dug a wine press in it, and built a watchtower. Then he leased it to tenants and went to another country. When the harvest time had come, he sent his slaves to the tenants to collect his produce. But the tenants seized his slaves and beat one, killed another, and stoned another. Again he sent other slaves, more than the first; and they treated them in the same way. Finally he sent his son to them, saying, 'They will respect my son.' But when the tenants saw the son, they said to themselves, 'This is the heir; come, let us kill him and get his inheritance.' So they seized him, threw him out of the vineyard, and killed him. Now when the owner of the vineyard comes, what will he do to those tenants?" They said to him, "He will put those wretches to a miserable death, and lease the vineyard to other tenants who will give him the produce at the harvest time."

Jesus said to them, "Have you never read in the scriptures:

'The stone that the builders rejected
        has become the cornerstone;
this was the Lord's doing,
        and it is amazing in our eyes'?

Therefore I tell you, the kingdom of God will be taken away from you and given to a people that produces the fruits of the kingdom." . . .

When the chief priests and the Pharisees heard his parables, they realized that he was speaking about them. They wanted to arrest him, but they feared the crowds, because they regarded him as a prophet.

Notice what you think and feel as you read the gospel.

Jesus' prophetic parable falls on hard hearts. He compares the religious leaders of his time to tenants who beat and kill all those sent to them by the owner of the vineyard, including the owner's son. Even the priests and Pharisees declare the tenants deserve death. Jesus quotes the scripture passage about the rejected stone that becomes the cornerstone, a metaphor for himself. The religious leaders resent him but are afraid to arrest him because of the crowds who believe in him.

Pray as you are led for yourself and others.

"Lord, your awareness of past, present, and future is whole and true. I cannot see my way ahead. Would you lead me? And will you guide all those you have given me in the ways that they should go? . . ." (Continue in your own words.)

Listen to Jesus.

I am with you, beloved servant, my friend. Your love for others comes from me. You are producing the fruit of the harvest, love. Give it to me, and I will give it back to you abundantly, and it will flow out upon others. What else is Jesus saying to you?

Ask God to show you how to live today.

"I do give you my love. You, rejected, broken, and glorified, are my cornerstone. Let me be amazed by you all day long. Amen."

Saturday, March 3, 2018

Know that God is present and ready to converse.

"Jesus, thank you for coming to me. Do you have a story that will ring true in my heart and change my life? Let me receive your Word, Lord."

Read the gospel: Luke 15:1–3, 11–32.

Now all the tax collectors and sinners were coming near to listen to Jesus. And the Pharisees and the scribes were grumbling and saying, "This fellow welcomes sinners and eats with them." . . .

Then Jesus said, "There was a man who had two sons. The younger of them said to his father, 'Father, give me the share of the property that will belong to me.' So he divided his property between them. A few days later the younger son gathered all he had and travelled to a distant country, and there he squandered his property in dissolute living. When he had spent everything, a severe famine took place throughout that country, and he began to be in need. So he went and hired himself out to one of the citizens of that country, who sent him to his fields to feed the pigs. He would gladly have filled himself with the pods that the pigs were eating; and no one gave him anything. But when he came to himself he said, 'How many of my father's hired hands have bread enough and to spare, but here I am dying of hunger! I will get up and go to my father, and I will say to him, "Father, I have sinned against heaven and before you; I am no longer worthy to be called your son; treat me like one of your hired hands."' So he set off and went to his father. But while he was still far off, his father saw him and was filled with compassion; he ran and put his arms around him and kissed him. Then the son said to him, 'Father, I have sinned against heaven and before you; I am no longer worthy to be called your son.' But the father said to his slaves, 'Quickly, bring out a robe—the best one—and put it on him; put a ring on his finger and sandals on his feet. And get the fatted calf and kill it, and let us eat and celebrate; for this son of mine was dead and is alive again; he was lost and is found!' And they began to celebrate.

"Now his elder son was in the field; and when he came and approached the house, he heard music and dancing. He called one of the slaves and asked what was going on. He replied, 'Your brother has come, and your father has killed the fatted calf, because he has got him back safe and sound.' Then he became angry and refused to go in. His father came out and began to plead with him. But he answered his father, 'Listen! For all these years I have been working like a slave for you, and I have never disobeyed your command; yet you have never given me even a young goat so that I might celebrate with my friends. But when this son of yours came back, who has devoured your property with prostitutes, you killed the fatted calf for him!' Then the father said to him, 'Son, you are always with me, and all that is mine is yours. But we had to celebrate and rejoice, because this brother of yours was dead and has come to life; he was lost and has been found.'"

Notice what you think and feel as you read the gospel.

This parable extolls the mercy of God, who, like Jesus, welcomes the sinner who returns to him. The father is overjoyed at the return of the wayward son, making the dutiful son angry and jealous, but the father consoles him, too. His mercy is for all.

Pray as you are led for yourself and others.

"Thank you for having mercy upon me, Lord. I see myself in both sons, but more important, I see your mercy toward me. Together let us extend it to all we encounter today . . ." (Continue in your own words.)

Listen to Jesus.

No matter where you wander, you can always come home to me, dear one. I will welcome you with joy and bless you with eternal life. Pray for those who have walked away from God. What else is Jesus saying to you?

Ask God to show you how to live today.

"I offer you my day, Lord, my thoughts, words, deeds, joys, and suffering, as a prayer for all those you have given me and all those I encounter in my day. Amen."

Sunday, March 4, 2018
Third Sunday of Lent

Know that God is present and ready to converse.

"Lord, I am not worthy that you should come to me and speak to me through your Spirit and your Word. I will hear you now."

Read the gospel: John 2:13–25.

The Passover of the Jews was near, and Jesus went up to Jerusalem. In the temple he found people selling cattle, sheep, and doves, and the money changers seated at their tables. Making a whip of cords, he drove all of them out of the temple, both the sheep and the cattle. He also poured out the coins of the money changers and overturned their tables. He told those who were selling the doves, "Take these things out of here! Stop making my Father's house a marketplace!" His disciples remembered that it was written, "Zeal for your house will consume me." The Jews then said to him, "What sign can you show us for doing this?" Jesus answered them, "Destroy this temple, and in three days I will raise it up." The Jews then said, "This temple has been under construction for forty-six years, and will you raise it up in three days?" But he was speaking of the temple of his body. After he was raised from the dead, his disciples remembered that he had said this; and they believed the scripture and the word that Jesus had spoken.

When he was in Jerusalem during the Passover festival, many believed in his name because they saw the signs that he was doing. But Jesus on his part would not entrust himself to them, because he knew all people and needed no one to testify about anyone; for he himself knew what was in everyone.

Notice what you think and feel as you read the gospel.

Jesus is angered by those seeking to profit in the Temple, for it is his Father's house. He then prophesies the destruction of the Temple, while referring at the same time to his own death and resurrection on the third day. Many people came to believe in him because of the miracles he performed, but Jesus knew their hearts had not been won over.

Pray as you are led for yourself and others.

"Lord, I seek to worship the Father in spirit and in truth. Purge all worldliness from my soul. Call me to true holiness now, and call those you have given me . . ." (Continue in your own words.)

Listen to Jesus.

You have come to me and tasted my love and wisdom, beloved. I give them to you gladly. You comfort me with your love and earnestness to please me. You do please me, beloved. What else is Jesus saying to you?

Ask God to show you how to live today.

"Teach me to remain in your love in all the circumstances of my days, starting with this day. Lord, walk with me. Amen."

Monday, March 5, 2018

Know that God is present and ready to converse.

"Jesus, sometimes you speak sternly. If you speak sternly to me, let me truly hear you and learn from you."

Read the gospel: Luke 4:24–30.

And Jesus said, "Truly I tell you, no prophet is accepted in the prophet's home town. But the truth is, there were many widows in Israel in the time of Elijah, when the heaven was shut up for three years and six months, and there was a severe famine over all the land; yet Elijah was sent to none of them except to a widow at Zarephath in Sidon. There were also many lepers in Israel in the time of the prophet Elisha, and none of them was cleansed except Naaman the Syrian." When they heard this, all in the synagogue were filled with rage. They got up, drove him out of the town, and led him to the brow of the hill on which their town was built, so that they might hurl him off the cliff. But he passed through the midst of them and went on his way.

Notice what you think and feel as you read the gospel.

The people in the synagogue in Jesus' hometown do not accept him, even as a prophet. They are angry to the point of wanting to kill him, but he slips away. His time has not yet come.

Pray as you are led for yourself and others.

"I pray for all those who are angry with God. Let this be their time of mercy, Lord. And if I have anger in my heart toward you or any person, help me forgive, and please transform that anger into love . . ." (Continue in your own words.)

Listen to Jesus.

The Spirit dwells within you, beloved, enlightening you and changing you. Give yourself to this process, knowing it is not your work but mine. Trust me. What else is Jesus saying to you?

Ask God to show you how to live today.

"Lord, I want to do my part, but you seem to be telling me to let you do yours. It is my part to let go and trust you. Amen."

Tuesday, March 6, 2018

Know that God is present and ready to converse.

"Lord, the universe is full of beings, laws, forces, and spirits. What is important for me?"

Read the gospel: Matthew 18:21–35.

Then Peter came and said to Jesus, "Lord, if another member of the church sins against me, how often should I forgive? As many as seven times?" Jesus said to him, "Not seven times, but, I tell you, seventy-seven times.

"For this reason the kingdom of heaven may be compared to a king who wished to settle accounts with his slaves. When he began the reckoning, one who owed him ten thousand talents was brought to him; and, as he could not pay, his lord ordered him to be sold, together with his wife and children and all his possessions, and payment to be made. So the slave fell on his knees before him, saying, 'Have patience with me, and I will pay you everything.' And out of pity for him, the lord of that slave released him and forgave him the debt. But that same slave, as he went out, came upon one of his fellow slaves who owed him a hundred denarii; and seizing him by the throat, he said, 'Pay what you owe.' Then his fellow slave fell down and pleaded with him, 'Have patience with me, and I will pay you.' But he refused; then he went and threw him into prison until he should pay the debt. When his fellow slaves saw what had happened, they were greatly distressed, and they went and reported to their lord all that had taken place. Then his lord summoned him and said to him, 'You wicked slave! I forgave you all that debt because you pleaded with me. Should you not have had mercy on your fellow slave, as I had mercy on you?' And in anger his lord handed him over to be tortured until he should pay his entire debt. So my heavenly Father will also do to every one of you, if you do not forgive your brother or sister from your heart."

Notice what you think and feel as you read the gospel.

Peter wonders about forgiveness—how much forgiveness is appropriate? Jesus tells him he must forgive those who offend him an infinite number of times. His parable makes the point that one who is forgiven by God is in no position to withhold forgiveness from others. Those who are not merciful will be punished.

Pray as you are led for yourself and others.

"Lord, I open my heart to your mercy—to receive it and to dispense it liberally. You came to forgive sins and restore us to friendship with God. Our part is to forgive the sins of others. Let me do that now . . ." (Continue in your own words.)

Listen to Jesus.

I have made the mysteries of God understandable to you, dear child. You know what you need to know. Let it sink deeply within you and change what you think, say, and do. What else is Jesus saying to you?

Ask God to show you how to live today.

"I resolve to forgive someone today. Let me see it and do it, Lord. Amen."

Wednesday, March 7, 2018

Know that God is present and ready to converse.

"Lord, let me hear your Word today, obey, and teach it by my life."

Read the gospel: Matthew 5:17–19.

Jesus said, "Do not think that I have come to abolish the law or the prophets; I have come not to abolish but to fulfill. For truly I tell you, until heaven and earth pass away, not one letter, not one stroke of a letter, will pass from the law until all is accomplished. Therefore, whoever breaks one of the least of these commandments, and teaches others to do the same, will be called least in the kingdom of heaven; but whoever does them and teaches them will be called great in the kingdom of heaven."

Notice what you think and feel as you read the gospel.

Jesus says he fulfills the law and the prophets. He urges obedience to all God's commandments. Those who do not will be called least in the kingdom of heaven.

Pray as you are led for yourself and others.

"Lord, do I obey all your commandments? Do I minimize for myself and others the importance of obedience? Forgive me. Rescue me. Teach me to obey . . ." (Continue in your own words.)

Listen to Jesus.

My Father seeks to make you holy, perfectly holy, because that is what will make you happy, now and forever. Would you give yourself to God for that, beloved disciple? What else is Jesus saying to you?

Ask God to show you how to live today.

"I do give myself to you, Lord. Let it be for my good and the good of all those you have given me. Amen."

Thursday, March 8, 2018

Know that God is present and ready to converse.

"Jesus, I live in a world of spirits. Protect me from evil in every form. Let me be with you."

Read the gospel: Luke 11:14–23.

Now Jesus was casting out a demon that was mute; when the demon had gone out, the one who had been mute spoke, and the crowds were amazed. But some of them said, "He casts out demons by Beelzebul, the ruler of the demons." Others, to test him, kept demanding from him a sign from heaven. But he knew what they were thinking and said to them, "Every kingdom divided against itself becomes a desert, and house falls on house. If Satan also is divided against himself, how will his kingdom stand?—for you say that I cast out the demons by Beelzebul. Now if I cast out the demons by Beelzebul, by whom do your exorcists cast them out? Therefore they will be your judges. But if it is by the finger of God that I cast out the demons, then the kingdom of God has come to you. When a strong man, fully armed, guards his castle, his property is safe. But when one stronger than he attacks him and overpowers him, he takes away his armor in which he trusted and divides his plunder. Whoever is not with me is against me, and whoever does not gather with me scatters."

Notice what you think and feel as you read the gospel.

Jesus faces constant criticism for the good he does and is even accused of being in league with Satan. Jesus refutes these accusations, and he declares that he has vanquished evil, even Beelzebul, ruler of the demons.

Pray as you are led for yourself and others.

"Lord, I come to you now to seek your protection for me and for all those you have given me. Let evil hold no sway in our lives . . ." (Continue in your own words.)

Listen to Jesus.

Cling to me, child, and you are safe. Do not fear the arrow that flies by night, but reach out for the light that is the love of God. Let it fill your heart and you will be safe and become a safe harbor yourself for those I have given you. Do you believe me? What else is Jesus saying to you?

Ask God to show you how to live today.

"Lord, I do believe you, but you know my powers are limited. But in you, with you, I can do anything. Let me do some good today, Blessed Savior. Amen."

Friday, March 9, 2018

Know that God is present and ready to converse.

"Lord, you draw near to me now. I will receive the wisdom of your Word."

Read the gospel: Mark 12:28–34.

One of the scribes came near and heard them disputing with one another, and seeing that Jesus answered them well, he asked him, "Which commandment is the first of all?" Jesus answered, "The first is, 'Hear, O Israel: the Lord our God, the Lord is one; you shall love the Lord your God with all your heart, and with all your soul, and with all your mind, and with all your strength.' The second is this, 'You shall love your neighbor as yourself.' There is no other commandment greater than these." Then the scribe said to him, "You are right, Teacher; you have truly said that 'he is one, and besides him there is no other'; and 'to love him with all the heart, and with all the understanding, and with all the strength,' and 'to love one's neighbor as oneself,'—this is much more important than all whole burnt offerings and sacrifices." When Jesus saw that he answered wisely, he said to him, "You are not far from the kingdom of God." After that no one dared to ask him any question.

Notice what you think and feel as you read the gospel.

Jesus and the scribe agree that the commandments to love God with all your being and to love your neighbor as yourself far surpass all other laws, sacrifices, and rituals.

Pray as you are led for yourself and others.

"Lord, give me the grace to love God and others with all my might. In love, I present to you now those you have given me . . ." (Continue in your own words.)

Listen to Jesus.

It's easy to love God if you know God and how much God loves you. All things work together for good for you, my beloved, because you love God. What else is Jesus saying to you?

Ask God to show you how to live today.

"Let the love of God overflow to others today, Lord. And show me what it means to love my neighbor as myself. Amen."

Saturday, March 10, 2018

Know that God is present and ready to converse.

"Lord, you take the initiative, drawing me to prayer and to your Word. I will receive it with joy."

Read the gospel: Luke 18:9–14.

Jesus also told this parable to some who trusted in themselves that they were righteous and regarded others with contempt: "Two men went up to the temple to pray, one a Pharisee and the other a tax collector. The Pharisee, standing by himself, was praying thus, 'God, I thank you that I am not like other people: thieves, rogues, adulterers, or even like this tax collector. I fast twice a week; I give a tenth of all my income.' But the tax collector, standing far off, would not even look up to heaven, but was beating his breast and saying, 'God, be merciful to me, a sinner!' I tell you, this man went down to his home justified rather than the other; for all who exalt themselves will be humbled, but all who humble themselves will be exalted."

Notice what you think and feel as you read the gospel.

It is human nature to regard yourself as the Pharisee does, comparing yourself favorably to sinners and cataloging your virtues. Jesus says those who exalt themselves will be humbled. But those who humble themselves, like the tax collector beating his breast and begging for mercy, will be exalted.

Pray as you are led for yourself and others.

"Lord, your spiritual laws prevail still. To go down is to go up. Be merciful to me, a sinner. Be merciful to those who pride themselves on their virtues, for they are sinners too . . ." (Continue in your own words.)

Listen to Jesus.

Learn from me, for I am perfect, yet I extend mercy to all. Show mercy and do not judge, for the standard by which you judge will be held against you. What else is Jesus saying to you?

Ask God to show you how to live today.

"Lord, it is easy to make fleeting, unpremeditated judgments of others during my day. Arrest them in me before I make them. If I do make a judgment, let me unmake it with mercy. Amen."

Sunday, March 11, 2018
Fourth Sunday of Lent

Know that God is present and ready to converse.

"Glory to you, Father, Son, and Holy Spirit. I enter your presence with a heart open to your Word."

Read the gospel: John 3:14–21.

Jesus said, "And just as Moses lifted up the serpent in the wilderness, so must the Son of Man be lifted up, that whoever believes in him may have eternal life.

"For God so loved the world that he gave his only Son, so that everyone who believes in him may not perish but may have eternal life.

"Indeed, God did not send the Son into the world to condemn the world, but in order that the world might be saved through him. Those who believe in him are not condemned; but those who do not believe are condemned already, because they have not believed in the name of the only Son of God. And this is the judgment, that the light has come into the world, and people loved darkness rather than light because their deeds were evil. For all who do evil hate the light and do not come to the light, so that their deeds may not be exposed. But those who do what is true come to the light, so that it may be clearly seen that their deeds have been done in God."

Notice what you think and feel as you read the gospel.

Jesus speaks of his crucifixion and says that he will save all those who look to him. He is the Savior of the world, bringing mercy, light, and eternal life to all who come to him.

Pray as you are led for yourself and others.

"Lord, let me not be blind to my sins. Reveal to me the sins I hide from myself and let me be cleansed by repenting in your grace . . ." (Continue in your own words.)

Listen to Jesus.

I will do it, dear child. I am shedding my light upon you. Do you see it? What else is Jesus saying to you?

Ask God to show you how to live today.

"As I walk in your light today, Lord, let me see others with clarity and compassion, for they are your children. Thank you. Amen."

Monday, March 12, 2018

Know that God is present and ready to converse.

"Lord, I am with you. Let me receive your Word with faith."

Read the gospel: John 4:43–54.

When the two days were over, Jesus went from that place to Galilee (for Jesus himself had testified that a prophet has no honor in the prophet's own country). When he came to Galilee, the Galileans welcomed him, since they had seen all that he had done in Jerusalem at the festival; for they too had gone to the festival.

Then he came again to Cana in Galilee where he had changed the water into wine. Now there was a royal official whose son lay ill in Capernaum. When he heard that Jesus had come from Judea to Galilee, he went and begged him to come down and heal his son, for he was at the point of death. Then Jesus said to him, "Unless you see signs and wonders you will not believe." The official said to him, "Sir, come down before my little boy dies." Jesus said to him,

"Go; your son will live." The man believed the word that Jesus spoke to him and started on his way. As he was going down, his slaves met him and told him that his child was alive. So he asked them the hour when he began to recover, and they said to him, "Yesterday at one in the afternoon the fever left him." The father realized that this was the hour when Jesus had said to him, "Your son will live." So he himself believed, along with his whole household. Now this was the second sign that Jesus did after coming from Judea to Galilee.

Notice what you think and feel as you read the gospel.

Jesus apparently challenges the man, who seems as if he wants only a sign. But the man is worried that his sick son might die. Jesus pronounces the son healed, and the man believes; his son is healed when he arrives home, and his whole household believes in Jesus.

Pray as you are led for yourself and others.

"Lord, increase my faith. Help my unbelief. Let me believe what is true about God. I pray, too, that others will find true faith . . ." (Continue in your own words.)

Listen to Jesus.

I am pleased by faith, beloved. Faith may be small but it endures and it grows. It makes all the difference to me and to you. Believe me. What else is Jesus saying to you?

Ask God to show you how to live today.

"I am a person of little faith; I am afraid. Let me do something in faith today, Lord. Teach me to live in faith. Amen."

Tuesday, March 13, 2018

Know that God is present and ready to converse.

"God, you are with me before I can come to you. You see me as I am, full of needs only you can satisfy. Let me feed on your holy Word."

Read the gospel: John 5:1–16.

After this there was a festival of the Jews, and Jesus went up to Jerusalem. Now in Jerusalem by the Sheep Gate there is a pool, called in Hebrew Beth-zatha, which has five porticoes. In these lay many invalids—blind, lame, and paralyzed. One man was there who had been ill for thirty-eight years. When Jesus saw him lying there and knew that he had been there a long time, he said to him, "Do you want to be made well?" The sick man answered him, "Sir, I have no one to put me into the pool when the water is stirred up; and while I am making my way, someone else steps down ahead of me." Jesus said to him, "Stand up, take your mat and walk." At once the man was made well, and he took up his mat and began to walk. Now that day was a sabbath. So the Jews said to the man who had been cured, "It is the sabbath; it is not lawful for you to carry your mat." But he answered them, "The man who made me well said to me, 'Take up your mat and walk.'" They asked him, "Who is the man who said to you, 'Take it up and walk'?" Now the man who had been healed did not know who it was, for Jesus had disappeared in the crowd that was there. Later Jesus found him in the temple and said to him, "See, you have been made well! Do not sin any more, so that nothing worse happens to you." The man went away and told the Jews that it was Jesus who had made him well. Therefore the Jews started persecuting Jesus, because he was doing such things on the sabbath.

Notice what you think and feel as you read the gospel.

Jesus takes the initiative to heal the invalid by the miraculous pool, Beth-zatha. The local Jews find fault in this because he has healed on the Sabbath, and they begin to persecute him.

Pray as you are led for yourself and others.

"Lord, you know where I am sick and sinful. Heal me, forgive me, and let me glorify God . . ." (Continue in your own words.)

Listen to Jesus.

My beloved, I am with you. Offer yourself to God today for the good of others. In that you will find healing and forgiveness. What else is Jesus saying to you?

Ask God to show you how to live today.

"Lord, you have made me well. I am yours, your servant. Do with me what you will. Amen."

Wednesday, March 14, 2018

Know that God is present and ready to converse.

"Three-Person God, you are One. Let me be one with you by the healing power of your Word."

Read the gospel: John 5:17–30.

But Jesus answered them, "My Father is still working, and I also am working." For this reason the Jews were seeking all the more to kill him, because he was not only breaking the sabbath, but was also calling God his own Father, thereby making himself equal to God.

Jesus said to them, "Very truly, I tell you, the Son can do nothing on his own, but only what he sees the Father doing; for whatever the Father does, the Son does likewise. The Father loves the Son and shows him all that he himself is doing; and he will show him greater works than these, so that you will be astonished. Indeed, just as the Father raises the dead and gives them life, so also the Son gives life to whomsoever he wishes. The Father judges no one but has given all judgement to the Son, so that all may honor the Son just as they honor the Father. Anyone who does not honor the Son does not honor the Father who sent him. Very truly, I tell you, anyone who hears my word and believes him who sent me has eternal life, and does not come under judgement, but has passed from death to life.

"Very truly, I tell you, the hour is coming, and is now here, when the dead will hear the voice of the Son of God, and those who hear will live. For just as the Father has life in himself, so he has granted the Son also to have life in himself; and he has given him authority to execute judgement, because he is the Son of Man. Do not be astonished at this; for the hour is coming when all who are in their graves will hear his voice and will come out—those who have done good, to the resurrection of life, and those who have done evil, to the resurrection of condemnation.

"I can do nothing on my own. As I hear, I judge; and my judgement is just, because I seek to do not my own will but the will of him who sent me."

Notice what you think and feel as you read the gospel.

Jesus does the will and the work of his Father. To receive Jesus as the Son of God is to honor the Father who sent him. To receive him is to receive eternal life. Those who hear and believe have already passed from death to life. The judgment is coming, with resurrection to condemnation or to life.

Pray as you are led for yourself and others.

"Jesus, I believe you are the Son of God, one with God. Thank you for coming and doing your merciful works among us. I pray for those who resist you, that they may truly hear and believe . . ." (Continue in your own words.)

Listen to Jesus.

I hear your prayers, beloved. Your will and my will are the same. I will work as you ask. Trust me. What else is Jesus saying to you?

Ask God to show you how to live today.

"I seek to do not my will today but yours. If there are things I can do or say or pray, prompt me, Lord, and I will obey. Amen."

Thursday, March 15, 2018

Know that God is present and ready to converse.

"Lord, your being here with me speaks of the reality of God—Father, Son, and Holy Spirit. Speak to me also through your Word."

Read the gospel: John 5:31–47.

Jesus said, "If I testify about myself, my testimony is not true. There is another who testifies on my behalf, and I know that his testimony to me is true. You sent messengers to John, and he testified to the truth. Not that I accept such human testimony, but I say these things so that you may be saved. He was a burning and shining lamp, and you were willing to rejoice for a while in his light. But I have a testimony greater than John's. The works that the Father has given me to complete, the very works that I am doing, testify on my behalf that the Father has sent me. And the Father who sent me has himself testified on my behalf. You have never heard his voice or seen his form, and you do not have his word abiding in you, because you do not believe him whom he has sent.

"You search the scriptures because you think that in them you have eternal life; and it is they that testify on my behalf. Yet you refuse to come to me to have life. I do not accept glory from human beings. But I know that you do not have the love of God in you. I have come in my Father's name, and you do not accept me; if another comes in his own name, you will accept him. How can you believe when you accept glory from one another and do not seek the glory that comes from the one who alone is God? Do not think that I will accuse you before the Father; your accuser is Moses, on whom you have set your hope. If you believed Moses, you would believe me, for he wrote about me. But if you do not believe what he wrote, how will you believe what I say?"

Notice what you think and feel as you read the gospel.

Jesus has testimony from John, from his Father, from the works he does, and from scripture, including Moses—yet his hearers will not believe in him. They are stuck in their human ways of thinking.

Pray as you are led for yourself and others.

"What will make the unbelieving world give true consideration to you, Jesus? This is the time of gathering—gather them in, Lord . . ." (Continue in your own words.)

Listen to Jesus.

Yes, gathering is the purpose of this age, which is rapidly moving toward its end. Your faith in me has a great influence on those I have given you. Simply stay close to me, beloved. What else is Jesus saying to you?

Ask God to show you how to live today.

"I come to you to have life, Jesus; stay close to me. Amen."

Friday, March 16, 2018

Know that God is present and ready to converse.

"Increase my faith in you, Lord, for faith is a gift of God. Let your Word increase my faith."

Read the gospel: John 7:1–2, 10, 25–30.

After this Jesus went about in Galilee. He did not wish to go about in Judea because the Jews were looking for an opportunity to kill him. Now the Jewish festival of Booths was near. . . .

But after his brothers had gone to the festival, then he also went, not publicly but as it were in secret. . . .

Now some of the people of Jerusalem were saying, "Is not this the man whom they are trying to kill? And here he is, speaking openly, but they say nothing to him! Can it be that the authorities really know that this is the Messiah? Yet we know where this man is from; but when the Messiah comes, no one will know where he is from." Then Jesus cried out as he was teaching in the temple, "You know me, and you know where I am from. I have not come on my own. But the one who sent me is true, and you do not know him. I know him, because I am from him, and he sent me." Then they tried to arrest him, but no one laid hands on him, because his hour had not yet come.

Notice what you think and feel as you read the gospel.

In Judea, they are seeking an opportunity to kill Jesus, yet still he goes down to Jerusalem and speaks openly in the temple. Some of the people remark that he cannot be the Messiah because they know where he comes from and no one will know where the Messiah is from. Jesus admits that they know where he is from yet says that they do not know who sent him, the true God. But no one lays hands on him because his time has not yet come.

Pray as you are led for yourself and others.

"Jesus, so much of your life you faced rejection and contradiction, arguments, jealousy, and rage. Soon they will arrest you and crucify you. Lord, strengthen me against rejection. I offer it all to you on behalf of those I pray for now . . ." (Continue in your own words.)

Listen to Jesus.

Do not be afraid, dear friend. I am with you, especially in your sufferings. Let your suffering be one with mine for the redemption of others. What else is Jesus saying to you?

Ask God to show you how to live today.

"Remind me to lift my suffering to you today, and let it bear fruit to your glory. Amen."

Saturday, March 17, 2018

Know that God is present and ready to converse.

"Lord, dispel my darkness by your Word. Be my light."

Read the gospel: John 7:40–53.

When they heard Jesus' words, some in the crowd said, "This is really the prophet." Others said, "This is the Messiah." But some asked, "Surely the Messiah does not come from Galilee, does he? Has not the scripture said that the Messiah is descended from David and comes from Bethlehem, the village where David lived?" So there was a division in the crowd because of him. Some of them wanted to arrest him, but no one laid hands on him.

Then the temple police went back to the chief priests and Pharisees, who asked them, "Why did you not arrest him?" The police answered, "Never has anyone spoken like this!" Then the Pharisees replied, "Surely you have not been deceived too, have you? Has any one of the authorities or of the Pharisees believed in him? But this crowd, which does not know the law—they are accursed." Nicodemus, who had gone to Jesus before, and who was one of them, asked, "Our law does not judge people without first giving them a hearing to find out what they are doing, does it?" They replied, "Surely you are not also from Galilee, are you? Search and you will see that no prophet is to arise from Galilee." Then each of them went home.

Notice what you think and feel as you read the gospel.

The people argue among themselves with considerable ignorance, for Jesus is descended from David and from Bethlehem. Though commissioned to arrest Jesus by the chief priests, the temple police fail to do so, for they are amazed at Jesus: "Never has anyone spoken like this!" Nicodemus urges the people to hear and consider what Jesus says and does before they make judgments.

Pray as you are led for yourself and others.

"Lord, keep me open to you and your Word, that I may know and love the truth. I pray that all those you have given me may come to know and love your truth, for you, Jesus, are the Truth . . ." (Continue in your own words.)

Listen to Jesus.

People generally do what they want to do, and they shape their own thinking around their desires. I am asking you to do what I want and desire, for that will make you truly happy and it will do much good for others. What else is Jesus saying to you?

Ask God to show you how to live today.

"I wish I could just give you all my will in one moment, but I need to offer myself to you day by day, moment by moment. Take me, Lord. Amen."

Sunday, March 18, 2018
Fifth Sunday of Lent

Know that God is present and ready to converse.

"Speak the Word, O Lord, and I will come forth into your Resurrection and your Life."

Read the gospel: John 12:20–33.

Now among those who went up to worship at the festival were some Greeks. They came to Philip, who was from Bethsaida in Galilee, and said to him, "Sir, we wish to see Jesus." Philip went and told Andrew; then Andrew and Philip went and told Jesus. Jesus answered them, "The hour has come for the Son of Man to be glorified. Very truly, I tell you, unless a grain of wheat falls into the earth and dies, it remains just a single grain; but if it dies, it bears much fruit. Those who love their life lose it, and those who hate their life in this world will keep it for eternal life. Whoever serves me must follow me, and where I am, there will my servant be also. Whoever serves me, the Father will honor.

"Now my soul is troubled. And what should I say—'Father, save me from this hour'? No, it is for this reason that I have come to this hour. Father, glorify your name." Then a voice came from heaven, "I have glorified it, and I will glorify it again." The crowd standing there heard it and said that it was thunder. Others said, "An angel has spoken to him." Jesus answered, "This voice has come for your sake, not for mine. Now is the judgment of this world; now the ruler of this world will be driven out. And I, when I am lifted up from the earth, will draw all people to myself." He said this to indicate the kind of death he was to die.

Notice what you think and feel as you read the gospel.

Jesus teaches his disciples that, paradoxically, death is the way to life. They must be willing to lose their lives, as he will, to inherit eternal life.

Pray as you are led for yourself and others.

"Lord, I am willing to lose my life to gain my life. I pray for myself and all those who are afraid . . ." (Continue in your own words.)

Listen to Jesus.

My child, you too face death, with me or without me. Cling to me, follow me, and I will bring you through. I will bless those you pray for too, for the love you have for them is love I give you. What else is Jesus saying to you?

Ask God to show you how to live today.

"Help me cling to you, Lord, not to my life. Where you go, I will follow, for I am your servant. Help me to cast down my life today in service of others; let me be available to others today, my Jesus, and give me ways to care and to help. Amen."

Monday, March 19, 2018
Saint Joseph, Husband of Mary

Know that God is present and ready to converse.

"Lord, you guide me by your Word and your Spirit. I rejoice in your presence."

Read the gospel: Matthew 1:16, 18–21, 24a.

And Jacob [was] the father of Joseph the husband of Mary, of whom Jesus was born, who is called the Messiah. . . .

Now the birth of Jesus the Messiah took place in this way. When his mother Mary had been engaged to Joseph, but before they lived together, she was found to be with child from the Holy Spirit. Her husband Joseph, being a righteous man and unwilling to expose her to public disgrace, planned to dismiss her quietly. But just when he had resolved to do this, an angel of the Lord appeared to him in a dream and said, "Joseph, son of David, do not be afraid to take Mary as your wife, for the child conceived in her is from the Holy Spirit. She will bear a son, and you are to name him Jesus, for he will save his people from their sins." . . .

When Joseph awoke from sleep, he did as the angel of the Lord commanded him; he took her as his wife.

Notice what you think and feel as you read the gospel.

Joseph, a righteous man, wishes to protect the pregnant Mary from public disgrace by dismissing her quietly. But the angel in his dream tells him to go ahead and marry her, for the child is from the Holy Spirit. Joseph believes and obeys. It must have felt to Joseph like an undeniable word from God.

Pray as you are led for yourself and others.

"Sometimes a spiritual moment can have an unusual power of reality, more real than ordinary moments. Speak to your people, Lord, and let them know you and receive your guidance . . ." (Continue in your own words.)

Listen to Jesus.

I speak to you, beloved disciple. Let those who wish to hear, hear my voice. I am ready to guide each one in the way of life everlasting. What else is Jesus saying to you?

Ask God to show you how to live today.

"Lord, speak to me today, and open my heart that I may follow not my own ideas of righteousness but your perfect will. Amen."

Tuesday, March 20, 2018

Know that God is present and ready to converse.

"Jesus, wholly God and wholly man, you are mystery. Let me learn of you through your Word."

Read the gospel: John 8:21–30.

Again Jesus said to the Pharisees, "I am going away, and you will search for me, but you will die in your sin. Where I am going, you cannot come." Then the Jews said, "Is he going to kill himself? Is that what he means by saying, 'Where I am going, you cannot come'?" He said to them, "You are from below, I am from above; you are of this world, I am not of this world. I told you that you would die in your sins, for you will die in your sins unless you believe that I am he." They said to him, "Who are you?" Jesus said to them, "Why do I speak to you at all? I have much to say about you and much to condemn; but the one who sent me is true, and I declare to the world what I have heard from him." They did not understand that he was speaking to them about the Father. So Jesus said, "When you have lifted up the Son of Man, then you will realize that I am he, and that I do nothing on my own, but I speak these things as the Father instructed me. And the one who sent me is with me; he has not left me alone, for I always do what is pleasing to him." As he was saying these things, many believed in him.

Notice what you think and feel as you read the gospel.

The Jews do not understand what Jesus is telling them—about himself, about them. They are of this world, below; he is from the Father, above. He warns them that they will die in their sins unless they believe that he is the Messiah. He foretells his death and says it will be a clear sign to them who he is and who sent him. Many believed in him.

Pray as you are led for yourself and others.

"How wonderful that the Crucifixion is the proof of the Messiah! It shows that you are from the Father and bring love for all humanity. I pray that others may come to know this love . . ." (Continue in your own words.)

Listen to Jesus.

I gave myself for you. I give myself to you now. We are one with all who are in God. Eternal life has already begun in you, beloved. What else is Jesus saying to you?

Ask God to show you how to live today.

"Let this be a day to anticipate with love your passion and death. Make it real to me, so that it changes my life and brings me closer to you. Amen."

Wednesday, March 21, 2018

Know that God is present and ready to converse.

"Lord, I return to your Word, and I find you waiting here for me. Thank you."

Read the gospel: John 8:31–42

Then Jesus said to the Jews who had believed in him, "If you continue in my word, you are truly my disciples; and you will know the truth, and the truth will make you free." They answered him, "We are descendants of Abraham and have never been slaves to anyone. What do you mean by saying, 'You will be made free'?"

Jesus answered them, "Very truly, I tell you, everyone who commits sin is a slave to sin. The slave does not have a permanent place in the household; the son has a place there forever. So if the Son makes you free, you will be free indeed. I know that you are descendants of Abraham; yet you look for an opportunity to kill me, because there is no place in you for my word. I declare what I have seen in the Father's presence; as for you, you should do what you have heard from the Father."

They answered him, "Abraham is our father." Jesus said to them, "If you were Abraham's children, you would be doing what Abraham did, but now you are trying to kill me, a man who has told you the truth that I heard from God. This is not what Abraham did. You are indeed doing what your father does." They said to him, "We are not illegitimate children; we have one father, God himself." Jesus said to them, "If God were your Father, you would love me, for I came from God and now I am here. I did not come on my own, but he sent me."

Notice what you think and feel as you read the gospel.

Jesus tells his listeners that they should do what you have heard from the Father. They claim God as Father, but Jesus says that if this were true, they would love him, for he came from God. He is the truth that makes his disciples free.

Pray as you are led for yourself and others.

"Lord, I love you. Thank you for setting me free. I pray earnestly for those you have given me. Let them love you too and walk in your freedom. . . ." (Continue in your own words.)

Listen to Jesus.

Examine your life, beloved, and identify what enslaves you, what hinders your freedom. Seek my grace to remove those sins from your life. I want you to walk in truth and be free. What else is Jesus saying to you?

Ask God to show you how to live today.

"Let me take your words to heart, Lord. Help me examine my life and break free of the things that enslave me, especially habitual sins. Amen."

Thursday, March 22, 2018

Know that God is present and ready to converse.

"Jesus, Teacher, speak to me plainly through your holy Word. Holy Spirit, guide me."

Read the gospel: John 8:51–59.

Jesus said, "Very truly, I tell you, whoever keeps my word will never see death." The Jews said to him, "Now we know that you have a demon. Abraham died, and so did the prophets; yet you say, 'Whoever keeps my word will never taste death.' Are you greater than our father Abraham, who died? The prophets also died. Who do you claim to be?" Jesus answered, "If I glorify myself, my glory is nothing. It is my Father who glorifies me, he of whom you say, 'He is our God,' though you do not know him. But I know him; if I were to say that I do not know him, I would be a liar like you. But I do know him and I keep his word. Your ancestor Abraham rejoiced that he would see my day; he saw it and was glad." Then the Jews said to him, "You are not yet fifty years old, and have you seen Abraham?" Jesus said to them, "Very truly, I tell you, before Abraham was, I am." So they picked up stones to throw at him, but Jesus hid himself and went out of the temple.

Notice what you think and feel as you read the gospel.

The Jews continue to argue with Jesus. They cannot believe Jesus is the Son of God, one with the Father. When he tells them plainly who he is, they attempt to stone him for blasphemy.

Pray as you are led for yourself and others.

"Lord, I believe in you. Help me keep your word and never see death. I pray others also find saving faith in you . . ." (Continue in your own words.)

Listen to Jesus.

I ask my disciples to keep my commandments and to proclaim the Gospel to the whole world. I will help you do your part, dear friend. What else is Jesus saying to you?

Ask God to show you how to live today.

"Let me receive your help to keep your word and thus to do and say what you want. Thank you for being with me, Jesus. Amen."

Friday, March 23, 2018

Know that God is present and ready to converse.

"Son of God, you are good to me. I praise you for your glory."

Read the gospel: John 10:31–42.

The Jews took up stones again to stone him. Jesus replied, "I have shown you many good works from the Father. For which of these are you going to stone me?" The Jews answered, "It is not for a good work that we are going to stone you, but for blasphemy, because you, though only a human being, are making yourself God." Jesus answered, "Is it not written in your law, 'I said, you are gods'? If those to whom the word of

God came were called 'gods'—and the scripture cannot be annulled—can you say that the one whom the Father has sanctified and sent into the world is blaspheming because I said, 'I am God's Son'? If I am not doing the works of my Father, then do not believe me. But if I do them, even though you do not believe me, believe the works, so that you may know and understand that the Father is in me and I am in the Father." Then they tried to arrest him again, but he escaped from their hands.

He went away again across the Jordan to the place where John had been baptizing earlier, and he remained there. Many came to him, and they were saying, "John performed no sign, but everything that John said about this man was true." And many believed in him there.

Notice what you think and feel as you read the gospel.

Jesus answers his adversaries well, and he backs up his words with healings and mighty miracles. He says the Father sent him into the world to tell us that he is God's Son, and he does the good works of God, yet they call him a blasphemer and want to arrest him.

Pray as you are led for yourself and others.

"Lord, many oppose you and deny your divinity, often bitterly. I pray for them, and I thank you for being willing to suffer such rejection. I don't reject you, Jesus. I am yours . . ." (Continue in your own words.)

Listen to Jesus.

Your words show understanding and your heart consoles me. You are the reason I was willing to suffer and die. Those who follow me continue to suffer and die. They are precious to me. What else is Jesus saying to you?

Ask God to show you how to live today.

"Lord, let me walk your Way of the Cross today, in solidarity with all those who suffer for your name. Amen."

Saturday, March 24, 2018

Know that God is present and ready to converse.

"Jesus, I am often concerned with earthly things. Let me turn from them and contemplate heavenly things in your Word."

Read the gospel: John 11:45–56.

Many of the Jews therefore, who had come with Mary and had seen what Jesus did, believed in him. But some of them went to the Pharisees and told them what he had done. So the chief priests and the Pharisees called a meeting of the council, and said, "What are we to do? This man is performing many signs. If we let him go on like this, everyone will believe in him, and the Romans will come and destroy both our holy place and our nation." But one of them, Caiaphas, who was high priest that year, said to them, "You know nothing at all! You do not understand that it is better for you to have one man die for the people than to have the whole nation destroyed." He did not say this on his own, but being high priest that year he prophesied that Jesus was about to die for the nation, and not for the nation only, but to gather into one the dispersed children of God. So from that day on they planned to put him to death. Jesus therefore no longer walked about openly among the Jews, but went from there to a town called Ephraim in the region near the wilderness; and he remained there with the disciples.

Now the Passover of the Jews was near, and many went up from the country to Jerusalem before the Passover to purify themselves. They were looking for Jesus and were asking one another as they stood in the temple, "What do you think? Surely he will not come to the festival, will he?"

Notice what you think and feel as you read the gospel.

After Jesus raises Lazarus from the dead, some Jews report it to the council of priests. They are worried that so many are coming to believe in Jesus that the Romans will come and destroy their temple and their nation. Caiaphas, the high priest, says that one man could die as a scapegoat for the nation, unwittingly prophesying that Jesus was about to die not only for the nation but to gather into one all the children of God everywhere. The council plans to put Jesus to death.

Pray as you are led for yourself and others.

"What folly in human plans, Lord, even my own. I turn my life over to you to manage. Let me serve you and these others I pray for . . ." (Continue in your own words.)

Listen to Jesus.

Have no fear, beloved child, for I am with you. Rejoice in the providence of God. I will bless you as you follow me. What else is Jesus saying to you?

Ask God to show you how to live today.

"I resolve today to follow you, accepting the circumstances you give me, and trusting in God's providence to bring good even out of evil. Amen."

Sunday, March 25, 2018
Palm Sunday of the Lord's Passion

Know that God is present and ready to converse.

"Jesus, the gospels are your story. Let me know you through your Word."

Read the gospel: Mark 14:1–15 (Mk 14:1–15:47).

It was two days before the Passover and the festival of Unleavened Bread. The chief priests and the scribes were looking for a way to arrest Jesus by stealth and kill him; for they said, "Not during the festival, or there may be a riot among the people."

While he was at Bethany in the house of Simon the leper, as he sat at the table, a woman came with an alabaster jar of very costly ointment of nard, and she broke open the jar and poured the ointment on his head. But some were there who said to one another in anger, "Why was the ointment wasted in this way? For this ointment could have been sold for more than three hundred denarii, and the money given to the poor." And they scolded her. But Jesus said, "Let her alone; why do you trouble her? She has performed a good service for me. For you always have the poor with you, and you can show kindness to them whenever you wish; but you will not always have me. She has done what she could; she has anointed my body beforehand for its burial. Truly I tell you, wherever the good news is proclaimed in the whole world, what she has done will be told in remembrance of her."

Then Judas Iscariot, who was one of the twelve, went to the chief priests in order to betray him to them. When they heard it, they were greatly pleased, and promised to give him money. So he began to look for an opportunity to betray him.

On the first day of Unleavened Bread, when the Passover lamb is sacrificed, his disciples said to him, "Where do you want us to go and make the preparations for you to eat the Passover?" So he sent two of his disciples, saying to them, "Go into the city, and a man carrying a jar of water will meet you; follow him, and wherever he enters, say to the owner of the house, 'The Teacher asks, Where is my guest room where I may eat the Passover with my disciples?' He will show you a large room upstairs, furnished and ready. Make preparations for us there."

Notice what you think and feel as you read the gospel.

The chief priests and Pharisees are looking for a way to capture Jesus by stealth and kill him. A woman honors Jesus by pouring a costly ointment on his head. When some object to the waste of money, Jesus commends the woman for anointing his body for burial because he knows his time of death is near. Judas goes to the chief priests to betray him. Two of his disciples are directed by Jesus to find a room for their Passover meal.

Pray as you are led for yourself and others.

"Jesus, you know all and can do all things. Show me what I need to know and do. Let me be your hands and feet, serving and praying for those you have given me . . ." (Continue in your own words.)

Listen to Jesus.

Her extravagant love—that's what I appreciated about the woman who anointed my head in the house of Simon. True love doesn't count the cost but expresses itself in ways large and small. What else is Jesus saying to you?

Ask God to show you how to live today.

"Help me to love like that, Lord, for I want to please you. Thank you. Amen."

Monday, March 26, 2018

Know that God is present and ready to converse.

"Holy Spirit, be with me and help me discern the Word of Truth before me."

Read the gospel: John 12:1–11.

Six days before the Passover Jesus came to Bethany, the home of Lazarus, whom he had raised from the dead. There they gave a dinner for him. Martha served, and Lazarus was one of those at the table with him. Mary took a pound of costly perfume made of pure nard, anointed Jesus' feet, and wiped them with her hair. The house was filled with the fragrance of the perfume. But Judas Iscariot, one of his disciples (the one who was about to betray him), said, "Why was this perfume not sold for three hundred denarii and the money given to the poor?" (He said this not because he cared about the poor, but because he was a thief; he kept the common purse and used to steal what was put into it.) Jesus said, "Leave her alone. She bought it so that she might keep it for the day of my burial. You always have the poor with you, but you do not always have me."

When the great crowd of the Jews learned that he was there, they came not only because of Jesus but also to see Lazarus, whom he had raised from the dead. So the chief priests planned to put Lazarus to death as well, since it was on account of him that many of the Jews were deserting and were believing in Jesus.

Notice what you think and feel as you read the gospel.

Mary of Bethany anoints Jesus' feet with perfume. Judas complains the perfume should have been sold and the money given to the poor, though his real purpose was to have more money to steal from the common purse. Many were at the house to see both Jesus and Lazarus, whom Jesus had raised from the dead. The priests planned to put Lazarus to death as well. How threatened they must have felt by the growth of Jesus' following.

Pray as you are led for yourself and others.

"Lord, you must have felt fear as your time of Passion and Death neared. You were human too, divine Savior. I pray for all those who live in fear. Give them peace, Lord . . ." (Continue in your own words.)

Listen to Jesus.

Yes, I knew fear, but knowing my Father of perfect light and love allowed me to master the fear. I tell you that secret, beloved disciple. What else is Jesus saying to you?

Ask God to show you how to live today.

"Let me face my own fears as you did, Jesus. Let me trust in the Father's infinite love and kindness and the perfect wisdom of his providence in my life. Amen."

Tuesday, March 27, 2018

Know that God is present and ready to converse.

"Jesus, I am trying to follow you, to know and love you better, by reading your Word. Thank you for being here with me and guiding me."

Read the gospel: John 13:21–33, 36–38.

After saying this Jesus was troubled in spirit, and declared, "Very truly, I tell you, one of you will betray me." The disciples looked at one another, uncertain of whom he was speaking. One of his disciples—the one whom Jesus loved—was reclining next to him; Simon Peter therefore motioned to him to ask Jesus of whom he was speaking. So while reclining next to Jesus, he asked him, "Lord, who is it?" Jesus answered, "It is the one to whom I give this piece of bread when I have dipped it in the dish." So when he had dipped the piece of bread, he gave it to Judas son of Simon Iscariot. After he received the piece of bread, Satan entered into him. Jesus said to him, "Do quickly what you are going to do." Now no one at the table knew why he said this to him. Some thought that, because Judas had the common purse, Jesus was telling him, "Buy what we need for the festival"; or, that he should give something to the poor. So, after receiving the piece of bread, he immediately went out. And it was night. When he had gone out, Jesus said, "Now the Son of Man has been glorified, and God has been glorified in him. If God has been glorified in him, God will also glorify him in himself and will glorify him at once. Little children, I am with you only a little longer. You will look for me; and as I said to the Jews so now I say to you, 'Where I am going, you cannot come.'" . . .

Simon Peter said to him, "Lord, where are you going?" Jesus answered, "Where I am going, you cannot follow me now; but you will follow afterwards." Peter said to him, "Lord, why can I not follow you now? I will lay down my life for you." Jesus answered, "Will you lay down your life for me? Very truly, I tell you, before the cock crows, you will have denied me three times."

Notice what you think and feel as you read the gospel.

Jesus is troubled by Judas's betrayal, but he knows it is necessary. Jesus sees his Passion and Death as his glorification, part and parcel of his Resurrection and Ascension. He prepares his disciples for his departure and predicts Peter's denial of him.

Pray as you are led for yourself and others.

"Lord, keep me from thinking that I have achieved full commitment to you. I am just a person, full of weakness and ignorance. Give me strength, wisdom, faith, and love so that I may follow you . . ." (Continue in your own words.)

Listen to Jesus.

You are secure in me. If you stumble and fall, turn to me, and I will pick you up and love you. For you, too, are a little child to me, and you are my own. Spend time with me today. What else is Jesus saying to you?

Ask God to show you how to live today.

"Your love is my strength, Lord. Let me not dwell on my own failures today but receive your forgiveness and love you all the more. Amen."

Wednesday, March 28, 2018

Know that God is present and ready to converse.

"Lord of heaven and earth, be real to me as I meet you in your Word."

Read the gospel: Matthew 26:14–25.

Then one of the twelve, who was called Judas Iscariot, went to the chief priests and said, "What will you give me if I betray him to you?" They paid him thirty pieces of silver. And from that moment he began to look for an opportunity to betray him.

On the first day of Unleavened Bread the disciples came to Jesus, saying, "Where do you want us to make the preparations for you to eat the Passover?" He said, "Go into the city to a certain man, and say to him, 'The Teacher says, My time is near; I will keep the Passover at your house with my disciples.'" So the disciples did as Jesus had directed them, and they prepared the Passover meal.

When it was evening, he took his place with the twelve; and while they were eating, he said, "Truly I tell you, one of you will betray me." And they became greatly distressed and began to say to him one after another, "Surely not I, Lord?" He answered, "The one who has dipped his hand into the bowl with me will betray me. The Son of Man goes as it is written of him, but woe to that one by whom the Son of Man is betrayed! It would have been better for that one not to have been born." Judas, who betrayed him, said, "Surely not I, Rabbi?" He replied, "You have said so."

Notice what you think and feel as you read the gospel.

Judas betrays Jesus for thirty pieces of silver and then joins the disciples at the Passover feast. There Jesus talks about the one who will betray him, and they all worry it might be themselves. "Surely not I, Lord?" they ask Jesus. Jesus said it would be better for that man who betrays him never to have been born.

Pray as you are led for yourself and others.

"Lord, surely not I? Put your guard about me. Let me be constant and faithful in my devotion and service to you. I pray the same for all those who follow you and serve you . . ." (Continue in your own words.)

Listen to Jesus.

Be simple in your faith in me. Love me as a child loves. Do not overreach in trying to do or be something I have not asked of you. Be honest. Be yourself. And be mine. I love you always. What else is Jesus saying to you?

Ask God to show you how to live today.

"Help me to walk the simple way with you, my Jesus. Only you I need. Amen."

Thursday, March 29, 2018
Holy Thursday

Know that God is present and ready to converse.

"Jesus, thank you for coming. What have you to teach me, Lord?"

Read the gospel: John 13:1–15.

Now before the festival of the Passover, Jesus knew that his hour had come to depart from this world and go to the Father. Having loved his own who were in the world, he loved them to the end. The devil had already put it into the heart of Judas son of Simon Iscariot to betray him. And during supper Jesus, knowing that the Father had given all things into his hands, and that he had come from God and was going to God, got up from the table, took off his outer robe, and tied a towel around himself. Then he poured water into a basin and began to wash the disciples' feet and to wipe them with the towel that was tied around him. He came to Simon Peter, who said to him, "Lord, are you going to wash my feet?" Jesus answered, "You do not know now what I am doing, but later you will understand." Peter said to him, "You will never wash my feet." Jesus answered, "Unless I wash you, you have no share with me." Simon Peter said to him, "Lord, not my feet only but also my hands and my head!" Jesus said to him, "One who has bathed does not need to wash, except for the feet, but is entirely clean. And you are clean, though not all of you." For he knew who was to betray him; for this reason he said, "Not all of you are clean."

After he had washed their feet, had put on his robe, and had returned to the table, he said to them, "Do you know what I have done to you? You call me Teacher and Lord—and you are right, for that is what I am. So if I, your Lord and Teacher, have washed your feet, you also ought to wash one another's feet. For I have set you an example, that you also should do as I have done to you."

Notice what you think and feel as you read the gospel.

Jesus teaches by example as he washes the feet of his disciples. He chooses to spend his last hours by serving his friends, modeling humility.

Pray as you are led for yourself and others.

"Lord, I aspire to your humility. Give me a heart to serve others in every way I can. Let me do unto others as unto you . . ." (Continue in your own words.)

Listen to Jesus.

You don't need to pretend anything, dear child. Be what you are and trust me to form you into the person I want you to be. What else is Jesus saying to you?

Ask God to show you how to live today.

"Linger with me, Lord. I don't want you to leave. I don't want you to suffer and die. How can I help you? Amen."

Friday, March 30, 2018
Good Friday

Know that God is present and ready to converse.

"Let me contemplate your Passion, Lord, that I may love you more."

Read the gospel: John 18:1–19 (Jn 18:1–19:42).

After Jesus had spoken these words, he went out with his disciples across the Kidron valley to a place where there was a garden, which he and his disciples entered. Now Judas, who betrayed him, also knew the place, because Jesus often met there with his disciples. So Judas brought a detachment of soldiers together with police from the chief priests and the Pharisees, and they came there with lanterns and torches and weapons. Then Jesus, knowing all that was to happen to him, came forward and asked them, "Whom are you looking for?" They answered, "Jesus of Nazareth." Jesus replied, "I am he." Judas, who betrayed him, was standing with them. When Jesus said to them, "I am he," they stepped back and fell to the ground. Again he asked them, "Whom are you looking for?" And they said, "Jesus of Nazareth." Jesus answered, "I told you that I am he. So if you are looking for me, let these men go." This was to fulfill the word that he had spoken, "I did not lose a single one of those whom you gave me." Then Simon Peter, who had a sword, drew it, struck the high priest's slave, and cut off his right ear. The slave's name was Malchus. Jesus said to Peter, "Put your sword back into its sheath. Am I not to drink the cup that the Father has given me?"

So the soldiers, their officer, and the Jewish police arrested Jesus and bound him. First they took him to Annas, who was the father-in-law of Caiaphas, the high priest that year. Caiaphas was the one who had advised the Jews that it was better to have one person die for the people.

Simon Peter and another disciple followed Jesus. Since that disciple was known to the high priest, he went with Jesus into the courtyard of the high priest, but Peter was standing outside at the gate. So the other disciple, who was known to the high priest, went out, spoke to the woman who guarded the gate, and brought Peter in. The woman said to Peter, "You are not also one of this man's disciples, are you?" He said, "I am not." Now the slaves and the police had made a charcoal fire because it was cold, and they were standing round it and warming themselves. Peter also was standing with them and warming himself.

Then the high priest questioned Jesus about his disciples and about his teaching.

Notice what you think and feel as you read the gospel.

Judas betrays Jesus. He leads the soldiers to Jesus to arrest him. The disciples scatter, as Jesus is led before Annas and Caiaphas. Outside the gate, Peter denies being a disciple of Jesus.

Pray as you are led for yourself and others.

"Lord, you were treated unjustly, and it has just begun. Help me not be unjust with others. I pray for those I have wronged . . ." (Continue in your own words.)

Listen to Jesus.

If you can be good and loving in any situation, even a situation that is cruel and unjust, you elevate that situation, make it meaningful, and redeem it. That is what I do. Follow me. What else is Jesus saying to you?

Ask God to show you how to live today.

"Then help me to be good and loving in all my circumstances today, and this will be a day of glory for you. Thank you. Amen."

Saturday, March 31, 2018
Holy Saturday

Know that God is present and ready to converse.

"Crucified Savior, I know you live and are here with me now. I praise you."

Read the gospel: Mark 16:1–7.

When the sabbath was over, Mary Magdalene, and Mary the mother of James, and Salome bought spices, so that they might go and anoint him. And very early on the first day of the week, when the sun had risen, they went to the tomb. They had been saying to one another, "Who will roll away the stone for us from the entrance to the tomb?" When they looked up, they saw that the stone, which was very large, had already been rolled back. As they entered the tomb, they saw a young man, dressed in a white robe, sitting on the right side; and they were alarmed. But he said to them, "Do not be alarmed; you are looking for Jesus of Nazareth, who was crucified. He has been raised; he is not here. Look, there is the place they laid him. But go, tell his disciples and Peter that he is going ahead of you to Galilee; there you will see him, just as he told you."

Notice what you think and feel as you read the gospel.

The women find the stone rolled away and the tomb empty. A young man in a white robe tells them not to be alarmed, for Jesus has been raised. He asks them to tell the others to go to Galilee, for there they will see Jesus.

Pray as you are led for yourself and others.

"Jesus, the events of your death and resurrection are straightforward and mysterious at the same time. The miraculous invades the mundane world. Let it be so in my life, too . . ." (Continue in your own words.)

Listen to Jesus.

I will grant your prayers as you ask. I am alive and I live for you. And you will live for me forever in the glorious kingdom of heaven, prepared for you by my Father from all time. What else is Jesus saying to you?

Ask God to show you how to live today.

"Then let me love you and serve you today, Lord. Let me do your will until you call me to yourself. Amen."

Sunday, April 1, 2018
Easter Sunday

Know that God is present and ready to converse.

"You are always present with me, Lord, but sometimes I do not recognize you. Reveal yourself to me and teach me by your Word."

Read the gospel: John 20:1–9.

Early on the first day of the week, while it was still dark, Mary Magdalene came to the tomb and saw that the stone had been removed from the tomb. So she ran and went to Simon Peter and the other disciple, the one whom Jesus loved, and said to them, "They have taken the Lord out of the tomb, and we do not know where they have laid him." Then Peter and the other disciple set out and went toward the tomb. The two were running together, but the other disciple outran Peter and reached the tomb first. He bent down to look in and saw the linen wrappings lying there, but he did not go in. Then Simon Peter came, following him, and went into the tomb. He saw the linen wrappings lying there, and the cloth that had been on Jesus' head, not lying with the linen wrappings but rolled up in a place by itself. Then the other disciple, who reached the tomb first, also went in, and he saw and believed; for as yet they did not understand the scripture, that he must rise from the dead.

Notice what you think and feel as you read the gospel.

Mary Magdalene first discovers Jesus' tomb is empty. Peter and John run to see, and they find the tomb empty, as she reported. They begin to realize that Jesus has risen from the dead.

Pray as you are led for yourself and others.

"Lord, let my heart burn within me as I hear and read your holy scriptures. You are the Word of God, the Light that came into the darkness. Make me what you please. I wish to serve . . ." (Continue in your own words.)

Listen to Jesus.

I AM, and the universe was created by me, through me, and for me. I give meaning and glory to all that is. You can reach out to me, and I want you to, but you can only begin to approach me now. Seek me and I will draw you into myself, beloved. What else is Jesus saying to you?

Ask God to show you how to live today.

"You are too high for me, my God, but I aspire to know you. Let me continuously advance my knowledge of you, your goodness, and your glory. Amen."

The Easter Season

INTRODUCTION

Easter is the greatest feast of the Church year because it celebrates the victory of Jesus Christ over sin and death, a victory not just for himself but for all who believe in him. Jesus is the pioneer who leads us into eternal life. "Just as in Adam all die," wrote St. Paul, "so in Christ all will come to life again . . . Christ the first fruits and then, at his coming, all those who belong to him" (1 Cor 15:22–23). In the risen Christ, we are reconciled with God now and forever.

Our hearts and minds may wonder at the great mystery of resurrection. In the gospels, we read how the disciples received the amazing news that Jesus is not dead but lives. At first, many of them are skeptical, but they come to believe as Jesus shows himself to them again and again. For modern readers, their skepticism that turns to faith helps us to believe in this greatest of all miracles.

The season ends with Pentecost, the descent of the Holy Spirit to empower the disciples of Jesus to carry on his great work. The Spirit is given to us, too, as is the work. Let us pray the gospels of this season with joy and thanksgiving.

Monday, April 2, 2018

Know that God is present and ready to converse.

"Jesus, you meet me here. You have risen from the dead, and you are Lord."

Read the gospel: Matthew 28:8–15.

So they left the tomb quickly with fear and great joy, and ran to tell his disciples. Suddenly Jesus met them and said, "Greetings!" And they came to him, took hold of his feet, and worshipped him. Then Jesus said to them, "Do not be afraid; go and tell my brothers to go to Galilee; there they will see me."

While they were going, some of the guard went into the city and told the chief priests everything that had happened. After the priests had assembled with the elders, they devised a plan to give a large sum of money to the soldiers, telling them, "You must say, 'His disciples came by night and stole him away while we were asleep.' If this comes to the governor's ears, we will satisfy him and keep you out of trouble." So they took the money and did as they were directed. And this story is still told among the Jews to this day.

Notice what you think and feel as you read the gospel.

Now there is no doubt that Jesus is the Son of God, for he is alive. Everything Jesus said and promised to his disciples is validated. What awe, amazement, and wonder they must have felt. Of course, the chief priests find another explanation and spread it—how sad they could not recognize their own hour of salvation.

Pray as you are led for yourself and others.

"Risen Lord, I worship you. Let me be with you every day. How may I serve you? How may I serve those you give me? . . ." (Continue in your own words.)

Listen to Jesus.

Beloved, it pleases me that you wish to spend time with me. You recognize that I am the great good, for you and for all who come to me. Tell others what I have done and am doing for you. They will hear you. What else is Jesus saying to you?

Ask God to show you how to live today.

"I do want to spread your good news, dear Savior, Good Shepherd. Put your Spirit in my heart and your name on my lips today. Amen."

Tuesday, April 3, 2018

Know that God is present and ready to converse.

"Sometimes I feel you are far from me, Jesus. But you are never far from me. You are here. Alleluia."

Read the gospel: John 20:11–18.

But Mary stood weeping outside the tomb. As she wept, she bent over to look into the tomb; and she saw two angels in white, sitting where the body of Jesus had been lying, one at the head and the other at the feet. They said to her, "Woman, why are you weeping?" She said to them, "They have taken away my Lord, and I do not know where they have laid him." When she had said this, she turned round and saw Jesus standing there, but she did not know that it was Jesus. Jesus said to her, "Woman, why are you weeping? For whom are you looking?" Supposing him to be the gardener, she said to him, "Sir, if you have carried him away, tell me where you have laid him, and I will take him away." Jesus said to her, "Mary!" She turned and said to him in Hebrew, "Rabbouni!" (which means Teacher). Jesus said to her, "Do not hold on to me, because I have not yet ascended to the Father. But go to my brothers and say to them, 'I am ascending to my Father and your Father, to my God and your God.'" Mary Magdalene went and announced to the disciples, "I have seen the Lord"; and she told them that he had said these things to her.

Notice what you think and feel as you read the gospel.

Weeping that the body of Jesus is not in the tomb, Mary Magdalene encounters the angels and then Jesus himself. He calls her by name, and she recognizes him with joy. Jesus gives her a message to bring to the disciples, and she delivers it.

Pray as you are led for yourself and others.

"Rabbouni, teach me. The truths of God are too high for me. I need your Spirit to understand them. I pray that all those I love may come to knowledge of God . . ." (Continue in your own words.)

Listen to Jesus.

I will always give you what you need, dear friend. You don't know what you need, but I do, for I love you and watch over you jealously. I have prepared a place for you. Come to me. What else is Jesus saying to you?

Ask God to show you how to live today.

"I thank you for caring for me, Lord. Forgive me for not trusting you at times. Strengthen my faith, my love, my commitment to you and your service. Amen."

Wednesday, April 4, 2018

Know that God is present and ready to converse.

"Jesus, Word of God, you are present in the scriptures. You are present in the Holy Spirit. You are here with me now. I rejoice."

Read the gospel: Luke 24:13–35.

Now on that same day two of them were going to a village called Emmaus, about seven miles from Jerusalem, and talking with each other about all these things that had happened. While they were talking and discussing, Jesus himself came near and went with them, but their eyes were kept from recognizing him. And he said to them, "What are you discussing with each other while you walk along?" They stood still, looking sad. Then one of them, whose name was Cleopas, answered him, "Are you the only stranger in Jerusalem who does not know the things that have taken place there in these days?" He asked them, "What things?" They replied, "The things about Jesus of Nazareth, who was a prophet mighty in deed and word before God and all the people, and how our chief priests and leaders handed him over to be condemned to death and crucified him. But we had hoped that he was the one to redeem Israel. Yes, and besides all this, it is now the third day since these things took place. Moreover, some women of our group astounded us. They were at the tomb early this morning, and when they did not find his body there, they came back and told us that they had indeed seen a vision of angels who said that he was alive. Some of those who were with us went to the tomb and found it just as the women had said; but they did not see him." Then he said to them, "Oh, how foolish you are, and how slow of heart to believe all that the prophets have declared! Was it not necessary that the Messiah should suffer these things and then enter into his glory?" Then beginning with Moses and all the prophets, he interpreted to them the things about himself in all the scriptures.

As they came near the village to which they were going, he walked ahead as if he were going on. But they urged him strongly, saying, "Stay with us, because it is almost evening and the day is now nearly over." So he went in to stay with them. When he was at the table with them, he took bread, blessed and broke it, and gave it to them. Then their eyes were opened, and they recognized him; and he vanished from their sight. They said to each other, "Were not our hearts burning within us while he was talking to us on the road, while he was opening the scriptures to us?" That same hour they got up and returned to Jerusalem; and they found the eleven and their companions gathered together. They were saying, "The Lord has risen indeed, and he has appeared to Simon!" Then they told what had happened on the road, and how he had been made known to them in the breaking of the bread.

Notice what you think and feel as you read the gospel.

The disciples on the road to Emmaus are sad, troubled—everything seems chaotic. Their teacher died, but now people are saying he's not dead, and they're sad and confused. Jesus, in his love for them, unfolds the scripture, showing them how the recent events of his Passion, Death, and Resurrection are foretold. Then, having given them comfort and explanation, he feeds them, and they finally they recognize him.

Pray as you are led for yourself and others.

"Lord, let me recognize you in my life, at every turn, in good times and in bad. Set my heart on fire with love for you and your holy Word. Illuminate those you have given me . . ." (Continue in your own words.)

Listen to Jesus.

My heart is full of love for you and for those you love. I am eager to share it with you. Love is a power unlike any other. It transforms hardship and suffering, making them meaningful and good. It overcomes all fear. It endures for eternity. What else is Jesus saying to you?

Ask God to show you how to live today.

"Lord, my love is weak, but it is there. I love you. I love others. Strengthen me, feed me, help me grow in love today and every day that I may be like you. Amen."

Thursday, April 5, 2018

Know that God is present and ready to converse.

"Jesus, I am aware of your presence with me now. Let your peace be upon me as I hear your words."

Read the gospel: Luke 24:35–48.

Then the two disciples told what had happened on the road, and how he had been made known to them in the breaking of the bread.

While they were talking about this, Jesus himself stood among them and said to them, "Peace be with you." They were startled and terrified, and thought that they were seeing a ghost. He said to them, "Why are you frightened, and why do doubts arise in your hearts? Look at my hands and my feet; see that it is I myself. Touch me and see; for a ghost does not have flesh and bones as you see that I have." And when he had said this, he showed them his hands and his feet. While in their joy they were disbelieving and still wondering, he said to them, "Have you anything here to eat?" They gave him a piece of broiled fish, and he took it and ate in their presence.

Then he said to them, "These are my words that I spoke to you while I was still with you—that everything written about me in the law of Moses, the prophets, and the psalms must be fulfilled." Then he opened their minds to understand the scriptures, and he said to them, "Thus it is written, that the Messiah is to suffer and to rise from the dead on the third day, and that repentance and forgiveness of sins is to be proclaimed in his name to all nations, beginning from Jerusalem. You are witnesses of these things."

Notice what you think and feel as you read the gospel.

The risen Jesus appears to them in his flesh, and the disciples are filled with joy, but they still wonder. They cannot accept this reality. Then he asks for something to eat, and he eats a piece of fish! Then he opens their minds so that they may understand the scriptures referring to him, the Messiah.

Pray as you are led for yourself and others.

"Lord, you gave your disciples great gifts to spread the Gospel. They were just ordinary people before you transformed them. Transform me, too, and let me serve you, your great good news, and those you give me . . ." (Continue in your own words.)

Listen to Jesus.

I seek people who will carry my word to others, who in love serve the needs of the poor, the sick, the persecuted, the lonely. Will you? What else is Jesus saying to you?

Ask God to show you how to live today.

"Lord, yes, send me. I have known your touch, I have heard your words. Let me proclaim your salvation in everything I do and say. Amen."

Friday, April 6, 2018

Know that God is present and ready to converse.

"Jesus, you appeared to the disciples after you rose from the dead. Appear to me now as I open myself to you and your Word."

Read the gospel: John 21:1–14.

After these things Jesus showed himself again to the disciples by the Sea of Tiberias; and he showed himself in this way. Gathered there together were Simon Peter, Thomas called the Twin, Nathanael of Cana in Galilee, the sons of Zebedee, and two others of his disciples. Simon Peter said to them, "I am going fishing." They said to him, "We will go with you." They went out and got into the boat, but that night they caught nothing. Just after daybreak, Jesus stood on the beach; but the disciples did not know that it was Jesus. Jesus said to them, "Children, you have no fish, have you?" They answered him, "No." He said to them, "Cast the net to the right side of the boat, and you will find some." So they cast it, and now they were not able to haul it in because there were so many fish. That disciple whom Jesus loved said to Peter, "It is the Lord!" When Simon Peter heard that it was the Lord, he put on some clothes, for he was naked, and jumped into the lake. But the other disciples came in the boat, dragging the net full of fish, for they were not far from the land, only about a hundred yards off.

When they had gone ashore, they saw a charcoal fire there, with fish on it, and bread. Jesus said to them, "Bring some of the fish that you have just caught." So Simon Peter went aboard and hauled the net ashore, full of large fish, a hundred and fifty-three of them; and though there were so many, the net was not torn. Jesus said to them, "Come and have breakfast." Now none of the disciples dared to ask him, "Who are you?" because they knew it was the Lord. Jesus came and took the bread and gave it to them, and did the same with the fish. This was now the third time that Jesus appeared to the disciples after he was raised from the dead.

Notice what you think and feel as you read the gospel.

As if they don't know what to do with themselves and are still trying to absorb the reality that Jesus is alive, the disciples go out fishing. They catch nothing, until, shortly after daybreak, they encounter Jesus, who speaks to them from the shore, instructing them how to fish. They net a huge haul of fish, causing John to realize Jesus' identity. John tells Peter, and they all have breakfast with Jesus on the beach.

Pray as you are led for yourself and others.

"Jesus, let the reality of your Resurrection become clear to me. Let it become an unshakeable absolute in my life, a fulcrum for all I think, do, and say, for I wish to share you with others . . ." (Continue in your own words.)

Listen to Jesus.

Come to me, beloved. See my hands and feet and my pierced side. I am yours. You lack nothing, for you have me. Ask me for good things for yourself and for others. What else is Jesus saying to you?

Ask God to show you how to live today.

"Jesus, give me a strong gift of prayer, that I can pray in faith for good things that other people need. Amen."

Saturday, April 7, 2018

Know that God is present and ready to converse.

"Jesus, you want people to believe you rose from the dead. Yet the world is full of unbelief, and even your own doubt you. Forgive us, and help us embrace the truth of your Resurrection."

Read the gospel: Mark 16:9–15.

Now after he rose early on the first day of the week, Jesus appeared first to Mary Magdalene, from whom he had cast out seven demons. She went out and told those who had been with him, while they were mourning and weeping. But when they heard that he was alive and had been seen by her, they would not believe it.

After this he appeared in another form to two of them, as they were walking into the country. And they went back and told the rest, but they did not believe them.

Later he appeared to the eleven themselves as they were sitting at the table; and he upbraided them for their lack of faith and stubbornness, because they had not believed those who saw him after he had risen. And he said to them, "Go into all the world and proclaim the good news to the whole creation."

Notice what you think and feel as you read the gospel.

The disciples won't believe the testimony of those who have encountered the risen Jesus. Can we blame them? Jesus does and takes them to task for their doubt and obstinacy. Then he commissions them to tell the good news of his Resurrection to the whole world.

Pray as you are led for yourself and others.

"Jesus, I sometimes flounder in unbelief. I may profess faith, but I do not always act confident that you are present and trustworthy. Change me, that I may be a worthy servant and may please you. Let me be your hands in serving others . . ." (Continue in your own words.)

Listen to Jesus.

Without me you can do nothing, child. I know your frailties. No matter. I have chosen you, and I give you to my Father. We love you, and we give you love for others. We commission you to love. What else is Jesus saying to you?

Ask God to show you how to live today.

"Lord, help me to know and believe that you are with me, and your presence will give me strength to go into the world today to proclaim, in words and actions, your love. Amen."

Sunday, April 8, 2018
Second Sunday of Easter

Know that God is present and ready to converse.

"Jesus, Prince of Peace, breathe on me as I approach your Word."

Read the gospel: John 20:19–31.

When it was evening on that day, the first day of the week, and the doors of the house where the disciples had met were locked for fear of the Jews, Jesus came and stood among them and said, "Peace be with you." After he said this, he showed them his hands and his side. Then the disciples rejoiced when they saw the Lord. Jesus said to them again, "Peace be with you. As the Father has sent me, so I send you." When he had said this, he breathed on them and said to them, "Receive the Holy Spirit. If you forgive the sins of any, they are forgiven them; if you retain the sins of any, they are retained."

But Thomas (who was called the Twin), one of the twelve, was not with them when Jesus came. So the other disciples told him, "We have seen the Lord." But he said to them, "Unless I see the mark of the nails in his hands, and put my finger in the mark of the nails and my hand in his side, I will not believe."

A week later his disciples were again in the house, and Thomas was with them. Although the doors were shut, Jesus came and stood among them and said, "Peace be with you." Then he said to Thomas, "Put your finger here and see my hands. Reach out your hand and put it in my side. Do not doubt but believe." Thomas answered him, "My Lord and my God!" Jesus said to him, "Have you believed because you have seen me? Blessed are those who have not seen and yet have come to believe." Now Jesus did many other signs in the presence of his disciples, which are not written in this book. But these are written so that you may come to believe that Jesus is the Messiah, the Son of God, and that through believing you may have life in his name.

Notice what you think and feel as you read the gospel.

Jesus gives his disciples the Holy Spirit to help them carry on his ministry. But Thomas is skeptical, declaring he needs to see the wounds of Jesus to believe. A week later he does, and he acknowledges Jesus as Lord and God. Jesus declares that we who have not seen him and believe are truly blessed.

Pray as you are led for yourself and others.

"You have blessed me, Jesus, with faith. I pray that others may know you through faith, especially those you have given me . . ." (Continue in your own words.)

Listen to Jesus.

People will never stop coming to me in faith, for my Spirit is at work throughout the world. My people are my church, with authority and power from God. By believing in me, you have life. By following me, you enter the realm of light, goodness, and love. What else is Jesus saying to you?

Ask God to show you how to live today.

"Lord, I want to follow you and please you in all that I do. Give me light, goodness, and love, and help me to act in your service. Amen."

Monday, April 9, 2018
Annunciation of the Lord

Know that God is present and ready to converse.

"Son of the Most High, you meet me here. Let my heart receive your Word."

Read the gospel: Luke 1:26–38.

In the sixth month the angel Gabriel was sent by God to a town in Galilee called Nazareth, to a virgin engaged to a man whose name was Joseph, of the house of David. The virgin's name was Mary. And he came to her and said, "Greetings, favored one! The Lord is with you." But she was much perplexed by his words and pondered what sort of greeting this might be. The angel said to her, "Do not be afraid, Mary, for you have found favor with God. And now, you will conceive in your womb and bear a son, and you will name him Jesus. He will be great, and will be called the Son of the Most High, and the Lord God will give to him the throne of his ancestor David. He will reign over the house of Jacob forever, and of his kingdom there will be no end." Mary said to the angel, "How can this be, since I am a virgin?" The angel said to her, "The Holy Spirit will come upon you, and the power of the Most High will overshadow you; therefore the child to be born will be holy; he will be called Son of God. And now, your relative Elizabeth in her old age has also conceived a son; and this is the sixth month for her who was said to be barren. For nothing will be impossible with God." Then Mary said, "Here am I, the servant of the Lord; let it be with me according to your word." Then the angel departed from her.

Notice what you think and feel as you read the gospel.

Mary doesn't question the angel's prophecy about the Messiah, but she does question how she, as a virgin, can be a mother. The angel explains, tells Mary about her pregnant cousin Elizabeth (who was thought to be barren), and Mary yields her will to God's.

Pray as you are led for yourself and others.

"Lord, nothing is impossible with you, though you work in mysterious ways. I surrender my will to you, asking you to form me in your own image . . ." (Continue in your own words.)

Listen to Jesus.

As you give yourself to God, dearly beloved, you become a member of the Holy Family. As you do the will of God, you become my mother or my brother. Our love for one another makes us family forever. What else is Jesus saying to you?

Ask God to show you how to live today.

"God, let me look upon others today as family, showing your favor to everyone I encounter. Amen."

Tuesday, April 10, 2018

Know that God is present and ready to converse.

"Holy Spirit, open my eyes to the truth of your scripture, that I may worship glorious God."

Read the gospel: John 3:7b–15.

Jesus said, "Do not be astonished that I said to you, 'You must be born from above.' The wind blows where it chooses, and you hear the sound of it, but you do not know where it comes from or where it goes. So it is with everyone who is born of the Spirit." Nicodemus said to him, "How can these things be?" Jesus answered him, "Are you a teacher of Israel, and yet you do not understand these things?

"Very truly, I tell you, we speak of what we know and testify to what we have seen; yet you do not receive our testimony. If I have told you about earthly things and you do not believe, how can you believe if I tell you about heavenly things? No one has ascended into heaven except the one who descended from heaven, the Son of Man. And just as Moses lifted up the serpent in the wilderness, so must the Son of Man be lifted up, that whoever believes in him may have eternal life."

Notice what you think and feel as you read the gospel.

Nicodemus wants to understand Jesus, but he struggles. Jesus clearly declares to him who he is, the Son of Man. Will Nicodemus believe when he sees Jesus crucified?

Pray as you are led for yourself and others.

"I seek to be born of the Spirit, Jesus, and to go where the Spirit wills. Let me abandon my own will to serve you and those you have given me . . ." (Continue in your own words.)

Listen to Jesus.

I grant your prayers, dear child. The wind is with you. Follow me. I will show you wonderful things. What else is Jesus saying to you?

Ask God to show you how to live today.

"Lord, Master, you are good to me. I resolve to be good to others for your name's sake. Amen."

Wednesday, April 11, 2018

Know that God is present and ready to converse.

"You came to give me everlasting life, Lord, and you are here with me now. Give me your light."

Read the gospel: John 3:16–21.

Jesus said, "For God so loved the world that he gave his only Son, so that everyone who believes in him may not perish but may have eternal life.

"Indeed, God did not send the Son into the world to condemn the world, but in order that the world might be saved through him. Those who believe in him are not condemned; but those who do not believe are condemned already, because they have not believed in the name of the only Son of God. And this is the judgement, that the light has come into the world, and people loved darkness rather than light because their deeds were evil. For all who do evil hate the light and do not come to the light, so that their deeds may not be exposed. But those who do what is true come to the light, so that it may be clearly seen that their deeds have been done in God."

Notice what you think and feel as you read the gospel.

Love is the reason for Jesus, God's Son, to come among us as a man, as a Savior, as the bringer of eternal life. He did not come to condemn us but to lead us into his wonderful light, a loving relationship with God, and eternal life. Why should anyone prefer the darkness?

Pray as you are led for yourself and others.

"Lord, I repudiate the darkness in myself. Let me come to the light and abide in you. Let others turn away from darkness too and find you . . ." (Continue in your own words.)

Listen to Jesus.

My heart is full of mercy for all people, even those who are in darkness, even those who choose darkness. I want to open their eyes and show them the goodness of God. Keep praying for them, my friend. What else is Jesus saying to you?

Ask God to show you how to live today.

"Lord, I will pray as you prompt me today for those in darkness. Fill me with your own compassion for them. Amen."

Thursday, April 12, 2018

Know that God is present and ready to converse.

"Lord, I come to you in faith. You wait for me here in love. Let me receive your truth."

Read the gospel: John 3:31–36.

The one who comes from above is above all; the one who is of the earth belongs to the earth and speaks about earthly things. The one who comes from heaven is above all. He testifies to what he has seen and heard, yet no one accepts his testimony. Whoever has accepted his testimony has certified this, that God is true. He whom God has sent speaks the words of God, for he gives the Spirit without measure. The Father loves the Son and has placed all things in his hands. Whoever believes in the Son has eternal life; whoever disobeys the Son will not see life, but must endure God's wrath.

Notice what you think and feel as you read the gospel.

John declares Jesus to be a heavenly messenger, come from the Father to speak the truth to the world. God has given him all power, and Jesus wants to give people eternal life.

Pray as you are led for yourself and others.

"Who does not believe the words of Jesus, Lord? Who refuses the eternal life he offers? I pray for them . . ." (Continue in your own words.)

Listen to Jesus.

Faith is a gift from God, but it is a gift freely given to any who seek it. It is an act of will to seek the Lord. Whoever wills to come to God, let them come into eternal life. What else is Jesus saying to you?

Ask God to show you how to live today.

"Lord, renew my will to believe in you and obey you. Let me show my faith and love in acts of kindness to others today. Amen."

Friday, April 13, 2018

Know that God is present and ready to converse.

"Feed me the bread of heaven, Lord Jesus, for you come to me from God."

Read the gospel: John 6:1–15.

After this Jesus went to the other side of the Sea of Galilee, also called the Sea of Tiberias. A large crowd kept following him, because they saw the signs that he was doing for the sick. Jesus went up the mountain and sat down there with his disciples. Now the Passover, the festival of the Jews, was near. When he looked up and saw a large crowd coming towards him, Jesus said to Philip, "Where are we to buy bread for these people to eat?" He said this to test him, for he himself knew what he was going to do. Philip answered him, "Six months' wages would not buy enough bread for each of them to get a little." One of his disciples, Andrew, Simon Peter's brother, said to him, "There is a boy here who has five barley loaves and two fish. But what are they among so many people?" Jesus said, "Make the people sit down." Now there was a great deal of grass in the place; so they sat down, about five thousand in all. Then Jesus took the loaves, and when he had given thanks, he distributed them to those who were seated; so also the fish, as much as they wanted. When they were satisfied, he told his disciples, "Gather up the fragments left over, so that nothing may be lost." So they gathered them up, and from the fragments of the five barley loaves, left by those who had eaten, they filled twelve baskets. When the people saw the sign that he had done, they began to say, "This is indeed the prophet who is to come into the world."

When Jesus realized that they were about to come and take him by force to make him king, he withdrew again to the mountain by himself.

Notice what you think and feel as you read the gospel.

Jesus miraculously multiplies bread and fish to feed five thousand. The people want to take him by force to make him king. Jesus withdraws.

Pray as you are led for yourself and others.

"Jesus, many are hungry, many are sick, many are like sheep with no shepherd. Are you still working among us, Lord? I pray for those in need and offer myself to their service . . ." (Continue in your own words.)

Listen to Jesus.

You are called to serve others, beloved disciple, and in so doing you serve me. Keep your gaze on the kingdom of heaven even as you do your work on earth. Draw strength from above. What else is Jesus saying to you?

Ask God to show you how to live today.

"With you I can do anything, Lord. Help me think, speak, act, and pray as you would have me. I'm yours. Amen."

Saturday, April 14, 2018

Know that God is present and ready to converse.

"There is much to fear, Lord, so stay close to me and teach me your ways."

Read the gospel: John 6:16–21.

When evening came, Jesus' disciples went down to the lake, got into a boat, and started across the lake to Capernaum. It was now dark, and Jesus had not yet come to them. The lake became rough because a strong wind was blowing. When they had rowed about three or four miles, they saw Jesus walking on the lake and coming near the boat, and they were terrified. But he said to them, "It is I; do not be afraid." Then they wanted to take him into the boat, and immediately the boat reached the land towards which they were going.

Notice what you think and feel as you read the gospel.

The disciples encounter rough water as they travel by boat at night, heading for Capernaum. When they see Jesus coming toward them walking on the water, they are frightened. He reassures them, they take him into the boat, and immediately they reach their destination.

Pray as you are led for yourself and others.

"Let me trust you in my storms, Lord, for you are always near to save me. Your ways are wonderful. I pray for those experiencing storms, especially those in fear . . ." (Continue in your own words.)

Listen to Jesus.

The events of earthly life appear to many as natural, and they are. But the hand of God also moves in the world, most often unseen and unacknowledged. Supernatural things are seen as natural. I tell you this because I want you to trust me and believe in the power of your prayers. What else is Jesus saying to you?

Ask God to show you how to live today.

"Let me see the hand of God at work in the lives of those I love. I offer myself to you, Lord, as an instrument of your supernatural power. Amen."

Sunday, April 15, 2018
Third Sunday of Easter

Know that God is present and ready to converse.

"Breathe your peace upon me, Jesus, as I seek you in your Word."

Read the gospel: Luke 24:35–48.

Then Jesus' disciples told what had happened on the road, and how he had been made known to them in the breaking of the bread.

While they were talking about this, Jesus himself stood among them and said to them, "Peace be with you." They were startled and terrified, and thought that they were seeing a ghost. He said to them, "Why are you frightened, and why do doubts arise in your hearts? Look at my hands and my feet; see that it is I myself. Touch me and see; for a ghost does not have flesh and bones as you see that I have." And when he had said this, he showed them his hands and his feet. While in their joy they were disbelieving and still wondering, he said to them, "Have you anything here to eat?" They gave him a piece of broiled fish, and he took it and ate in their presence.

Then he said to them, "These are my words that I spoke to you while I was still with you—that everything written about me in the law of Moses, the prophets, and the psalms must be fulfilled." Then he opened their minds to understand the scriptures, and he said to them, "Thus it is written, that the Messiah is to suffer and to rise from the dead on the third day, and that repentance and forgiveness of sins is to be proclaimed in his name to all nations, beginning from Jerusalem. You are witnesses of these things."

Notice what you think and feel as you read the gospel.

When Jesus appears to his disciples, he greets them with "Peace," but his disciples are terrified. He reassures them of his Resurrection and his identity; he invites them to touch him, to see him as he is. He says he is the fulfillment of everything written about him in the scriptures and they have been the witnesses of these things.

Pray as you are led for yourself and others.

"Jesus, you are my Lord and my God. You have done wonderful things for me—you know me as I am and have made me your own. How may I witness to you? I will begin by praying for these people . . ." (Continue in your own words.)

Listen to Jesus.

I have given you grace to believe in me, my dear child. I give you also my love for others. Just live in my peace, and you will bless others and glorify me. What else is Jesus saying to you?

Ask God to show you how to live today.

"Help me live in your peace, Lord. You accept me; help me accept you, that my life may be your witness in the world."

Monday, April 16, 2018

Know that God is present and ready to converse.

"Lord, you provide for me. Give me, in the reading of your Word, the food that endures for eternal life."

Read the gospel: John 6:22–29.

The next day the crowd that had stayed on the other side of the lake saw that there had been only one boat there. They also saw that Jesus had not got into the boat with his disciples, but that his disciples had gone away alone. Then some boats from Tiberias came near the place where they had eaten the bread after the Lord had given thanks. So when the crowd saw that neither Jesus nor his disciples were there, they themselves got into the boats and went to Capernaum looking for Jesus.

When they found him on the other side of the lake, they said to him, "Rabbi, when did you come here?" Jesus answered them, "Very truly, I tell you, you are looking for me, not because you saw signs, but because you ate your fill of the loaves. Do not work for the food that perishes, but for the food that endures for eternal life, which the Son of Man will give you. For it is on him that God the Father has set his seal." Then they said to him, "What must we do to perform the works of God?" Jesus answered them, "This is the work of God, that you believe in him whom he has sent."

Notice what you think and feel as you read the gospel.

Jesus reproves the crowd for following him merely to be fed. He exhorts them to work for the food that endures forever. They ask what they should do to perform the works of God, and he answers that they should believe in the one God has sent, the Son of Man.

Pray as you are led for yourself and others.

"Lord, I come to you once again to be fed. Strengthen me and those you have given me that we may do the works of God . . . " (Continue in your own words.)

Listen to Jesus.

I give you the strength and the faith you need, beloved. Stay close to me, loving me. That pleases me. Love is also the food that endures for eternal life. What else is Jesus saying to you?

Ask God to show you how to live today.

"I resolve to walk in faith and love today, my God. Lead me on my way. Thank you. Amen."

Tuesday, April 17, 2018

Know that God is present and ready to converse.

"Father, feed me the bread of heaven, your holy Word."

Read the gospel: John 6:30–35.

So they said to Jesus, "What sign are you going to give us then, so that we may see it and believe you? What work are you performing? Our ancestors ate the manna in the wilderness; as it is written, 'He gave them bread from heaven to eat.'" Then Jesus said to them, "Very truly, I tell you, it was not Moses who gave you the bread from heaven, but it is my Father who gives you the true bread from heaven. For the bread of God is that which comes down from heaven and gives life to the world." They said to him, "Sir, give us this bread always."

Jesus said to them, "I am the bread of life. Whoever comes to me will never be hungry, and whoever believes in me will never be thirsty."

Notice what you think and feel as you read the gospel.

The people want a sign; Jesus gives them himself as the bread of life that will never fail them. The people must only come to him and believe in him.

Pray as you are led for yourself and others.

"Lord, make my heart long for you and love you above all else. Give your bread to those I pray for now . . ." (Continue in your own words.)

Listen to Jesus.

You are right to turn to me and not to yourself. I will never disappoint you, but you must come to me, my dear child. I am the bread of life. What else is Jesus saying to you?

Ask God to show you how to live today.

"Thank you, dear Jesus. I come to you worshiping. Lead me on your way. Amen."

Wednesday, April 18, 2018

Know that God is present and ready to converse.

"Father, I submit to your will. Teach me by your Word."

Read the gospel: John 6:35–40.

Jesus said to them, "I am the bread of life. Whoever comes to me will never be hungry, and whoever believes in me will never be thirsty. But I said to you that you have seen me and yet do not believe. Everything that the Father gives me will come to me, and anyone who comes to me I will never drive away; for I have come down from heaven, not to do my own will, but the will of him who sent me. And this is the will of him who sent me, that I should lose nothing of all that he has given me, but raise it up on the last day. This is indeed the will of my Father, that all who see the Son and believe in him may have eternal life; and I will raise them up on the last day."

Notice what you think and feel as you read the gospel.

The Father's will is that we belong to Jesus, that we may be raised on the last day to eternal life. Jesus' words are extraordinary, filled with promises to those who come to him.

Pray as you are led for yourself and others.

"Lord, I thank you for the many who have come to you in faith. You will not lose any of us. But I pray for those who have not yet come to you . . ." (Continue in your own words.)

Listen to Jesus.

Beloved disciple, all human history is a great drama of wills. Do not resist God's will, but in love, give yourself to God and save yourself from death. What else is Jesus saying to you?

Ask God to show you how to live today.

"Lord, I give you myself this moment—heart, mind, soul, and body. Make me your instrument this day. Amen."

Thursday, April 19, 2018

Know that God is present and ready to converse.

"Lord, teach me your way of life. I hunger for the truth of your Word."

Read the gospel: John 6:44–51.

Jesus said, "No one can come to me unless drawn by the Father who sent me; and I will raise that person up on the last day. It is written in the prophets, 'And they shall all be taught by God.' Everyone who has heard and learned from the Father comes to me. Not that anyone has seen the Father except the one who is from God; he has seen the Father. Very truly, I tell you, whoever believes has eternal life. I am the bread of life. Your ancestors ate the manna in the wilderness, and they died. This is the bread that comes down from heaven, so that one may eat of it and not die. I am the living bread that came down from heaven. Whoever eats of this bread will live forever; and the bread that I will give for the life of the world is my flesh."

Notice what you think and feel as you read the gospel.

The bread of eternal life is the flesh of Jesus Christ—he asks us to believe this to gain that life. He fulfills the miracle of manna in the wilderness because the bread that is Jesus confers eternal life. How Jesus' words must have puzzled, shocked, and offended many who heard them!

Pray as you are led for yourself and others.

"Lord, I think I understand my need to feed on you. As you gave yourself to me, I give myself to you for the good of those you have given me . . ." (Continue in your own words.)

Listen to Jesus.

Beloved, I love it when you come to me and abandon yourself to me. It is my opportunity to love you and enjoy you. Here, take my heart. I love you. What else is Jesus saying to you?

Ask God to show you how to live today.

"Lord, let me love others today with your heart. Dwell in me and use me to bring your life to the world, that good may come and God be glorified. Amen."

Friday, April 20, 2018

Know that God is present and ready to converse.

"Lord, unlock my understanding that I may find you in your Word."

Read the gospel: John 6:52–59.

The Jews then disputed among themselves, saying, "How can this man give us his flesh to eat?" So Jesus said to them, "Very truly, I tell you, unless you eat the flesh of the Son of Man and drink his blood, you have no life in you. Those who eat my flesh and drink my blood have eternal life, and I will raise them up on the last day; for my flesh is true food and my blood is true drink. Those who eat my flesh and drink my blood abide in me, and I in them. Just as the living Father sent me, and I live because of the Father, so whoever eats me will live because of me. This is the bread that came down from heaven, not like that which your ancestors ate, and they died. But the one who eats this bread will live forever." He said these things while he was teaching in the synagogue at Capernaum.

Notice what you think and feel as you read the gospel.

Jesus' hearers are baffled by his claim that his flesh is the bread of life, that they must eat it to live. Jesus baffles them further by proclaiming that they must also drink his blood to have eternal life.

Pray as you are led for yourself and others.

"Lord, thank you for the Eucharist, your Body and Blood, available to all who desire to abide in you. Let me be childlike in receiving it, as I now receive your Word. Let the sacrament be honored by all who love you . . ." (Continue in your own words.)

Listen to Jesus.

Those who come to me, child, must come to me in faith. Those who lack faith may ask the Father for it, and God will give them the Holy Spirit and every good thing they require. Walk in simple faith, beloved. What else is Jesus saying to you?

Ask God to show you how to live today.

"Lord, I believe. Shine the light of your Spirit upon the darkness of unbelief in my soul, and let my eye be focused only on you. Amen."

Saturday, April 21, 2018

Know that God is present and ready to converse.

"Lord, I open my heart now to your Spirit and your life. I depend upon you."

Read the gospel: John 6:60–69.

When many of Jesus' disciples heard it, they said, "This teaching is difficult; who can accept it?" But Jesus, being aware that his disciples were complaining about it, said to them, "Does this offend you? Then what if you were to see the Son of Man ascending to where he was before? It is the spirit that gives life; the flesh is useless. The words that I have spoken to you are spirit and life. But among you there are some who do not believe." For Jesus knew from the first who were the ones that did not believe, and who was the one that would betray him. And he said, "For this reason I have told you that no one can come to me unless it is granted by the Father."

Because of this many of his disciples turned back and no longer went about with him. So Jesus asked the twelve, "Do you also wish to go away?" Simon Peter answered him, "Lord, to whom can we go? You have the words of eternal life. We have come to believe and know that you are the Holy One of God."

Notice what you think and feel as you read the gospel.

Even Jesus' disciples complain about his insistence that they receive his words literally, that his believers must eat his flesh and drink his blood. Though all are baffled, the twelve do not leave Jesus, for they believe he is the Holy One of God.

Pray as you are led for yourself and others.

"Many do not believe in Jesus or believe in him weakly, with rationalizations and excuses. Blow on them and all of us with your Holy Spirit, Lord, that all the living may know that you are Almighty God. I pray especially for . . ." (Continue in your own words.)

Listen to Jesus.

My followers are the light in a darkening world. Sometimes you don't feel it, but you are a beam of light and hope to some who walk in darkness. Ask me for faith, hope, and love to share with others, and you shall have them. What else is Jesus saying to you?

Ask God to show you how to live today.

"Lord, give me faith, hope, and love, and the will and the wisdom to share them with others. How wonderful that God is good and always leading his people to goodness. Alleluia. Amen."

Sunday, April 22, 2018
Fourth Sunday of Easter

Know that God is present and ready to converse.

"Risen Savior, I come to your Word as I come to you. Lead me."

Read the gospel: John 10:11–18.

Jesus said, "I am the good shepherd. The good shepherd lays down his life for the sheep. The hired hand, who is not the shepherd and does not own the sheep, sees the wolf coming and leaves the sheep and runs away—and the wolf snatches them and scatters them. The hired hand runs away because a hired hand does not care for the sheep. I am the good shepherd. I know my own and my own know me, just as the Father knows me and I know the Father. And I lay down my life for the sheep. I have other sheep that do not belong to this fold. I must bring them also, and they will listen to my voice. So there will be one flock, one shepherd. For this reason the Father loves me, because I lay down my life in order to take it up again. No one takes it from me, but I lay it down of my own accord. I have power to lay it down, and I have power to take it up again. I have received this command from my Father."

Notice what you think and feel as you read the gospel.

Jesus proclaims himself the good shepherd who lays down his life for the sheep. He does not run away from his own when the wolf comes but protects them with his very life. He knows his own and his own know him, just as he knows and is known by his Father. He has other sheep who will also hear his voice and come, so we may be one flock under one shepherd.

Pray as you are led for yourself and others.

"How beautiful the love between Father and Son, Lord. What happiness! Let me join you in that love and extend it to others, including . . ." (Continue in your own words.)

Listen to Jesus.

Love endures. Love grows by the giving of it. Do not hoard your love, dear one. Give it away irresponsibly, as I have done and do. Love is the substance of eternal life. Join me. What else is Jesus saying to you?

Ask God to show you how to live today.

"Lord, you exhort me to rise above my small and selfish self, to lay down my life as you do. I implore you to help me do it. Let it surprise those who know me and glorify you. Amen."

Monday, April 23, 2018

Know that God is present and ready to converse.

"Lord, I know your voice, and I am ready to hear your holy Word."

Read the gospel: John 10:1–10.

Jesus said, "Very truly, I tell you, anyone who does not enter the sheepfold by the gate but climbs in by another way is a thief and a bandit. The one who enters by the gate is the shepherd of the sheep. The gatekeeper opens the gate for him, and the sheep hear his voice. He calls his own sheep by name and leads them out. When he has brought out all his own, he goes ahead of them, and the sheep follow him because they know his voice. They will not follow a stranger, but they will run from him because they do not know the voice of strangers." Jesus used this figure of speech with them, but they did not understand what he was saying to them.

So again Jesus said to them, "Very truly, I tell you, I am the gate for the sheep. All who came before me are thieves and bandits; but the sheep did not listen to them. I am the gate. Whoever enters by me will be saved, and will come in and go out and find pasture. The thief comes only to steal and kill and destroy. I came that they may have life, and have it abundantly."

Notice what you think and feel as you read the gospel.

Jesus calls himself both the shepherd and the gate of the sheepfold. He knows his sheep and his sheep know him. They will not follow a stranger, who comes to steal and destroy. The sheep follow him because he gives them life, abundantly.

Pray as you are led for yourself and others.

"Lord, I love it when you speak to me. I rejoice that you know me yet still love me. Help me to follow you closely, ignoring the other voices that would tear me away from you. We love each other. Let me extend your love to these . . ." (Continue in your own words.)

Listen to Jesus.

I am happy to speak to you, beloved disciple. Following me, you travel to eternal life. Listening to me and loving me, you do good in the world, a stay against the wicked. Do not lose heart. Abide in me. All things are possible for God. What else is Jesus saying to you?

Ask God to show you how to live today.

"Lord, how may I tell or show others that you are the good shepherd, the gate to eternal life? So many shrug off your message. Give me new words and actions that others may come to you. Thank you. Amen."

Tuesday, April 24, 2018

Know that God is present and ready to converse.

"Jesus, you are one with the Father, your Father and my Father. Let me hear your voice in this Word."

Read the gospel: John 10:22–30.

At that time the festival of the Dedication took place in Jerusalem. It was winter, and Jesus was walking in the temple, in the portico of Solomon. So the Jews gathered around him and said to him, "How long will you keep us in suspense? If you are the Messiah, tell us plainly." Jesus answered, "I have told you, and you do not believe. The works that I do in my Father's name testify to me; but you do not believe, because you do not belong to my sheep. My sheep hear my voice. I know them, and they follow me. I give them eternal life, and they will never perish. No one will snatch them out of my hand. What my Father has given me is greater than all else, and no one can snatch it out of the Father's hand. The Father and I are one."

Notice what you think and feel as you read the gospel.

Jesus admits to being the Messiah, but they keep asking because they do not believe. Those who do believe and who follow him will never perish. They are safe with him, for he is the shepherd of his sheep. Those who believe are a gift to him from his Father, and he and his Father are one.

Pray as you are led for yourself and others.

"What mystery of goodness and love, Lord. You saved me and keep me safe, forever. Thank you. How may I show you my thanks? . . ." (Continue in your own words.)

Listen to Jesus.

Just stay close to me, dear child. Persevere in faith and love, and eternal life will come soon. Nothing can harm you. You will never perish. I promise you that. What else is Jesus saying to you?

Ask God to show you how to live today.

"Let me be one with you and the Father, Lord. Let your Spirit move in me today, and let me do something for someone in need that pleases you. Amen."

Wednesday, April 25, 2018
Saint Mark, the Evangelist

Know that God is present and ready to converse.

"Lord, give me faith to receive your holy Word and please you by my response. Thank you for being here with me now."

Read the gospel: Mark 16:15–20.

And Jesus said to them, "Go into all the world and proclaim the good news to the whole creation. The one who believes and is baptized will be saved; but the one who does not believe will be condemned. And these signs will accompany those who believe: by using my name they will cast out demons; they will speak in new tongues; they will pick up snakes in their hands, and if they drink any deadly thing, it will not hurt them; they will lay their hands on the sick, and they will recover."

So then the Lord Jesus, after he had spoken to them, was taken up into heaven and sat down at the right hand of God. And they went out and proclaimed the good news everywhere, while the Lord worked with them and confirmed the message by the signs that accompanied it.

Notice what you think and feel as you read the gospel.

Jesus commissions his disciples, explaining to them the power of faith in him for personal salvation or, failing that, condemnation. Among believers, Jesus promises that faith will confer powers to do good and evangelize effectively. Then Jesus ascends to his Father, and the disciples obey his great commission.

Pray as you are led for yourself and others.

"Lord, I believe your Gospel of salvation. Let my faith bear fruit that does good in the world. I offer myself to you for the good of others, especially . . ." (Continue in your own words.)

Listen to Jesus.

With a little faith, you can do much. Act upon it with love, and I will bless your efforts. Remain in hope, for it is my good pleasure to give you the kingdom. I love you. What else is Jesus saying to you?

Ask God to show you how to live today.

"Let me stay near you, Lord, and be conscious of opportunities to do your work in the world. Amen."

Thursday, April 26, 2018

Know that God is present and ready to converse.

"Lord, let me be blessed to receive you in your Word."

Read the gospel: John 13:16–20.

Jesus said, "Very truly, I tell you, servants are not greater than their master, nor are messengers greater than the one who sent them. If you know these things, you are blessed if you do them. I am not speaking of all of you; I know whom I have chosen. But it is to fulfill the scripture, 'The one who ate my bread has lifted his heel against me.' I tell you this now, before it occurs, so that when it does occur, you may believe that I am he. Very truly, I tell you, whoever receives one whom I send receives me; and whoever receives me receives him who sent me."

Notice what you think and feel as you read the gospel.

Jesus expresses solidarity with the messengers, the disciples, and the Father who sent him. This is the great Communion of Saints. It's important to act upon what we know, for blessings result.

Pray as you are led for yourself and others.

"Thank you for enfolding me in the Holy Family, Lord. I pray that you enfold others, including those of my own family, into your family. I think of these . . ." (Continue in your own words.)

Listen to Jesus.

Beloved disciple, I put this love in your heart. I also give you power to act. How may I help you today? Ask me for what you need. What else is Jesus saying to you?

Ask God to show you how to live today.

"Lord, let me receive you, that I may bring your love to others, and accompany me on the way, dear Jesus. Amen."

Friday, April 27, 2018

Know that God is present and ready to converse.

"Lord, banish my doubts as I hear your Word and take it into my mind, heart, soul, and spirit."

Read the gospel: John 14:1–6.

Jesus said, "Do not let your hearts be troubled. Believe in God, believe also in me. In my Father's house there are many dwelling places. If it were not so, would I have told you that I go to prepare a place for you? And if I go and prepare a place for you, I will come again and will take you to myself, so that where I am, there you may be also. And you know the way to the place where I am going." Thomas said to him, "Lord, we do not know where you are going. How can we know the way?" Jesus said to him, "I am the way, and the truth, and the life. No one comes to the Father except through me."

Notice what you think and feel as you read the gospel.

Jesus makes such beautiful promises to the disciples, about the place he will prepare for them and his returning to collect them. Thomas protests that they do not know the way to that place. Jesus attests that he is the way, the truth, and the life. The disciples know him, and that's all they need.

Pray as you are led for yourself and others.

"Lord, I long to be with you forever, as you promise. Keep me close to you, so that I can follow you and receive life everlasting. I pray too for . . ." (Continue in your own words.)

Listen to Jesus.

Yes, keep your eyes on me, my child. I have all those things to give you, and I have already begun to do so. Do not let your heart be troubled by your circumstances. Trust me. What else is Jesus saying to you?

Ask God to show you how to live today.

"Thank you, Lord. You know me. Today I will abide in you and not be troubled by doubts or circumstances. Amen"

Saturday, April 28, 2018

Know that God is present and ready to converse.

"You are everywhere, God, but I cannot see you. May I see you in your Word?"

Read the gospel: John 14:7–14.

Jesus said, "If you know me, you will know my Father also. From now on you do know him and have seen him."

Philip said to him, "Lord, show us the Father, and we will be satisfied." Jesus said to him, "Have I been with you all this time, Philip, and you still do not know me? Whoever has seen me has seen the Father. How can you say, 'Show us the Father'? Do you not believe that I am in the Father and the Father is in me? The words that I say to you I do not speak on my own; but the Father who dwells in me does his works. Believe me that I am in the Father and the Father is in me; but if you do not, then believe me because of the works themselves. Very truly, I tell you, the one who believes in me will also do the works that I do and, in fact, will do greater works than these, because I am going to the Father. I will do whatever you ask in my name, so that the Father may be glorified in the Son. If in my name you ask me for anything, I will do it."

Notice what you think and feel as you read the gospel.

Speaking for all the disciples, Philip asks Jesus to show them the Father. Jesus tells him that they can see the Father in him, for he is one with the Father. Whoever believes in the unity of Father and Son will do the works that Jesus does, and even greater works once he has ascended to the Father. He promises to do whatever we ask in his name, to the glory of the Father.

Pray as you are led for yourself and others.

"Lord, inspire my prayers that I may please you and do the works you wish me to do. How may I glorify you? . . ." (Continue in your own words.)

Listen to Jesus.

You glorify God by your faith and the loving actions that spring from it. Strive to do everything you do for love of God and others. Give me those people you love and worry about. What else is Jesus saying to you?

Ask God to show you how to live today.

"Fill my heart with the love of your heart, dear Lord, and I will please you today and glorify our Father. Amen."

Sunday, April 29, 2018
Fifth Sunday of Easter

Know that God is present and ready to converse.

"Lord, open my eyes that I may see you in a fresh and real way by the reading of your Word."

Read the gospel: John 15:1–8.

Jesus said, "I am the true vine, and my Father is the vinegrower. He removes every branch in me that bears no fruit. Every branch that bears fruit he prunes to make it bear more fruit. You have already been cleansed by the word that I have spoken to you. Abide in me as I abide in you. Just as the branch cannot bear fruit by itself unless it abides in the vine, neither can you unless you abide in me. I am the vine, you are the branches. Those who abide in me and I in them bear much fruit, because apart from me you can do nothing. Whoever does not abide in me is thrown away like a branch and withers; such branches are gathered, thrown into the fire, and burned. If you abide in me, and my words abide in you, ask for whatever you wish, and it will be done for you. My Father is glorified by this, that you bear much fruit and become my disciples."

Notice what you think and feel as you read the gospel.

Jesus tells us the secret of fruitfulness is abiding in him. He is the vine and we are the branches, he says, and the Father removes the branches that do not bear fruit. And those that do bear fruit must be pruned to bear more. Those who abide in him will bear much fruit and glorify God. Abiding in him also results in fruitful prayer.

Pray as you are led for yourself and others.

"So I cling to you, dear Jesus, and ask for courage as the Father prunes my unfruitful branches. Let me embrace your simplicities of faith, hope, and love. Let others come to you, as well. I think of . . ." (Continue in your own words.)

Listen to Jesus.

Dear child, I hear your prayers and grant them. You are right not to stop hoping for those who appear to have rejected me. I work mysteriously. All things are possible for me and for you. Each day seek to abide in me. What else is Jesus saying to you?

Ask God to show you how to live today.

"You are good, my Lord. Thank you for the hope you put in my heart for those who need you. Let me grow in your wisdom and bear fruit in your love. Amen."

Monday, April 30, 2018

Know that God is present and ready to converse.

"I love you, Lord of hosts, Master of heaven and earth. Instruct me by your Word."

Read the gospel: John 14:21–26.

Jesus said, "They who have my commandments and keep them are those who love me; and those who love me will be loved by my Father, and I will love them and reveal myself to them." Judas (not Iscariot) said to him, "Lord, how is it that you will reveal yourself to us, and not to the world?" Jesus answered him, "Those who love me will keep my word, and my Father will love them, and we will come to them and make our home with them. Whoever does not love me does not keep my words; and the word that you hear is not mine, but is from the Father who sent me.

"I have said these things to you while I am still with you. But the Advocate, the Holy Spirit, whom the Father will send in my name, will teach you everything, and remind you of all that I have said to you."

Notice what you think and feel as you read the gospel.

Jesus tells his disciples that love of God and God's Son compel obedience to his commandments, which are all about loving. To those who love and obey him, Jesus will reveal himself, but not to those who do not love him. They will remain in darkness, while the Holy Spirit will teach obedient believers everything.

Pray as you are led for yourself and others.

"Lord, you know I want to know you more and more, because I love you with all my might. I pity those who do not love you. I pray especially for these . . ." (Continue in your own words.)

Listen to Jesus.

Love is all, dear disciple. Receive all the love I shower upon you. All that I give you, rejoice in it, for it comes from my love for your good. I hear your prayers for others, and I will show them great mercy. What else is Jesus saying to you?

Ask God to show you how to live today.

"Then let me love others as you do today, my Jesus. I give myself to you for them. Teach me your incredible love. Amen."

Tuesday, May 1, 2018

Know that God is present and ready to converse.

"Lord, I am ready to receive your wisdom in your blessed Word. Let the words of your Son burn in my heart and make me new."

Read the gospel: John 14:27–31a.

Jesus said, "Peace I leave with you; my peace I give to you. I do not give to you as the world gives. Do not let your hearts be troubled, and do not let them be afraid. You heard me say to you, 'I am going away, and I am coming to you.' If you loved me, you would rejoice that I am going to the Father, because the Father is greater than I. And now I have told you this before it occurs, so that when it does occur, you may believe. I will no longer talk much with you, for the ruler of this world is coming. He has no power over me; but I do as the Father has commanded me, so that the world may know that I love the Father."

Notice what you think and feel as you read the gospel.

Jesus comforts his disciples on the eve of his departure, but they will not understand his words until after his Crucifixion, Death, and Resurrection have taken place.

Pray as you are led for yourself and others.

"Lord, I do not know your ways or my future. I can only trust in you. Strengthen me and those you have given me . . ." (Continue in your own words.)

Listen to Jesus.

Beloved, don't be afraid. I am with you. I know your inmost heart and all you fear and love and hope for. Place yourself today in my hands and I will perform mighty deeds for you and those you love. What else is Jesus saying to you?

Ask God to show you how to live today.

"Thank you, Jesus. I am yours. Let your peace fill me today, that I, too, may do the will of the Father without fear. Amen."

Wednesday, May 2, 2018

Know that God is present and ready to converse.

"Lord, I worship you now for you are with me. Consecrate me by your Word."

Read the gospel: John 15:1–8.

Jesus said, "I am the true vine, and my Father is the vinegrower. He removes every branch in me that bears no fruit. Every branch that bears fruit he prunes to make it bear more fruit. You have already been cleansed by the word that I have spoken to you. Abide in me as I abide in you. Just as the branch cannot bear fruit by itself unless it abides in the vine, neither can you unless you abide in me. I am the vine, you are the branches. Those who abide in me and I in them bear much fruit, because apart from me you can do nothing. Whoever does not abide in me is thrown away like a branch and withers; such branches are gathered, thrown into the fire, and burned. If you abide in me, and my words abide in you, ask for whatever you wish, and it will be done for you. My Father is glorified by this, that you bear much fruit and become my disciples."

Notice what you think and feel as you read the gospel.
Jesus uses the metaphor of the vine to describe humanity's relationship to God. He is the vine, and we are the branches. If we are not fruitful, the Father, the vinegrower, cuts us off and casts us aside. The secret to fruitfulness is abiding in Jesus, the vine. If we abide in him and his words abide in us, whatever we ask will be done for us. This glorifies God.

Pray as you are led for yourself and others.
"What amazing freedom and power you give me, Jesus. I ask but one thing: that I may abide in you now and forever. I believe all good things will follow for me and those I love . . ." (Continue in your own words.)

Listen to Jesus.
It is easy to abide in me, my dear child, but it is also difficult, for you are walking in a dark world, full of evil and ignorance. Cling to me and together we will glorify our Father. What else is Jesus saying to you?

Ask God to show you how to live today.
"I know the darkness, Lord, outside and inside. Cleanse me by your Word; light my way today and help me do what pleases you. Amen."

Thursday, May 3, 2018
Saints Philip and James, Apostles

Know that God is present and ready to converse.
"Mighty Trinity, three Persons in One God, I long to see you and understand your mystery. Holy Spirit, enlighten me by your Word."

Read the gospel: John 14:6–14.
Jesus said to Thomas, "I am the way, and the truth, and the life. No one comes to the Father except through me. If you know me, you will know my Father also. From now on you do know him and have seen him."

Philip said to him, "Lord, show us the Father, and we will be satisfied." Jesus said to him, "Have I been with you all this time, Philip, and you still do not know me? Whoever has seen me has seen the Father. How can you say, 'Show us the Father'? Do you not believe that I am in the Father and the Father is in me? The words that I say to you I do not speak on my own; but the Father who dwells in me does his works.

Believe me that I am in the Father and the Father is in me; but if you do not, then believe me because of the works themselves. Very truly, I tell you, the one who believes in me will also do the works that I do and, in fact, will do greater works than these, because I am going to the Father. I will do whatever you ask in my name, so that the Father may be glorified in the Son. If in my name you ask me for anything, I will do it."

Notice what you think and feel as you read the gospel.

Jesus is the key to the mystery of God, and to know him, he says, is to know the Father. His words are truth because they come from the Father. Our part is to believe him, and when we pray in his name, whatever we ask will be granted.

Pray as you are led for yourself and others.

"Lord, I have heard your words and believe in you, the Father, and the Holy Spirit. I ask you for a peaceful world, with people everywhere turning to the one true God . . ." (Continue in your own words.)

Listen to Jesus.

What I told to my disciples was also meant for you, beloved servant and friend. You are right to take my words to heart. My words will change you, free you, and make you fruitful in good works. Let us glorify God together. What else is Jesus saying to you?

Ask God to show you how to live today.

"Lord, I want what you promise. I give myself and all I have to you. Just stay with me and help me walk in your holy way. Amen."

Friday, May 4, 2018

Know that God is present and ready to converse.

"Master of the Universe, I place my soul in your hands. Show me what I need to know and do to please you."

Read the gospel: John 15:12–17.

Jesus said, "This is my commandment, that you love one another as I have loved you. No one has greater love than this, to lay down one's life for one's friends. You are my friends if you do what I command you. I do not call you servants any longer, because the servant does not know what the master is doing; but I have called you friends, because I have made known to you everything that I have heard from my Father. You did not choose me but I chose you. And I appointed you to go and bear fruit, fruit that will last, so that the Father will give you whatever you ask him in my name. I am giving you these commands so that you may love one another."

Notice what you think and feel as you read the gospel.

Jesus commands us to love one another, even to give our lives for love of others. To do so makes us his friends, no longer servants. This is our appointed destiny, and our loving will bear fruit that will last forever.

Pray as you are led for yourself and others.

"You grant me the power of prayer, Lord. In your name, I bring to God a great number of people who need healing in their bodies, minds, and souls. I think particularly of . . ." (Continue in your own words.)

Listen to Jesus.

Dear friend, when you serve others, you serve me. Everyone has needs, even those who appear strong and well, just as you have needs. Look upon everyone with love and mercy, and you will see me. What else is Jesus saying to you?

Ask God to show you how to live today.

"Lord, you have chosen me to bear fruit—to love as you love. Let me see you in others today, and, when I do, let me serve you to the best of my ability. I rejoice that I can please you by loving others. Amen."

Saturday, May 5, 2018

Know that God is present and ready to converse.

"Eternal Wisdom, Jesus, Word of the Father, speak to my heart that I may be prepared to live as you did in the world."

Read the gospel: John 15:18–21.

Jesus said, "If the world hates you, be aware that it hated me before it hated you. If you belonged to the world, the world would love you as its own. Because you do not belong to the world, but I have chosen you out of the world—therefore the world hates you. Remember the word that I said to you, 'Servants are not greater than their master.' If they persecuted me, they will persecute you; if they kept my word, they will keep yours also. But they will do all these things to you on account of my name, because they do not know him who sent me."

Notice what you think and feel as you read the gospel.

Jesus warns his disciples of the hatred of the world. As the world hated him, it will hate us. We will not escape the contempt and persecution of those who do not know God.

Pray as you are led for yourself and others.

"Thank you for helping it all make sense, Lord. Like you, I pray now for those who hate me and hurt me, especially for those who are far from God . . ." (Continue in your own words.)

Listen to Jesus.

Join me in my suffering, beloved servant, and you will receive the crown of life, the joy of the everlasting kingdom. You will be hated for a season but loved for all eternity. You have made the right choice to follow me. What else is Jesus saying to you?

Ask God to show you how to live today.

"Lord, you give me strength to go on. Let me do whatever I can to lessen the hatred and the darkness and the suffering I encounter in my own life. Today and tomorrow. Amen."

Sunday, May 6, 2018
Sixth Sunday of Easter

Know that God is present and ready to converse.

"Lord, I want you to love me. I want to love you and please you. Guide me by your Word."

Read the gospel: John 15:9–17.

Jesus said, "As the Father has loved me, so I have loved you; abide in my love. If you keep my commandments, you will abide in my love, just as I have kept my Father's commandments and abide in his love. I have said these things to you so that my joy may be in you, and that your joy may be complete.

"This is my commandment, that you love one another as I have loved you. No one has greater love than this, to lay down one's life for one's friends. You are my friends if you do what I command you. I do not call you servants any longer, because the servant does not know what the master is doing; but I have called you friends, because I have made known to you everything that I have heard from my Father. You did not choose me but I chose you. And I appointed you to go and bear fruit, fruit that will last, so that the Father will give you whatever you ask him in my name. I am giving you these commands so that you may love one another."

Notice what you think and feel as you read the gospel.

Jesus declares that he loves us as the Father loves him. By loving one another we abide in his love. The greatest love is to lay down your life for your friends, as he did. By obeying this commandment, we become his friends, more than servants, and we will be fruitful and granted whatever we ask of God.

Pray as you are led for yourself and others.

"Lord, give me your love and help me to love others as you do. I have failed much in this. How may I give myself for love of others? Let me begin by praying for these . . ." (Continue in your own words.)

Listen to Jesus.

Dear friend, do not be discouraged if your love is not yet perfect. Practice it as you can, and I will replenish it. Let service to others become a habit. Be generous with all you have. Let it flow from love, my love. What else is Jesus saying to you?

Ask God to show you how to live today.

"Jesus, I am willing to lay down my life today for love of another. Guide me in this encounter and action. Be present in my journey today. Amen."

Monday, May 7, 2018

Know that God is present and ready to converse.

"Holy Spirit, you are with me as Jesus promised. Guide me into all the truth of God."

Read the gospel: John 15:26–16:4a.

Jesus said, "When the Advocate comes, whom I will send to you from the Father, the Spirit of truth who comes from the Father, he will testify on my behalf. You also are to testify because you have been with me from the beginning.

"I have said these things to you to keep you from stumbling. They will put you out of the synagogues. Indeed, an hour is coming when those who kill you will think that by doing so they are offering worship to God. And they will do this because they have not known the Father or me. But I have said these things to you so that when their hour comes you may remember that I told you about them.

"I did not say these things to you from the beginning, because I was with you."

Notice what you think and feel as you read the gospel.

Jesus cares about his own, and he has provided for them. He acknowledges they will face fierce opposition, even from those who think they are acting in God's name.

Pray as you are led for yourself and others.

"Lord, the world has not changed. I pray for all those who face persecution. May they have the strength of your Spirit. I pray also for those you have given me . . ." (Continue in your own words.)

Listen to Jesus.

Dwell in quiet confidence, my beloved, for I care for you as I have cared for all my disciples. Be not afraid, for I have overcome the world. What else is Jesus saying to you?

Ask God to show you how to live today.

"Lord, even when I face trials, let me walk in the quiet peace of your Spirit today, loving you. Amen."

Tuesday, May 8, 2018

Know that God is present and ready to converse.

"I can do nothing good on my own, Lord. Be with me and guide me to yourself."

Read the gospel: John 16:5–11.

Jesus said, "But now I am going to him who sent me; yet none of you asks me, 'Where are you going?' But because I have said these things to you, sorrow has filled your hearts. Nevertheless, I tell you the truth: it is to your advantage that I go away, for if I do not go away, the Advocate will not come to you; but if I go, I will send him to you. And when he comes, he will prove the world wrong about sin and righteousness and judgement: about sin, because they do not believe in me; about righteousness, because I am going to the Father and you will see me no longer; about judgement, because the ruler of this world has been condemned."

Notice what you think and feel as you read the gospel.

Understandably the disciples are anxious about Jesus' leaving them. He explains to them that it is better he should go away, that the Advocate may come to them. When he was present, they had to rely on him; when the Advocate comes, they will have God within themselves, empowering them.

Pray as you are led for yourself and others.

"Lord, I receive your gift of the Spirit. Let it work in me for the good of others, especially . . ." (Continue in your own words.)

Listen to Jesus.

God is one, but we are three Persons, loving and working together with one will. Abandon yourself to God's will, my child. We will lead you to heaven. What else is Jesus saying to you?

Ask God to show you how to live today.

"Lord, strip me of all my own plans and let me do only what you want me to do today. I surrender myself to you. Amen."

Wednesday, May 9, 2018

Know that God is present and ready to converse.

"Ever-present Lord God Almighty, let me know your glory. Let me understand your Word."

Read the gospel: John 16:12–15.

Jesus said, "I still have many things to say to you, but you cannot bear them now. When the Spirit of truth comes, he will guide you into all the truth; for he will not speak on his own, but will speak whatever he hears, and he will declare to you the things that are to come. He will glorify me, because he will take what is mine and declare it to you. All that the Father has is mine. For this reason I said that he will take what is mine and declare it to you."

Notice what you think and feel as you read the gospel.

Jesus speaks of knowing God as a learning process in the believer, with the Spirit as our teacher. The Spirit will tell us even the things that are to come!

Pray as you are led for yourself and others.

"Lord, I know you are going to come again to establish your just kingdom among us. Come soon, Lord, and let all people know your mercy . . ." (Continue in your own words.)

Listen to Jesus.

All that I have promised will come to pass. Time rules the world, but it does not touch eternity. Do not be anxious or discouraged. Do today what I give you to do. I love you. What else is Jesus saying to you?

Ask God to show you how to live today.

"I love you too, Lord. You are Truth. Help me speak your truth to others. Amen."

Thursday, May 10, 2018

Know that God is present and ready to converse.

"I need you now, Lord, to help me understand your Word. Teach me."

Read the gospel: John 16:16–20.

Jesus said, "A little while, and you will no longer see me, and again a little while, and you will see me." Then some of his disciples said to one another, "What does he mean by saying to us, 'A little while, and you will no longer see me, and again a little while, and you will see me'; and 'Because I am going to the Father'?" They said, "What does he mean by this 'a little while'? We do not know what he is talking about." Jesus knew that they wanted to ask him, so he said to them, "Are you discussing among yourselves what I meant when I said, 'A little while, and you will no longer see me, and again a little while, and you will see me'? Very truly, I tell you, you will weep and mourn, but the world will rejoice; you will have pain, but your pain will turn into joy."

Notice what you think and feel as you read the gospel.

The disciples are confused by Jesus' words about his future, as they don't know what "a little while" means. He puts it in emotional terms—they will weep and mourn first, while the world rejoices, but then their pain will turn to joy.

Pray as you are led for yourself and others.

"Lord, your prophecy of the future is true for all who follow you. Even now it is not fulfilled in my own life. But I trust you, and I entrust to you all those you have given me . . ." (Continue in your own words.)

Listen to Jesus.

Come to me often, beloved. I am the joy you need in your life and hereafter. My joy will give you strength to serve. What else is Jesus saying to you?

Ask God to show you how to live today.

"Let joy be my watchword for today, Lord. I reach out and accept your joy. Thank you. Amen."

Friday, May 11, 2018

Know that God is present and ready to converse.

"Lord, I rejoice in your presence. Speak to me today."

Read the gospel: John 16:20–23.

Jesus said, "Very truly, I tell you, you will weep and mourn, but the world will rejoice; you will have pain, but your pain will turn into joy. When a woman is in labor, she has pain, because her hour has come. But when her child is born, she no longer remembers the anguish because of the joy of having brought a human being into the world. So you have pain now; but I will see you again, and your hearts will rejoice, and no one will take your joy from you. On that day you will ask nothing of me. Very truly, I tell you, if you ask anything of the Father in my name, he will give it to you."

Notice what you think and feel as you read the gospel.

Jesus continues to prepare his disciples for his departure to the Father. They are being entrusted by him to do his work, but he promises that God will be with them, granting their prayers.

Pray as you are led for yourself and others.

"Father, in Jesus' name I ask you to help and heal all those I give you today . . ." (Continue in your own words.)

Listen to Jesus.

Child, as you look to God, you receive from God. But your true duty, your true call, is to love God. Everything comes from that. What else is Jesus saying to you?

Ask God to show you how to live today.

"Lord, help me to love you as you want me to. I have failed so many times in that simple duty. Forgive me and make me new. Amen."

Saturday, May 12, 2018

Know that God is present and ready to converse.

"Loving Father, I ask you to form me and mold me to do your will, for you have called me to love."

Read the gospel: John 16:23b–28.

Jesus said, "On that day you will ask nothing of me. Very truly, I tell you, if you ask anything of the Father in my name, he will give it to you. Until now you have not asked for anything in my name. Ask and you will receive, so that your joy may be complete.

"I have said these things to you in figures of speech. The hour is coming when I will no longer speak to you in figures, but will tell you plainly of the Father. On that day you will ask in my name. I do not say to you that I will ask the Father on your behalf; for the Father himself loves you, because you have loved me and have believed that I came from God. I came from the Father and have come into the world; again, I am leaving the world and am going to the Father."

Notice what you think and feel as you read the gospel.

Jesus teaches his disciples about his Father's love for them. The Father loves them because they loved Jesus and believed he came to them from God.

Pray as you are led for yourself and others.

"Lord, I forget about the primacy of love in the heavenly scheme of things. Don't let love get pushed out of my life, my heart. Fill me now with love for all those I pray for . . ." (Continue in your own words.)

Listen to Jesus.

Love is an act of the will, my beloved. Will becomes action for good, and feelings may follow. What else is Jesus saying to you?

Ask God to show you how to live today.

"I will to love today, Lord. Show me the actions for good and help me do them. I praise you, Savior. Amen."

Sunday, May 13, 2018
Ascension of the Lord

Know that God is present and ready to converse.

"Jesus, seated at the right hand of the Father, be with me now as I read your holy Word."

Read the gospel: Mark 16:15–20.

And Jesus said to them, "Go into all the world and preach the gospel to the whole creation. He who believes and is baptized will be saved; but he who does not believe will be condemned. And these signs will accompany those who believe: in my name they will cast our demons; they will pick up serpents, and if they drink any deadly thing, it will not hurt them; they will lay hands on the sick, and they will recover."

So then the Lord Jesus, after he had spoken to them, was taken up into heaven, and sat down at the right hand of God. And they went forth and preached everywhere, while the Lord worked with them and confirmed the message by the signs that attended it. Amen.

Notice what you think and feel as you read the gospel.

Jesus gives power to his disciples to do his work when he is gone, then he is taken up into heaven. They go forth in obedience, and the Lord works with them.

Pray as you are led for yourself and others.

"What work do you have for me, Lord? Please work with me, for I am very frail . . ." (Continue in your own words.)

Listen to Jesus.

In your weakness, you are strong through me. Give yourself to me, dear disciple. Come to me as a child. I will lift you up and together we will do much good. What else is Jesus saying to you?

Ask God to show you how to live today.

"Let me rejoice in my weakness, then, Lord, and turn it all over to you. Make of me what you will. Amen."

Monday, May 14, 2018
Saint Matthias, Apostle

Know that God is present and ready to converse.

"Jesus, let me abide in you and in your love. Thank you for being with me now."

Read the gospel: John 15:9–17.

Jesus said, "As the Father has loved me, so I have loved you; abide in my love. If you keep my commandments, you will abide in my love, just as I have kept my Father's commandments and abide in his love. I have said these things to you so that my joy may be in you, and that your joy may be complete.

"This is my commandment, that you love one another as I have loved you. No one has greater love than this, to lay down one's life for one's friends. You are my friends if you do what I command you. I do not call you servants any longer, because the servant does not know what the master is doing; but I have called you friends, because I have made known to you everything that I have heard from my Father. You did not choose me but I chose you. And I appointed you to go and bear fruit, fruit that will last, so that the Father will give you whatever you ask him in my name. I am giving you these commands so that you may love one another."

Notice what you think and feel as you read the gospel.

Jesus speaks of the love of God and commands his disciples to abide in his love as he has abided in his Father's love. That is the path to joy: loving others, serving others even to death. If we participate in God's love, we are the friends of Jesus and will bear the fruits of love.

Pray as you are led for yourself and others.

"Jesus, make my heart like your heart. I need to obey your commandment of love. I pray in love for all those you have given me . . ." (Continue in your own words.)

Listen to Jesus.

Let love be your light, my dear disciple, though the world be dark and hateful. I have chosen you and raised you up to be my friend forever. Live in my love. What else is Jesus saying to you?

Ask God to show you how to live today.
"Lord, how may I lay down my life for my friends? Let me be willing and able to do that, even today. Amen."

Tuesday, May 15, 2018

Know that God is present and ready to converse.
"God of the living, let me know you. Let me receive your Word into my heart today."

Read the gospel: John 17:1–11a.
After Jesus had spoken these words, he looked up to heaven and said, "Father, the hour has come; glorify your Son so that the Son may glorify you, since you have given him authority over all people, to give eternal life to all whom you have given him. And this is eternal life, that they may know you, the only true God, and Jesus Christ whom you have sent. I glorified you on earth by finishing the work that you gave me to do. So now, Father, glorify me in your own presence with the glory that I had in your presence before the world existed.

"I have made your name known to those whom you gave me from the world. They were yours, and you gave them to me, and they have kept your word. Now they know that everything you have given me is from you; for the words that you gave to me I have given to them, and they have received them and know in truth that I came from you; and they have believed that you sent me. I am asking on their behalf; I am not asking on behalf of the world, but on behalf of those whom you gave me, because they are yours. All mine are yours, and yours are mine; and I have been glorified in them. And now I am no longer in the world, but they are in the world, and I am coming to you. Holy Father, protect them in your name that you have given me, so that they may be one, as we are one."

Notice what you think and feel as you read the gospel.
Jesus prays to his Father for his disciples, asking God to protect them. He says they have eternal life and are separated from the world of darkness and death.

Pray as you are led for yourself and others.
"Lord, I accept your protection and your truth. By prayer I extend them to all those you have given me. I give them all to you . . ." (Continue in your own words.)

Listen to Jesus.

I have given to you eternal life, child. Live in that life now. Come to know the glory of God. Be one with us. What else is Jesus saying to you?

Ask God to show you how to live today.

"Lord, you give such priceless gifts, and all I need to do is receive them. Help me to receive them and give them to others. Amen."

Wednesday, May 16, 2018

Know that God is present and ready to converse.

"One God, Almighty Creator, Savior, and Sustainer of all, let me hear your Word now. Sanctify me in your truth."

Read the gospel: John 17:11b–19.

Jesus said, "And now I am no longer in the world, but they are in the world, and I am coming to you. Holy Father, protect them in your name that you have given me, so that they may be one, as we are one. While I was with them, I protected them in your name that you have given me. I guarded them, and not one of them was lost except the one destined to be lost, so that the scripture might be fulfilled. But now I am coming to you, and I speak these things in the world so that they may have my joy made complete in themselves. I have given them your word, and the world has hated them because they do not belong to the world, just as I do not belong to the world. I am not asking you to take them out of the world, but I ask you to protect them from the evil one. They do not belong to the world, just as I do not belong to the world. Sanctify them in the truth; your word is truth. As you have sent me into the world, so I have sent them into the world. And for their sakes I sanctify myself, so that they also may be sanctified in truth."

Notice what you think and feel as you read the gospel.

Jesus prays to the Father for his own, that they may be protected in the world and from the world, one with him, full of his joy, and made holy in the truth. He is sending them into the world on behalf of that truth.

Pray as you are led for yourself and others.

"Lord, let me walk in truth. Lead me in the way of truth. Let me be real as I serve you from my heart and mind. With my heart and mind I now pray for those you have given me . . ." (Continue in your own words.)

Listen to Jesus.

You are a child in God's family. The most important thing is that God loves you, for you love me, and I give you love for others. You lack nothing. What else is Jesus saying to you?

Ask God to show you how to live today.

"Then let me love others in truth today, Lord. Let my will be one with yours. Amen."

Thursday, May 17, 2018

Know that God is present and ready to converse.

"Glorious Father, you have shared your glory with your Son, Jesus. Let me glorify God as I receive and believe your Word."

Read the gospel: John 17:20–26.

Jesus said, "I ask not only on behalf of these, but also on behalf of those who will believe in me through their word, that they may all be one. As you, Father, are in me and I am in you, may they also be in us, so that the world may believe that you have sent me. The glory that you have given me I have given them, so that they may be one, as we are one, I in them and you in me, that they may become completely one, so that the world may know that you have sent me and have loved them even as you have loved me. Father, I desire that those also, whom you have given me, may be with me where I am, to see my glory, which you have given me because you loved me before the foundation of the world.

"Righteous Father, the world does not know you, but I know you; and these know that you have sent me. I made your name known to them, and I will make it known, so that the love with which you have loved me may be in them, and I in them."

Notice what you think and feel as you read the gospel.

Jesus enfolds all later believers into his family of faith and love, that we all may be one in God and in one another. This will be the sign to the world, he says, that God is, and God is love.

Pray as you are led for yourself and others.

"Lord, I thank you for including me in your infinite love. Send me out to do your loving will . . ." (Continue in your own words.)

Listen to Jesus.

Love knows no limits. All love derives from the infinite love of God. You are learning to love, dear follower. Cling to me and learn how to love. What else is Jesus saying to you?

Ask God to show you how to live today.

"Lord, I have far to go, but you are with me. I glorify you. Amen."

Friday, May 18, 2018

Know that God is present and ready to converse.

"God of Love, feed me by your word of love."

Read the gospel: John 21:15–19.

When they had finished breakfast, Jesus said to Simon Peter, "Simon son of John, do you love me more than these?" He said to him, "Yes, Lord; you know that I love you." Jesus said to him, "Feed my lambs." A second time he said to him, "Simon son of John, do you love me?" He said to him, "Yes, Lord; you know that I love you." Jesus said to him, "Tend my sheep." He said to him the third time, "Simon son of John, do you love me?" Peter felt hurt because he said to him the third time, "Do you love me?" And he said to him, "Lord, you know everything; you know that I love you." Jesus said to him, "Feed my sheep. Very truly, I tell you, when you were younger, you used to fasten your own belt and to go wherever you wished. But when you grow old, you will stretch out your hands, and someone else will fasten a belt around you and take you where you do not wish to go." (He said this to indicate the kind of death by which he would glorify God.) After this he said to him, "Follow me."

Notice what you think and feel as you read the gospel.

Jesus requires one thing of Peter: love. True love translates into service to those Jesus loves, those in need. To love Jesus is to follow him and, in the power of the Holy Spirit, to go where we cannot know. This is what it means to love and serve God.

Pray as you are led for yourself and others.

"Lord, increase my love for you, that I may serve others with all my strength, that I may trust you in every danger. I pray for those you have given me, especially . . ." (Continue in your own words.)

Listen to Jesus.

The world does not know that love is the greatest power. I give you God's love, dear disciple, because you have committed to following me. Go out and serve. You will bear fruit to the glory of God. What else is Jesus saying to you?

Ask God to show you how to live today.

"Lord, I thank you for your love, for your words. Let me truly take them in today that I may please you and help others. Amen."

Saturday, May 19, 2018

Know that God is present and ready to converse.

"Eternal Word of God, Jesus Christ, you walked among us and spoke to us. Let me hear you now."

Read the gospel: John 21:20–25.

Peter turned and saw the disciple whom Jesus loved following them; he was the one who had reclined next to Jesus at the supper and had said, "Lord, who is it that is going to betray you?" When Peter saw him, he said to Jesus, "Lord, what about him?" Jesus said to him, "If it is my will that he remain until I come, what is that to you? Follow me!" So the rumor spread in the community that this disciple would not die. Yet Jesus did not say to him that he would not die, but, "If it is my will that he remain until I come, what is that to you?"

This is the disciple who is testifying to these things and has written them, and we know that his testimony is true. But there are also many other things that Jesus did; if every one of them were written down, I suppose that the world itself could not contain the books that would be written.

Notice what you think and feel as you read the gospel.

John the Evangelist calls himself "the disciple whom Jesus loved," knowing full well that Jesus loved every one of them—and every one of us. The gospels are the story of this great love, which all the world cannot contain.

Pray as you are led for yourself and others.

"Lord, confirm your great love for me that I may feel it in my heart and soul, and then let me reflect your love upon all those you have given me. I commit to loving these . . ." (Continue in your own words.)

Listen to Jesus.

My Word tells you all you need to know about love and loving. You are right to desire to grow in love. Come back to me every day and I will fill you to overflowing. What else is Jesus saying to you?

Ask God to show you how to live today.

"How do I show your love to others today, dear Jesus? Show me and lead me in every opportunity. Amen."

Sunday, May 20, 2018
Pentecost Sunday

Know that God is present and ready to converse.

"Lord, breathe upon me your Holy Spirit and make me willing to serve you in the world."

Read the gospel: John 20:19–23.

When it was evening on that day, the first day of the week, and the doors of the house where the disciples had met were locked for fear of the Jews, Jesus came and stood among them and said, "Peace be with you." After he said this, he showed them his hands and his side. Then the disciples rejoiced when they saw the Lord. Jesus said to them again, "Peace be with you. As the Father has sent me, so I send you." When he had said this, he breathed on them and said to them, "Receive the Holy Spirit. If you forgive the sins of any, they are forgiven them; if you retain the sins of any, they are retained."

Notice what you think and feel as you read the gospel.

Jesus, risen from the dead but not yet ascended to heaven, appears among the disciples and by his breath gives them the Holy Spirit. The Holy Spirit confers the power to serve others, even at the spiritual level.

Pray as you are led for yourself and others.

"Lord, let the Holy Spirit be in my prayer now as I pray for those you have given me. Please prosper the spiritual health of these . . ." (Continue in your own words.)

Listen to Jesus.

My beloved follower, stay with me, learn from me every day. I can make your life so simple and true. Follow me. What else is Jesus saying to you?

Ask God to show you how to live today.

"I long for that life simple and true, Jesus. Let me see others with your eyes today and serve them as you would. Amen."

Ordinary Time

INTRODUCTION

The second period of Ordinary Time immediately follows Pentecost. The Holy Spirit has fallen upon the disciples while they prayed in the upper room. For the disciples, Pentecost was even more transforming than Easter, for the Holy Spirit gave them, as Jesus had promised, power to carry the Good News to every nation on earth. So began the age of grace.

Our own journeys are similarly wrapped up with Christ's command to follow him every day. This is our own time of grace as we seek to do his work in today's world. By praying with the Word of God in this season, we may discover how we, too, can serve the Master. The last Sunday of Ordinary Time is the Feast of Christ the King, whose coming and kingdom we await.

Monday, May 21, 2018

Know that God is present and ready to converse.

"Jesus, serving you in the world can be difficult. Please strengthen me by your holy Word."

Read the gospel: Mark 9:14–29.

When they came to the disciples, they saw a great crowd around them, and some scribes arguing with them. When the whole crowd saw Jesus, they were immediately overcome with awe, and they ran forward to greet him. He asked them, "What are you arguing about with them?" Someone from the crowd answered him, "Teacher, I brought you my son; he has a spirit that makes him unable to speak; and whenever it seizes him, it dashes him down; and he foams and grinds his teeth and becomes rigid; and I asked your disciples to cast it out, but they could not do so." He answered them, "You faithless generation, how much longer must I be among you? How much longer must I put up with you? Bring him to me." And they brought the boy to him. When the spirit saw him, immediately it threw the boy into convulsions, and he fell on the ground and rolled about, foaming at the mouth. Jesus asked the father, "How long has this been happening to him?" And he said, "From childhood. It has often cast him into the fire and into the water, to destroy him; but if you are able to do anything, have pity on us and help us." Jesus said to him, "If you are able!—All things can be done for the one who believes."' Immediately the father of the child cried out, "I believe; help my unbelief!" When Jesus saw that a crowd came running together, he rebuked the unclean spirit, saying to it, "You spirit that keep this boy from speaking and hearing, I command you, come out of him, and never enter him again!" After crying out and convulsing him terribly, it came out, and the boy was like a corpse, so that most of them said, "He is dead." But Jesus took him by the hand and lifted him up, and he was able to stand. When he had entered the house, his disciples asked him privately, "Why could we not cast it out?" He said to them, "This kind can come out only through prayer."

Notice what you think and feel as you read the gospel.

Jesus is unhappy that his own disciples lack the faith necessary to cast out the demon from the boy. With faith, Jesus tells the boy's father, all things are possible. The father believes, but he asks Jesus to help his unbelief. Then Jesus explains to his disciples that power comes through prayer, implying that great faith also comes by prayer.

Pray as you are led for yourself and others.

"Lord, so I pray for faith, shore it up that I may do good and fulfill your will in my life. Keep me in prayer. I pray for those you have given me . . ." (Continue in your own words.)

Listen to Jesus.

Faith, hope, and love flow to you from the Word of God. Do not abandon your reading, child. Listen to me; learn to know and love me more. Then pray, and all things will be possible to you. What else is Jesus saying to you?

Ask God to show you how to live today.

"Dear Jesus, I am praying now that my heart may put you and your words first in all the decisions of my day, in all the decisions of my life. Amen."

Tuesday, May 22, 2018

Know that God is present and ready to converse.

"I welcome your presence with me now, Lord. What may I learn from your eternal Word?"

Read the gospel: Mark 9:30–37.

Jesus and his disciples went on from there and passed through Galilee. He did not want anyone to know it; for he was teaching his disciples, saying to them, "The Son of Man is to be betrayed into human hands, and they will kill him, and three days after being killed, he will rise again." But they did not understand what he was saying and were afraid to ask him.

Then they came to Capernaum; and when he was in the house he asked them, "What were you arguing about on the way?" But they were silent, for on the way they had argued with one another about who was the greatest. He sat down, called the twelve, and said to them, "Whoever wants to be first must be last of all and servant of all." Then he took a little child and put it among them; and taking it in his arms, he said to them, "Whoever welcomes one such child in my name welcomes me, and whoever welcomes me welcomes not me but the one who sent me."

Notice what you think and feel as you read the gospel.

Jesus foretells his Passion, Death, and Resurrection, but his disciples are blocked in their understanding. They argue on the way about who among them is greatest. When they arrive, Jesus tells the twelve that the secret of being the greatest is to be servant of all, for he himself is present in the least of those around us—the poor, the sick, and the vulnerable, like the little child.

Pray as you are led for yourself and others.

"Lord, I pray today for the most vulnerable people I know. Give me grace and wisdom to receive them as you received the little child. I pray for . . . " (Continue in your own words.)

Listen to Jesus.

This is your daily bread, beloved disciple: to welcome others and serve them. In so doing, I come to you and my Father comes to you, and we will remain with you forever. To be close to others is to be close to God. What else is Jesus saying to you?

Ask God to show you how to live today.

"Lord, teach me to truly welcome others. I wish to learn today. Amen."

Wednesday, May 23, 2018

Know that God is present and ready to converse.

"Lord, I look to you for wisdom. Let me understand your Word."

Read the gospel: Mark 9:38–40.

John said to Jesus, "Teacher, we saw someone casting out demons in your name, and we tried to stop him, because he was not following us." But Jesus said, "Do not stop him; for no one who does a deed of power in my name will be able soon afterwards to speak evil of me. Whoever is not against us is for us."

Notice what you think and feel as you read the gospel.

The disciples want exclusive power as followers of Jesus, but Jesus opens their minds to the ways of God. There is no competition; there are many ways to serve God and others.

Pray as you are led for yourself and others.

"Lord, let me be at peace and not judge your servants. Let me cede control to you and rejoice to see your will being done. I pray for those I have criticized, including . . ." (Continue in your own words.)

Listen to Jesus.

Fallen human nature conflicts with God's nature, my child. Know what is human in yourself and ask God to transform you. Holiness is God's nature, and it is without strife or striving. It is empty of self. What else is Jesus saying to you?

Ask God to show you how to live today.

"Lord, I fall short of holiness. I worship you, for you are holy as I am not. I give myself to you to make me what you want, even today. Amen."

Thursday, May 24, 2018

Know that God is present and ready to converse.

"Lord, I stand before you a child. Your child. Let me hear your Word in my deepest being."

Read the gospel: Mark 9:41–50.

Jesus said, "For truly I tell you, whoever gives you a cup of water to drink because you bear the name of Christ will by no means lose the reward.

"If any of you put a stumbling block before one of these little ones who believe in me, it would be better for you if a great millstone were hung around your neck and you were thrown into the sea. If your hand causes you to stumble, cut it off; it is better for you to enter life maimed than to have two hands and to go to hell, to the unquenchable fire. And if your foot causes you to stumble, cut it off; it is better for you to enter life lame than to have two feet and to be thrown into hell. And if your eye causes you to stumble, tear it out; it is better for you to enter the kingdom of God with one eye than to have two eyes and to be thrown into hell, where their worm never dies, and the fire is never quenched.

"For everyone will be salted with fire. Salt is good; but if salt has lost its saltiness, how can you season it? Have salt in yourselves, and be at peace with one another."

Notice what you think and feel as you read the gospel.

Jesus demands holiness at any personal cost, for sin is punished. The goal of any follower must be holiness.

Pray as you are led for yourself and others.

"Lord, I desire the holiness you demand. Help me make the necessary sacrifices to achieve it, to please you. I pray also for those I love, that you make them holy . . ." (Continue in your own words.)

Listen to Jesus.

Holiness begins in humility and utter dependence upon God, dearly beloved. You know your besetting sins. Give them to me. What else is Jesus saying to you?

Ask God to show you how to live today.

"I long to live as you ask, Lord. Make me aware of moments to obey, moments to sacrifice, and moments to love. Amen."

Friday, May 25, 2018

Know that God is present and ready to converse.

"Jesus, you are here to speak to me. I open my heart to your word."

Read the gospel: Mark 10:1–12.

Jesus left that place and went to the region of Judea and beyond the Jordan. And crowds again gathered around him; and, as was his custom, he again taught them.

Some Pharisees came, and to test him they asked, "Is it lawful for a man to divorce his wife?" He answered them, "What did Moses command you?" They said, "Moses allowed a man to write a certificate of dismissal and to divorce her." But Jesus said to them, "Because of your hardness of heart he wrote this commandment for you. But from the beginning of creation, 'God made them male and female.' 'For this reason a man shall leave his father and mother and be joined to his wife, and the two shall become one flesh.' So they are no longer two, but one flesh. Therefore what God has joined together, let no one separate."

Then in the house the disciples asked him again about this matter. He said to them, "Whoever divorces his wife and marries another commits adultery against her; and if she divorces her husband and marries another, she commits adultery."

Notice what you think and feel as you read the gospel.

Jesus refuses to compromise his moral teaching regarding marriage and divorce. He speaks of God's original intention in creating them male and female, that they may be one flesh, never to separate.

Pray as you are led for yourself and others.

"Lord, have mercy on those of us who have divorced or experienced the damage divorce causes. Help us to heal . . ." (Continue in your own words.)

Listen to Jesus.

I know you, my dear disciple, and I know your heart. In your weakness, cling to me. I am healing. I am holiness. I will restore you and make you whole. What else is Jesus saying to you?

Ask God to show you how to live today.

"I cling to you today, Lord; let nothing separate us. Walk with me and show me how to do your will. Amen."

Saturday, May 26, 2018

Know that God is present and ready to converse.

"I come to you in your Word, Jesus, that you might touch me and bless me."

Read the gospel: Mark 10:13–16.

People were bringing little children to Jesus in order that he might touch them; and the disciples spoke sternly to them. But when Jesus saw this, he was indignant and said to them, "Let the little children come to me; do not stop them; for it is to such as these that the kingdom of God belongs. Truly I tell you, whoever does not receive the kingdom of God as a little child will never enter it." And he took them up in his arms, laid his hands on them, and blessed them.

Notice what you think and feel as you read the gospel.

Jesus has time for children, and he uses them as an example of how we should all be. He exhorts us to receive the kingdom of God as little children.

Pray as you are led for yourself and others.

"Childlike, I seek the kingdom, Lord; take my hand and lead me. I pray for the children you have given me . . ." (Continue in your own words.)

Listen to Jesus.

You can make religion hard, but I make it easy. Throw away everything and take on purity of heart. Love me. Trust me. Cling to me. I love you, my child. What else is Jesus saying to you?

Ask God to show you how to live today.

"Lord, let me receive your kingdom, your love, as a child would—with joy and simplicity—and show me how to share your love with others today. Amen."

Sunday, May 27, 2018
The Most Holy Trinity

Know that God is present and ready to converse.

"Almighty Trinity, Father, Son, and Holy Spirit, you are one God, present with me now."

Read the gospel: Matthew 28:16–20.

Now the eleven disciples went to Galilee, to the mountain to which Jesus had directed them. When they saw him, they worshipped him; but some doubted. And Jesus came and said to them, "All authority in heaven and on earth has been given to me. Go therefore and make disciples of all nations, baptizing them in the name of the Father and of the Son and of the Holy Spirit, and teaching them to obey everything that I have commanded you. And remember, I am with you always, to the end of the age."

Notice what you think and feel as you read the gospel.

Jesus teaches his disciples to baptize in the name of the Father, Son, and Holy Spirit. He asks them to make disciples of all nations. He asks them to remember that he is with them always, even to the end of the age.

Pray as you are led for yourself and others.

"Lord, thank you for being with me now, for I am living at the end of the age. I pray for all those who will come after me, for the children and for their children. Stay with them . . ." (Continue in your own words.)

Listen to Jesus.

The world is rapidly changing everywhere, but God's purposes shall be accomplished. Seek peace and rely on God, dear one. You will not be disappointed. What else is Jesus saying to you?

Ask God to show you how to live today.

"Lord, let me not be subject to discouragement as I see the violence and strife around me. By your grace, I will trust in the love and power of the Holy Trinity: Father, Son, and Holy Spirit. Amen."

Monday, May 28, 2018

Know that God is present and ready to converse.

"Jesus, I know you are with me always, and you love me. Help me to love you better than I ever have."

Read the gospel: Mark 10:17–27.

As Jesus was setting out on a journey, a man ran up and knelt before him, and asked him, "Good Teacher, what must I do to inherit eternal life?" Jesus said to him, "Why do you call me good? No one is good but God alone. You know the commandments: 'You shall not murder; You shall not commit adultery; You shall not steal; You shall not bear false witness; You shall not defraud; Honor your father and mother.'" He said to him, "Teacher, I have kept all these since my youth." Jesus, looking at him, loved him and said, "You lack one thing; go, sell what you own, and give the money to the poor, and you will have treasure in heaven; then come, follow me." When he heard this, he was shocked and went away grieving, for he had many possessions.

Then Jesus looked around and said to his disciples, "How hard it will be for those who have wealth to enter the kingdom of God!" And the disciples were perplexed at these words. But Jesus said to them again, "Children, how hard it is to enter the kingdom of God! It is easier for a camel to go through the eye of a needle than for someone who is rich to enter the kingdom of God." They were greatly astounded and said to one another, "Then who can be saved?" Jesus looked at them and said, "For mortals it is impossible, but not for God; for God all things are possible."

Notice what you think and feel as you read the gospel.

An apparently good young man approaches Jesus to ask him what he must do to gain eternal life. Jesus begins by questioning the man's choice of works in calling him "Good Teacher." The rest of Jesus' words raise a very high standard for goodness, including selling all he owns, giving the money to the poor, and following Jesus. This instruction was more than the man could bear. The disciples wonder how anyone can be saved, but Jesus reassures them that all things are possible for God.

Pray as you are led for yourself and others.

"Lord, you look upon your followers with love and want them to be holy as God is holy. For the sake of your love, help me, because all things are possible for you. Let me begin by praying for those who need my prayers . . ." (Continue in your own words.)

Listen to Jesus.

Take one day at a time, beloved, and fill it with the fruits of faith, hope, and love. Find little ways to express those things, and virtue will grow within you. What else is Jesus saying to you?

Ask God to show you how to live today.

"Open my eyes to the little things I can do today for others. Then help me do them. Amen."

Tuesday, May 29, 2018

Know that God is present and ready to converse.

"Lord, you have blessed me in this life. Help me follow you more closely by the reading of your Word."

Read the gospel: Mark 10:28–31.

Peter began to say to Jesus, "Look, we have left everything and followed you." Jesus said, "Truly I tell you, there is no one who has left house or brothers or sisters or mother or father or children or fields, for my sake and for the sake of the good news, who will not receive a hundredfold now in this age—houses, brothers and sisters, mothers and children, and fields, with persecutions—and in the age to come eternal life. But many who are first will be last, and the last will be first."

Notice what you think and feel as you read the gospel.

Jesus speaks to Peter of the rewards of following him—in this life and in the eternal age to come. But his saying that many who are first will be last and vice versa suggests that we cannot expect what seems fair and just either in this life or the next. If we follow Jesus, we will be blessed beyond measure—that's all we need to know.

Pray as you are led for yourself and others.

"Lord, thank you for blessing me in so many ways. I seek blessings for those in need among those you have given me . . ." (Continue in your own words.)

Listen to Jesus.

I hold you in my hand, dear one. In me you are safe and secure forever. Give to me those in need of my love and protection. For your sake, I will take them in. We are family. What else is Jesus saying to you?

Ask God to show you how to live today.

"Let me walk in the confidence you give me, Lord. Let me rely on your promises and see others with your loving eyes. Amen."

Wednesday, May 30, 2018

Know that God is present and ready to converse.

"Lord, you are here with me now. Open my heart to hear your holy Word."

Read the gospel: Mark 10:32–45.

The disciples were on the road, going up to Jerusalem, and Jesus was walking ahead of them; they were amazed, and those who followed were afraid. He took the twelve aside again and began to tell them what was to happen to him, saying, "See, we are going up to Jerusalem, and the Son of Man will be handed over to the chief priests and the scribes, and they will condemn him to death; then they will hand him over to the Gentiles; they will mock him, and spit upon him, and flog him, and kill him; and after three days he will rise again."

James and John, the sons of Zebedee, came forward to him and said to him, "Teacher, we want you to do for us whatever we ask of you." And he said to them, "What is it you want me to do for you?" And they said to him, "Grant us to sit, one at your right hand and one at your left, in your glory." But Jesus said to them, "You do not know what you are asking. Are you able to drink the cup that I drink, or be baptized with the baptism that I am baptized with?" They replied, "We are able." Then Jesus said to them, "The cup that I drink you will drink; and with the baptism with which I am baptized, you will be baptized; but to sit at my right hand or at my left is not mine to grant, but it is for those for whom it has been prepared."

When the ten heard this, they began to be angry with James and John. So Jesus called them and said to them, "You know that among the Gentiles those whom they recognize as their rulers lord it over them, and their great ones are tyrants over them. But it is not so among you; but whoever wishes to become great among you must be your servant, and whoever wishes to be first among you must be slave of all. For the Son of Man came not to be served but to serve, and to give his life as a ransom for many."

Notice what you think and feel as you read the gospel.

The disciples do not hear Jesus as he prophesies his Passion, Death, and Resurrection. Their minds cannot absorb it. Instead they are thinking of themselves, their rewards in the kingdom. Jesus says they don't know what they are asking, because they too must drink the cup of suffering. They say they can, and Jesus agrees, but his Father will decide how his followers will be rewarded.

Pray as you are led for yourself and others.

"Lord, let me deeply understand that following you means drinking the cup of suffering. Let me rejoice in the suffering that comes to me. Let me learn from it. Let me pray for those who suffer now . . ." (Continue in your own words.)

Listen to Jesus.

No life is free of suffering. But, dear disciple, offer your suffering to God for the good of others. This is my way. It will give you peace and bear much fruit to the glory of God. What else is Jesus saying to you?

Ask God to show you how to live today.

"Thank you, Jesus. As I look forward to my day, I offer all suffering to God for the good of all those you have given me. Amen."

Thursday, May 31, 2018
Visitation of the Blessed Virgin Mary

Know that God is present and ready to converse.

"Lord, let me receive your Word with true humility, for that is the source of strength and wisdom."

Read the gospel: Luke 1:39–56.

In those days Mary set out and went with haste to a Judean town in the hill country, where she entered the house of Zechariah and greeted Elizabeth. When Elizabeth heard Mary's greeting, the child leapt in her womb. And Elizabeth was filled with the Holy Spirit and exclaimed with a loud cry, "Blessed are you among women, and blessed is the fruit of your womb. And why has this happened to me, that the mother of my Lord comes to me? For as soon as I heard the sound of your greeting, the child in my womb leapt for joy. And blessed is she who believed that there would be a fulfillment of what was spoken to her by the Lord."

And Mary said,

"My soul magnifies the Lord,
and my spirit rejoices in God my Savior,
for he has looked with favor on the lowliness of his servant.
Surely, from now on all generations will call me blessed;
for the Mighty One has done great things for me,
and holy is his name.
His mercy is for those who fear him
from generation to generation.
He has shown strength with his arm;
he has scattered the proud in the thoughts of their hearts.
He has brought down the powerful from their thrones,
and lifted up the lowly;
he has filled the hungry with good things,
and sent the rich away empty.
He has helped his servant Israel,
in remembrance of his mercy,
according to the promise he made to our ancestors,
to Abraham and to his descendants forever."

And Mary remained with her for about three months and then returned to her home.

Notice what you think and feel as you read the gospel.

The Lord fulfills his high purposes through humble women. Mary is full of wisdom about the ways of God in the world, and responds with praise.

Pray as you are led for yourself and others.

"Lord, you have done great things for me, sending my Savior, Jesus Christ. Let me receive you today, Lord, and let all those you have given me do the same . . ." (Continue in your own words.)

Listen to Jesus.

Dear child, I am yours, and I love all those whom I have given you and you have given back to me. Trust me to draw them to myself. What else is Jesus saying to you?

Ask God to show you how to live today.

"Today I will trust the mighty and merciful ways of God. Thank you, Lord, the Almighty. Amen."

Friday, June 1, 2018

Know that God is present and ready to converse.

Lord, you have forgiven me. Let me forgive others from my heart so that I may draw nearer to you.

Read the gospel: Mark 11:11–26.

Then Jesus entered Jerusalem and went into the temple; and when he had looked around at everything, as it was already late, he went out to Bethany with the twelve.

On the following day, when they came from Bethany, he was hungry. Seeing in the distance a fig tree in leaf, he went to see whether perhaps he would find anything on it. When he came to it, he found nothing but leaves, for it was not the season for figs. He said to it, "May no one ever eat fruit from you again." And his disciples heard it.

Then they came to Jerusalem. And he entered the temple and began to drive out those who were selling and those who were buying in the temple, and he overturned the tables of the money-changers and the seats of those who sold doves; and he would not allow anyone to carry anything through the temple. He was teaching and saying, "Is it not written,

> 'My house shall be called a house of prayer for all the nations'?
> But you have made it a den of robbers."

And when the chief priests and the scribes heard it, they kept looking for a way to kill him; for they were afraid of him, because the whole crowd was spellbound by his teaching. And when evening came, Jesus and his disciples went out of the city.

In the morning as they passed by, they saw the fig tree withered away to its roots. Then Peter remembered and said to him, "Rabbi, look! The fig tree that you cursed has withered." Jesus answered them, "Have faith in God. Truly I tell you, if you say to this mountain, 'Be taken up and thrown into the sea,' and if you do not doubt in your heart, but believe that what you say will come to pass, it will be done for you. So I tell you, whatever you ask for in prayer, believe that you have received it, and it will be yours.

"Whenever you stand praying, forgive, if you have anything against anyone; so that your Father in heaven may also forgive you your trespasses."

Notice what you think and feel as you read the gospel.

Jesus expresses righteous anger toward the money changers in the Temple, but why rebuke the fig tree? It turns out to be a lesson in having faith in God and the power of prayer. And whenever we pray, we must forgive so that we may also be forgiven by God.

Pray as you are led for yourself and others.

"Jesus, help me forgive all those who have hurt or offended me, and I ask you for forgiveness for all I have hurt or offended. I think of . . ." (Continue in your own words.)

Listen to Jesus.

I grant you mercy, beloved. Let forgiveness be a part of your daily prayer. It will bring you health and life. What else is Jesus saying to you?

Ask God to show you how to live today.

"Let me show forgiveness from the instant of hurt or offense, Lord. Keep a watch over my heart and mind and tongue, so that I do not fall into temptation. Amen."

Saturday, June 2, 2018

Know that God is present and ready to converse.

"Your Father has given to you all power and might, Lord Jesus. Arm me with strength by your Word."

Read the gospel: Mark 11:27–33.

Again Jesus and his disciples came to Jerusalem. As he was walking in the temple, the chief priests, the scribes, and the elders came to him and said, "By what authority are you doing these things? Who gave you this authority to do them?" Jesus said to them, "I will ask you one question; answer me, and I will tell you by what authority I do these things. Did the baptism of John come from heaven, or was it of human origin? Answer me." They argued with one another, "If we say, 'From heaven,' he will say, 'Why then did you not believe him?' But shall we say, 'Of human origin'?"—they were afraid of the crowd, for all regarded John as truly a prophet. So they answered Jesus, "We do not know." And Jesus said to them, "Neither will I tell you by what authority I am doing these things."

Notice what you think and feel as you read the gospel.

When the chief priests, scribes, and elders—the Jewish authorities—question Jesus about the source of his authority, he turns the questions back on them, for he knows they are trying to trap him. They claim ignorance because they are afraid of the people—how genuine can their authority be?

Pray as you are led for yourself and others.

"Lord, your Word is truth. Your authority is of the Father, and thus you are afraid of no one. Lead me, and those you have given me, to complete, trusting surrender to the will of God . . ." (Continue in your own words.)

Listen to Jesus.

Dear disciple, I do the will of the Father, who made you, who knows you, who loves you. Trust in me, and you will fear no evil. What else is Jesus saying to you?

Ask God to show you how to live today.

"Jesus, help me to know and do God's will fearlessly today. Amen."

Sunday, June 3, 2018
The Body and Blood of Christ

Know that God is present and ready to converse.

"Bread of Heaven, feed me by your Word."

Read the gospel: Mark 14:12–16, 22–26.

On the first day of Unleavened Bread, when the Passover lamb is sacrificed, his disciples said to him, "Where do you want us to go and make the preparations for you to eat the Passover?" So he sent two of his disciples, saying to them, "Go into the city, and a man carrying a jar of water will meet you; follow him, and wherever he enters, say to the owner of the house, 'The Teacher asks, Where is my guest room where I may eat the Passover with my disciples?' He will show you a large room upstairs, furnished and ready. Make preparations for us there." So the disciples set out and went to the city, and found everything as he had told them; and they prepared the Passover meal. . . .

While they were eating, he took a loaf of bread, and after blessing it he broke it, gave it to them, and said, "Take; this is my body." Then he took a cup, and after giving thanks he gave it to them, and all of them drank from it. He said to them, "This is my blood of the covenant, which is poured out for many. Truly I tell you, I will never again drink of the fruit of the vine until that day when I drink it new in the kingdom of God."

When they had sung the hymn, they went out to the Mount of Olives.

Notice what you think and feel as you read the gospel.

On the feast of Passover, Jesus institutes the great sacrament of the Eucharist, transforming bread and wine into his own body and blood and giving it to his disciples.

Pray as you are led for yourself and others.

"Lord, may I receive your Body and Blood today—spiritually if not literally? I receive you into my soul, Blessed Redeemer . . ." (Continue in your own words.)

Listen to Jesus.

I love you, child, for you follow me. We give ourselves to one another. Follow me to paradise. What else is Jesus saying to you?

Ask God to show you how to live today.

"I stumble when I follow you, Lord. Help me to walk straight in your path. Amen."

Monday, June 4, 2018

Know that God is present and ready to converse.

"Lord, I thank you for being with me, being mine. Teach me by your Word."

Read the gospel: Mark 12:1–12.

Then Jesus began to speak to them in parables. "A man planted a vineyard, put a fence around it, dug a pit for the wine press, and built a watch tower; then he leased it to tenants and went to another country. When the season came, he sent a slave to the tenants to collect from them his share of the produce of the vineyard. But they seized him, and beat him, and sent him away empty-handed. And again he sent another slave to them; this one they beat over the head and insulted. Then he sent another, and that one they killed. And so it was with many others; some they beat, and others they killed. He had still one other, a beloved son. Finally he sent him to them, saying, 'They will respect my son.' But those tenants said to one another, 'This is the heir; come, let us kill him, and the inheritance will be ours.' So they seized him, killed him, and threw him out of the vineyard. What then will the owner of the vineyard do? He will come and destroy the tenants and give the vineyard to others. Have you not read this scripture:

'The stone that the builders rejected
  has become the cornerstone;
this was the Lord's doing,
  and it is amazing in our eyes'?"

When they realized that he had told this parable against them, they wanted to arrest him, but they feared the crowd. So they left him and went away.

Notice what you think and feel as you read the gospel.

Jesus summarizes in parable form the historical relationship between God and Israel. He warns his hearers that the owner will come and destroy the unrighteous tenants and give the vineyard to others. Then Jesus quotes scripture, saying the Lord will use the rejected stone as the cornerstone of the new building.

Pray as you are led for yourself and others.

"Jesus, like the rejected stone, I too am small and imperfect. In your mercy, Lord, do a work in me and allow me to serve God and bear fruit to his glory. Let me be a servant to those you have given me . . ." (Continue in your own words.)

Listen to Jesus.

It is wonderful how my Father and I work in the hearts of those who follow me. Follow me today, beloved disciple, and we shall bear fruit. What else is Jesus saying to you?

Ask God to show you how to live today.

"Lord, you have led me into your vineyard, and you allow me to serve you. Let me give you thanks and praise all day! Amen."

Tuesday, June 5, 2018

Know that God is present and ready to converse.

"Lord, here with me now, let your Word teach, change, and amaze me."

Read the gospel: Mark 12:13–17.

Then they sent to Jesus some Pharisees and some Herodians to trap him in what he said. And they came and said to him, "Teacher, we know that you are sincere, and show deference to no one; for you do not regard people with partiality, but teach the way of God in accordance with truth. Is it lawful to pay taxes to the emperor, or not? Should we pay them, or should we not?" But knowing their hypocrisy, he said to them, "Why are you putting me to the test? Bring me a denarius and let me see it." And they brought one. Then he said to them, "Whose head is this, and whose title?" They answered, "The emperor's." Jesus said to them, "Give to the emperor the things that are the emperor's, and to God the things that are God's." And they were utterly amazed at him.

Notice what you think and feel as you read the gospel.

The Pharisees and Herodians try to trap Jesus in a question that seems to pit God against the Roman emperor. He recognizes the trap and escapes it.

Pray as you are led for yourself and others.

"Lord, I have questions too about how to live best and serve. Please show me what I should know and draw me and those you have given me to yourself . . ." (Continue in your own words.)

Listen to Jesus.

My child, rely on simplicity. Simply love God and all those you encounter. That is the life of my followers. What else is Jesus saying to you?

Ask God to show you how to live today.

"When your love is my foundation, my works, however small, are blessed and bear fruit. Show me as we go, Lord. Amen."

Wednesday, June 6, 2018

Know that God is present and ready to converse.

"Jesus, I open myself now to both the scriptures and the power of God."

Read the gospel: Mark 12:18–27.

Some Sadducees, who say there is no resurrection, came to Jesus and asked him a question, saying, "Teacher, Moses wrote for us that if a man's brother dies, leaving a wife but no child, the man shall marry the widow and raise up children for his brother. There were seven brothers; the first married and, when he died, left no children; and the second married her and died, leaving no children; and the third likewise; none of the seven left children. Last of all the woman herself died. In the resurrection whose wife will she be? For the seven had married her."

Jesus said to them, "Is not this the reason you are wrong, that you know neither the scriptures nor the power of God? For when they rise from the dead, they neither marry nor are given in marriage, but are like angels in heaven. And as for the dead being raised, have you not read in the book of Moses, in the story about the bush, how God said to him, 'I am the God of Abraham, the God of Isaac, and the God of Jacob'? He is God not of the dead, but of the living; you are quite wrong."

Notice what you think and feel as you read the gospel.

The Sadducees ask Jesus a question to trap him. He doesn't deflect it but simply declares that those who are risen from the dead do not marry but are like the angels.

Pray as you are led for yourself and others.

"Lord, you speak with the authority of knowing both God and the scriptures. I long to see things as you see them and to act as you act. Let it be to your glory and the good of others . . ." (Continue in your own words.)

Listen to Jesus.

I pour my life into you, dear one, and I give you light in your darkness. I know your heart and receive it gratefully. I give you mine. What else is Jesus saying to you?

Ask God to show you how to live today.

"I look forward to walking today in your life, light, and love. I praise your holy name, Jesus. Amen."

Thursday, June 7, 2018

Know that God is present and ready to converse.

"Lord, your Word is truth. Teach me wisdom."

Read the gospel: Mark 12:28–34.

One of the scribes came near and heard the Sadducees disputing with one another, and seeing that Jesus answered them well, he asked him, "Which commandment is the first of all?" Jesus answered, "The first is, 'Hear, O Israel: the Lord our God, the Lord is one; you shall love the

Lord your God with all your heart, and with all your soul, and with all your mind, and with all your strength.' The second is this, 'You shall love your neighbor as yourself.' There is no other commandment greater than these." Then the scribe said to him, "You are right, Teacher; you have truly said that 'he is one, and besides him there is no other'; and 'to love him with all the heart, and with all the understanding, and with all the strength,' and 'to love one's neighbor as oneself,'—this is much more important than all whole burnt offerings and sacrifices." When Jesus saw that he answered wisely, he said to him, "You are not far from the kingdom of God." After that no one dared to ask him any question.

Notice what you think and feel as you read the gospel.

The scribe asks a question not to trick Jesus about the commandments, but to learn from him, and Jesus answers him by quoting the two greatest commandments from Moses—to love God and others with everything we have. The scribe commends Jesus' answer and even adds to it. Jesus tells him he is not far from the kingdom of God.

Pray as you are led for yourself and others.

"Lord of Love, all love comes from you, for you are Love. Fill me with love for you and love for those you have given me . . ." (Continue in your own words.)

Listen to Jesus.

This love you ask for is the work of a lifetime, but it is also a work of one day—today. Take what love you find within and act on it today. You will be happy, for God is working in you and with you. What else is Jesus saying to you?

Ask God to show you how to live today.

"Lord, you have already shown me how to live today. By your grace, I will act in love today. Amen."

Friday, June 8, 2018
Sacred Heart of Jesus

Know that God is present and ready to converse.

"Jesus, make my heart like yours through the cleansing power of the Word."

Read the gospel: John 19:31–37.

Since it was the day of Preparation, the Jews did not want the bodies left on the cross during the sabbath, especially because that sabbath was a day of great solemnity. So they asked Pilate to have the legs of the crucified men broken and the bodies removed. Then the soldiers came and broke the legs of the first and of the other who had been crucified with him. But when they came to Jesus and saw that he was already dead, they did not break his legs. Instead, one of the soldiers pierced his side with a spear, and at once blood and water came out. (He who saw this has testified so that you also may believe. His testimony is true, and he knows that he tells the truth.) These things occurred so that the scripture might be fulfilled, "None of his bones shall be broken." And again another passage of scripture says, "They will look on the one whom they have pierced."

Notice what you think and feel as you read the gospel.

When the soldier pierces Jesus' side with a spear, blood and water flow out. John the Evangelist was present and saw great significance to this event, as it fulfilled Old Testament prophesy. It also focused attention on the water and the blood that is salvation and the life of the Church.

Pray as you are led for yourself and others.

"Wash me again with your water, Lord, and cleanse my soul with your blood. I pray the same for all those I love and encounter, today and every day . . ." (Continue in your own words.)

Listen to Jesus.

A heart of love, beloved, is a heart that bleeds. When you bleed in love for others, you participate in my love for them. Continue in this way. What else is Jesus saying to you?

Ask God to show you how to live today.

"Lord, in your love I don't feel pain, but it hurts me that others do not know your love. How can I help? Amen."

Saturday, June 9, 2018
Immaculate Heart of the Blessed Virgin Mary

Know that God is present and ready to converse.

"Let me treasure all the incidents in Jesus' life as Mary did. Come Holy Spirit!"

Read the gospel: Luke 2:41–51.

Now every year Jesus' parents went to Jerusalem for the festival of the Passover. And when he was twelve years old, they went up as usual for the festival. When the festival was ended and they started to return, the boy Jesus stayed behind in Jerusalem, but his parents did not know it. Assuming that he was in the group of travelers, they went a day's journey. Then they started to look for him among their relatives and friends. When they did not find him, they returned to Jerusalem to search for him. After three days they found him in the temple, sitting among the teachers, listening to them and asking them questions. And all who heard him were amazed at his understanding and his answers. When his parents saw him they were astonished; and his mother said to him, "Child, why have you treated us like this? Look, your father and I have been searching for you in great anxiety." He said to them, "Why were you searching for me? Did you not know that I must be in my Father's house?" But they did not understand what he said to them. Then he went down with them and came to Nazareth, and was obedient to them. His mother treasured all these things in her heart.

Notice what you think and feel as you read the gospel.

Jesus seems to get ahead of himself in beginning his ministry by teaching the teachers in the Temple. Mary and Joseph are astonished to find their lost boy doing this; Jesus simply answers that he must be in his Father's house, but he continues with them obediently.

Pray as you are led for yourself and others.

"I pray today especially for the children you have given me, Lord. Let them be parented with wisdom and love. Let them be obedient and grow up in God . . ." (Continue in your own words.)

Listen to Jesus.

You are part of my holy family, dear disciple, for you do the will of God. With me, my mother, and all the saints, you are one with God and already know the kingdom of heaven. I am happy for you and with you. What else is Jesus saying to you?

Ask God to show you how to live today.

"How may I extend my loving care to children today, Lord? Help me to truly appreciate them as you did. Amen."

Sunday, June 10, 2018
Tenth Sunday in Ordinary Time

Know that God is present and ready to converse.

"Jesus, sometimes you were surrounded by chaos, but you brought order out of it. Please do that for me as I read your Word."

Read the gospel: Mark 3:20–35.

And the crowd came together again, so that they could not even eat. When Jesus' family heard it, they went out to restrain him, for people were saying, "He has gone out of his mind." And the scribes who came down from Jerusalem said, "He has Beelzebul, and by the ruler of the demons he casts out demons." And he called them to him, and spoke to them in parables, "How can Satan cast out Satan? If a kingdom is divided against itself, that kingdom cannot stand. And if a house is divided against itself, that house will not be able to stand. And if Satan has risen up against himself and is divided, he cannot stand, but his end has come. But no one can enter a strong man's house and plunder his property without first tying up the strong man; then indeed the house can be plundered.

"Truly I tell you, people will be forgiven for their sins and whatever blasphemies they utter; but whoever blasphemes against the Holy Spirit can never have forgiveness, but is guilty of an eternal sin"— for they had said, "He has an unclean spirit."

Then his mother and his brothers came; and standing outside, they sent to him and called him. A crowd was sitting around him; and they said to him, "Your mother and your brothers and sisters are outside, asking for you." And he replied, "Who are my mother and my brothers?" And looking at those who sat around him, he said, "Here are my mother and my brothers! Whoever does the will of God is my brother and sister and mother."

Notice what you think and feel as you read the gospel.

Among the crowds, members of Jesus' family question his sanity. The scribes accuse him of being in league with Satan. Jesus warns them against blasphemy against the Holy Spirit, for he acted in the power of the Holy Spirit, not demonic spirits. With his family standing outside, Jesus proclaimed that those who do the will of God are members of his family.

Pray as you are led for yourself and others.

"It is marvelous to see Jesus acting and speaking with power in this scripture. What begins in chaos ends in perfect serenity. Jesus, remain with me now as I pray . . ." (Continue in your own words.)

Listen to Jesus.

I am with you, for you believe in me and love me. I will remain with you always. I give you the Holy Spirit so that you can do the works of love I do, for I work through you. What else is Jesus saying to you?

Ask God to show you how to live today.

"Help me to be true to your call today, my Jesus. I am yours. Amen."

Monday, June 11, 2018

Know that God is present and ready to converse.

"Blessed Lord, how can I be truly happy?"

Read the gospel: Matthew 5:1–12.

When Jesus saw the crowds, he went up the mountain; and after he sat down, his disciples came to him. Then he began to speak, and taught them, saying:

> "Blessed are the poor in spirit, for theirs is the kingdom of heaven.
>
> "Blessed are those who mourn, for they will be comforted.
>
> "Blessed are the meek, for they will inherit the earth.
>
> "Blessed are those who hunger and thirst for righteousness, for they will be filled.
>
> "Blessed are the merciful, for they will receive mercy.
>
> "Blessed are the pure in heart, for they will see God.
>
> "Blessed are the peacemakers, for they will be called children of God.
>
> "Blessed are those who are persecuted for righteousness' sake, for theirs is the kingdom of heaven.
>
> "Blessed are you when people revile you and persecute you and utter all kinds of evil against you falsely on my account. Rejoice and be glad, for your reward is great in heaven, for in the same way they persecuted the prophets who were before you."

Notice what you think and feel as you read the gospel.

Jesus' teaching about morality goes far beyond the Ten Commandments and the laws of the Jews. He declares that those who are poor, mourning, meek, hungry for righteousness, merciful, pure, peaceable, or persecuted are the blessed ones, both now and in the kingdom hereafter. If we want happiness, Jesus says, follow his way.

Pray as you are led for yourself and others.

"Lord, you ask much. Help me to understand it deeply, receive it, and live it. Perhaps I should start with 'poor of spirit.' I think that means I must recognize my need for you . . ." (Continue in your own words.)

Listen to Jesus.

I love to delight you with the rewards of following me. Take it a little at a time, and you will see too that the time is short. We shall be together forever. Let us go. What else is Jesus saying to you?

Ask God to show you how to live today.

"Let me follow you today in true meekness of heart, for that is your way. Amen."

Tuesday, June 12, 2018

Know that God is present and ready to converse.

"Teacher, I am present with you here. May I be truly open to your Word."

Read the gospel: Matthew 5:13–16.

Jesus said, "You are the salt of the earth; but if salt has lost its taste, how can its saltiness be restored? It is no longer good for anything, but is thrown out and trampled underfoot.

"You are the light of the world. A city built on a hill cannot be hidden. No one after lighting a lamp puts it under the bushel basket, but on the lampstand, and it gives light to all in the house. In the same way, let your light shine before others, so that they may see your good works and give glory to your Father in heaven."

Notice what you think and feel as you read the gospel.

Jesus commends his followers, letting them know how important they are in the world. The metaphors suggest that they are goodness, truth, and testimony to God's glory. He urges them to continue in that way.

Pray as you are led for yourself and others.

"Let me remember your call to be salt of the earth, Lord, for the world needs it. Let all your disciples shine their light, which is you, before others . . ." (Continue in your own words.)

Listen to Jesus.

As long as you follow me and imitate me, my child, you will do good works that glorify our Father. Others will notice and benefit from your service. What else is Jesus saying to you?

Ask God to show you how to live today.

"Let my mind be stayed on you, Lord, for it is so easy for me to forget that I belong to you and that I must seek to do all things with you. Amen."

Wednesday, June 13, 2018

Know that God is present and ready to converse.

"Lord, be with me as I read your Word, for I long to keep your commandments."

Read the gospel: Matthew 5:17–19.

Jesus said, "Do not think that I have come to abolish the law or the prophets; I have come not to abolish but to fulfill. For truly I tell you, until heaven and earth pass away, not one letter, not one stroke of a letter, will pass from the law until all is accomplished. Therefore, whoever breaks one of the least of these commandments, and teaches others to do the same, will be called least in the kingdom of heaven; but whoever does them and teaches them will be called great in the kingdom of heaven."

Notice what you think and feel as you read the gospel.

Jesus places high value on the scriptures, the law, and the prophets, and he identifies himself with that tradition. He prophesies that everything the scriptures say will be accomplished before the end. To keep the commandments and teach others to do the same will make a person great in the kingdom.

Pray as you are led for yourself and others.

"Alleluia, Lord, for I attend to your Word with all my heart. I pray that believers and nonbelievers everywhere may be awakened by the scripture and see the truths of God . . ." (Continue in your own words.)

Listen to Jesus.

To understand and love the scripture, dearly beloved, you must have a willing heart. You are right to pray for those who do not. I have tried to gather people into my kingdom. I will continue to extend the mercy of God to whoever asks, seeks, or is willing to receive it. What else is Jesus saying to you?

Ask God to show you how to live today.

"Lord, let me join you in extending mercy to any who will receive it, and even those who cannot yet. Let me live in hope today with your mercy upon me. Amen."

Thursday, June 14, 2018

Know that God is present and ready to converse.

"Lord, you call me by your Word to keep the commandments. Help me understand by your Holy Spirit."

Read the gospel: Matthew 5:20–26.

Jesus said, "For I tell you, unless your righteousness exceeds that of the scribes and Pharisees, you will never enter the kingdom of heaven.

"You have heard that it was said to those of ancient times, 'You shall not murder'; and 'whoever murders shall be liable to judgement.' But I say to you that if you are angry with a brother or sister, you will be liable to judgement; and if you insult a brother or sister, you will be liable to the council; and if you say, 'You fool,' you will be liable to the hell of fire. So when you are offering your gift at the altar, if you remember that your brother or sister has something against you, leave your gift there before the altar and go; first be reconciled to your brother or sister, and then come and offer your gift. Come to terms quickly with your accuser while you are on the way to court with him, or your accuser may hand you over to the judge, and the judge to the guard, and you will be thrown into prison. Truly I tell you, you will never get out until you have paid the last penny."

Notice what you think and feel as you read the gospel.

Jesus repudiates legalism in religious practice, seeing the commandments of Moses as minimal guideposts and obedience to them as inadequate. He asks the crowd listening to him for a heart transformation: he asks them to go far beyond obedience to the commandments in showing real love and mercy to others.

Pray as you are led for yourself and others.

"Lord, I long to obey the commandments of scripture, including yours, from my heart. Transform me by your persistent grace that I may be a blessing to many, including . . ." (Continue in your own words.)

Listen to Jesus.

Your desire for yourself is my desire for you, dear one. To seek an obedient heart, full of grace and truth, is the beginning of finding it. Follow me. What else is Jesus saying to you?

Ask God to show you how to live today.

"I am glad to know you, Lord. Let me concentrate today on being reconciled to someone who has something against me. Help me be reconciled. Amen."

Friday, June 15, 2018

Know that God is present and ready to converse.

"Jesus, you are the great successor of Moses. I sit at your feet to receive your teaching."

Read the gospel: Matthew 5:27–32.

Jesus said, "You have heard that it was said, 'You shall not commit adultery.' But I say to you that everyone who looks at a woman with lust has already committed adultery with her in his heart. If your right eye causes you to sin, tear it out and throw it away; it is better for you to lose one of your members than for your whole body to be thrown into hell. And if your right hand causes you to sin, cut it off and throw it away; it is better for you to lose one of your members than for your whole body to go into hell.

"It was also said, 'Whoever divorces his wife, let him give her a certificate of divorce.' But I say to you that anyone who divorces his wife, except on the ground of unchastity, causes her to commit adultery; and whoever marries a divorced woman commits adultery."

Notice what you think and feel as you read the gospel.

Jesus continues his great discourse on morality, aligning his own teaching with that of Moses but also going far beyond it. Adultery breaks the law of Moses; lust for another is already adultery in Jesus' formulation.

Pray as you are led for yourself and others.

"Lord, I must throw myself upon your mercy and beg for your grace, for I long to obey your commandments. I pray for holiness, Lord, for myself and all those you have given me . . ." (Continue in your own words.)

Listen to Jesus.

If holiness is what God wants and you want it too, why would God not give it to you and to those you pray for? Cry out for the grace to be holy. To be holy is to be close to God and please God. Desire that above all. What else is Jesus saying to you?

Ask God to show you how to live today.

"Lord, I do want holiness. Perhaps the first step for me is to realize I am not even close to holiness. I need your help. Lead me into holiness, Lord. Amen."

Saturday, June 16, 2018

Know that God is present and ready to converse.

"Jesus, too often my actions are guided by my own thoughts and desires, but I open myself now to the idea that what I want and what I do might be changed by your mighty Word."

Read the gospel: Matthew 5:33–37.

Jesus said, "Again, you have heard that it was said to those of ancient times, 'You shall not swear falsely, but carry out the vows you have made to the Lord.' But I say to you, Do not swear at all, either by heaven, for it is the throne of God, or by the earth, for it is his footstool, or by Jerusalem, for it is the city of the great King. And do not swear by your head, for you cannot make one hair white or black. Let your word be 'Yes, Yes' or 'No, No'; anything more than this comes from the evil one."

Notice what you think and feel as you read the gospel.

Jesus speaks of the futility of human will and plans, as if a person can make God do his or her own will. It is vain to swear by God or by anything else. Instead say merely yes or no and trust in God's loving providence.

Pray as you are led for yourself and others.

"Lord, I say yes to you and your ways and no to the evil one. Let those I love reject evil and grow ever closer to you . . ." (Continue in your own words.)

Listen to Jesus.

I speak of simplicity and humility as well as trust in God. Do not make yourself out to be more than you are. Yet you are a child of the great King and will inherit the kingdom hereafter. What else is Jesus saying to you?

Ask God to show you how to live today.

"I am happy to be your child, Lord. Let me do everything today with simplicity and humility, knowing I am your own. Amen."

Sunday, June 17, 2018
Eleventh Sunday in Ordinary Time

Know that God is present and ready to converse.

"God, I wish to advance in love for you as you will it. Sanctify me by your Word."

Read the gospel: Mark 4:26–34.

Jesus also said, "The kingdom of God is as if someone would scatter seed on the ground, and would sleep and rise night and day, and the seed would sprout and grow, he does not know how. The earth produces of itself, first the stalk, then the head, then the full grain in the head. But when the grain is ripe, at once he goes in with his sickle, because the harvest has come."

He also said, "With what can we compare the kingdom of God, or what parable will we use for it? It is like a mustard seed, which, when sown upon the ground, is the smallest of all the seeds on earth; yet when it is sown it grows up and becomes the greatest of all shrubs, and puts forth large branches, so that the birds of the air can make nests in its shade."

With many such parables he spoke the word to them, as they were able to hear it; he did not speak to them except in parables, but he explained everything in private to his disciples.

Notice what you think and feel as you read the gospel.

Jesus speaks of spiritual growth as a gift and a work of God. He compares it to the natural process of seeds growing and becoming whatever grain or plant they were intended to become. As this happens in nature in the right circumstances, it also happens in the spiritual lives of humans as God wills.

Pray as you are led for yourself and others.

"Lord, I believe you want me to grow in faith. Do not let me do anything to hinder your will as I give myself to your growing and ripening process. I pray, too, for others' growth . . ." (Continue in your own words.)

Listen to Jesus.

You are growing in my care, dear disciple. Look how far we've come—the harvest is near. What else is Jesus saying to you?

Ask God to show you how to live today.

"Lord, you give me my own will, yet I cannot do what you can do. Help me give my will to you in small ways and large so that you can make me grow in ways that truly please you. Amen."

Monday, June 18, 2018

Know that God is present and ready to converse.

"Lord, you are here with me now. I resolve to listen to your Word and act upon it today."

Read the gospel: Matthew 5:38–42.

Jesus said, "You have heard that it was said, 'An eye for an eye and a tooth for a tooth.' But I say to you, Do not resist an evildoer. But if anyone strikes you on the right cheek, turn the other also; and if anyone wants to sue you and take your coat, give your cloak as well; and if anyone forces you to go one mile, go also the second mile. Give to everyone who begs from you, and do not refuse anyone who wants to borrow from you."

Notice what you think and feel as you read the gospel.

Jesus teaches personal pacifism. Do not resist an evildoer but give more than asked, more than required by justice. This is the hard commandment of the Lord.

Pray as you are led for yourself and others.

"I throw myself on your mercy, Jesus, for I have no power to obey you well. I pray that you encourage me and empower me to obey you. Also encourage and empower those you have given me . . ." (Continue in your own words.)

Listen to Jesus.

Do not be discouraged, child. I hold up for you my own way. Walk with me the way I walked, knowing I am with you at all times. When you fail, rely on my mercy. Rejoice with me as you succeed. What else is Jesus saying to you?

Ask God to show you how to live today.

"I want to make you happy, Lord, at any cost. Let me find a way to give you cause to rejoice today. Thank you. Amen."

Tuesday, June 19, 2018

Know that God is present and ready to converse.

"Lord, your Word is a lamp to my feet. Give me your light today."

Read the gospel: Matthew 5:43–48.

Jesus said, "You have heard that it was said, 'You shall love your neighbor and hate your enemy.' But I say to you, Love your enemies and pray for those who persecute you, so that you may be children of your Father in heaven; for he makes his sun rise on the evil and on the good, and sends rain on the righteous and on the unrighteous. For if you love those who love you, what reward do you have? Do not even the tax-collectors do the same? And if you greet only your brothers and sisters, what more are you doing than others? Do not even the Gentiles do the same? Be perfect, therefore, as your heavenly Father is perfect."

Notice what you think and feel as you read the gospel.

In his great sermon, Jesus continues to urge his followers to be perfect and holy as God is. All love is from God, and we are to love God, our own, and our enemies, as our heavenly Father does.

Pray as you are led for yourself and others.

"Lord, I hear you, and I pray now for the ones who have slighted me or persecuted me or opposed me in any way, especially . . ." (Continue in your own words.)

Listen to Jesus.

It is good for you to release anger and forgive those who have harmed you. For you, too, need forgiveness. This is a powerful key to happiness, pleasing God and bringing about great joy in heaven, for you are not alone. What else is Jesus saying to you?

Ask God to show you how to live today.

"Let me walk in the awareness of being one of many who love and serve the Lord. Let me encourage my brothers and sisters today. Amen."

Wednesday, June 20, 2018

Know that God is present and ready to converse.

"Jesus, in communion with your Father and the Holy Spirit, manifest yourself to me as I encounter your holy Word."

Read the gospel: Matthew 6:1–6, 16–18.

Jesus said, "Beware of practicing your piety before others in order to be seen by them; for then you have no reward from your Father in heaven.

"So whenever you give alms, do not sound a trumpet before you, as the hypocrites do in the synagogues and in the streets, so that they may be praised by others. Truly I tell you, they have received their reward. But when you give alms, do not let your left hand know what your right hand is doing, so that your alms may be done in secret; and your Father who sees in secret will reward you. . . .

"And whenever you pray, do not be like the hypocrites; for they love to stand and pray in the synagogues and at the street corners, so that they may be seen by others. Truly I tell you, they have received their reward. But whenever you pray, go into your room and shut the door and pray to your Father who is in secret; and your Father who sees in secret will reward you.

"And whenever you fast, do not look dismal, like the hypocrites, for they disfigure their faces so as to show others that they are fasting. Truly I tell you, they have received their reward. But when you fast, put oil on your head and wash your face, so that your fasting may be seen not by others but by your Father who is in secret; and your Father who sees in secret will reward you."

Notice what you think and feel as you read the gospel.

Jesus repudiates the religiosity of hypocrites. We are to seek true holiness, not the appearance of it. The desire to appear pious renders pious acts worthless in God's eyes. We are to seek God's favor alone.

Pray as you are led for yourself and others.

"Lord, forgive me all my hypocrisy. I call it now to mind. Give me your Spirit so that I can be my genuine self, the person you love and bless. I pray today for all who hide themselves behind facades . . ." (Continue in your own words.)

Listen to Jesus.

You are God's own beloved child. Live your life before God, not before those whom you want to admire you. That admiration is worthless. God's approval is all. What else is Jesus saying to you?

Ask God to show you how to live today.

"Lord, give me moments of authenticity today. Because you are with me, Lord, I can live as I am. Help me be truly authentic, what you want me to be. Amen."

Thursday, June 21, 2018

Know that God is present and ready to converse.

"Jesus, let my prayer be meaningful and powerful, for I rely upon you."

Read the gospel: Matthew 6:7–15.

Jesus said, "When you are praying, do not heap up empty phrases as the Gentiles do; for they think that they will be heard because of their many words. Do not be like them, for your Father knows what you need before you ask him.

"Pray then in this way:

Our Father in heaven,
hallowed be your name.
Your kingdom come.
Your will be done,
on earth as it is in heaven.
Give us this day our daily bread.
And forgive us our debts,
as we also have forgiven our debtors.
And do not bring us to the time of trial,
but rescue us from the evil one.

For if you forgive others their trespasses, your heavenly Father will also forgive you; but if you do not forgive others, neither will your Father forgive your trespasses."

Notice what you think and feel as you read the gospel.

Jesus teaches his followers to pray, honoring our Father, urging his will be done, asking for what we need, begging forgiveness, and requesting rescue from evil.

Pray as you are led for yourself and others.

"Hallowed be your name, Lord. Give me grace to forgive others—past, present, and future. I now forgive . . ." (Continue in your own words.)

Listen to Jesus.

Forgiveness is a great exercise in the progress of holiness. It purifies you and frees your spirit to love God more and more. It is the recognition that you, too, are broken and at the mercy of God. Forgive, dear one. I forgive you. What else is Jesus saying to you?

Ask God to show you how to live today.

"Let me examine my heart in the light of your Spirit, Lord, and forgive and forgive again. Hallowed be your name. Amen."

Friday, June 22, 2018

Know that God is present and ready to converse.

"Heavenly Father, who often seems far off, I know you are with me now. Give me wisdom and grace to remain in your presence now and after our time together."

Read the gospel: Matthew 6:19–23.

Jesus said, "Do not store up for yourselves treasures on earth, where moth and rust consume and where thieves break in and steal; but store up for yourselves treasures in heaven, where neither moth nor rust consumes and where thieves do not break in and steal. For where your treasure is, there your heart will be also.

"The eye is the lamp of the body. So, if your eye is healthy, your whole body will be full of light; but if your eye is unhealthy, your whole body will be full of darkness. If then the light in you is darkness, how great is the darkness!"

Notice what you think and feel as you read the gospel.

Jesus knows that possessions and money distract us from loving God and living well. He suggests we focus our eyes on what is good and beautiful—God alone—and then our whole body will be full of light.

Pray as you are led for yourself and others.

"I desire to want you alone, dear Lord, and to let the selfishness drop away from me. Grant me purity of desire, Lord, and grant it too for all those you have given me . . ." (Continue in your own words.)

Listen to Jesus.

You are lifting up your heart to God, beloved, and God hears your prayer with happiness. I love you with all my heart. Cherish our moments and take them with you in good times and, especially, in bad. What else is Jesus saying to you?

Ask God to show you how to live today.

"Your love is my treasure. Help me be worthy of your love during the crucial moments of my day. I give all my moments to you. Amen."

Saturday, June 23, 2018

Know that God is present and ready to converse.

"Master of the universe, you are my Creator and Savior. I place myself before you to receive your wisdom and grace, and I open myself to your holy Word."

Read the gospel: Matthew 6:24–34.

Jesus said, "No one can serve two masters; for a slave will either hate the one and love the other, or be devoted to the one and despise the other. You cannot serve God and wealth.

"Therefore I tell you, do not worry about your life, what you will eat or what you will drink, or about your body, what you will wear. Is not life more than food, and the body more than clothing? Look at the birds of the air; they neither sow nor reap nor gather into barns, and yet your heavenly Father feeds them. Are you not of more value than they? And can any of you by worrying add a single hour to your span of life? And why do you worry about clothing? Consider the lilies of the field, how they grow; they neither toil nor spin, yet I tell you, even Solomon in all his glory was not clothed like one of these. But if God so clothes the grass of the field, which is alive today and tomorrow is thrown into the oven, will he not much more clothe you—you of little faith? Therefore do not worry, saying, 'What will we eat?' or 'What will we drink?' or 'What will we wear?' For it is the Gentiles who strive for all these things; and indeed your heavenly Father knows that you need all these things. But strive first for the kingdom of God and his righteousness, and all these things will be given to you as well.

"So do not worry about tomorrow, for tomorrow will bring worries of its own. Today's trouble is enough for today."

Notice what you think and feel as you read the gospel.

Jesus preaches that God wants our full devotion. We should not be distracted, worried, or bothered by the elements of our lives like food, drink, clothing, our bodies, our resources, our savings, or our future. Just seek to serve God, and God will take care of everything.

Pray as you are led for yourself and others.

"Lord, this is the day you made for me. Give me grace to seek you and serve you single-mindedly. I entrust to you all those you want me to pray for, including . . ." (Continue in your own words.)

Listen to Jesus.

I draw you into the present, my child. You dwell in your past and imagine your future obsessively, neglecting today. You fear punishment and failure. Have no fears about past or future, for God loves you and cares for you and will continue to care for you. Seek God today and again tomorrow. What else is Jesus saying to you?

Ask God to show you how to live today.

"Lord, I commit myself to today alone, starting from this moment. Help me to be attentive to you, as you share this day with me. Amen."

Sunday, June 24, 2018
Nativity of John the Baptist

Know that God is present and ready to converse.

"Almighty God, your Word accomplishes your purposes in history. Accomplish your purposes in me as I read your Word."

Read the gospel: Luke 1:57–66, 80.

Now the time came for Elizabeth to give birth, and she bore a son. Her neighbors and relatives heard that the Lord had shown his great mercy to her, and they rejoiced with her.

On the eighth day they came to circumcise the child, and they were going to name him Zechariah after his father. But his mother said, "No; he is to be called John." They said to her, "None of your relatives has this name." Then they began motioning to his father to find out what name he wanted to give him. He asked for a writing tablet and wrote, "His name is John." And all of them were amazed. Immediately his mouth was opened and his tongue freed, and he began to speak, praising God. Fear came over all their neighbors, and all these things were talked about throughout the entire hill country of Judea. All who heard them pondered them and said, "What then will this child become?" For, indeed, the hand of the Lord was with him.

The child grew and became strong in spirit, and he was in the wilderness until the day he appeared publicly to Israel.

Notice what you think and feel as you read the gospel.

Elizabeth, thought barren, gives birth to a son. Zechariah, his father, struck mute for unbelief, regains his speech when he declares that the boy is to be named John. This is the birth of John the Baptist, the one who would announce the Savior of Israel and the whole world, Jesus.

Pray as you are led for yourself and others.

"Lord, as John became strong in spirit as he grew, let me and all those you have given me also become strong in spirit, so that we may serve your great purposes . . ." (Continue in your own words.)

Listen to Jesus.

What will you become? You are right to take your life seriously and to realize the great value of those around you. Because you are made in the image of God, I have given you myself—my life, suffering, and resurrection—to save you from sin and death. Will you give yourself to me for the good of others? What else is Jesus saying to you?

Ask God to show you how to live today.

"I worship you, Lord, and wish to be obedient to you. Help me give myself to others now and today. To God be the glory. Amen."

Monday, June 25, 2018

Know that God is present and ready to converse.

"Great Teacher, Spirit of God, I cannot understand your Word unless you are with me. Let me hear you now."

Read the gospel: Matthew 7:1–5.

Jesus said, "Do not judge, so that you may not be judged. For with the judgement you make you will be judged, and the measure you give will be the measure you get. Why do you see the speck in your neighbor's eye, but do not notice the log in your own eye? Or how can you say to your neighbor, 'Let me take the speck out of your eye,' while the log is in your own eye? You hypocrite, first take the log out of your own eye, and then you will see clearly to take the speck out of your neighbor's eye."

Notice what you think and feel as you read the gospel.

Jesus unfolds the mechanisms of holiness step by step; this step has to do with judging others. Do not judge, he says, for we will be judged by the same measure. Attend to your own faults, not those of others.

Pray as you are led for yourself and others.

"Lord, I do not do well in keeping this commandment, for I am much concerned with the faults of others. I pray for forgiveness of my own faults and a new mind full of grace that I may ignore or forgive what I perceive to be fault in others . . ." (Continue in your own words.)

Listen to Jesus.

Welcome to the joy of the Lord. Mercy is God's, and you may enter into God's mercy, both for yourself and others. Practice mercy every day. Pray for it. I wish it to be a part of your whole approach to life, to others. What else is Jesus saying to you?

Ask God to show you how to live today.

"Instead of judging someone, Jesus, let me show him or her mercy, in my mind, in my words, in my actions. Thank you for your mercy to me. Amen."

Tuesday, June 26, 2018

Know that God is present and ready to converse.

"Lord, thank you for being who you are, holy and mighty God. Let me value you and your Word as I ought."

Read the gospel: Matthew 7:6, 12–14.

Jesus said, "Do not give what is holy to dogs; and do not throw your pearls before swine, or they will trample them under foot and turn and maul you. . . .

"In everything do to others as you would have them do to you; for this is the law and the prophets.

"Enter through the narrow gate; for the gate is wide and the road is easy that leads to destruction, and there are many who take it. For the gate is narrow and the road is hard that leads to life, and there are few who find it."

Notice what you think and feel as you read the gospel.

Jesus urges prudence as we practice our faith, lest we provoke others to harm us. Scripture tells us to do unto others as we would have them do to us. Don't expect it to be easy—the narrow gate and hard road lead to life. Go that way.

Pray as you are led for yourself and others.

"Lord, I pray for all those who are on the easy road that leads to destruction. Let them turn to the hard road that leads to life. May many find life . . ." (Continue in your own words.)

Listen to Jesus.

Your heart is with me, beloved; your prayers accomplish much in the lives of others. Embrace the mystery of prayer wholeheartedly. I will hear you and do it. What else is Jesus saying to you?

Ask God to show you how to live today.

"Where and how have I taken the easy road, Lord? How may I correct my ways and walk the hard road to life eternal? Amen."

Wednesday, June 27, 2018

Know that God is present and ready to converse.

"How may I know you better and understand your will for my journey? I seek you today in your Word."

Read the gospel: Matthew 7:15–20.

Jesus said, "Beware of false prophets, who come to you in sheep's clothing but inwardly are ravenous wolves. You will know them by their fruits. Are grapes gathered from thorns, or figs from thistles? In the same way, every good tree bears good fruit, but the bad tree bears bad fruit. A good tree cannot bear bad fruit, nor can a bad tree bear good fruit. Every tree that does not bear good fruit is cut down and thrown into the fire. Thus you will know them by their fruits."

Notice what you think and feel as you read the gospel.

Jesus warns his hearers about being taken in by false prophets. Watch them, he says, and observe their fruit. Good trees bear good fruit; bad trees bear bad fruit and will be thrown into the fire.

Pray as you are led for yourself and others.

"Jesus, you are the Truth, and only in you may I bear good fruit. Let me bear good fruit for the good of others, especially those in need . . ." (Continue in your own words.)

Listen to Jesus.

When you have choices, decisions, or judgments to make, beloved, turn to me for guidance. Place matters in my hands, and I will help you make the best choices. This is another great power of prayer. We are companions. What else is Jesus saying to you?

Ask God to show you how to live today.

"I face choices now, Lord, and will make choices during my day. Guide me to good choices that bear good fruit. Thank you. Amen."

Thursday, June 28, 2018

Know that God is present and ready to converse.

"Father, Son, and Holy Spirit, I seek to know you truly and to remain with you always. May I find you in your Word."

Read the gospel: Matthew 7:21–29.

Jesus said, "Not everyone who says to me, 'Lord, Lord,' will enter the kingdom of heaven, but only one who does the will of my Father in heaven. On that day many will say to me, 'Lord, Lord, did we not prophesy in your name, and cast out demons in your name, and do many deeds of power in your name?' Then I will declare to them, 'I never knew you; go away from me, you evildoers.'

"Everyone then who hears these words of mine and acts on them will be like a wise man who built his house on rock. The rain fell, the floods came, and the winds blew and beat on that house, but it did not fall, because it had been founded on rock. And everyone who hears these words of mine and does not act on them will be like a foolish man who built his house on sand. The rain fell, and the floods came, and the winds blew and beat against that house, and it fell—and great was its fall!"

Now when Jesus had finished saying these things, the crowds were astounded at his teaching, for he taught them as one having authority, and not as their scribes.

Notice what you think and feel as you read the gospel.

Jesus says his followers must do the will of his Father, not their own will. His followers must know him, not just use his name. Those who hear his words and act on them are building their house on rock and will not perish in the flood.

Pray as you are led for yourself and others.

"Lord, you have called me to know you and do your will—call my name again today, please, remind me to spend time with you. I pray also for those who speak your name but fail to do your will—who build their houses on sand. Save them . . ." (Continue in your own words.)

Listen to Jesus.

Beloved, you and I cannot control the hearts and minds of others so that they do the will of God. My Father has granted free will to human beings, and people do as they wish for better or for worse. You have chosen me and I have chosen you. You are on the rock; cling to me. What else is Jesus saying to you?

Ask God to show you how to live today.

"I praise you, Jesus. This world is full of light and full of darkness too. I ask you to guide my feet along your lighted path. Amen."

Friday, June 29, 2018
Saints Peter and Paul, Apostles

Know that God is present and ready to converse.

"Jesus, you are the Son of the living God, present now to teach me by your Word."

Read the gospel: Matthew 16:13–19.

Now when Jesus came into the district of Caesarea Philippi, he asked his disciples, "Who do people say that the Son of Man is?" And they said, "Some say John the Baptist, but others Elijah, and still others Jeremiah or one of the prophets." He said to them, "But who do you say that I am?" Simon Peter answered, "You are the Messiah, the Son of the living God." And Jesus answered him, "Blessed are you, Simon son of Jonah! For flesh and blood has not revealed this to you, but my Father in heaven.

And I tell you, you are Peter, and on this rock I will build my church, and the gates of Hades will not prevail against it. I will give you the keys of the kingdom of heaven, and whatever you bind on earth will be bound in heaven, and whatever you loose on earth will be loosed in heaven."

Notice what you think and feel as you read the gospel.

Jesus points out to his disciples that there are many rumors about who he is, and he asks them who they think he is. Peter answers quickly that Jesus is the Messiah. Jesus tells Peter that God has revealed it to him and that Jesus will build his church upon Peter and give him the keys of the kingdom of heaven.

Pray as you are led for yourself and others.

"Lord, I pray for all the leaders of your Church, from pope to parish council. Let them lead all people to you with the power of wisdom, faith, and love . . ." (Continue in your own words.)

Listen to Jesus.

I will never abandon my Church, for it proclaims me as Savior to the whole world. The Church will confront darkness and trouble until the end of time, but it will not fail. What else is Jesus saying to you?

Ask God to show you how to live today.

"Jesus, not even Peter and Paul were perfect, but those whom you call out to be leaders of your Church you give grace to do your will. When Church leaders fail, help me to respond—whether by forgiving, bearing patiently with, or admonishing—always in your love and mercy. Amen."

Saturday, June 30, 2018

Know that God is present and ready to converse.

"Jesus, I approach you today with reverence and hope. Speak to me by your mighty Word."

Read the gospel: Matthew 8:5–17.

When Jesus entered Capernaum, a centurion came to him, appealing to him and saying, "Lord, my servant is lying at home paralyzed, in terrible distress." And he said to him, "I will come and cure him." The centurion answered, "Lord, I am not worthy to have you come under my roof; but only speak the word, and my servant will be healed. For I also am a man under authority, with soldiers under me; and I say to one, 'Go,' and he goes, and to another, 'Come,' and he comes, and to my slave, 'Do this,' and the slave does it." When Jesus heard him, he was amazed and said to those who followed him, "Truly I tell you, in no one in Israel have I found such faith. I tell you, many will come from east and west and will eat with Abraham and Isaac and Jacob in the kingdom of heaven, while the heirs of the kingdom will be thrown into the outer darkness, where there will be weeping and gnashing of teeth." And to the centurion Jesus said, "Go; let it be done for you according to your faith." And the servant was healed in that hour.

When Jesus entered Peter's house, he saw his mother-in-law lying in bed with a fever; he touched her hand, and the fever left her, and she got up and began to serve him. That evening they brought to him many who were possessed by demons; and he cast out the spirits with a word, and cured all who were sick. This was to fulfill what had been spoken through the prophet Isaiah, "He took our infirmities and bore our diseases."

Notice what you think and feel as you read the gospel.

Jesus is impressed with the centurion's faith in God and love of his servant. The humble centurion also shows understanding of Jesus' authority—Jesus can heal from a distance. After Jesus proclaims that many non-Jews from the east and west will enter the kingdom of heaven, he heals the servant. Then he heals Peter's mother-in-law and many more.

Pray as you are led for yourself and others.

"Jesus, you took our infirmities and bore our diseases, as the prophet said. I pray now for those who need healing, including . . ." (Continue in your own words.)

Listen to Jesus.

I am the Word who created you in love; I know you, and I can heal all your ills. I am the same today as I always was. I was present with the Father from the beginning. And with the Holy Spirit we are present now and forever. We love you and invite you to love us. Enter our universe of love. What else is Jesus saying to you?

Ask God to show you how to live today.

"Lord, your glory overwhelms me. I am not worthy to have you come under my roof, but say the word and I shall be healed. Amen."

Sunday, July 1, 2018
Thirteenth Sunday in Ordinary Time

Know that God is present and ready to converse.

"Lord, I believe in you, in your truth and your love. Feed me by your Word."

Read the gospel: Mark 5:21–43.

When Jesus had crossed again in the boat to the other side, a great crowd gathered round him; and he was by the lake. Then one of the leaders of the synagogue named Jairus came and, when he saw him, fell at his feet and begged him repeatedly, "My little daughter is at the point of death. Come and lay your hands on her, so that she may be made well, and live." So he went with him.

And a large crowd followed him and pressed in on him. Now there was a woman who had been suffering from hemorrhages for twelve years. She had endured much under many physicians, and had spent all that she had; and she was no better, but rather grew worse. She had heard about Jesus, and came up behind him in the crowd and touched his cloak, for she said, "If I but touch his clothes, I will be made well." Immediately her hemorrhage stopped; and she felt in her body that she was healed of her disease. Immediately aware that power had gone forth from him, Jesus turned about in the crowd and said, "Who touched my clothes?" And his disciples said to him, "You see the crowd pressing in on you; how can you say, 'Who touched me?'" He looked all round to see who had done it. But the woman, knowing what had happened to her, came in fear and trembling, fell down before him, and told him the whole truth. He said to her, "Daughter, your faith has made you well; go in peace, and be healed of your disease."

While he was still speaking, some people came from the leader's house to say, "Your daughter is dead. Why trouble the teacher any further?" But overhearing what they said, Jesus said to the leader of the synagogue, "Do not fear, only believe." He allowed no one to follow him except Peter, James, and John, the brother of James. When they came to the house of the leader of the synagogue, he saw a commotion, people weeping and wailing loudly. When he had entered, he said to them, "Why do you make a commotion and weep? The child is not dead but sleeping." And they laughed at him. Then he put them all outside, and took the child's father and mother and those who were with him, and went in where the child was. He took her by the hand and said to her, "Talitha cum," which means, "Little girl, get up!" And immediately the girl got up and began to walk about (she was twelve years of age). At this they were overcome with amazement. He strictly ordered them that no one should know this, and told them to give her something to eat.

Notice what you think and feel as you read the gospel.

These are two mighty works of Jesus, both occasioned by faith which Jesus requests and responds to. The long-suffering woman believes that only to touch Jesus' garment will heal her, and it does. The leader of the synagogue believes Jesus can heal or raise his daughter from death even when others laugh at the idea, and Jesus raises her. Jesus rewards great faith.

Pray as you are led for yourself and others.

"I believe, Lord; help my unbelief, that you may be real and mighty in my life and the lives of those you have given me . . ." (Continue in your own words.)

Listen to Jesus.

I give you what you ask for, beloved disciple and friend. I give you what you need. As for your faith, I increase it as you use it. Don't be afraid to trust in me. What else is Jesus saying to you?

Ask God to show you how to live today.

"Today I resolve to trust in you, looking to you for ways to serve others. Stay with me, Lord. Amen."

Monday, July 2, 2018

Know that God is present and ready to converse.

"Lord, I desire to be with you, for you are the Resurrection and the Life. Receive me."

Read the gospel: Matthew 8:18–22.

Now when Jesus saw great crowds around him, he gave orders to go over to the other side. A scribe then approached and said, "Teacher, I will follow you wherever you go." And Jesus said to him, "Foxes have holes, and birds of the air have nests; but the Son of Man has nowhere to lay his head." Another of his disciples said to him, "Lord, first let me go and bury my father." But Jesus said to him, "Follow me, and let the dead bury their own dead."

Notice what you think and feel as you read the gospel.

A scribe wishes to follow Jesus, and Jesus tells him of the hardships of a traveling ministry. Another disciple would follow him, but first he wishes to bury his father. Jesus says, "Follow me, and let the dead bury their own dead."

Pray as you are led for yourself and others.

"Lord, what does it mean to follow you today? How may I follow you without excuse and without fear of hardship? I await your instruction and your grace . . ." (Continue in your own words.)

Listen to Jesus.

Anyone who seeks me finds me. I am always here, mighty to save, full of light, mercy, and love. You need only to turn away from yourself and come to me. Be with me now. What else is Jesus saying?

Ask God to show you how to live today.

"I want to follow you in a real way today, Lord. I want to walk with you. Show me my stumbling blocks and give me grace to overcome them. Amen."

Tuesday, July 3, 2018

Know that God is present and ready to converse.

"My God, even in my belief doubts come. You are the living God even though I cannot see you."

Read the gospel: Matthew 8:23–27.

And when Jesus got into the boat, his disciples followed him. A windstorm arose on the sea, so great that the boat was being swamped by the waves; but he was asleep. And they went and woke him up, saying, "Lord, save us! We are perishing!" And he said to them, "Why are you afraid, you of little faith?" Then he got up and rebuked the winds and the sea; and there was a dead calm. They were amazed, saying, "What sort of man is this, that even the winds and the sea obey him?"

Notice what you think and feel as you read the gospel.

In the storm on the sea, the disciples are afraid. When they awaken Jesus, he takes them to task for their little faith. He calms the wind and the waves by his command, and they are amazed.

Pray as you are led for yourself and others.

"Jesus, I beg you, calm the storms in my life, or if that is not your will, be with me in the boat. I pray also for others who are facing heavy weather, especially . . ." (Continue in your own words.)

Listen to Jesus.

I am with you. I reward the faith of those who come to God, who look to God in their hard times and good times. Your faith pleases me, dear one. Stay with me, and you will be showered with happiness. What else is Jesus saying to you?

Ask God to show you how to live today.

"Lord, give me the faith to manage this day and to do your will in it. I want to please you, for you have blessed me. Amen."

Wednesday, July 4, 2018

Know that God is present and ready to converse.

"Jesus, disrupt my life. Put me on the path of life. Touch me, Word of God."

Read the gospel: Matthew 8:28–34.

When Jesus came to the other side, to the country of the Gadarenes, two demoniacs coming out of the tombs met him. They were so fierce that no one could pass that way. Suddenly they shouted, "What have you to do with us, Son of God? Have you come here to torment us before the time?" Now a large herd of swine was feeding at some distance from them. The demons begged him, "If you cast us out, send us into the herd of swine." And he said to them, "Go!" So they came out and entered the swine; and suddenly, the whole herd rushed down the steep bank into the lake and perished in the water. The swineherds ran off, and on going into the town, they told the whole story about what had happened to the demoniacs. Then the whole town came out to meet Jesus; and when they saw him, they begged him to leave their neighborhood.

Notice what you think and feel as you read the gospel.

Jesus casts demons out of two possessed people and sends the demons into a herd of swine, which rushes down into the lake and drowns. When the swineherds tell the news in town, they all come out to meet Jesus and beg him to leave.

Pray as you are led for yourself and others.

"Lord, people reject even the good you do. I will not reject you; I need you to work your mighty deeds of compassion among those you have given me. I think of . . ." (Continue in your own words.)

Listen to Jesus.

People cling to their familiar ways. They ignore or explain away the reality of God and the works of God. This is true even among those who say they believe, who do believe. So many have so little faith. Do you have faith in God? What else is Jesus saying to you?

Ask God to show you how to live today.

"I want to have and show my faith in you today, Lord. How can I do that? You will make it clear to me. Thank you. Amen."

Thursday, July 5, 2018

Know that God is present and ready to converse.

"I come into your presence, Lord, with hope. I know your holy Word will touch me in the way I need it."

Read the gospel: Matthew 9:1–8.

And after getting into a boat Jesus crossed the sea and came to his own town.

And just then some people were carrying a paralyzed man lying on a bed. When Jesus saw their faith, he said to the paralytic, "Take heart, son; your sins are forgiven." Then some of the scribes said to themselves, "This man is blaspheming." But Jesus, perceiving their thoughts, said, "Why do you think evil in your hearts? For which is easier, to say, 'Your sins are forgiven,' or to say, "Stand up and walk'? But so that you may know that the Son of Man has authority on earth to forgive sins"—he then said to the paralytic—"Stand up, take your bed and go to your home." And he stood up and went to his home. When the crowds saw it, they were filled with awe, and they glorified God, who had given such authority to human beings.

Notice what you think and feel as you read the gospel.

As God, Jesus has the power both to forgive and to heal. He makes that clear in this incident. Those watching him are awestruck, and they glorify God.

Pray as you are led for yourself and others.

"Lord, I come to you with requests for many things, but today I seek forgiveness first, not just for me but for all those you have given me . . ." (Continue in your own words.)

Listen to Jesus.

Your faith does good, even for those who do not believe in me themselves. Persist in believing for others' sake. I will have mercy, and I will heal them. That is what God sent me here to do. I give you my Spirit now. What else is Jesus saying to you?

Ask God to show you how to live today.

"I wish to walk in your spirit today, Lord, seeing things as you do, responding as you would. May I have that privilege? Amen."

Friday, July 6, 2018

Know that God is present and ready to converse.

"I need you, Lord, to call me again to your service. I am listening."

Read the gospel: Matthew 9:9–13.

As Jesus was walking along, he saw a man called Matthew sitting at the tax booth; and he said to him, "Follow me." And he got up and followed him.

And as he sat at dinner in the house, many tax collectors and sinners came and were sitting with him and his disciples. When the Pharisees saw this, they said to his disciples, "Why does your teacher eat with tax collectors and sinners?" But when he heard this, he said, "Those who are well have no need of a physician, but those who are sick. Go and learn what this means, 'I desire mercy, not sacrifice.' For I have come to call not the righteous but sinners."

Notice what you think and feel as you read the gospel.

Jesus calls Matthew, a loathed tax collector, to follow him, and he does so immediately. Jesus and his disciples sit at dinner in Matthew's house with many other tax collectors and sinners. Of course, the Pharisees criticize their association with sinners, but Jesus sets them straight by quoting scripture: "I desire mercy, not sacrifice." He came to call sinners.

Pray as you are led for yourself and others.

"I qualify as a sinner, Jesus. Thank you for calling me. Please extend your mercy to the people I pray for now . . ." (Continue in your own words.)

Listen to Jesus.

If God is merciful, who can refuse mercy to others? To follow me is to learn mercy, both to receive it and to give it. Do not withhold mercy even from those who do not ask for it. Mercy is not pity. It is humble and loving forgiveness. What else is Jesus saying to you?

Ask God to show you how to live today.

"By your grace, Savior, I will walk in mercy. I will see others with eyes of mercy and act accordingly. Amen."

Saturday, July 7, 2018

Know that God is present and ready to converse.

"Jesus, you are with me, and I rejoice."

Read the gospel: Matthew 9:14–17.

Then the disciples of John came to Jesus, saying, "Why do we and the Pharisees fast often, but your disciples do not fast?" And Jesus said to them, "The wedding guests cannot mourn as long as the bridegroom is with them, can they? The days will come when the bridegroom is taken away from them, and then they will fast. No one sews a piece of unshrunk cloth on an old cloak, for the patch pulls away from the cloak, and a worse tear is made. Neither is new wine put into old wineskins; otherwise, the skins burst, and the wine is spilled, and the skins are destroyed; but new wine is put into fresh wineskins, and so both are preserved."

Notice what you think and feel as you read the gospel.

Jesus responds to the question about his disciples not fasting by comparing himself to a bridegroom and them to wedding guests. This is a time of feasting, but when he is gone they will fast. But now is a time of something new, the coming of the Messiah, and old ways must give way to new ways.

Pray as you are led for yourself and others.

"Jesus, Bridegroom, renew my life and my love. Let all whom you have given me know the joy you bring . . ." (Continue in your own words.)

Listen to Jesus.

You may have joy, and you may have mourning, but even your mourning is joy when you have me. And you do have me, for I am here always and I will never abandon you, even if you seek to abandon me. I hold you in my hand. What else is Jesus saying to you?

Ask God to show you how to live today.

"Thank you for your faithfulness, Jesus. I will trust in you today and speak of your goodness to others. Amen."

Sunday, July 8, 2018
Fourteenth Sunday in Ordinary Time

Know that God is present and ready to converse.

"Lord, your mercy is new every morning. Let your Word be fresh air to my spirit."

Read the gospel: Mark 6:1–6.

Jesus left that place and came to his home town, and his disciples followed him. On the sabbath he began to teach in the synagogue, and many who heard him were astounded. They said, "Where did this man get all this? What is this wisdom that has been given to him? What deeds of power are being done by his hands! Is not this the carpenter, the son of Mary and brother of James and Joses and Judas and Simon, and are not his sisters here with us?" And they took offence at him. Then Jesus said to them, "Prophets are not without honor, except in their home town, and among their own kin, and in their own house." And he could do no deed of power there, except that he laid his hands on a few sick people and cured them. And he was amazed at their unbelief.

Then he went about among the villages teaching.

Notice what you think and feel as you read the gospel.

Familiar with Jesus, the people of his home town cannot accept him as a prophet. Jesus understands this, but he is amazed at their lack of faith. He leaves to visit other villages.

Pray as you are led for yourself and others.

"Lord, I pray for all those who are dry or stale in their faith, for those who know you from a distance, even as a mere memory . . ."

Listen to Jesus.

Many grow cold, for this world is full of darkness and fear. People fear even the light and love I bring them from my Father. Yet this is the age of grace, and many have turned to me and will continue to do so. Persevere to the end, beloved. What else is Jesus saying to you?

Ask God to show you how to live today.

"Today with your help, my Jesus, I will persevere in faith, hope, and love. Those gifts come only from you. Amen."

Monday, July 9, 2018

Know that God is present and ready to converse.

"Lord, your Word is full of stories, true stories of your earthly ministry. Teach me."

Read the gospel: Matthew 9:18–26.

While he was saying these things to them, suddenly a leader of the synagogue came in and knelt before him, saying, "My daughter has just died; but come and lay your hand on her, and she will live." And Jesus got up and followed him, with his disciples. Then suddenly a woman who had been suffering from hemorrhages for twelve years came up behind him and touched the fringe of his cloak, for she said to herself, "If I only touch his cloak, I will be made well." Jesus turned, and seeing her he said, "Take heart, daughter; your faith has made you well." And instantly the woman was made well. When Jesus came to the leader's house and saw the flute-players and the crowd making a commotion, he said, "Go away; for the girl is not dead but sleeping." And they laughed at him. But when the crowd had been put outside, he went in and took her by the hand, and the girl got up. And the report of this spread throughout that district.

Notice what you think and feel as you read the gospel.

No person ever did or claimed to do the things that Jesus did. He heals and he raises from the dead. He responds to faith in him and faith in God. His fame is still spreading.

Pray as you are led for yourself and others.

"I praise you for your Word, Lord. May it penetrate every district of the world. May many hearts be ignited with faith in you . . ." (Continue in your own words.)

Listen to Jesus.

I call my followers sons and daughters because I am a Father to you: Father, Mother, Spouse, Teacher, Master, and Friend. I am also your Savior, delivering you from sin, darkness, and death to give you the kingdom of everlasting life in the family of God. Enter into the joy of the Lord. What else is Jesus saying to you?

Ask God to show you how to live today.

"You are my beloved, Jesus. What I cherish most is you. You heal me and save me from death. How may I express my love for you today? Amen."

Tuesday, July 10, 2018

Know that God is present and ready to converse.

"Almighty God, your Spirit envelops the whole earth, the entire universe. I look to you now."

Read the gospel: Matthew 9:32–38.

After they had gone away, a demoniac who was mute was brought to Jesus. And when the demon had been cast out, the one who had been mute spoke; and the crowds were amazed and said, "Never has anything like this been seen in Israel." But the Pharisees said, "By the ruler of the demons he casts out the demons."

Then Jesus went about all the cities and villages, teaching in their synagogues, and proclaiming the good news of the kingdom, and curing every disease and every sickness. When he saw the crowds, he had compassion for them, because they were harassed and helpless, like sheep without a shepherd. Then he said to his disciples, "The harvest is plentiful, but the laborers are few; therefore ask the Lord of the harvest to send out laborers into his harvest."

Notice what you think and feel as you read the gospel.

Jesus amazes the crowds by restoring the voice of the mute, but the Pharisees call it the work of the devil. Yet Jesus persists in his healing and preaching ministry because he loves the people. He knows they need a shepherd, and when he is gone they will need others to gather them in to the Lord's harvest.

Pray as you are led for yourself and others.

"I ask you, Lord, to send out many laborers into your harvest, that no one may be lost. Raise up shepherds like yourself, Jesus, and gather all your sheep . . ." (Continue in your own words.)

Listen to Jesus.

Look for those who are harassed and helpless, my friend, and do for them what you can. Do not be discouraged by the multitudes of those who suffer on earth. I bless you with hope and the power to change things for good. In this way you will glorify God. What else is Jesus saying to you?

Ask God to show you how to live today.

"I will look for those in need, my Jesus, and do what I can. I will live in hope because you are with me. Amen."

Wednesday, July 11, 2018

Know that God is present and ready to converse.

"Lord, you are near me. Lead me into your kingdom by your Word."

Read the gospel: Matthew 10:1–7.

Then Jesus summoned his twelve disciples and gave them authority over unclean spirits, to cast them out, and to cure every disease and every sickness. These are the names of the twelve apostles: first, Simon, also known as Peter, and his brother Andrew; James son of Zebedee, and his brother John; Philip and Bartholomew; Thomas and Matthew the tax collector; James son of Alphaeus, and Thaddaeus; Simon the Cananaean, and Judas Iscariot, the one who betrayed him.

These twelve Jesus sent out with the following instructions: "Go nowhere among the Gentiles, and enter no town of the Samaritans, but go rather to the lost sheep of the house of Israel. As you go, proclaim the good news, 'The kingdom of heaven has come near.'"

Notice what you think and feel as you read the gospel.

Jesus commissions his twelve disciples to do the work of his ministry with power and authority like his own. As they perform good works of healing, he instructs them to proclaim the good news that the kingdom of heaven has come near.

Pray as you are led for yourself and others.

"I am very small, Master, but I am ready to obey your call. Send me . . ." (Continue in your own words.)

Listen to Jesus.

I love you, dear disciple, and I do send you. I send you among your own people and among the lost sheep. Hold the hope of the kingdom in your heart as you go. Do not be concerned how your words and your works are received. They will bear fruit in their own good time. What else is Jesus saying to you?

Ask God to show you how to live today.

"If you go with me, Lord, I will have the courage to go out and serve. You will teach me what I need to know. Amen."

Thursday, July 12, 2018

Know that God is present and ready to converse.

"Teacher, your Word is Truth. Let me receive it with my whole being."

Read the gospel: Matthew 10:7–15.

Jesus said to the twelve, "As you go, proclaim the good news, 'The kingdom of heaven has come near.' Cure the sick, raise the dead, cleanse the lepers, cast out demons. You received without payment; give without payment. Take no gold, or silver, or copper in your belts, no bag for your journey, or two tunics, or sandals, or a staff; for laborers deserve their food. Whatever town or village you enter, find out who in it is worthy, and stay there until you leave. As you enter the house, greet it. If the house is worthy, let your peace come upon it; but if it is not worthy, let your peace return to you. If anyone will not welcome you or listen to your words, shake off the dust from your feet as you leave that house or town. Truly I tell you, it will be more tolerable for the land of Sodom and Gomorrah on the day of judgement than for that town."

Notice what you think and feel as you read the gospel.

Jesus speaks to his disciples about carrying on his work, proclaiming the Gospel, and doing every kind of good work among those who suffer. They are to give as they have received, freely and without concern for themselves. Some will welcome them and some will not.

Pray as you are led for yourself and others.

"Lord, I pray for all your laborers on the journey. I think of . . ." (Continue in your own words.)

Listen to Jesus.

My work must continue because the mercy of God still blankets the earth. You may be a part of my work. What else is Jesus saying to you?

Ask God to show you how to live today.

"I offer myself to your service, my Lord and Master. Make me worthy to serve those you love. Amen."

Friday, July 13, 2018

Know that God is present and ready to converse.

"Great is your faithfulness, dear Lord. Teach me faithfulness by your Word."

Read the gospel: Matthew 10:16–23.

Jesus said to the twelve, "See, I am sending you out like sheep into the midst of wolves; so be wise as serpents and innocent as doves. Beware of them, for they will hand you over to councils and flog you in their synagogues; and you will be dragged before governors and kings because of me, as a testimony to them and the Gentiles. When they hand you over, do not worry about how you are to speak or what you are to say; for what you are to say will be given to you at that time; for it is not you who speak, but the Spirit of your Father speaking through you. Brother will betray brother to death, and a father his child, and children will rise against parents and have them put to death; and you will be hated by all because of my name. But the one who endures to the end will be saved. When they persecute you in one town, flee to the next; for truly I tell you, you will not have gone through all the towns of Israel before the Son of Man comes."

Notice what you think and feel as you read the gospel.

Jesus speaks to his disciples about the dangers and suffering involved in serving him. They will face peril, betrayal, and hatred because of him. But they will receive the Spirit to speak the truth and persevere to the end. The ones who endure to the end will be saved.

Pray as you are led for yourself and others.

"I have known suffering, Jesus. I pray now for grace to endure to the end, serving as you will . . ." (Continue in your own words.)

Listen to Jesus.

The world appears to be a chaotic crowd of people, and so it is. But these crowds are composed of individuals I love. Some return my love, but many do not know me yet. Tell them about me, person by person, and my grace will do the rest. What else is Jesus saying to you?

Ask God to show you how to live today.

"I will focus on individuals today, Lord. Give me an opportunity to speak of you. Thank you. Amen."

Saturday, July 14, 2018

Know that God is present and ready to converse.

"Father, Son, and Holy Spirit, you are one Lord. I seek you in your Word."

Read the gospel: Matthew 10:24–33.

Jesus said, "A disciple is not above the teacher, nor a slave above the master; it is enough for the disciple to be like the teacher, and the slave like the master. If they have called the master of the house Beelzebul, how much more will they malign those of his household!

"So have no fear of them; for nothing is covered up that will not be uncovered, and nothing secret that will not become known. What I say to you in the dark, tell in the light; and what you hear whispered, proclaim from the housetops. Do not fear those who kill the body but cannot kill the soul; rather fear him who can destroy both soul and body in hell. Are not two sparrows sold for a penny? Yet not one of them will fall to the ground unperceived by your Father. And even the hairs of your head are all counted. So do not be afraid; you are of more value than many sparrows.

"Everyone therefore who acknowledges me before others, I also will acknowledge before my Father in heaven; but whoever denies me before others, I also will deny before my Father in heaven."

Notice what you think and feel as you read the gospel.

As Jesus speaks of the suffering his followers will encounter in the world, he emphasizes that they should not be fearful. They might be killed in body but not in soul. God values them infinitely, and Jesus will acknowledge to his Father in heaven those who acknowledge him.

Pray as you are led for yourself and others.

"Forgive the times I have denied you, Lord, either by my words or by my silence. I pray for all those who are afraid to acknowledge you . . ." (Continue in your own words.)

Listen to Jesus.

The Spirit of God brings light to the inner person. Love overcomes all fear. This light and this love are signs of the kingdom of God in its everlasting truth. Do not be afraid of it. You may enter. What else is Jesus saying to you?

Ask God to show you how to live today.

"Transform me by your truth today, that I may serve you and others without fear. Amen."

Sunday, July 15, 2018
Fifteenth Sunday in Ordinary Time

Know that God is present and ready to converse.

"Lord, let my prayer be pleasing to you, and be with me in my comings and goings all day."

Read the gospel: Mark 6:7–13.

Jesus called the twelve and began to send them out two by two, and gave them authority over the unclean spirits. He ordered them to take nothing for their journey except a staff; no bread, no bag, no money in their belts; but to wear sandals and not to put on two tunics. He said to them, "Wherever you enter a house, stay there until you leave the place. If any place will not welcome you and they refuse to hear you, as you leave, shake off the dust that is on your feet as a testimony against them." So they went out and proclaimed that all should repent. They cast out many demons, and anointed with oil many who were sick and cured them.

Notice what you think and feel as you read the gospel.

Jesus sends out the twelve with power and authority but nothing for themselves. They are to preach repentance, cast out demons, and heal the sick. If people will not hear them, they are to leave.

Pray as you are led for yourself and others.

"Lord, give me wisdom to know when to come and go, when to speak and when to be silent, as I seek to bear your good news to others . . ." (Continue in your own words.)

Listen to Jesus.

Beloved disciple, be in this world just as you are, for you are the person I love. When you speak about me, begin with yourself, for that is all you know. What else is Jesus saying to you?

Ask God to show you how to live today.

"Let me be who I am today, dear Jesus, nothing more and nothing less than who you made me. With your help I will speak the truth, yours and mine, in words and in action, to all I encounter. Amen."

Monday, July 16, 2018

Know that God is present and ready to converse.

"Lord, I am glad you are here to instruct me by your Word. Help me to receive what you will."

Read the gospel: Matthew 10:34–11:1.

Jesus said, "Do not think that I have come to bring peace to the earth; I have not come to bring peace, but a sword.

> For I have come to set a man against his father,
> and a daughter against her mother,
> and a daughter-in-law against her mother-in-law;
> and one's foes will be members of one's own household.

Whoever loves father or mother more than me is not worthy of me; and whoever loves son or daughter more than me is not worthy of me; and whoever does not take up the cross and follow me is not worthy of me. Those who find their life will lose it, and those who lose their life for my sake will find it.

"Whoever welcomes you welcomes me, and whoever welcomes me welcomes the one who sent me. Whoever welcomes a prophet in the name of a prophet will receive a prophet's reward; and whoever welcomes a righteous person in the name of a righteous person will receive the reward of the righteous; and whoever gives even a cup of cold water to one of these little ones in the name of a disciple—truly I tell you, none of these will lose their reward."

Now when Jesus had finished instructing his twelve disciples, he went on from there to teach and proclaim his message in their cities.

Notice what you think and feel as you read the gospel.

Jesus reminds his disciples that they must love him first and make him the priority in their interaction with others, even over their own family members. He knows his message will cause dissension and even wars. He says righteousness will be rewarded.

Pray as you are led for yourself and others.

"Lord, the world is at war. I do not understand it. All I can do is ask you to work your will in history and in my own family . . ." (Continue in your own words.)

Listen to Jesus.

The things that trouble you, dear one, give them to me, for I am the Lord, the Savior of the world, and I am fulfilling my purposes despite the warring and unrighteousness of nations and people. Do good with your life and trust me with everything else. What else is Jesus saying to you?

Ask God to show you how to live today.

"Lord, I give you my troubles, for you are the Almighty One, the only hope for peace. Let me be a peacemaker today. Amen."

Tuesday, July 17, 2018

Know that God is present and ready to converse.

"Lord, you are the judge of the whole world. You know everything. I trust in your mercy."

Read the gospel: Matthew 11:20–24.

Then Jesus began to reproach the cities in which most of his deeds of power had been done, because they did not repent. "Woe to you, Chorazin! Woe to you, Bethsaida! For if the deeds of power done in you had been done in Tyre and Sidon, they would have repented long ago in sackcloth and ashes. But I tell you, on the day of judgement it will be more tolerable for Tyre and Sidon than for you. And you, Capernaum, will you be exalted to heaven? No, you will be brought down to Hades. For if the deeds of power done in you had been done in Sodom, it would have remained until this day. But I tell you that on the day of judgement it will be more tolerable for the land of Sodom than for you."

Notice what you think and feel as you read the gospel.

Jesus reproaches the cities he has visited that have not repented. He prophesies that because they did not receive him as Messiah and Savior, these cities will be destroyed, for they had a greater opportunity to repent than Tyre, Sidon, and Sodom—notoriously wicked cities of the Old Testament.

Pray as you are led for yourself and others.

"Lord, the world is in flames because of human evil. Let me in no way be a part of that evil. Instead let me be peaceful and true, helping others when I can . . ." (Continue in your own words.)

Listen to Jesus.

I look with clear eyes upon the righteous and unrighteous of this world. Nothing escapes me. Yet I let the good be good and the evil be evil until the end. Then comes the judgment, when nothing shall be forgotten or passed over. As for you, fly to my mercy and endeavor to do good every day. What else is Jesus saying to you?

Ask God to show you how to live today.

"Lord, help me to walk today in godly fear, for much is at stake. I am a living actor in the story of your divine love. You are my Lord and Master, my shepherd and my shield. Amen."

Wednesday, July 18, 2018

Know that God is present and ready to converse.

"Jesus, I come to your Word to know God and learn to please God. Give me understanding as I read."

Read the gospel: Matthew 11:25–27.

At that time Jesus said, "I thank you, Father, Lord of heaven and earth, because you have hidden these things from the wise and the intelligent and have revealed them to infants; yes, Father, for such was your gracious will. All things have been handed over to me by my Father; and no one knows the Son except the Father, and no one knows the Father except the Son and anyone to whom the Son chooses to reveal him."

Notice what you think and feel as you read the gospel.

Jesus thanks his Father that he hides his truth from the wise and intelligent and reveals it to infants. No one knows his Father except him and those to whom he chooses to reveal the Father.

Pray as you are led for yourself and others.

"Jesus, the knowledge I seek depends on you. Let me know and love you and our Father. Let the wise and intelligent realize that relationship with you is the beginning of true knowledge . . ." (Continue in your own words.)

Listen to Jesus.

My Father has given me all authority and all power. As I have from the beginning, I am still seeking souls to follow me in my way. It is a hard and narrow way. It is a joyful way to life. Beloved, as you follow me, rejoice that I have chosen you. What else is Jesus saying to you?

Ask God to show you how to live today.

"Lord, let me be an infant as I follow you today, for I long to know God and love God and please God in all I do, today and always. Amen."

Thursday, July 19, 2018

Know that God is present and ready to converse.

"Praise to you, almighty God, for you are the creator and master of the universe, and yet you are here for me today. I open my heart to you."

Read the gospel: Matthew 11:28–30.

Jesus said, "Come to me, all you that are weary and are carrying heavy burdens, and I will give you rest. Take my yoke upon you, and learn from me; for I am gentle and humble in heart, and you will find rest for your souls. For my yoke is easy, and my burden is light."

Notice what you think and feel as you read the gospel.

Jesus invites his hearers to come to him, knowing they are weary and carrying heavy burdens. If they take his yoke and learn from him, they will find rest. He is gentle and humble in heart.

Pray as you are led for yourself and others.

"Jesus, I want my heart to be like yours, gentle and humble at all times. I take your yoke upon me now, this moment. Lead me . . ." (Continue in your own words.)

Listen to Jesus.

I speak much of the heart, for it is the origin of all that is good and all that is evil in a person. My heart is pure, so I offer it to you. When you ask, I give you a new heart, peaceful and loving and strong to serve. What else is Jesus saying to you?

Ask God to show you how to live today.

"Lord, I do ask for your heart, that I may see and love others and serve them as you do. Amen."

Friday, July 20, 2018

Know that God is present and ready to converse.

"Jesus, come what may, I am resolved to follow you. That is why I am here with you now. Teach me."

Read the gospel: Matthew 12:1–8.

At that time Jesus went through the cornfields on the sabbath; his disciples were hungry, and they began to pluck heads of grain and to eat. When the Pharisees saw it, they said to him, "Look, your disciples are doing what is not lawful to do on the sabbath." He said to them, "Have you not read what David did when he and his companions were hungry? He entered the house of God and ate the bread of the Presence, which it was not lawful for him or his companions to eat, but only for the priests. Or have you not read in the law that on the sabbath the priests in the temple break the sabbath and yet are guiltless? I tell you, something greater than the temple is here. But if you had known what this means, 'I desire mercy and not sacrifice,' you would not have condemned the guiltless. For the Son of Man is lord of the sabbath."

Notice what you think and feel as you read the gospel.

Jesus defends his disciples and himself by asserting his rule over all. The Pharisees say they are breaking the Sabbath by eating grain from the fields. Jesus quotes scripture to liberate them from man-made religiosity and show them the spiritual side of religion: God desires mercy, not sacrifice.

Pray as you are led for yourself and others.

"Lord, let me have a heart of mercy and not be bound by hollow laws. Let me not judge others in their own practices. I think of . . ." (Continue in your own words.)

Listen to Jesus.

Those who walk with me are free. Those who love me are the children of God. You need not fear the opinions of others. Nothing shall harm you, for you are mine. What else is Jesus saying to you?

Ask God to show you how to live today.

"I seek to walk with you, know you, and love you, Jesus. That is enough for me. Amen."

Saturday, July 21, 2018

Know that God is present and ready to converse.

"I come to you now seeking hope and strength for my life. I will hear you now."

Read the gospel: Matthew 12:14–21.

When Jesus became aware of this, he departed. Many crowds followed him, and he cured all of them, and he ordered them not to make him known. This was to fulfill what had been spoken through the prophet Isaiah:

> "Here is my servant, whom I have chosen,
> my beloved, with whom my soul is well pleased.
> I will put my Spirit upon him,
> and he will proclaim justice to the Gentiles.
> He will not wrangle or cry aloud,
> nor will anyone hear his voice in the streets.
> He will not break a bruised reed
> or quench a smoldering wick
> until he brings justice to victory.
> And in his name the Gentiles will hope."

Notice what you think and feel as you read the gospel.

Jesus does his healings as quietly as he can. He doesn't need to draw attention to himself, because he is the beloved Son of the Father, serving in the Spirit of God. In his quiet way he will bring justice to victory. He is the hope of all peoples.

Pray as you are led for yourself and others.

"Lord, come to me in your quietness and let us love one another. I pray for all those who lack hope . . ." (Continue in your own words.)

Listen to Jesus.

I am with you, dear disciple, and I love you. I understand you and all those I have given you to love and pray for. Love and prayer are very quiet, aren't they? But they bring victory. Rely on it. Follow me. What else is Jesus saying to you?

Ask God to show you how to live today.

"Teach me to be quiet today, dear Jesus; help me to look for your justice, hope for your victory over suffering and evil, and pray for those in need. Amen."

Sunday, July 22, 2018
Sixteenth Sunday in Ordinary Time

Know that God is present and ready to converse.

"Be with me, Lord, in my work and in my rest. Thank you for being here now."

Read the gospel: Mark 6:30–34.

The apostles gathered around Jesus, and told him all that they had done and taught. He said to them, "Come away to a deserted place all by yourselves and rest a while." For many were coming and going, and they had no leisure even to eat. And they went away in the boat to a deserted place by themselves. Now many saw them going and recognized them, and they hurried there on foot from all the towns and arrived ahead of them. As he went ashore, he saw a great crowd; and he had compassion for them, because they were like sheep without a shepherd; and he began to teach them many things.

Notice what you think and feel as you read the gospel.

After they return from the mission Jesus sent them on, the apostles need to get away from the crowds and rest a while. Yet seeing the great crowd gathering, Jesus has compassion on the people and begins to teach them.

Pray as you are led for yourself and others.

"Lord, give me energy to work, and peace to rest in your service. I pray now for all those who have no shepherd . . ." (Continue in your own words.)

Listen to Jesus.

You can do only what you can do. Try to do it with compassion, because people respond to genuine love. And the love of God is your only message. Speak your heart and move on in peace. What else is Jesus saying to you?

Ask God to show you how to live today.

"Thank you for your peace, Lord Jesus. It gives me strength. I offer my whole self to you and to your people today. Amen."

Monday, July 23, 2018

Know that God is present and ready to converse.

"Risen Lord, you promised to be with me always, and here you are. I rejoice."

Read the gospel: Matthew 12:38–42.

Then some of the scribes and Pharisees said to Jesus, "Teacher, we wish to see a sign from you." But he answered them, "An evil and adulterous generation asks for a sign, but no sign will be given to it except the sign of the prophet Jonah. For just as Jonah was for three days and three nights in the belly of the sea monster, so for three days and three nights the Son of Man will be in the heart of the earth. The people of Nineveh will rise up at the judgement with this generation and condemn it, because they repented at the proclamation of Jonah, and see, something greater than Jonah is here! The queen of the South will rise up at the judgement with this generation and condemn it, because she came from the ends of the earth to listen to the wisdom of Solomon, and see, something greater than Solomon is here!"

Notice what you think and feel as you read the gospel.

Jesus disapproves of those who ask for a sign from him, yet he does prophesy the great sign of his Passion, Death, and Resurrection, calling it the sign of Jonah. But he is so much greater than Jonah or Solomon, for he is the very Son of God. Instead of seeking a sign, these scribes and Pharisees should repent.

Pray as you are led for yourself and others.

"I have faith that you work in my life, Lord, for I have received many blessings. I pray for those in need, and I think especially of these . . ." (Continue in your own words.)

Listen to Jesus.

I do work in your life, my beloved, my friend, and you can see it with eyes of faith. It pleases me when you rely on faith in me. It allows me to guide you to make the best decisions for yourself and for those who depend on you. Trust me to be always here for you. What else is Jesus saying to you?

Ask God to show you how to live today.

"Guide me today, Jesus, through the tangled way, and let me think, speak, and act in ways that glorify you and help others. Amen."

Tuesday, July 24, 2018

Know that God is present and ready to converse.

"I come before you, Lord, and I seek to do your will."

Read the gospel: Matthew 12:46–50.

While Jesus was still speaking to the crowds, his mother and his brothers were standing outside, wanting to speak to him. Someone told him, "Look, your mother and your brothers are standing outside, wanting to speak to you." But to the one who had told him this, Jesus replied, "Who is my mother, and who are my brothers?" And pointing to his disciples, he said, "Here are my mother and my brothers! For whoever does the will of my Father in heaven is my brother and sister and mother."

Notice what you think and feel as you read the gospel.

Jesus opens his family to all who do the will of his Father in heaven. They are his true mothers and brothers.

Pray as you are led for yourself and others.

"I thank you for including me in your holy family, Jesus. Help me be worthy of you. Help others learn to do your Father's will . . ." (Continue in your own words.)

Listen to Jesus.

If your heart and mind want to do my God's will, you shall. Be led by the Holy Spirit in love, peace, joy, faithfulness, perseverance, and hope. You will be blessed and bless others. This is my will for you, child. What else is Jesus saying to you?

Ask God to show you how to live today.

"I will set my heart and mind on these things, Friend, Brother, Savior. Lead me. Amen."

Wednesday, July 25, 2018
Saint James, Apostle

Know that God is present and ready to converse.

"Lord, I come before you with a small and often selfish heart. Transform me by your Word."

Read the gospel: Matthew 20:20–28.

Then the mother of the sons of Zebedee came to Jesus with her sons, and kneeling before him, she asked a favor of him. And he said to her, "What do you want?" She said to him, "Declare that these two sons of mine will sit, one at your right hand and one at your left, in your kingdom." But Jesus answered, "You do not know what you are asking. Are you able to drink the cup that I am about to drink?" They said to him, "We are able." He said to them, "You will indeed drink my cup, but to sit at my right hand and at my left, this is not mine to grant, but it is for those for whom it has been prepared by my Father."

When the ten heard it, they were angry with the two brothers. But Jesus called them to him and said, "You know that the rulers of the Gentiles lord it over them, and their great ones are tyrants over them. It will not be so among you; but whoever wishes to be great among you must be your servant, and whoever wishes to be first among you must be your slave; just as the Son of Man came not to be served but to serve, and to give his life a ransom for many."

Notice what you think and feel as you read the gospel.

The mother of James and John, the sons of Zebedee, asks Jesus to give them preferential treatment. Without anger or disapproval, he turns her question into an occasion for teaching. He asks the sons of Zebedee if they can drink the cup of suffering he is about to drink. They may not understand that, but they say they can—and Jesus agrees. Then he explains to all the disciples that the great among them must be servants.

Pray as you are led for yourself and others.

"Lord, forgive my wishes to be first and great. I give myself now to humble service, imitating you. I pray that all who serve you may serve in humility . . ." (Continue in your own words.)

Listen to Jesus.

You may aspire to greatness, beloved, but let it be for me and for others, not for yourself. Pray often for pure motives, and you will learn to walk humbly in my ways. What else is Jesus saying to you?

Ask God to show you how to live today.

"Teach me how to discern my own motives, Lord, and cleanse them that I may be pleasing to you. Thank you. Amen."

Thursday, July 26, 2018

Know that God is present and ready to converse.

"Jesus, open my eyes to your Word, that through it I may understand and love you better."

Read the gospel: Matthew 13:10–17.

Then the disciples came and asked Jesus, "Why do you speak to them in parables?" He answered, "To you it has been given to know the secrets of the kingdom of heaven, but to them it has not been given. For to those who have, more will be given, and they will have an abundance; but from those who have nothing, even what they have will be taken away. The reason I speak to them in parables is that 'seeing they do not perceive, and hearing they do not listen, nor do they understand.' With them indeed is fulfilled the prophecy of Isaiah that says:

'You will indeed listen, but never understand,
  and you will indeed look, but never perceive.
For this people's heart has grown dull,
  and their ears are hard of hearing,
    and they have shut their eyes;
    so that they might not look with their eyes,
  and listen with their ears,
and understand with their heart and turn—
  and I would heal them.'

But blessed are your eyes, for they see, and your ears, for they hear. Truly I tell you, many prophets and righteous people longed to see what you see, but did not see it, and to hear what you hear, but did not hear it."

Notice what you think and feel as you read the gospel.

The disciples ask Jesus why he speaks to the people in parables and riddles. His answer is difficult, for it seems counter to God's purposes.

He quotes from Isaiah a long passage criticizing those who do not turn to God because of their dull hearts. Those whose hearts are dull toward God cannot understand his Word and cannot come to him. But Jesus' disciples are blessed to know him.

Pray as you are led for yourself and others.

"Lord, remove all dullness from my heart that I may truly know, understand, and obey you. I pray now for all those whose hearts are dull toward God and your Word. Let them yearn for you . . ." (Continue in your own words.)

Listen to Jesus.

I do desire that all may turn to God with all their hearts. I will receive them and grant them eternal life. But I do not force them. They must be willing. What else is Jesus saying to you?

Ask God to show you how to live today.

"Lord, I turn my eyes to seek you, I strain my ears to hear you. Heal my blindness and deafness, that I may know and share your abundant blessing. Amen."

Friday, July 27, 2018

Know that God is present and ready to converse.

"Jesus, there are many hindrances to understanding your Word. Help me avoid them, for I long to know and serve you."

Read the gospel: Matthew 13:18–23.

Jesus said, "Hear then the parable of the sower. When anyone hears the word of the kingdom and does not understand it, the evil one comes and snatches away what is sown in the heart; this is what was sown on the path. As for what was sown on rocky ground, this is the one who hears the word and immediately receives it with joy; yet such a person has no root, but endures only for a while, and when trouble or persecution arises on account of the word, that person immediately falls away. As for what was sown among thorns, this is the one who hears the word, but the cares of the world and the lure of wealth choke the word, and it yields nothing. But as for what was sown on good soil, this is the one who hears the word and understands it, who indeed bears fruit and yields, in one case a hundredfold, in another sixty, and in another thirty."

Notice what you think and feel as you read the gospel.

In the parable of the sower, Jesus speaks of all the ways that the word of the kingdom fails to take root in a person, including evil, trouble, persecution, worry, and greed. The word takes root only in good soil, and then it bears much fruit.

Pray as you are led for yourself and others.

"Lord, let my heart be that good soil, that I may understand your word deeply and bear fruit to God's glory. I pray for those who struggle with understanding your words. Prepare their hearts to receive you . . ." (Continue in your own words.)

Listen to Jesus.

I have spoken plainly, and my deeds have spoken as well. Some people do not want to hear me and receive me because they do not want to change. They are deceived about what makes them happy. When they need me, they come, and I heal and save them and make them my own. Pray for the deceived. What else is Jesus saying to you?

Ask God to show you how to live today.

"May all souls turn to the light of your truth, Lord. Let me grow in your light today, knowing you are with me. Amen."

Saturday, July 28, 2018

Know that God is present and ready to converse.

"You are my way, my truth, and my life, Jesus Christ. I will hear you now."

Read the gospel: Matthew 13:24–30.

Jesus put before them another parable: "The kingdom of heaven may be compared to someone who sowed good seed in his field; but while everybody was asleep, an enemy came and sowed weeds among the wheat, and then went away. So when the plants came up and bore grain, then the weeds appeared as well. And the slaves of the householder came and said to him, 'Master, did you not sow good seed in your field? Where, then, did these weeds come from?' He answered, 'An enemy has done this.' The slaves said to him, 'Then do you want us to go and gather them?' But he replied, 'No; for in gathering the weeds you would uproot the wheat along with them. Let both of them grow together until the harvest; and at harvest time I will tell the reapers, Collect the weeds first and bind them in bundles to be burned, but gather the wheat into my barn.'"

Notice what you think and feel as you read the gospel.

Jesus' parable about the wheat and the weeds makes it plain that those God calls to the kingdom will grow like wheat, but they will grow among weeds sown by the enemy. At the harvest the weeds will be collected, bundled, and burned, but the wheat will be gathered into the barn. For a time God allows evil, but in the end comes judgment.

Pray as you are led for yourself and others.

"Lord, as I grow let me not be dismayed by the weeds around me. Let me trust in you without judging others. I pray for those who do not yet trust in you . . ." (Continue in your own words.)

Listen to Jesus.

You can live without fear, dear disciple, because you trust in me. You have come in under the mercy of God. Stay close to me and share my blessings with others. What else is Jesus saying to you?

Ask God to show you how to live today.

"I will share your blessings, Lord. Let me find many ways today to do so. Amen."

Sunday, July 29, 2018
Seventeenth Sunday in Ordinary Time

Know that God is present and ready to converse.

"Bread of heaven, feed me by your Word."

Read the gospel: John 6:1–15.

After this Jesus went to the other side of the Sea of Galilee, also called the Sea of Tiberias. A large crowd kept following him, because they saw the signs that he was doing for the sick. Jesus went up the mountain and sat down there with his disciples. Now the Passover, the festival of the Jews, was near. When he looked up and saw a large crowd coming towards him, Jesus said to Philip, "Where are we to buy bread for these people to eat?" He said this to test him, for he himself knew what he was going to do. Philip answered him, "Six months' wages would not buy enough bread for each of them to get a little." One of his disciples, Andrew, Simon Peter's brother, said to him, "There is a boy here who has five barley loaves and two fish. But what are they among so many people?" Jesus said, "Make the people sit down." Now there was a great deal of grass in the place; so they sat down, about five thousand in all. Then Jesus took the loaves, and when he had given thanks, he distributed them to those who were seated; so also the fish, as much as they wanted. When they were satisfied, he told his disciples, "Gather up the fragments left over, so that nothing may be lost." So they gathered them up, and from the fragments of the five barley loaves, left by those who had eaten, they filled twelve baskets. When the people saw the sign that he had done, they began to say, "This is indeed the prophet who is to come into the world."

When Jesus realized that they were about to come and take him by force to make him king, he withdrew again to the mountain by himself.

Notice what you think and feel as you read the gospel.

Jesus feeds five thousand people with five barley loaves and two fish, with twelve baskets left over. The people recognize him as the promised Messiah, and they want to make him king. Jesus withdraws.

Pray as you are led for yourself and others.

"Lord, let me learn to trust in you to meet all the needs in my life and in the lives of those you have given me . . ." (Continue in your own words.)

Listen to Jesus.

To strengthen your faith, I subject you to tests as I do with all my disciples. You will face troubles and have needs and fears. These are the times to come to me and ask me for help. I will do it. Remember these times and let your trust in me grow. What else is Jesus saying to you?

Ask God to show you how to live today.

"Let me face my troubles, needs, and fears with confidence in you. I praise you now for your constant love and kindness. Amen."

Monday, July 30, 2018

Know that God is present and ready to converse.

"What do you want to teach me today, Lord? Open my mind and heart to your Word."

Read the gospel: Matthew 13:31–35.

He put before them another parable, "The kingdom of heaven is like a mustard seed that someone took and sowed in his field; it is the smallest of all the seeds, but when it has grown it is the greatest of shrubs and becomes a tree, so that the birds of the air come and make nests in its branches."

He told them another parable: "The kingdom of heaven is like yeast that a woman took and mixed in with three measures of flour until all of it was leavened."

Jesus told the crowds all these things in parables; without a parable he told them nothing. This was to fulfill what had been spoken through the prophet:

> "I will open my mouth to speak in parables;
> I will proclaim what has been hidden from the foundation of the world."

Notice what you think and feel as you read the gospel.

Jesus compares the kingdom of God to things that grow large. He proclaims truth hidden from the foundation of the world. The kingdom of heaven is growing in numbers and the kingdom of heaven enlarges within a believer.

Pray as you are led for yourself and others.

"Grow in me, dear Jesus, and draw many, many into your everlasting kingdom. I pray for those who have walked away from you . . ." (Continue in your own words.)

Listen to Jesus.

You hear and understand, dear disciple. It is my work that you grow in holiness, faith, hope, and love. These are my gifts to you. Others will see that you are mine. What else is Jesus saying to you?

Ask God to show you how to live today.

"Thank you, Redeemer, for your care for me and for many. Let me always honor you and never dishonor your name. Amen."

Tuesday, July 31, 2018

Know that God is present and ready to converse.

"Lord, I open my ears to listen to your holy Word. Speak to me."

Read the gospel: Matthew 13:36–43.

Then he left the crowds and went into the house. And his disciples approached him, saying, "Explain to us the parable of the weeds of the field." He answered, "The one who sows the good seed is the Son of Man; the field is the world, and the good seed are the children of the kingdom; the weeds are the children of the evil one, and the enemy who sowed them is the devil; the harvest is the end of the age, and the reapers are angels. Just as the weeds are collected and burned up with fire, so will it be at the end of the age. The Son of Man will send his angels, and they will collect out of his kingdom all causes of sin and all evildoers, and they will throw them into the furnace of fire, where there will be weeping and gnashing of teeth. Then the righteous will shine like the sun in the kingdom of their Father. Let anyone with ears listen!"

Notice what you think and feel as you read the gospel.

Jesus explains the parable of the wheat and weeds. The good seed are the children of the kingdom; the weeds are of the evil one. At the end of the age all will be gathered and receive justice—for the weeds, destruction, and for the righteous, the kingdom of their Father. Jesus wants people to hear this and take it to heart.

Pray as you are led for yourself and others.

"I do take your words to heart. I long for final justice because I know of your mercy and your wisdom, Lord. Let your kingdom come! . . ." (Continue in your own words.)

Listen to Jesus.

Many refuse to understand that judgment is coming at the end of this age. Many rush into sin without fear of God's judgment or punishment. Indeed, they choose punishment for themselves. I wait for them to choose me. What else is Jesus saying to you?

Ask God to show you how to live today.

"Lord, it is frightening to contemplate the final judgment. I seek to turn away from sin, and I pray that others do also, so that we may all shine like the sun in your everlasting kingdom. Amen."

Wednesday, August 1, 2018

Know that God is present and ready to converse.

"Lord God in heaven, you are a precious gift to me. Help me respond to your love with all my heart."

Read the gospel: Matthew 13:44–46.

Jesus said, "The kingdom of heaven is like treasure hidden in a field, which someone found and hid; then in his joy he goes and sells all that he has and buys that field.

"Again, the kingdom of heaven is like a merchant in search of fine pearls; on finding one pearl of great value, he went and sold all that he had and bought it."

Notice what you think and feel as you read the gospel.

Jesus uses a couple of economic metaphors to illustrate the value of the kingdom of God. When you find treasure, you'll sell everything you have to acquire that treasure. To acquire the kingdom of heaven is worth selling all you have. Nothing else matters in the end.

Pray as you are led for yourself and others.

"Lord, make me willing to sell or abandon all that I have, all that I am, to enter the kingdom of heaven. I pray that all those you have given me will value your gift of the kingdom . . ." (Continue in your own words.)

Listen to Jesus.

You have chosen well, dearly beloved. It grieves me that some do not choose to receive the gift of the kingdom, that some remain closed to faith, repentance, sacrifice, and change. How will they come to realize that the love of God is the only thing that matters? What else is Jesus saying to you?

Ask God to show you how to live today.

"Lord, I pray for those you speak of. Is there anything I can do? Amen."

Thursday, August 2, 2018

Know that God is present and ready to converse.

"Jesus, you speak in parables. Give me understanding of your Word. Give me what you want me to have as I read and pray."

Read the gospel: Matthew 13:47–53.

Jesus said, "Again, the kingdom of heaven is like a net that was thrown into the sea and caught fish of every kind; when it was full, they drew it ashore, sat down, and put the good into baskets but threw out the bad. So it will be at the end of the age. The angels will come out and separate the evil from the righteous and throw them into the furnace of fire, where there will be weeping and gnashing of teeth.

"Have you understood all this?" They answered, "Yes." And he said to them, "Therefore every scribe who has been trained for the kingdom of heaven is like the master of a household who brings out of his treasure what is new and what is old." When Jesus had finished these parables, he left that place.

Notice what you think and feel as you read the gospel.

The kingdom is a net full of things good and bad which the angels will sort at the end of the age. Evil will be thrown into a furnace. The kingdom is made up of treasure, both old and new.

Pray as you are led for yourself and others.

"Thank you for the treasure, old and new, Lord. I wish to share it with those you have given me . . ." (Continue in your own words.)

Listen to Jesus.

There is great treasure in my Word. Reading and praying with the scripture gives you strength and wisdom because you are drawing close to me. As you know and love the Word of God, you know and love me. I love you, too. What else is Jesus saying to you?

Ask God to show you how to live today.

"Train me for the kingdom, Lord; teach me how to share with others the treasure you've shared with me. Amen."

Friday, August 3, 2018

Know that God is present and ready to converse.

"Jesus, you lived thousands of years ago, thousands of miles away, yet you are here with me now. I draw near."

Read the gospel: Matthew 13:54–58.

He came to his home town and began to teach the people in their synagogue, so that they were astounded and said, "Where did this man get this wisdom and these deeds of power? Is not this the carpenter's son? Is not his mother called Mary? And are not his brothers James and Joseph and Simon and Judas? And are not all his sisters with us? Where then did this man get all this?" And they took offence at him. But Jesus said to them, "Prophets are not without honor except in their own country and in their own house." And he did not do many deeds of power there, because of their unbelief.

Notice what you think and feel as you read the gospel.

Familiarity breeds contempt? The people of his home town are skeptical about Jesus because they think they know him. They limit Jesus' work by their unbelief.

Pray as you are led for yourself and others.

"I, too, limit your work in my life by my unbelief. I am sorry. Help me and all those who hold onto our unbelief. I give myself and all of them to you now . . ." (Continue in your own words.)

Listen to Jesus.

Faith is a door you must open. I am here waiting for you, child. Are you coming in? What else is Jesus saying to you?

Ask God to show you how to live today.

"I love you, gentle Savior. You are patient with me. Let me be patient with those I encounter today, especially in difficult situations. Amen."

Saturday, August 4, 2018

Know that God is present and ready to converse.

"Jesus, evil seems to run rampant in this world. May I find safe harbor in you, your Word?"

Read the gospel: Matthew 14:1–12.

At that time Herod the ruler heard reports about Jesus; and he said to his servants, "This is John the Baptist; he has been raised from the dead, and for this reason these powers are at work in him." For Herod had arrested John, bound him, and put him in prison on account of Herodias, his brother Philip's wife, because John had been telling him, "It is not lawful for you to have her." Though Herod wanted to put him to death, he feared the crowd, because they regarded him as a prophet. But when Herod's birthday came, the daughter of Herodias danced before the company, and she pleased Herod so much that he promised on oath to grant her whatever she might ask. Prompted by her mother, she said, "Give me the head of John the Baptist here on a platter." The king was grieved, yet out of regard for his oaths and for the guests, he commanded it to be given; he sent and had John beheaded in the prison. The head was brought on a platter and given to the girl, who brought it to her mother. His disciples came and took the body and buried it; then they went and told Jesus.

Notice what you think and feel as you read the gospel.

Herod is vain, paranoid, evil, and mad, yet he is allowed by God to exercise power over John the Baptist. He has him killed for his own birthday party. His disciples bury John's body and then tell Jesus. Jesus could not have been surprised that Herod had killed John, but he must have grieved. Herod was so deranged that he thought Jesus was John raised from the dead. Ironically, Jesus himself would rise from the dead after his bloody crucifixion.

Pray as you are led for yourself and others.

"Evil has power in this world, Lord, but you have the ultimate victory. Deliver me and those you have given me from evil, and keep our eyes fixed on your kingdom . . ." (Continue in your own words.)

Listen to Jesus.

Evil is chaos, and the heart is capable of unspeakable evil. Evil is a self-devouring madness, full of lies and fear. Know that, and come to me, child. I am good, simple, and true. In me is deliverance from all evil. What else is Jesus saying to you?

Ask God to show you how to live today.

"Lord, I come. Save me from evil today. Root it out of my heart, every bit. Amen."

Sunday, August 5, 2018
Eighteenth Sunday in Ordinary Time

Know that God is present and ready to converse.

"Lord, as I come before you in your Word, I ask you to give me what you have for me. Thank you."

Read the gospel: John 6:24–35.

So when the crowd saw that neither Jesus nor his disciples were there, they themselves got into the boats and went to Capernaum looking for Jesus.

When they found him on the other side of the lake, they said to him, "Rabbi, when did you come here?" Jesus answered them, "Very truly, I tell you, you are looking for me, not because you saw signs, but because you ate your fill of the loaves. Do not work for the food that perishes, but for the food that endures for eternal life, which the Son of Man will give you. For it is on him that God the Father has set his seal." Then they said to him, "What must we do to perform the works of God?" Jesus answered them, "This is the work of God, that you believe in him whom he has sent." So they said to him, "What sign are you going to give us then, so that we may see it and believe you? What work are you performing? Our ancestors ate the manna in the wilderness; as it is written, 'He gave them bread from heaven to eat.'" Then Jesus said to them, "Very truly, I tell you, it was not Moses who gave you the bread from heaven, but it is my Father who gives you the true bread from heaven. For the bread of God is that which comes down from heaven and gives life to the world." They said to him, "Sir, give us this bread always."

Jesus said to them, "I am the bread of life. Whoever comes to me will never be hungry, and whoever believes in me will never be thirsty."

Notice what you think and feel as you read the gospel.

After Jesus feeds the crowd, they follow him, because they want to eat. Jesus directs them to seek the food that endures for eternal life, which comes by faith in him. He is the true bread from heaven that gives life to the world.

Pray as you are led for yourself and others.

"Lord, give me the bread of life today. And let me break it and give it to others, especially those you have given me . . ." (Continue in your own words.)

Listen to Jesus.

I love to feed you every day, beloved, because my daily bread strengthens you more and more. Do you come to me every day? Come. I give you eternal life, one day at a time. What else is Jesus saying to you?

Ask God to show you how to live today.

"Today I will walk with you, Lord. I believe in you. Let my words and actions speak of you. Amen."

Monday, August 6, 2018
Transfiguration of the Lord

Know that God is present and ready to converse.

"Father, I wish to listen to your beloved Son. I turn to the Word of God."

Read the gospel: Mark 9:2–10.

Six days later, Jesus took with him Peter and James and John, and led them up a high mountain apart, by themselves. And he was transfigured before them, and his clothes became dazzling white, such as no one on earth could bleach them. And there appeared to them Elijah with Moses, who were talking with Jesus. Then Peter said to Jesus, "Rabbi, it is good for us to be here; let us make three dwellings, one for you, one for Moses, and one for Elijah." He did not know what to say, for they were terrified. Then a cloud overshadowed them, and from the cloud there came a voice, "This is my Son, the Beloved; listen to him!" Suddenly when they looked around, they saw no one with them any more, but only Jesus.

As they were coming down the mountain, he ordered them to tell no one about what they had seen, until after the Son of Man had risen from the dead. So they kept the matter to themselves, questioning what this rising from the dead could mean.

Notice what you think and feel as you read the gospel.

As Peter, James, and John look on, Jesus is mysteriously transfigured, becoming dazzling white in conversation with Moses and Elijah. The disciples are terrified. Then from a cloud comes a voice, "This is my Son, the Beloved. Listen to him." Afterward, Jesus asks them not to speak of it until after he rises from the dead. Again they do not understand.

Pray as you are led for yourself and others.

"Risen Lord, you dwell in the glory of your Father. I worship you. I give you all I am and all I love . . ." (Continue in your own words.)

Listen to Jesus.

People underestimate the glory of God and the goodness of God's purposes. God is not hindered by the thoughts of men and women, not even by the lack of faith among those who believe. Let your doubts fall away and trust in your Father and my Father. What else is Jesus saying to you?

Ask God to show you how to live today.

"Lord, my feelings are inconsequential. You are all. Let me be mindful of that today. Amen."

Tuesday, August 7, 2018

Know that God is present and ready to converse.

"Son of God, I come to you in storm or calm. Reach out to me with your Word."

Read the gospel: Matthew 14:22–36.

Immediately Jesus made the disciples get into the boat and go on ahead to the other side, while he dismissed the crowds. And after he had dismissed the crowds, he went up the mountain by himself to pray. When evening came, he was there alone, but by this time the boat, battered by the waves, was far from the land, for the wind was against them. And early in the morning he came walking towards them on the lake. But when the disciples saw him walking on the lake, they were terrified, saying, "It is a ghost!" And they cried out in fear. But immediately Jesus spoke to them and said, "Take heart, it is I; do not be afraid."

Peter answered him, "Lord, if it is you, command me to come to you on the water." He said, "Come." So Peter got out of the boat, started walking on the water, and came towards Jesus. But when he noticed the strong wind, he became frightened, and beginning to sink, he cried out, "Lord, save me!" Jesus immediately reached out his hand and caught him, saying to him, "You of little faith, why did you doubt?" When they got into the boat, the wind ceased. And those in the boat worshipped him, saying, "Truly you are the Son of God."

When they had crossed over, they came to land at Gennesaret. After the people of that place recognized him, they sent word throughout the region and brought all who were sick to him, and begged him that they might touch even the fringe of his cloak; and all who touched it were healed.

Notice what you think and feel as you read the gospel.

Jesus walks to the boat on the water of the lake. Peter impulsively joins him. Jesus saves him when he starts to sink, and asks him why he doubts.

Pray as you are led for yourself and others.

"Lord, how much good do I forfeit for lack of faith? I resolve to believe in you with all my heart. I pray for all of us with too little faith . . ." (Continue in your own words.)

Listen to Jesus.

I love to find faith in people. People believe in many things that are not deserving of faith, but God is. Hearts resist faith in God, my child. As you realize that, come to me. I will strengthen your faith. What else is Jesus saying to you?

Ask God to show you how to live today.

"You are the Lord, Jesus. I depend on you completely. I give myself to you completely. Let me walk in faith. Amen."

Wednesday, August 8, 2018

Know that God is present and ready to converse.

"Lord, I come to you again asking mercy. Touch me by your Word."

Read the gospel: Matthew 15:21–28.

Jesus left that place and went away to the district of Tyre and Sidon. Just then a Canaanite woman from that region came out and started shouting, "Have mercy on me, Lord, Son of David; my daughter is tormented by a demon." But he did not answer her at all. And his disciples came and urged him, saying, "Send her away, for she keeps shouting after us." He answered, "I was sent only to the lost sheep of the house of Israel." But she came and knelt before him, saying, "Lord, help me." He answered, "It is not fair to take the children's food and throw it to the dogs." She said, "Yes, Lord, yet even the dogs eat the crumbs that fall from their masters' table." Then Jesus answered her, "Woman, great is your faith! Let it be done for you as you wish." And her daughter was healed instantly.

Notice what you think and feel as you read the gospel.

Because the Canaanite woman persists in asking, Jesus grants her request and heals her daughter. He commends her faith.

Pray as you are led for yourself and others.

"Lord, give me persistent faith that pleases you. I pray for all those you have given me, that they may look to you in faith for themselves and their loved ones . . ." (Continue in your own words.)

Listen to Jesus.

You can turn to me. You can trust me. I am faithful and will never let you go. Be true to me and true to the work I have given you. Together we will bear fruit to the glory of our Father. What else is Jesus saying to you?

Ask God to show you how to live today.

"When I waver, Lord, strengthen me. Let me see clearly what you would have me do today. I love you. Amen."

Thursday, August 9, 2018

Know that God is present and ready to converse.

"Living God, you sent your Son to save us. May all the world receive your good news."

Read the gospel: Matthew 16:13–23.

Now when Jesus came into the district of Caesarea Philippi, he asked his disciples, "Who do people say that the Son of Man is?" And they said, "Some say John the Baptist, but others Elijah, and still others Jeremiah or one of the prophets." He said to them, "But who do you say that I am?" Simon Peter answered, "You are the Messiah, the Son of the living God." And Jesus answered him, "Blessed are you, Simon son of Jonah! For flesh and blood has not revealed this to you, but my Father in heaven. And I tell you, you are Peter, and on this rock I will build my church, and the gates of Hades will not prevail against it. I will give you the keys of the kingdom of heaven, and whatever you bind on earth will be bound in heaven, and whatever you loose on earth will be loosed in heaven." Then he sternly ordered the disciples not to tell anyone that he was the Messiah.

From that time on, Jesus began to show his disciples that he must go to Jerusalem and undergo great suffering at the hands of the elders and chief priests and scribes, and be killed, and on the third day be raised. And Peter took him aside and began to rebuke him, saying, "God forbid it, Lord! This must never happen to you." But he turned and said to Peter, "Get behind me, Satan! You are a stumbling block to me; for you are setting your mind not on divine things but on human things."

Notice what you think and feel as you read the gospel.

Peter acknowledges that Jesus is the Son of the living God, and Jesus blesses him and prophesies that Peter will be the rock on which he builds his church. Jesus also prophesies his own Passion, Death, and Resurrection in Jerusalem. He rebukes Peter for denying it.

Pray as you are led for yourself and others.

"Lord, I set my mind on many human things. Turn my mind to the divine. In your Spirit I pray for these . . ." (Continue in your own words.)

Listen to Jesus.

Power to do good comes from God, beloved disciple. My Father wants to do good through you. Seek God and you will find that power. God will work through you. What else is Jesus saying to you?

Ask God to show you how to live today.

"I seek you, Lord. Let me be moved by divine power, not by my own. Amen."

Friday, August 10, 2018

Know that God is present and ready to converse.

"What is the secret of living a life that pleases God? I will seek it in your Word."

Read the gospel: John 12:24–26.

Jesus said, "Very truly, I tell you, unless a grain of wheat falls into the earth and dies, it remains just a single grain; but if it dies, it bears much fruit. Those who love their life lose it, and those who hate their life in this world will keep it for eternal life. Whoever serves me must follow me, and where I am, there will my servant be also. Whoever serves me, the Father will honor."

Notice what you think and feel as you read the gospel.

Jesus speaks of godly fruitfulness. One must die to this world to live eternal life. Follow him and receive honor from the Father.

Pray as you are led for yourself and others.

"Lord, give me your view of life, that I might willingly turn away from my life and seek your life. I pray for all I love. May we follow you closely . . ." (Continue in your own words.)

Listen to Jesus.

People cling to things of this world and do not see them passing away. Things and people pass away, so do not set your heart on them. Love others, but love them for eternity, as children of God. Great peace and joy are found in letting go of this world. What else is Jesus saying to you?

Ask God to show you how to live today.

"I receive your wisdom, Lord and Savior. I have nowhere else to go but to you. Lead me by the hand. Amen."

Saturday, August 11, 2018

Know that God is present and ready to converse.

"I have faith, Lord, so I come to you. But I have only a little, so I come to you for more."

Read the gospel: Matthew 17:14–20.

When they came to the crowd, a man came to him, knelt before him, and said, "Lord, have mercy on my son, for he is an epileptic and he suffers terribly; he often falls into the fire and often into the water. And I brought him to your disciples, but they could not cure him." Jesus answered, "You faithless and perverse generation, how much longer must I be with you? How much longer must I put up with you? Bring him here to me." And Jesus rebuked the demon, and it came out of him, and the boy was cured instantly. Then the disciples came to Jesus privately and said, "Why could we not cast it out?" He said to them, "Because of your little faith. For truly I tell you, if you have faith the size of a mustard seed, you will say to this mountain, 'Move from here to there,' and it will move; and nothing will be impossible for you."

Notice what you think and feel as you read the gospel.

Jesus disciples cannot cure a man's epileptic son, and Jesus is exasperated by their lack of faith. He tells them faith the size of a mustard seed can move mountains.

Pray as you are led for yourself and others.

"Lord, I want to please you with true faith. Give me a little faith and send me out to serve you in some way. I begin by praying for others . . ." (Continue in your own words.)

Listen to Jesus.

Those who are filled with the things of this world, the teachings and aspirations the world promotes, lose the little faith they had in God. When they lose faith, they lose power to do the works of God. Turn to me with all your heart and mind, and you will learn the power of faith. What else is Jesus saying to you?

Ask God to show you how to live today.

"I turn to you today, Lord. I empty myself of worldly things and open myself to your grace and truth. Amen."

Sunday, August 12, 2018
Nineteenth Sunday in Ordinary Time

Know that God is present and ready to converse.

"Jesus, I am drawn to you by our Father. Let me eat the Bread of Life."

Read the gospel: John 6:41–51.

Then the Jews began to complain about him because he said, "I am the bread that came down from heaven." They were saying, "Is not this Jesus, the son of Joseph, whose father and mother we know? How can he now say, 'I have come down from heaven'?" Jesus answered them, "Do not complain among yourselves. No one can come to me unless drawn by the Father who sent me; and I will raise that person up on the last day. It is written in the prophets, 'And they shall all be taught by God.' Everyone who has heard and learned from the Father comes to me. Not that anyone has seen the Father except the one who is from God; he has seen the Father. Very truly, I tell you, whoever believes has eternal life. I am the bread of life. Your ancestors ate the manna in the wilderness, and they died. This is the bread that comes down from heaven, so that one may eat of it and not die. I am the living bread that came down from heaven. Whoever eats of this bread will live forever; and the bread that I will give for the life of the world is my flesh."

Notice what you think and feel as you read the gospel.

Jesus amplifies for complainers what he meant by calling himself the bread of heaven. To them he's just the Jesus they know from the village. He tells them he comes from God and whoever comes to him and believes has eternal life. The bread that he gives for the life of the world is his flesh.

Pray as you are led for yourself and others.

"Lord, I come, I believe, I receive the life you give me by the sacrifice of your flesh. I pray that others come to you as well . . ." (Continue in your own words.)

Listen to Jesus.

The way of God is always the way of love. It is love that brought me to the world, and it is love that causes me to remain with you. It is love that draws me to you. The love of God is the bread of life. Feed on me, dear one. What else is Jesus saying to you?

Ask God to show you how to live today.

"Lord, instill your great love in me, and let me act upon it today. Amen."

Monday, August 13, 2018

Know that God is present and ready to converse.

"Sometimes, Lord, your words distress me. Let me receive them with an open heart and an open mind."

Read the gospel: Matthew 17:22–27.

As they were gathering in Galilee, Jesus said to them, "The Son of Man is going to be betrayed into human hands, and they will kill him, and on the third day he will be raised." And they were greatly distressed.

When they reached Capernaum, the collectors of the temple tax came to Peter and said, "Does your teacher not pay the temple tax?" He said, "Yes, he does." And when he came home, Jesus spoke of it first, asking, "What do you think, Simon? From whom do kings of the earth take toll or tribute? From their children or from others?" When Peter said, "From others," Jesus said to him, "Then the children are free. However, so that we do not give offence to them, go to the lake and cast a hook; take the first fish that comes up; and when you open its mouth, you will find a coin; take that and give it to them for you and me."

Notice what you think and feel as you read the gospel.

Jesus prophesies his Death and Resurrection, and his disciples are distressed. Then Jesus provides Peter with a coin for the temple tax in the mouth of a fish.

Pray as you are led for yourself and others.

"I know you were betrayed, killed, and raised, Lord. What does that mean for me today? It means I will entrust those I love to your care . . ." (Continue in your own words.)

Listen to Jesus.

You must trust me for everything, but I am faithful even when you are not. I see what you cannot. When you are powerless, I act, and I act through you. Do not be distressed, for I am with you. I love you as my own. What else is Jesus saying to you?

Ask God to show you how to live today.

"Let me love others then, Lord. Let me find practical ways to show love to others. Amen."

Tuesday, August 14, 2018

Know that God is present and ready to converse.

"Lord, let me come as a child and receive your holy Word."

Read the gospel: Matthew 18:1–5, 10, 12–14.

At that time the disciples came to Jesus and asked, "Who is the greatest in the kingdom of heaven?" He called a child, whom he put among them, and said, "Truly I tell you, unless you change and become like children, you will never enter the kingdom of heaven. Whoever becomes humble like this child is the greatest in the kingdom of heaven. Whoever welcomes one such child in my name welcomes me.

"Take care that you do not despise one of these little ones; for, I tell you, in heaven their angels continually see the face of my Father in heaven. What do you think? If a shepherd has a hundred sheep, and one of them has gone astray, does he not leave the ninety-nine on the mountains and go in search of the one that went astray? And if he finds it, truly I tell you, he rejoices over it more than over the ninety-nine that never went astray. So it is not the will of your Father in heaven that one of these little ones should be lost."

Notice what you think and feel as you read the gospel.

Jesus tells his disciples that the great ones in the kingdom of heaven are like children. Humility is greatness. To welcome such a child is to welcome Jesus Christ. He asks his disciples not to despise but to care for children.

Pray as you are led for yourself and others.

"Lord, I pray earnestly for the children in my life . . ." (Continue in your own words.)

Listen to Jesus.

I was a child on earth, and my mother cared for me. I loved then and love her still. Be like her. What else is Jesus saying to you?

Ask God to show you how to live today.

"Mother of Jesus, I pray for grace such as you had to love children, those in my own family and those in other families. Amen."

Wednesday, August 15, 2018
Assumption of the Blessed Virgin Mary

Know that God is present and ready to converse.

"Lord, I make myself small to reach up to you. I sit at your feet."

Read the gospel: Luke 1:39–56.

In those days Mary set out and went with haste to a Judean town in the hill country, where she entered the house of Zechariah and greeted Elizabeth. When Elizabeth heard Mary's greeting, the child leapt in her womb. And Elizabeth was filled with the Holy Spirit and exclaimed with a loud cry, "Blessed are you among women, and blessed is the fruit of your womb. And why has this happened to me, that the mother of my Lord comes to me? For as soon as I heard the sound of your greeting, the child in my womb leapt for joy. And blessed is she who believed that there would be a fulfillment of what was spoken to her by the Lord."

And Mary said,

"My soul magnifies the Lord,
and my spirit rejoices in God my Savior,
for he has looked with favor on the lowliness of his servant.
Surely, from now on all generations will call me blessed;
for the Mighty One has done great things for me,
and holy is his name.
His mercy is for those who fear him
from generation to generation.
He has shown strength with his arm;
he has scattered the proud in the thoughts of their hearts.
He has brought down the powerful from their thrones,
and lifted up the lowly;
he has filled the hungry with good things,
and sent the rich away empty.
He has helped his servant Israel,
in remembrance of his mercy,
according to the promise he made to our ancestors,
to Abraham and to his descendants forever."

And Mary remained with her for about three months and then returned to her home.

Notice what you think and feel as you read the gospel.

Mary and Elizabeth are being used by God as instruments in his great plan of salvation. Elizabeth blesses Mary, and Mary sings the praises of God, for he looks with favor on the lowly and needy and keeps his promises forever.

Pray as you are led for yourself and others.

"Give me the grace of humility, Lord, that I might be your beloved servant . . ." (Continue in your own words.)

Listen to Jesus.

By your humility in serving God and others, you possess power to pass on the mercy of God to many generations of those who will come after you. Such is the power of the meek. The meek are not weak; they are mighty with the power of God. What else is Jesus saying to you?

Ask God to show you how to live today.

"Teach me meekness, Lord, in the moments of my day, in my words and my actions. Amen."

Thursday, August 16, 2018

Know that God is present and ready to converse.

"Lord, you have forgiven me. Teach me to forgive others."

Read the gospel: Matthew 18:21–19:1.

Then Peter came and said to him, "Lord, if another member of the church sins against me, how often should I forgive? As many as seven times?" Jesus said to him, "Not seven times, but, I tell you, seventy-seven times.

"For this reason the kingdom of heaven may be compared to a king who wished to settle accounts with his slaves. When he began the reckoning, one who owed him ten thousand talents was brought to him; and, as he could not pay, his lord ordered him to be sold, together with his wife and children and all his possessions, and payment to be made. So the slave fell on his knees before him, saying, 'Have patience with me, and I will pay you everything.' And out of pity for him, the lord of that slave released him and forgave him the debt. But that same slave, as he went out, came upon one of his fellow slaves who owed him a hundred denarii; and seizing him by the throat, he said, 'Pay what you owe.' Then his fellow slave fell down and pleaded with him, 'Have patience with me, and I will pay you.' But he refused; then he went and threw him into prison until he should pay the debt. When his fellow slaves saw what had happened, they were greatly distressed, and they went and reported to their lord all that had taken place. Then his lord summoned him and said to him, 'You wicked slave! I forgave you all that debt because you pleaded with me. Should you not have had mercy on your fellow slave, as I had mercy on you?' And in anger his lord handed him over to be tortured until he should pay his entire debt. So my heavenly Father will also do to every one of you, if you do not forgive your brother or sister from your heart."

When Jesus had finished saying these things, he left Galilee and went to the region of Judea beyond the Jordan.

Notice what you think and feel as you read the gospel.

Jesus teaches the need to forgive others. The mercy of God depends on it. We must forgive from our hearts.

Pray as you are led for yourself and others.

"Lord, I now extend forgiveness from my heart to all who have hurt me in any way. Let your mercy feed my own . . ." (Continue in your own words.)

Listen to Jesus.

To say that God is love is to say that God is mercy. His mercy is new every morning. He extends his mercy freely. Imitate God, my dear disciple. What else is Jesus saying to you?

Ask God to show you how to live today.

"Sometimes my heart is clogged with negative feelings I am not quite aware of. Let them be banished by mercy today, Lord. Let me hold nothing against anyone. Thank you. Amen."

Friday, August 17, 2018

Know that God is present and ready to converse.

"Lord, let my heart be soft to receive your Word. You are with me here."

Read the gospel: Matthew 19:3–12.

Some Pharisees came to Jesus, and to test him they asked, "Is it lawful for a man to divorce his wife for any cause?" He answered, "Have you not read that the one who made them at the beginning 'made them male and female,' and said, 'For this reason a man shall leave his father and mother and be joined to his wife, and the two shall become one flesh'? So they are no longer two, but one flesh. Therefore what God has joined together, let no one separate." They said to him, "Why then did Moses command us to give a certificate of dismissal and to divorce her?" He said to them, "It was because you were so hard-hearted that Moses allowed you to divorce your wives, but at the beginning it was not so. And I say to you, whoever divorces his wife, except for unchastity, and marries another commits adultery."

His disciples said to him, "If such is the case of a man with his wife, it is better not to marry." But he said to them, "Not everyone can accept this teaching, but only those to whom it is given. For there are eunuchs who have been so from birth, and there are eunuchs who have been made eunuchs by others, and there are eunuchs who have made themselves eunuchs for the sake of the kingdom of heaven. Let anyone accept this who can."

Notice what you think and feel as you read the gospel.

Jesus teaches that the bond of marriage should not be broken. His disciples find this difficult to accept and suggest it would be better not to marry. Jesus does not deny this option.

Pray as you are led for yourself and others.

"Lord, I pray for marriages, especially those in jeopardy . . ." (Continue in your own words.)

Listen to Jesus.

I am the bridegroom; you are the bride. I have loved you from the beginning and will love you to the end. There will indeed be no end, for we shall be together in paradise, perfect in love. Practice love in your life while you can. What else is Jesus saying to you?

Ask God to show you how to live today.

"I shall practice love today, Jesus. Fill me with love to share. Amen."

Saturday, August 18, 2018

Know that God is present and ready to converse.

"I am your child, Lord. Teach me."

Read the gospel: Matthew 19:13–15.

Then little children were being brought to Jesus in order that he might lay his hands on them and pray. The disciples spoke sternly to those who brought them; but Jesus said, "Let the little children come to me, and do not stop them; for it is to such as these that the kingdom of heaven belongs." And he laid his hands on them and went on his way.

Notice what you think and feel as you read the gospel.

Jesus receives the children, saying that they are like those to whom the kingdom of heaven belongs.

Pray as you are led for yourself and others.

"Jesus, lay your hands on me and bless me today. Bless these people, too, for they need you . . ." (Continue in your own words.)

Listen to Jesus.

Be simple, beloved follower. Look solely to me. Speak only truth. Strive to love and to give. Live one day at a time. Rejoice, for I walk with you. What else is Jesus saying to you?

Ask God to show you how to live today.

"Let me be simple, Lord, today and every day. Let me follow you with the heart of a child. Amen."

Sunday, August 19, 2018
Twentieth Sunday in Ordinary Time

Know that God is present and ready to converse.

"Jesus, I will recognize you in the breaking of the bread, your Word."

Read the gospel: John 6:51–58.

Jesus said, "I am the living bread that came down from heaven. Whoever eats of this bread will live forever; and the bread that I will give for the life of the world is my flesh."

The Jews then disputed among themselves, saying, "How can this man give us his flesh to eat?" So Jesus said to them, "Very truly, I tell you, unless you eat the flesh of the Son of Man and drink his blood, you have no life in you. Those who eat my flesh and drink my blood have eternal life, and I will raise them up on the last day; for my flesh is true food and my blood is true drink. Those who eat my flesh and drink my blood abide in me, and I in them. Just as the living Father sent me, and I live because of the Father, so whoever eats me will live because of me. This is the bread that came down from heaven, not like that which your ancestors ate, and they died. But the one who eats this bread will live forever."

Notice what you think and feel as you read the gospel.

The Jews hearing him have trouble with Jesus' saying that those who will live forever must eat his flesh. He is very literal about this, repeating it many times. To inherit eternal life they must eat his flesh and drink his blood, true food and true drink. To do so is to abide in him forever.

Pray as you are led for yourself and others.

"Lord, I resolve to obey you. Let me eat and drink of your flesh and blood, according to your will. Give your life to me and to these . . ." (Continue in your own words.)

Listen to Jesus.

Have faith in the Eucharist, dear disciple. There I make it so easy for you. The Eucharist is our communion, our gifts of self to one another. This happens in the spirit and is real and powerful. What else is Jesus saying to you?

Ask God to show you how to live today.

"I will draw strength from your flesh and blood, Lord, and I will give it all to your service. Amen."

Monday, August 20, 2018

Know that God is present and ready to converse.

"Lord, as I read your Word make me willing to do your will."

Read the gospel: Matthew 19:16–22.

Then someone came to Jesus and said, "Teacher, what good deed must I do to have eternal life?" And he said to him, "Why do you ask me about what is good? There is only one who is good. If you wish to enter into life, keep the commandments." He said to him, "Which ones?" And Jesus said, "You shall not murder; You shall not commit adultery; You shall not steal; You shall not bear false witness; Honor your father and mother; also, You shall love your neighbor as yourself." The young man said to him, "I have kept all these; what do I still lack?" Jesus said to him, "If you wish to be perfect, go, sell your possessions, and give the money to the poor, and you will have treasure in heaven; then come, follow me." When the young man heard this word, he went away grieving, for he had many possessions.

Notice what you think and feel as you read the gospel.

A rich young man asks Jesus how to have eternal life. Jesus tells him to keep the commandments. When the young man says he has done so, Jesus invites him to sell everything, give to the poor, and follow him—the young man is unable to do so.

Pray as you are led for yourself and others.

"How do you wish I shall obey you in this, dear Lord? You have blessed me, and all I have is yours. How can I give to the poor? . . ." (Continue in your own words.)

Listen to Jesus.

If you would follow me, you must set your heart on me alone. I am the fountain of abundance, and as you serve me, I will bless you. I will care for you and yours all your days. What else is Jesus saying to you?

Ask God to show you how to live today.

"I set my heart upon you alone, Lord. All I own I give to you. All I am is yours. I shall give to others. Amen."

Tuesday, August 21, 2018

Know that God is present and ready to converse.

"What truth do you have for me today, dear Jesus? I open my heart to you now."

Read the gospel: Matthew 19:23–30.

Then Jesus said to his disciples, "Truly I tell you, it will be hard for a rich person to enter the kingdom of heaven. Again I tell you, it is easier for a camel to go through the eye of a needle than for someone who is rich to enter the kingdom of God." When the disciples heard this, they were greatly astounded and said, "Then who can be saved?" But Jesus looked at them and said, "For mortals it is impossible, but for God all things are possible."

Then Peter said in reply, "Look, we have left everything and followed you. What then will we have?" Jesus said to them, "Truly I tell you, at the renewal of all things, when the Son of Man is seated on the throne of his glory, you who have followed me will also sit on twelve thrones, judging the twelve tribes of Israel. And everyone who has left houses or brothers or sisters or father or mother or children or fields, for my name's sake, will receive a hundredfold, and will inherit eternal life. But many who are first will be last, and the last will be first."

Notice what you think and feel as you read the gospel.

The disciples are astounded by Jesus' teaching about wealth, that it is hard for a rich person to enter heaven. The disciples ask Jesus what reward they will get for leaving everything and following him. He tells them they will rule with him. Then he says that all those who make sacrifices for his sake will receive great rewards and eternal life.

Pray as you are led for yourself and others.

"Lord, let me give generously at every opportunity, for I want the rewards that last forever . . ." (Continue in your own words.)

Listen to Jesus.

My promises to you are the same as my promises to my disciples, for you are my disciple. I love you very much. I know it is hard to give. Don't be afraid of it. You cannot cling to things. They are not your goal. I am, for I am your life. Possessions will get in the way of that life. What else is Jesus saying to you?

Ask God to show you how to live today.

"Lord, give me wisdom as I seek to obey your word. I choose to walk in your way of life. Amen."

Wednesday, August 22, 2018

Know that God is present and ready to converse.

"Lord, fill my heart with gratitude for your Word and let me be your servant."

Read the gospel: Matthew 20:1–16.

Jesus said, "For the kingdom of heaven is like a landowner who went out early in the morning to hire laborers for his vineyard. After agreeing with the laborers for the usual daily wage, he sent them into his vineyard. When he went out about nine o'clock, he saw others standing idle in the marketplace; and he said to them, 'You also go into the vineyard, and I will pay you whatever is right.' So they went. When he went out again about noon and about three o'clock, he did the same. And about five o'clock he went out and found others standing around; and he said to them, 'Why are you standing here idle all day?' They said to him, 'Because no one has hired us.' He said to them, 'You also go into the vineyard.' When evening came, the owner of the vineyard said to his manager, 'Call the laborers and give them their pay, beginning with the last and then going to the first.' When those hired about five o'clock came, each of them received the usual daily wage. Now when the first came, they thought they would receive more; but each of them also received the usual daily wage. And when they received it, they grumbled against the landowner, saying, 'These last worked only one hour, and you have made them equal to us who have borne the burden of the day and the scorching heat.' But he replied to one of them, 'Friend, I am doing you no wrong; did you not agree with me for the usual daily wage? Take what belongs to you and go; I choose to give to this last the same as I give to you. Am I not allowed to do what I choose with what belongs to me? Or are you envious because I am generous?' So the last will be first, and the first will be last."

Notice what you think and feel as you read the gospel.

Jesus' parable is about the generosity of God. He is ready to give the kingdom of heaven to all who come and serve him. Human beings do not understand or possess generosity as God does.

Pray as you are led for yourself and others.

"Am I envious of others' blessings, Lord? Forgive me. I pray for the envious now . . ." (Continue in your own words.)

Listen to Jesus.

I gave my life for you, and I give you life and promise you eternal life. Live by my promises. Learn how to love me more. That is the great reward. Love is what gives you eternal life. Do you understand me, beloved? What else is Jesus saying to you?

Ask God to show you how to live today.

"Generous Lord, I thank you. Let me work to show you my gratitude for the life you have placed inside of me. Amen."

Thursday, August 23, 2018

Know that God is present and ready to converse.

"Jesus Christ, you are calling to me by your Word. Let me not take it lightly."

Read the gospel: Matthew 22:1–14.

Once more Jesus spoke to them in parables, saying: "The kingdom of heaven may be compared to a king who gave a wedding banquet for his son. He sent his slaves to call those who had been invited to the wedding banquet, but they would not come. Again he sent other slaves, saying, 'Tell those who have been invited: Look, I have prepared my dinner, my oxen and my fat calves have been slaughtered, and everything is ready; come to the wedding banquet.' But they made light of it and went away, one to his farm, another to his business, while the rest seized his slaves, maltreated them, and killed them. The king was enraged. He sent his troops, destroyed those murderers, and burned their city. Then he said to his slaves, 'The wedding is ready, but those invited were not worthy. Go therefore into the main streets, and invite everyone you find to the wedding banquet.' Those slaves went out into the streets and gathered all whom they found, both good and bad; so the wedding hall was filled with guests.

"But when the king came in to see the guests, he noticed a man there who was not wearing a wedding robe, and he said to him, 'Friend, how did you get in here without a wedding robe?' And he was speechless. Then the king said to the attendants, 'Bind him hand and foot, and throw him into the outer darkness, where there will be weeping and gnashing of teeth.' For many are called, but few are chosen."

Notice what you think and feel as you read the gospel.

Jesus' parable affirms that many are called to the kingdom of heaven, but a great many have excuses related to this world. So who does come? Those in the streets, both good and bad.

Pray as you are led for yourself and others.

"Lord, you found me in the street. I praise you. Gather many, many more into your kingdom, including those you have given to me to pray for . . ." (Continue in your own words.)

Listen to Jesus.

Such is the way of the world, to distract people's hearts from God and from what really makes for happiness. Blessed are the poor, for it is easier for them to recognize they have nothing to protect and they need saving. I give them hope and then the kingdom. What else is Jesus saying to you?

Ask God to show you how to live today.

"Lord, you have called us, poor as we are, to your banquet. But what will I wear? Help me remember, in every moment of the day, to put on Christ—to serve you in love. Amen."

Friday, August 24, 2018
Saint Bartholomew, Apostle

Know that God is present and ready to converse.

"Prayer allows my spirit to enter the kingdom of heaven, Lord. Thank you."

Read the gospel: John 1:45–51.

Philip found Nathanael and said to him, "We have found him about whom Moses in the law and also the prophets wrote, Jesus son of Joseph from Nazareth." Nathanael said to him, "Can anything good come out of Nazareth?" Philip said to him, "Come and see." When Jesus saw Nathanael coming towards him, he said of him, "Here is truly an Israelite in whom there is no deceit!" Nathanael asked him, "Where did you come to know me?" Jesus answered, "I saw you under the fig tree before Philip called you." Nathanael replied, "Rabbi, you are the Son of God! You are the King of Israel!" Jesus answered, "Do you believe because I told you that I saw you under the fig tree? You will see greater things than these." And he said to him, "Very truly, I tell you, you will see heaven opened and the angels of God ascending and descending upon the Son of Man."

Notice what you think and feel as you read the gospel.

Jesus hears Nathanael's prayer though he is far off because Jesus is God, one with Father, Son, and Holy Spirit. Nathanael believes Jesus is the Son of God, and Jesus prophesies of the glory he will receive, with the heavens opened and the angels ascending and descending upon him.

Pray as you are led for yourself and others.

"Lord, I hope in glory. Let the hearts of those I love hunger for your glory . . ." (Continue in your own words.)

Listen to Jesus.

The glory of God is the goodness of God. My hour of glory was my suffering and death because love in obedience to my Father moved me to give myself as ransom for the sins of the world. By that I merited my place at the right hand of the Father. Follow me. What else is Jesus saying to you?

Ask God to show you how to live today.

"Lord, help me bear my cross today, following you. I rejoice to be your servant. Amen."

Saturday, August 25, 2018

Know that God is present and ready to converse.

"Lord, you are my teacher. I will humbly hear your Word."

Read the gospel: Matthew 23:1–12.

Then Jesus said to the crowds and to his disciples, "The scribes and the Pharisees sit on Moses' seat; therefore, do whatever they teach you and follow it; but do not do as they do, for they do not practice what they teach. They tie up heavy burdens, hard to bear, and lay them on the shoulders of others; but they themselves are unwilling to lift a finger to move them. They do all their deeds to be seen by others; for they make their phylacteries broad and their fringes long. They love to have the place of honor at banquets and the best seats in the synagogues, and to be greeted with respect in the marketplaces, and to have people call them rabbi. But you are not to be called rabbi, for you have one teacher, and you are all students. And call no one your father on earth, for you have one Father—the one in heaven. Nor are you to be called instructors, for you have one instructor, the Messiah. The greatest among you will be your servant. All who exalt themselves will be humbled, and all who humble themselves will be exalted."

Notice what you think and feel as you read the gospel.

Jesus describes the hypocrisy of the scribes and Pharisees to the crowds and to his disciples. Obey them for they are in authority, he says, but do not be like them. Don't seek honor among people, but humble yourself. Then you shall be exalted.

Pray as you are led for yourself and others.

"I pray for the proud and hypocritical, including myself. Teach us true humility, Jesus . . ." (Continue in your own words.)

Listen to Jesus.

Do you notice the sin and the inclination for sin in your own heart? You are human, dear disciple. Don't be discouraged by your faults, for it can be pride to abhor them. Instead, accept yourself as one needing to be made holy—and you cannot make yourself holy. Come to me and I will wash you whiter than snow. What else is Jesus saying to you?

Ask God to show you how to live today.

"Let me concentrate today on recognizing my sins and faults. I will surrender them to you one by one. Amen."

Sunday, August 26, 2018
Twenty-First Sunday in Ordinary Time

Know that God is present and ready to converse.

"Lord, your words are spirit and life. Let me hear them and remain with you."

Read the gospel: John 6:60–69.

When many of Jesus' disciples heard it, they said, "This teaching is difficult; who can accept it?" But Jesus, being aware that his disciples were complaining about it, said to them, "Does this offend you? Then what if you were to see the Son of Man ascending to where he was before? It is the spirit that gives life; the flesh is useless. The words that I have spoken to you are spirit and life. But among you there are some who do not believe." For Jesus knew from the first who were the ones that did not believe, and who was the one that would betray him. And he said, "For this reason I have told you that no one can come to me unless it is granted by the Father."

Because of this many of his disciples turned back and no longer went about with him. So Jesus asked the twelve, "Do you also wish to go away?" Simon Peter answered him, "Lord, to whom can we go? You have the words of eternal life. We have come to believe and know that you are the Holy One of God."

Notice what you think and feel as you read the gospel.

Some of the disciples are scandalized that Jesus insists they must eat his flesh and drink his blood to have life. Many disciples leave him, but the twelve remain, for they recognize that only Jesus has the words of eternal life. He is the Holy One of God.

Pray as you are led for yourself and others.

"I have nowhere else to go, Lord. Let your words of truth go throughout the world and gather in many to your kingdom . . ." (Continue in your own words.)

Listen to Jesus.

Beloved, do you love me? That love comes by the spirit, the Holy Spirit within your spirit. This is my life. And by this life you may learn a host of virtues, all deriving from the love of God. You will act in my name and bear fruit to God's glory. Love me. What else is Jesus saying to you?

Ask God to show you how to live today.

"Keep love in the forefront of my mind and heart today, my Jesus. Show me how to act in every situation. Amen."

Monday, August 27, 2018

Know that God is present and ready to converse.

"I come to your Word for truth, Lord. Thank you for being present now."

Read the gospel: Matthew 23:13–22.

Jesus said, "But woe to you, scribes and Pharisees, hypocrites! For you lock people out of the kingdom of heaven. For you do not go in yourselves, and when others are going in, you stop them. Woe to you, scribes and Pharisees, hypocrites! For you cross sea and land to make a single convert, and you make the new convert twice as much a child of hell as yourselves.

"Woe to you, blind guides, who say, 'Whoever swears by the sanctuary is bound by nothing, but whoever swears by the gold of the sanctuary is bound by the oath.' You blind fools! For which is greater, the gold or the sanctuary that has made the gold sacred? And you say, 'Whoever swears by the altar is bound by nothing, but whoever swears by the gift that is on the altar is bound by the oath.' How blind you are! For which is greater, the gift or the altar that makes the gift sacred? So whoever swears by the altar, swears by it and by everything on it; and whoever swears by the sanctuary, swears by it and by the one who dwells in it; and whoever swears by heaven, swears by the throne of God and by the one who is seated upon it."

Notice what you think and feel as you read the gospel.

Jesus condemns the scribes and Pharisees as hypocrites, absurd rule-makers, and blind fools. They lock people out of the kingdom of heaven and will not enter it themselves.

Pray as you are led for yourself and others.

"Lord, forgive the Pharisee in me and let me live in the freedom of your love. Holy Spirit, move in me to walk in you, not in the flesh . . ." (Continue in your own words.)

Listen to Jesus.

Beloved, I deal harshly with those who lead my people away from me, with those who harden their hearts against me—for I know their hearts. But all who take refuge in me rejoice, for I am their shield. Seek the kingdom, then, in all you do, and I will bless you. What else is Jesus saying to you?

Ask God to show you how to live today.

"Thank you for your wisdom, Lord. Give me light to discern how to act and pray today. Amen."

Tuesday, August 28, 2018

Know that God is present and ready to converse.

"Lord, I come to the washing of your Word. You are here with me now. Thank you."

Read the gospel: Matthew 23:23–26.

Jesus said, "Woe to you, scribes and Pharisees, hypocrites! For you tithe mint, dill, and cummin, and have neglected the weightier matters of the law: justice and mercy and faith. It is these you ought to have practiced without neglecting the others. You blind guides! You strain out a gnat but swallow a camel!

"Woe to you, scribes and Pharisees, hypocrites! For you clean the outside of the cup and of the plate, but inside they are full of greed and self-indulgence. You blind Pharisee! First clean the inside of the cup, so that the outside also may become clean."

Notice what you think and feel as you read the gospel.

Jesus condemns the scribes and Pharisees for practicing and teaching petty observances but neglecting what's really important: justice, mercy, and faith. He condemns their hypocritical practices, which are full of greed and self-indulgence. He then tells them to start cleaning the inside and the rest will take care of itself.

Pray as you are led for yourself and others.

"I repent of my greed and self-indulgence, Lord, and seek with all my heart justice, mercy, and faith. I ask for these gifts for myself and for all those motivated by greed and self-indulgence . . ." (Continue in your own words.)

Listen to Jesus.

Sin begins inside you, often leading to sinful actions. That is why you need to root evil thoughts out of your heart as soon as you recognize them. My Spirit will help you see them, but it will take an act of your will, strengthened by my grace, to overcome them. Turn to me, and you will be made clean, worthy of the kingdom of heaven. What else is Jesus saying to you?

Ask God to show you how to live today.

"Lord, I resolve to obey you today. Help me see my sins before they become actions, and give me the grace and strength to reject my sins and, moment by moment, turn to you. Amen."

Wednesday, August 29, 2018
Martyrdom of John the Baptist

Know that God is present and ready to converse.

"Lord, you raise up righteous and holy people, truthful and courageous. Choose me."

Read the gospel: Mark 6:17–29.

For Herod himself had sent men who arrested John, bound him, and put him in prison on account of Herodias, his brother Philip's wife, because Herod had married her. For John had been telling Herod, "It is not lawful for you to have your brother's wife." And Herodias had a grudge against him, and wanted to kill him. But she could not, for Herod feared John, knowing that he was a righteous and holy man, and he protected him. When he heard him, he was greatly perplexed; and yet he liked to listen to him. But an opportunity came when Herod on his birthday gave a banquet for his courtiers and officers and for the leaders of Galilee. When his daughter Herodias came in and danced, she pleased Herod and his guests; and the king said to the girl, "Ask me for whatever you wish, and I will give it." And he solemnly swore to her, "Whatever you ask me, I will give you, even half of my kingdom." She went out and said to her mother, "What should I ask for?" She replied, "The head of John the baptizer." Immediately she rushed back to the king and requested, "I want you to give me at once the head of John the Baptist on a platter." The king was deeply grieved; yet out of regard for his oaths and for the guests, he did not want to refuse her. Immediately the king sent a soldier of the guard with orders to bring John's head. He went and beheaded him in the prison, brought his head on a platter, and gave it to the girl. Then the girl gave it to her mother. When his disciples heard about it, they came and took his body, and laid it in a tomb.

Notice what you think and feel as you read the gospel.

John the Baptist spoke truth to power and was martyred for it in an absurd and grotesque way.

Pray as you are led for yourself and others.

"Lord, give me the honesty and courage of John, for I long to serve you well, even if I suffer for it. I pray for all those suffering now for their faith in you . . ." (Continue in your own words.)

Listen to Jesus.

Do not be afraid of persecution or suffering you receive because of me. I am with you and will give you whatever you need to endure it. If killed, you will receive honor in heaven. If not killed, you will also receive honor in heaven. Beloved, cling to me and find safety and everlasting life. What else is Jesus saying to you?

Ask God to show you how to live today.

"Do I ever suffer in your name, Lord? I am willing if it be your will. Prepare me, Lord. Thank you. Amen."

Thursday, August 30, 2018

Know that God is present and ready to converse.

"Lord, I am ready. Keep me faithful to your Word."

Read the gospel: Matthew 24:42–51.

Jesus said, "Keep awake therefore, for you do not know on what day your Lord is coming. But understand this: if the owner of the house had known in what part of the night the thief was coming, he would have stayed awake and would not have let his house be broken into.

Therefore you also must be ready, for the Son of Man is coming at an unexpected hour.

"Who then is the faithful and wise slave, whom his master has put in charge of his household, to give the other slaves their allowance of food at the proper time? Blessed is that slave whom his master will find at work when he arrives. Truly I tell you, he will put that one in charge of all his possessions. But if that wicked slave says to himself, 'My master is delayed,' and he begins to beat his fellow slaves, and eats and drinks with drunkards, the master of that slave will come on a day when he does not expect him and at an hour that he does not know. He will cut him in pieces and put him with the hypocrites, where there will be weeping and gnashing of teeth."

Notice what you think and feel as you read the gospel.

Jesus tells his disciples to be ready for his return, using the examples of the faithful slave and the wicked slave. Serving God is a high-stakes business and must be taken seriously.

Pray as you are led for yourself and others.

"Lord, I aspire to be faithful and wise in your service. Enable me . . ." (Continue in your own words.)

Listen to Jesus.

I grant you the sincere prayer from your heart, beloved. The affairs of the world can cause your faith and love to wither. Your own heart can betray you. But you will walk with me. What else is Jesus saying to you?

Ask God to show you how to live today.

"I shall walk with you today, dear Lord and Master. Let me do your will today, every day, one day at a time. Amen."

Friday, August 31, 2018

Know that God is present and ready to converse.

"Lord, I wish to know you through the reading of your Word. Thank you for being here with me."

Read the gospel: Matthew 25:1–13.

Jesus said, "Then the kingdom of heaven will be like this. Ten bridesmaids took their lamps and went to meet the bridegroom. Five of them were foolish, and five were wise. When the foolish took their lamps, they took no oil with them; but the wise took flasks of oil with their lamps. As the bridegroom was delayed, all of them became drowsy and slept. But at midnight there was a shout, 'Look! Here is the bridegroom! Come out to meet him.' Then all those bridesmaids got up and trimmed their lamps. The foolish said to the wise, 'Give us some of your oil, for our lamps are going out.' But the wise replied, 'No! there will not be enough for you and for us; you had better go to the dealers and buy some for yourselves.' And while they went to buy it, the bridegroom came, and those who were ready went with him into the wedding banquet; and the door was shut. Later the other bridesmaids came also, saying, 'Lord, lord, open to us.' But he replied, 'Truly I tell you, I do not know you.' Keep awake therefore, for you know neither the day nor the hour."

Notice what you think and feel as you read the gospel.

Jesus' parable of the bridesmaids is about readiness, about waiting wisely for the return of the bridegroom, as he often referred to himself. The foolish ones have no oil in their lamps, so they can't go out to meet the bridegroom at midnight, but the wise ones are prepared. The bridegroom tells the foolish ones, "I do not know you."

Pray as you are led for yourself and others.

"By your grace, Lord, I will stay awake. Come soon, Lord, but first gather to yourself all who will come . . ." (Continue in your own words.)

Listen to Jesus.

I know you, my child, and I let you know me. Come to me often and love me, speak to me, rejoice with me, and mourn with me. These are the things lovers do. As we spend time together, you will know me more and more. What else is Jesus saying to you?

Ask God to show you how to live today.

"Today I will spend time with you, and I will take you with me. You will improve all the encounters and duties of my day. Thank you for the peace you give me, Lord. Amen."

Saturday, September 1, 2018

Know that God is present and ready to converse.

"Lord, I live to please you. Show me how to please you."

Read the gospel: Matthew 25:14–30.

Jesus said, "For it is as if a man, going on a journey, summoned his slaves and entrusted his property to them; to one he gave five talents, to another two, to another one, to each according to his ability. Then he went away. The one who had received the five talents went off at once and traded with them, and made five more talents. In the same way, the one who had the two talents made two more talents. But the one who had received the one talent went off and dug a hole in the ground and hid his master's money. After a long time the master of those slaves came and settled accounts with them. Then the one who had received the five talents came forward, bringing five more talents, saying, 'Master, you handed over to me five talents; see, I have made five more talents.' His master said to him, 'Well done, good and trustworthy slave; you have been trustworthy in a few things, I will put you in charge of many things; enter into the joy of your master.' And the one with the two talents also came forward, saying, 'Master, you handed over to me two talents; see, I have made two more talents.' His master said to him, 'Well done, good and trustworthy slave; you have been trustworthy in a few things, I will put you in charge of many things; enter into the joy of your master.' Then the one who had received the one talent also came forward, saying, 'Master, I knew that you were a harsh man, reaping where you did not sow, and gathering where you did not scatter seed; so I was afraid, and I went and hid your talent in the ground. Here you have what is yours.' But his master replied, 'You wicked and lazy slave! You knew, did you, that I reap where I did not sow, and gather where I did not scatter? Then you ought to have invested my money with the bankers, and on my return I would have received what was my own with interest. So take the talent from him, and give it to the one with the ten talents. For to all those who have, more will be given, and they will have an abundance; but from those who have nothing, even what they have will be taken away. As for this worthless slave, throw him into the outer darkness, where there will be weeping and gnashing of teeth.'"

Notice what you think and feel as you read the gospel.

Jesus tells a parable about using one's gifts in his service. Those who do the best they can with the gifts they are given are rewarded when the master returns. The one who buries his gift, the master rebukes and punishes.

Pray as you are led for yourself and others.

"Jesus, the wicked servant failed because he was afraid. Let me not be afraid to act on the gifts or talents you have given me . . ." (Continue in your own words.)

Listen to Jesus.

I long to say to you, beloved disciple, "Well done, good and trustworthy servant; enter into my joy." How do you propose to use your gifts? Do you need any help from me? Just ask. What else is Jesus saying to you?

Ask God to show you how to live today.

"I do ask you to help me identify and use my gifts well in your service. Help me discern the best ways to serve. Amen."

Sunday, September 2, 2018
Twenty-Second Sunday in Ordinary Time

Know that God is present and ready to converse.

"Savior, teach me the ways of righteousness by your holy Word."

Read the gospel: Mark 7:1–8, 14–15, 21–23.

Now when the Pharisees and some of the scribes who had come from Jerusalem gathered around Jesus, they noticed that some of his disciples were eating with defiled hands, that is, without washing them. (For the Pharisees, and all the Jews, do not eat unless they thoroughly wash their hands, thus observing the tradition of the elders; and they do not eat anything from the market unless they wash it; and there are also many other traditions that they observe, the washing of cups, pots, and bronze kettles.) So the Pharisees and the scribes asked him, "Why do your disciples not live according to the tradition of the elders, but eat with defiled hands?" He said to them, "Isaiah prophesied rightly about you hypocrites, as it is written,

> 'This people honors me with their lips,
> but their hearts are far from me;
> in vain do they worship me,
> teaching human precepts as doctrines.'

You abandon the commandment of God and hold to human tradition." . . .

Then he called the crowd again and said to them, "Listen to me, all of you, and understand: there is nothing outside a person that by going in can defile, but the things that come out are what defile. . . .

"For it is from within, from the human heart, that evil intentions come: fornication, theft, murder, adultery, avarice, wickedness, deceit, licentiousness, envy, slander, pride, folly. All these evil things come from within, and they defile a person."

Notice what you think and feel as you read the gospel.

Jesus talks about phony religion, which is full of man-made rules and ignores the commandments of God. You can observe ritual washings, but they will not make you clean. One is defiled by the evils that come from within the heart.

Pray as you are led for yourself and others.

"I am a sinner, Lord, seeking forgiveness and cleansing. I turn from my sins, and I pray that others may turn to you also . . ." (Continue in your own words.)

Listen to Jesus.

Turn to me in the sacrament of Penance, dear one, and I will give you grace to do better. Cooperate with my grace and you will see change. Return to me often to confess your sins. What else is Jesus saying to you?

Ask God to show you how to live today.

"Lord, give me the grace to honor you with my heart today. Amen."

Monday, September 3, 2018

Know that God is present and ready to converse.

"Jesus, let me never take you for granted. Let me be near you always."

Read the gospel: Luke 4:16–30.

When Jesus came to Nazareth, where he had been brought up, he went to the synagogue on the sabbath day, as was his custom. He stood up to read, and the scroll of the prophet Isaiah was given to him. He unrolled the scroll and found the place where it was written:

"The Spirit of the Lord is upon me,
because he has anointed me
to bring good news to the poor.
He has sent me to proclaim release to the captives

and recovery of sight to the blind,
to let the oppressed go free,
to proclaim the year of the Lord's favor."

And he rolled up the scroll, gave it back to the attendant, and sat down. The eyes of all in the synagogue were fixed on him. Then he began to say to them, "Today this scripture has been fulfilled in your hearing." All spoke well of him and were amazed at the gracious words that came from his mouth. They said, "Is not this Joseph's son?" He said to them, "Doubtless you will quote to me this proverb, 'Doctor, cure yourself!' And you will say, 'Do here also in your home town the things that we have heard you did at Capernaum.'" And he said, "Truly I tell you, no prophet is accepted in the prophet's home town. But the truth is, there were many widows in Israel in the time of Elijah, when the heaven was shut up for three years and six months, and there was a severe famine over all the land; yet Elijah was sent to none of them except to a widow at Zarephath in Sidon. There were also many lepers in Israel in the time of the prophet Elisha, and none of them was cleansed except Naaman the Syrian." When they heard this, all in the synagogue were filled with rage. They got up, drove him out of the town, and led him to the brow of the hill on which their town was built, so that they might hurl him off the cliff. But he passed through the midst of them and went on his way.

Notice what you think and feel as you read the gospel.

Jesus has a close call in his home town because the people do not accept him as a prophet. Somehow he passes through the midst of them untouched and leaves. They were enraged because he attributes Isaiah's words about the Messiah to himself. At first they speak well of him, but then they realize they know him, Joseph's son. How can he be the Messiah?

Pray as you are led for yourself and others.

"Messiah, you bring me good news, sight, and freedom. Let me proclaim your goodness to others . . ." (Continue in your own words.)

Listen to Jesus.

I am able and willing to save many, my beloved. Some will hear you now, and some will not. Some will despise you. Some will ignore you. Some will think about what you have said about me, and they will come to me later. Thank you for speaking of me. You speak with your actions too. What else is Jesus saying to you?

Ask God to show you how to live today.

"Teach me to speak and act according to your will. You have done so much for me, Lord. Amen."

Tuesday, September 4, 2018

Know that God is present and ready to converse.

"Lord, you give me your Word with authority. I will hear you now."

Read the gospel: Luke 4:31–37.

Jesus went down to Capernaum, a city in Galilee, and was teaching them on the sabbath. They were astounded at his teaching, because he spoke with authority. In the synagogue there was a man who had the spirit of an unclean demon, and he cried out with a loud voice, "Let us alone! What have you to do with us, Jesus of Nazareth? Have you come to destroy us? I know who you are, the Holy One of God." But Jesus rebuked him, saying, "Be silent, and come out of him!" When the demon had thrown him down before them, he came out of him without having done him any harm. They were all amazed and kept saying to one another, "What kind of utterance is this? For with authority and power he commands the unclean spirits, and out they come!" And a report about him began to reach every place in the region.

Notice what you think and feel as you read the gospel.

Jesus, because he is the Messiah, the Holy One of God, speaks and acts with authority, astounding the people of Capernaum. His fame spreads.

Pray as you are led for yourself and others.

"Lord, you are the Truth of God. How I long for all to receive you. So many need you . . ." (Continue in your own words.)

Listen to Jesus.

I speak, I heal, I forgive, I call, and I am willing, but I cannot make people come to me. Dear disciple, stay strong in faith and love, stay hopeful about those who do not come to me. And pray for them. You will see marvels. What else is Jesus saying to you?

Ask God to show you how to live today.

"Help me remember, Lord, your power and authority, and I will walk in hope today even in the darkness of the world. Amen."

Wednesday, September 5, 2018

Know that God is present and ready to converse.

"Lord, I was looking for you, and I find you already here, waiting for me. Let me hear your good news."

Read the gospel: Luke 4:38–44.

After leaving the synagogue Jesus entered Simon's house. Now Simon's mother-in-law was suffering from a high fever, and they asked him about her. Then he stood over her and rebuked the fever, and it left her. Immediately she got up and began to serve them.

As the sun was setting, all those who had any who were sick with various kinds of diseases brought them to him; and he laid his hands on each of them and cured them. Demons also came out of many, shouting, "You are the Son of God!" But he rebuked them and would not allow them to speak, because they knew that he was the Messiah.

At daybreak he departed and went into a deserted place. And the crowds were looking for him; and when they reached him, they wanted to prevent him from leaving them. But he said to them, "I must proclaim the good news of the kingdom of God to the other cities also; for I was sent for this purpose." So he continued proclaiming the message in the synagogues of Judea.

Notice what you think and feel as you read the gospel.

Jesus heals and proclaims the good news of the kingdom of God in a deserted place. The people don't want him to leave, but he must go and continue doing what God sent him to do.

Pray as you are led for yourself and others.

"Lord, you did your duty with love and obedience. Let me do that today, as I pray for those you have given me . . ." (Continue in your own words.)

Listen to Jesus.

People sometimes find that life is very difficult, full of suffering and disappointment. And it is. But there is peace and joy even in the midst of suffering. Surrender to the will of God, beloved, keep God's commandments, and you will know his peace and joy. What else is Jesus saying to you?

Ask God to show you how to live today.

"Lord, I will go with you today, surrendering to your will, because I don't want to go without you. Amen."

Thursday, September 6, 2018

Know that God is present and ready to converse.

"Lord, I come to you today to hear the Word of God. Let me receive it and obey it."

Read the gospel: Luke 5:1–11.

Once while Jesus was standing beside the lake of Gennesaret, and the crowd was pressing in on him to hear the word of God, he saw two boats there at the shore of the lake; the fishermen had gone out of them and were washing their nets. He got into one of the boats, the one belonging to Simon, and asked him to put out a little way from the shore. Then he sat down and taught the crowds from the boat. When he had finished speaking, he said to Simon, "Put out into the deep water and let down your nets for a catch." Simon answered, "Master, we have worked all night long but have caught nothing. Yet if you say so, I will let down the nets." When they had done this, they caught so many fish that their nets were beginning to break. So they signaled to their partners in the other boat to come and help them. And they came and filled both boats, so that they began to sink. But when Simon Peter saw it, he fell down at Jesus' knees, saying, "Go away from me, Lord, for I am a sinful man!" For he and all who were with him were amazed at the catch of fish that they had taken; and so also were James and John, sons of Zebedee, who were partners with Simon. Then Jesus said to Simon, "Do not be afraid; from now on you will be catching people." When they had brought their boats to shore, they left everything and followed him.

Notice what you think and feel as you read the gospel.

Jesus is not shy about performing a dramatic sign to make a point. The point is that his disciples will carry on his work of proclaiming the word of God, and that many will hear and believe. The fish they caught when they followed Jesus' orders represent the unimaginable numbers of people who will come to faith in him.

Pray as you are led for yourself and others.

"Lord, are you still fishing for the souls of people? Send me. I pray for all who do not yet know you, or who have turned aside from your way . . ." (Continue in your own words.)

Listen to Jesus.

It is not easy to walk with me, beloved. You know that. My disciples pay a price, often a great price, but their work and witness is vital to the project of salvation, and the reward is infinitely greater than all the sacrifices. What else is Jesus saying to you?

Ask God to show you how to live today.

"Prepare me to go out to preach the good news, Lord, with actions and words. Amen."

Friday, September 7, 2018

Know that God is present and ready to converse.

"Lord, I come to you to get to know and love you better. Speak to my heart."

Read the gospel: Luke 5:33–39.

Then the Pharisees and their scribes said to Jesus, "John's disciples, like the disciples of the Pharisees, frequently fast and pray, but your disciples eat and drink." Jesus said to them, "You cannot make wedding guests fast while the bridegroom is with them, can you? The days will come when the bridegroom will be taken away from them, and then they will fast in those days." He also told them a parable: "No one tears a piece from a new garment and sews it on an old garment; otherwise the new will be torn, and the piece from the new will not match the old. And no one puts new wine into old wineskins; otherwise the new wine will burst the skins and will be spilled, and the skins will be destroyed. But new wine must be put into fresh wineskins. And no one after drinking old wine desires new wine, but says, 'The old is good.'"

Notice what you think and feel as you read the gospel.

Jesus compares himself to a bridegroom and his disciples to wedding guests. His disciples cannot fast as long as he is present; later they will. The patch on the old garment and the new wine in fresh wineskins suggest that the spiritual universe has changed since Jesus.

Pray as you are led for yourself and others.

"Help me discern what is good, old or new, Jesus. How may I serve you and those you have given me? . . ." (Continue in your own words.)

Listen to Jesus.

Rejoice with me today, dear disciple, because we are together and I do my work through you. What is my work? To love at every opportunity. If you love from the heart, you will show it in your words and actions. What else is Jesus saying to you?

Ask God to show you how to live today.

"I will listen for your voice all day, Lord, for you speak to me when I need it. Amen."

Saturday, September 8, 2018
Nativity of the Blessed Virgin Mary

Know that God is present and ready to converse.

"Almighty God, you work your will through your Word. I give my will to you."

Read the gospel: Matthew 1:1–16, 18–23.

An account of the genealogy of Jesus the Messiah, the son of David, the son of Abraham.

Abraham was the father of Isaac, and Isaac the father of Jacob, and Jacob the father of Judah and his brothers, and Judah the father of Perez and Zerah by Tamar, and Perez the father of Hezron, and Hezron the father of Aram, and Aram the father of Aminadab, and Aminadab the father of Nahshon, and Nahshon the father of Salmon, and Salmon the father of Boaz by Rahab, and Boaz the father of Obed by Ruth, and Obed the father of Jesse, and Jesse the father of King David.

And David was the father of Solomon by the wife of Uriah, and Solomon the father of Rehoboam, and Rehoboam the father of Abijah, and Abijah the father of Asaph, and Asaph the father of Jehoshaphat, and Jehoshaphat the father of Joram, and Joram the father of Uzziah, and Uzziah the father of Jotham, and Jotham the father of Ahaz, and Ahaz the father of Hezekiah, and Hezekiah the father of Manasseh, and Manasseh the father of Amos, and Amos the father of Josiah, and Josiah the father of Jechoniah and his brothers, at the time of the deportation to Babylon.

And after the deportation to Babylon: Jechoniah was the father of Salathiel, and Salathiel the father of Zerubbabel, and Zerubbabel the father of Abiud, and Abiud the father of Eliakim, and Eliakim the father of Azor, and Azor the father of Zadok, and Zadok the father of Achim, and Achim the father of Eliud, and Eliud the father of Eleazar, and Eleazar the father of Matthan, and Matthan the father of Jacob, and Jacob the father of Joseph the husband of Mary, of whom Jesus was born, who is called the Messiah. . . .

Now the birth of Jesus the Messiah took place in this way. When his mother Mary had been engaged to Joseph, but before they lived together, she was found to be with child from the Holy Spirit. Her husband Joseph, being a righteous man and unwilling to expose her to public disgrace, planned to dismiss her quietly. But just when he had resolved to do this, an angel of the Lord appeared to him in a dream and said, "Joseph, son of David, do not be afraid to take Mary as your wife, for the child conceived in her is from the Holy Spirit. She will bear a son, and you are to name him Jesus, for he will save his people from their sins." All this took place to fulfill what had been spoken by the Lord through the prophet:

"Look, the virgin shall conceive and bear a son,
and they shall name him Emmanuel,"

which means, "God is with us."

Notice what you think and feel as you read the gospel.

Jesus, the Son of God by the Holy Spirit, was, through his earthly father, the descendant of many, both good and bad. Joseph, a good man, is guided by an angel in a dream, and he obeys, for he believes that Jesus will save his people.

Pray as you are led for yourself and others.

"Jesus, your mother, Mary, was born that she could give birth to you, that her body could shelter you and give you a loving welcome. Grant me that same love for you, that I may carry you to others . . ." (Continue in your own words.)

Listen to Jesus.

Dear child, I welcome you into my family. Seek me in word and sacrament, and you will know that I am with you. What else is Jesus saying to you?

Ask God to show you how to live today.

"Emmanuel, dwell in me today and help me accept and follow your will. Be with me now and forever. Amen."

Sunday, September 9, 2018
Twenty-Third Sunday in Ordinary Time

Know that God is present and ready to converse.

"Lord, you do everything well. Guide my prayer."

Read the gospel: Mark 7:31–37.

Then Jesus returned from the region of Tyre, and went by way of Sidon towards the Sea of Galilee, in the region of the Decapolis. They brought to him a deaf man who had an impediment in his speech; and they begged him to lay his hand on him. He took him aside in private, away from the crowd, and put his fingers into his ears, and he spat and touched his tongue. Then looking up to heaven, he sighed and said to him, "Ephphatha," that is, "Be opened." And immediately his ears were opened, his tongue was released, and he spoke plainly. Then Jesus ordered them to tell no one; but the more he ordered them, the more zealously they proclaimed it. They were astounded beyond measure, saying, "He has done everything well; he even makes the deaf to hear and the mute to speak."

Notice what you think and feel as you read the gospel.

Jesus uses an unusual method to heal a deaf man with a speech impediment. The people are astounded and rapidly tell others.

Pray as you are led for yourself and others.

"Lord, heal me so I may hear your words more clearly and speak your praise more joyfully. I pray for those in need of healing today . . ." (Continue in your own words.)

Listen to Jesus.

Even now I work on the earth, as my Father works and the Holy Spirit works. We have one purpose: to bring all people into the kingdom of God. We draw them with love. You do so also, beloved. What else is Jesus saying to you?

Ask God to show you how to live today.

"Open my heart to love you, my God, and to love all those I encounter. I praise you. Amen."

Monday, September 10, 2018

Know that God is present and ready to converse.

"Lord, you did your works among sinful men and women. You speak your Word to sinners like me. Thank you."

Read the gospel: Luke 6:6–11.

On another sabbath Jesus entered the synagogue and taught, and there was a man there whose right hand was withered. The scribes and the Pharisees watched him to see whether he would cure on the sabbath, so that they might find an accusation against him. Even though he knew what they were thinking, he said to the man who had the withered hand, "Come and stand here." He got up and stood there. Then Jesus said to them, "I ask you, is it lawful to do good or to do harm on the sabbath, to save life or to destroy it?" After looking around at all of them, he said to him, "Stretch out your hand." He did so, and his hand was restored. But they were filled with fury and discussed with one another what they might do to Jesus.

Notice what you think and feel as you read the gospel.

The scribes and Pharisees do not rejoice that Jesus heals the man with the withered hand. They hate Jesus. They will not even answer his questions. After he restores the man's hand, they are furious and discuss how to hurt Jesus.

Pray as you are led for yourself and others.

"Lord, I pray earnestly for all who hate you. Save them, Lord, for they don't understand . . ." (Continue in your own words.)

Listen to Jesus.

You are my beloved disciple, friend. I have called you to faith in me, I call you to love others with my love; I call you to hope for my return. The kingdom of heaven is coming. Watch and pray. What else is Jesus saying to you?

Ask God to show you how to live today.

"Let me see the coming of your kingdom today, Lord. Let me see it in others; let me see it in me. Thank you. Amen."

Tuesday, September 11, 2018

Know that God is present and ready to converse.

"Jesus, you have chosen me—you love me and speak to me. Make me your disciple by your Word."

Read the gospel: Luke 6:12–19.

Now during those days Jesus went out to the mountain to pray; and he spent the night in prayer to God. And when day came, he called his disciples and chose twelve of them, whom he also named apostles: Simon, whom he named Peter, and his brother Andrew, and James, and John, and Philip, and Bartholomew, and Matthew, and Thomas, and James son of Alphaeus, and Simon, who was called the Zealot, and Judas son of James, and Judas Iscariot, who became a traitor.

He came down with them and stood on a level place, with a great crowd of his disciples and a great multitude of people from all Judea, Jerusalem, and the coast of Tyre and Sidon. They had come to hear him and to be healed of their diseases; and those who were troubled with unclean spirits were cured. And all in the crowd were trying to touch him, for power came out from him and healed all of them.

Notice what you think and feel as you read the gospel.

Jesus prays all night, then chooses twelve disciples to be his apostles, including Judas. Then he goes down to the great multitude and heals all of them.

Pray as you are led for yourself and others.

"All are in need of healing, Lord, inside and outside. I pray especially for those who need spiritual and psychological healing . . ." (Continue in your own words.)

Listen to Jesus.

I am healing you, too, beloved, making you whole. I am the fountain of holiness, and I give you this pure water to drink. Pray with me. Stay with me as long as you can. We need our time together. What else is Jesus saying to you?

Ask God to show you how to live today.

"Give me this water, Lord, and keep me close by you everywhere I go. Amen."

Wednesday, September 12, 2018

Know that God is present and ready to converse.

"Teach me your blessedness, Lord. Open me to receive your wisdom by your Word."

Read the gospel: Luke 6:20–26.

Then Jesus looked up at his disciples and said:

"Blessed are you who are poor,
for yours is the kingdom of God.
"Blessed are you who are hungry now,
for you will be filled.
"Blessed are you who weep now,

for you will laugh.

"Blessed are you when people hate you, and when they exclude you, revile you, and defame you on account of the Son of Man. Rejoice on that day and leap for joy, for surely your reward is great in heaven; for that is what their ancestors did to the prophets.

"But woe to you who are rich,
for you have received your consolation.
"Woe to you who are full now,
for you will be hungry.
"Woe to you who are laughing now,
for you will mourn and weep.

"Woe to you when all speak well of you, for that is what their ancestors did to the false prophets."

Notice what you think and feel as you read the gospel.

Jesus must have amazed his listeners with these words, for they seem the opposite of common sense. His wisdom is informed by his knowledge of his loving Father and the eternity he has prepared for all who follow his way of love. Adversity on the path is better than comfort because the reward for those who are poor and suffer, especially for Jesus' sake, is great in heaven.

Pray as you are led for yourself and others.

"Lord, give me your vision of blessedness, and let me rejoice to suffer for your sake. I pray for those who are comfortable and complacent without God . . ." (Continue in your own words.)

Listen to Jesus.

You are learning to have my heart, dear disciple. I will reward your faithfulness with eternal life in companionship with God, the angels, and the saints. You will have troubles now, but rejoice in the prospect of the kingdom of heaven. What else is Jesus saying to you?

Ask God to show you how to live today.

"Let me experience my troubles in this way, Lord, accepting and even rejoicing, for I have treasure in heaven. Amen."

Thursday, September 13, 2018

Know that God is present and ready to converse.

"Jesus, Teacher, I shall sit at your feet and hear your Word."

Read the gospel: Luke 6:27–38.

Jesus said, "But I say to you that listen, Love your enemies, do good to those who hate you, bless those who curse you, pray for those who abuse you. If anyone strikes you on the cheek, offer the other also; and from anyone who takes away your coat do not withhold even your shirt. Give to everyone who begs from you; and if anyone takes away your goods, do not ask for them again. Do to others as you would have them do to you.

"If you love those who love you, what credit is that to you? For even sinners love those who love them. If you do good to those who do good to you, what credit is that to you? For even sinners do the same. If you lend to those from whom you hope to receive, what credit is that to you? Even sinners lend to sinners, to receive as much again. But love your enemies, do good, and lend, expecting nothing in return. Your reward will be great, and you will be children of the Most High; for he is kind to the ungrateful and the wicked. Be merciful, just as your Father is merciful.

"Do not judge, and you will not be judged; do not condemn, and you will not be condemned. Forgive, and you will be forgiven; give, and it will be given to you. A good measure, pressed down, shaken together, running over, will be put into your lap; for the measure you give will be the measure you get back."

Notice what you think and feel as you read the gospel.

Jesus establishes the highest possible standards for moral behavior, as he exemplified in his life, ministry, passion, and death. He teaches how to respond to evil with love.

Pray as you are led for yourself and others.

"Lord, I pray for all those who have hurt me. Bless them with your loving presence . . ." (Continue in your own words.)

Listen to Jesus.

You will encounter difficult people and difficult situations. In fact, you may sometimes look for them because they are opportunities for you to show them the love of God, the love I put into your heart. This is honoring me and living the Gospel before others. What else is Jesus saying to you?

Ask God to show you how to live today.

"Help me to hold your teaching in my heart as I encounter difficult people today, Savior. Help me live to your high standard of morality today and every day. I bless your name, Lord. Amen."

Friday, September 14, 2018
Exaltation of the Holy Cross

Know that God is present and ready to converse.

"Jesus, Messiah, you were indeed a prophet in your earthly ministry. I will listen to your Word."

Read the gospel: John 3:13–17.

Jesus said, "No one has ascended into heaven except the one who descended from heaven, the Son of Man. And just as Moses lifted up the serpent in the wilderness, so must the Son of Man be lifted up, that whoever believes in him may have eternal life.

"For God so loved the world that he gave his only Son, so that everyone who believes in him may not perish but may have eternal life.

"Indeed, God did not send the Son into the world to condemn the world, but in order that the world might be saved through him."

Notice what you think and feel as you read the gospel.

Jesus pronounces that he is from heaven, from God. Just as Moses lifted up the serpent in the wilderness to save his people, so Jesus must be lifted up on a cross to save us and give us eternal life. Jesus is here not to condemn people but to save all who believe in him.

Pray as you are led for yourself and others.

"Lord, sometimes it is difficult to believe in you, especially at certain times in our lives. I pray for those whose faith is wavering . . ." (Continue in your own words.)

Listen to Jesus.

I came and did what my Father sent me to do. The world remained in darkness, but many came into my light, receiving the gifts of God. I give you life, peace, truth, faith, hope, love, and much, much more. You belong to my family, dear disciple. What else is Jesus saying to you?

Ask God to show you how to live today.

"Give me a heart today to invite another into your holy family. Put me before a person who needs to know you. Amen."

Saturday, September 15, 2018
Our Lady of Sorrows

Know that God is present and ready to converse.

"Jesus, you speak in the gospels as no one ever has or ever will. Your Word speaks to me across the centuries."

Read the gospel: John 19:25b–27.

Meanwhile, standing near the cross of Jesus were his mother, and his mother's sister, Mary the wife of Clopas, and Mary Magdalene. When Jesus saw his mother and the disciple whom he loved standing beside her, he said to his mother, "Woman, here is your son." Then he said to the disciple, "Here is your mother." And from that hour the disciple took her into his own home.

Notice what you think and feel as you read the gospel.

Even as he suffers before dying, Jesus did not forget his grieving mother. He puts her in the care of John the apostle and John in her care. Did Mary teach John her perfect way of love?

Pray as you are led for yourself and others.

"Lord, you want me to care for others, even those not in my own family. I pray for those who have no family or who are abandoned or abused . . ." (Continue in your own words.)

Listen to Jesus.

There are many needy people in the world, beloved disciple. I need a great army of workers to feed, heal, and care for the needy. Would you join that army? It is the way to joy and eternal life. What else is Jesus saying to you?

Ask God to show you how to live today.

"I offer myself today. I just need your guidance as to how best to serve, how best to please you, Lord. Amen."

Sunday, September 16, 2018
Twenty-Fourth Sunday in Ordinary Time

Know that God is present and ready to converse.

"Son of God, Jesus, manifest yourself to me by your mighty Word."

Read the gospel: Mark 8:27–35.

Jesus went on with his disciples to the villages of Caesarea Philippi; and on the way he asked his disciples, "Who do people say that I am?" And they answered him, "John the Baptist; and others, Elijah; and still others, one of the prophets." He asked them, "But who do you say that I am?" Peter answered him, "You are the Messiah." And he sternly ordered them not to tell anyone about him.

Then he began to teach them that the Son of Man must undergo great suffering, and be rejected by the elders, the chief priests, and the scribes, and be killed, and after three days rise again. He said all this quite openly. And Peter took him aside and began to rebuke him. But turning and looking at his disciples, he rebuked Peter and said, "Get behind me, Satan! For you are setting your mind not on divine things but on human things."

He called the crowd with his disciples, and said to them, "If any want to become my followers, let them deny themselves and take up their cross and follow me. For those who want to save their life will lose it, and those who lose their life for my sake, and for the sake of the gospel, will save it."

Notice what you think and feel as you read the gospel.

Jesus commends Peter's acknowledgment that he is the Messiah, then he prophesies his Passion, Death, and Resurrection. When Peter rebukes him, he rebukes Peter. Jesus tells the crowd and his disciples that if they want to follow him, they must deny themselves and take up their crosses. To save your life, you must lose it.

Pray as you are led for yourself and others.

"I desire to deny myself in obedience to your Word, Lord. I offer my self-denial on behalf of those who do not yet follow you . . ." (Continue in your own words.)

Listen to Jesus.

Love thinks about others without regard to the suffering of self. Take up your cross and follow me. If you want to know love, God's and others', deny yourself and follow me. I am here with you, beloved disciple. What else is Jesus saying to you?

Ask God to show you how to live today.

"Lead me as I deny myself, Lord. You know what is best. Let me rejoice with you. Amen."

Monday, September 17, 2018

Know that God is present and ready to converse.

"Give me humility as I approach you, Lord, and hear your blessed Word."

Read the gospel: Luke 7:1–10.

After Jesus had finished all his sayings in the hearing of the people, he entered Capernaum. A centurion there had a slave whom he valued highly, and who was ill and close to death. When he heard about Jesus, he sent some Jewish elders to him, asking him to come and heal his slave. When they came to Jesus, they appealed to him earnestly, saying, "He is worthy of having you do this for him, for he loves our people, and it is he who built our synagogue for us." And Jesus went with them, but when he was not far from the house, the centurion sent friends to say to him, "Lord, do not trouble yourself, for I am not worthy to have you come under my roof; therefore I did not presume to come to you. But only speak the word, and let my servant be healed. For I also am a man set under authority, with soldiers under me; and I say to one, 'Go,' and he goes, and to another, 'Come,' and he comes, and to my slave, 'Do this,' and the slave does it." When Jesus heard this he was amazed at him, and turning to the crowd that followed him, he said, "I tell you, not even in Israel have I found such faith." When those who had been sent returned to the house, they found the slave in good health.

Notice what you think and feel as you read the gospel.

Jesus is impressed by the centurion and pays him high compliments. Why? The centurion loves his slave, so he seeks out Jesus to heal him. The centurion is humble, counting himself unworthy to have Jesus visit his house, but he has faith in Jesus' power.

Pray as you are led for yourself and others.

"Lord, give me the love, humility, and faith of the centurion, for I long to please you. I pray for those you have given me who are ill, especially the dying . . ." (Continue in your own words.)

Listen to Jesus.

Like the centurion, you, too, delight me when you come to me in prayer, beloved. You pray because you love and believe. I hear your prayers and do my work, sometimes in mysterious ways. You will understand later. What else is Jesus saying to you?

Ask God to show you how to live today.

"Let me find moments to love and pray in faith today, Lord. Many are in need. Amen."

Tuesday, September 18, 2018

Know that God is present and ready to converse.

"Compassionate Savior, you are here with me now. Let me love you as I hear the Word of God in my heart and mind."

Read the gospel: Luke 7:11–17.

Soon afterwards Jesus went to a town called Nain, and his disciples and a large crowd went with him. As he approached the gate of the town, a man who had died was being carried out. He was his mother's only son, and she was a widow; and with her was a large crowd from the town. When the Lord saw her, he had compassion for her and said to her, "Do not weep." Then he came forward and touched the bier, and the bearers stood still. And he said, "Young man, I say to you, rise!" The dead man sat up and began to speak, and Jesus gave him to his mother. Fear seized all of them; and they glorified God, saying, "A great prophet has risen among us!" and "God has looked favorably on his people!" This word about him spread throughout Judea and all the surrounding country.

Notice what you think and feel as you read the gospel.

Jesus has compassion not for the dead man but for the widow whose only son had died. He consoles her and then touches the dead man, raising him to life. Jesus gives him to his mother. No wonder Jesus' fame spread throughout all the country.

Pray as you are led for yourself and others.

"You were your mother's only son, Jesus. You must have thought of her and her grief at losing you. I pray for those in grief, especially mothers . . ." (Continue in your own words.)

Listen to Jesus.

I love mothers for they understand love, the sorrows of love as well as joys. I honor my own mother and offer her to you as your mother too. What else is Jesus saying to you?

Ask God to show you how to live today.

"I seek to understand love as your mother does, Lord. Let me know her love for you in my heart. Amen."

Wednesday, September 19, 2018

Know that God is present and ready to converse.

"Lord, I receive you and your holy Word now."

Read the gospel: Luke 7:31–35.

Jesus said, "To what then will I compare the people of this generation, and what are they like? They are like children sitting in the market-place and calling to one another,

'We played the flute for you, and you did not dance;
we wailed, and you did not weep.'

For John the Baptist has come eating no bread and drinking no wine, and you say, 'He has a demon'; the Son of Man has come eating and drinking, and you say, 'Look, a glutton and a drunkard, a friend of tax collectors and sinners!' Nevertheless, wisdom is vindicated by all her children."

Notice what you think and feel as you read the gospel.

Jesus knows he just can't win with some people. They aren't happy with any kind of message he brings. They find fault with him no matter what he does.

Pray as you are led for yourself and others.

"Lift the veils of darkness from my eyes, Lord, and from the eyes of those who find fault. I pray for . . ." (Continue in your own words.)

Listen to Jesus.

I speak to you softly, beloved follower. You hear my words, and you learn to love me. I would have you love all people as I do, for that is the greatest witness to me. Let others criticize you. They can criticize us both. Just love. What else is Jesus saying to you?

Ask God to show you how to live today.

"So I will love today, Lord, because you ask me to and because you give me the power to love. Amen."

Thursday, September 20, 2018

Know that God is present and ready to converse.

"Jesus, do you have something to say just to me?"

Read the gospel: Luke 7:36–50.

One of the Pharisees asked Jesus to eat with him, and he went into the Pharisee's house and took his place at the table. And a woman in the city, who was a sinner, having learned that he was eating in the Pharisee's house, brought an alabaster jar of ointment. She stood behind him at his feet, weeping, and began to bathe his feet with her tears and to dry them with her hair. Then she continued kissing his feet and anointing them with the ointment. Now when the Pharisee who had invited him saw it, he said to himself, "If this man were a prophet, he would have known who and what kind of woman this is who is touching him—that she is a sinner." Jesus spoke up and said to him, "Simon, I have something to say to you." "Teacher," he replied, "speak." "A certain creditor had two debtors; one owed five hundred denarii, and the other fifty. When they could not pay, he cancelled the debts for both of them. Now which of them will love him more?" Simon answered, "I suppose the one for whom he cancelled the greater debt." And Jesus said to him, "You have judged rightly." Then turning towards the woman, he said to Simon, "Do you see this woman? I entered your house; you gave me no water for my feet, but she has bathed my feet with her tears and dried them with her hair. You gave me no kiss, but from the time I came in she has not stopped kissing my feet. You did not anoint my head with oil, but she has anointed my feet with ointment. Therefore, I tell you, her sins, which were many, have been forgiven; hence she has shown great love. But the one to whom little is forgiven, loves little." Then he said to her, "Your sins are forgiven." But those who were at the table with him began to say among themselves, "Who is this who even forgives sins?" And he said to the woman, "Your faith has saved you; go in peace."

Notice what you think and feel as you read the gospel.

Jesus instructs the Pharisee who doubts that he is a prophet because he allows a sinful woman to anoint his feet. He tells everyone at the table that he has forgiven the woman's many sins, so she loves much and gives lavishly.

Pray as you are led for yourself and others.

"Jesus is the Messiah, the Son of God, with power to forgive sins. I ask forgiveness for . . ." (Continue in your own words.)

Listen to Jesus.

You cannot love me too much, dear disciple. When you come to me, I am very happy. When you stay with me I am happier still. I have much to share with you. Let's start with love. What else is Jesus saying to you?

Ask God to show you how to live today.

"I am grateful for your forgiveness, Lord. Let me not judge others who have also sinned. I will forgive them as you do. Amen."

Friday, September 21, 2018
Saint Matthew, Apostle and Evangelist

Know that God is present and ready to converse.

"Merciful Lord, I come to you for mercy. I find you here in your Word."

Read the gospel: Matthew 9:9–13.

As Jesus was walking along, he saw a man called Matthew sitting at the tax booth; and he said to him, "Follow me." And he got up and followed him.

And as he sat at dinner in the house, many tax collectors and sinners came and were sitting with him and his disciples. When the Pharisees saw this, they said to his disciples, "Why does your teacher eat with tax collectors and sinners?" But when he heard this, he said, "Those who are well have no need of a physician, but those who are sick. Go and learn what this means, 'I desire mercy, not sacrifice.' For I have come to call not the righteous but sinners."

Notice what you think and feel as you read the gospel.

Jesus calls Matthew to follow him, then eats with Matthew's friends at his house. Of course the Pharisees complain about Jesus' eating with sinners. Jesus says he came to call not the righteous but sinners.

Pray as you are led for yourself and others.

"I am a sinner, Lord, and you have called me. Thank you for forgiving me. I pray that you will also be merciful to these . . ." (Continue in your own words.)

Listen to Jesus.

Do not be afraid of what people say, my child. I was criticized for everything I said and did. My Father in heaven is criticized. My most faithful followers endure criticism and persecution. Just show everyone mercy, and rejoice in your reward. What else is Jesus saying to you?

Ask God to show you how to live today.

"Dear Jesus, help me to navigate through the good and evil of my day. I long to please you and serve you. Amen."

Saturday, September 22, 2018

Know that God is present and ready to converse.

"Lord, prepare my heart to receive your Word, that I may bear fruit to your glory."

Read the gospel: Luke 8:4–15.

When a great crowd gathered and people from town after town came to him, Jesus said in a parable: "A sower went out to sow his seed; and as he sowed, some fell on the path and was trampled on, and the birds of the air ate it up. Some fell on the rock; and as it grew up, it withered for lack of moisture. Some fell among thorns, and the thorns grew with it and choked it. Some fell into good soil, and when it grew, it produced a hundredfold." As he said this, he called out, "Let anyone with ears to hear listen!"

Then his disciples asked him what this parable meant. He said, "To you it has been given to know the secrets of the kingdom of God; but to others I speak in parables, so that

'looking they may not perceive,
and listening they may not understand.'

"Now the parable is this: The seed is the word of God. The ones on the path are those who have heard; then the devil comes and takes away the word from their hearts, so that they may not believe and be saved. The ones on the rock are those who, when they hear the word, receive it with joy. But these have no root; they believe only for a while and in a time of testing fall away. As for what fell among the thorns, these are the ones who hear; but as they go on their way, they are choked by the cares and riches and pleasures of life, and their fruit does not mature. But as for that in the good soil, these are the ones who, when they hear the word, hold it fast in an honest and good heart, and bear fruit with patient endurance."

Notice what you think and feel as you read the gospel.

Jesus tells a parable about receiving the Word of God fruitfully. It's not just hearing; it's holding the Word fast in an honest and good heart, then bearing fruit with patient endurance. That takes effort.

Pray as you are led for yourself and others.

"Jesus, make my heart wholly honest and good so that I can endure and bear fruit. I pray for others who seek to follow you, too, that you let your Word take root in their hearts . . ." (Continue in your own words.)

Listen to Jesus.

Sometimes people need to come to the end of themselves to turn to me, to the Word of God. Adversity often prepares a heart to receive me. But some grow angry and rebel. Yet I seek to gather souls with mercy and wisdom. What else is Jesus saying to you?

Ask God to show you how to live today.

"Give me mercy and wisdom to speak to those in adversity, Lord. Help me open their hearts to you. Amen."

Sunday, September 23, 2018
Twenty-Fifth Sunday in Ordinary Time

Know that God is present and ready to converse.

"Lord, I welcome your Word into my heart."

Read the gospel: Mark 9:30–37.

Jesus and his disciples went on from there and passed through Galilee. He did not want anyone to know it; for he was teaching his disciples, saying to them, "The Son of Man is to be betrayed into human hands, and they will kill him, and three days after being killed, he will rise again." But they did not understand what he was saying and were afraid to ask him.

Then they came to Capernaum; and when he was in the house he asked them, "What were you arguing about on the way?" But they were silent, for on the way they had argued with one another about who was the greatest. He sat down, called the twelve, and said to them, "Whoever wants to be first must be last of all and servant of all." Then he took a little child and put it among them; and taking it in his arms, he said to them, "Whoever welcomes one such child in my name welcomes me, and whoever welcomes me welcomes not me but the one who sent me."

Notice what you think and feel as you read the gospel.

Jesus prophesies his Passion, Death, and Resurrection, but his disciples don't hear it. Instead they argue among themselves about who is the greatest among them. Jesus tells them the one who would be first must be last and servant of all. He illustrates this by taking a child into his arms.

Pray as you are led for yourself and others.

"I am your servant, Jesus. I will care for your children. I pray now for . . ." (Continue in your own words.)

Listen to Jesus.

Do not seek greatness as defined by the world, my child. Seek to serve. Let your ambition and resources focus on the needs of others. Align with others to serve the needy, the poor, the abused, the captive, the hungry, the ill, the persecuted. In them you welcome me. What else is Jesus saying to you?

Ask God to show you how to live today.

"Lord, please help me to see, understand, and act in your service. Give me a new start today and steady my hand. Amen."

Monday, September 24, 2018

Know that God is present and ready to converse.

"Give me ears to hear you, Lord, as I contemplate your holy Word."

Read the gospel: Luke 8:16–18.

Jesus said, "No one after lighting a lamp hides it under a jar, or puts it under a bed, but puts it on a lampstand, so that those who enter may see the light. For nothing is hidden that will not be disclosed, nor is anything secret that will not become known and come to light. Then pay attention to how you listen; for to those who have, more will be given; and from those who do not have, even what they seem to have will be taken away."

Notice what you think and feel as you read the gospel.

Jesus urges his hearers to let their light shine in the world. He says to pay attention to how we listen, for those who receive will receive even more.

Pray as you are led for yourself and others.

"Lord, I am listening. Fill me with your light so others may see you in me. I pray for those in darkness . . . " (Continue in your own words.)

Listen to Jesus.

Life is difficult for all, beloved. Wealth, health, and comforts do not make life easy and pleasant. Troubles come in every way, if not now, then later. How do you escape troubles? No one can. But you can walk with me, serving others. We will find the way through. What else is Jesus saying to you?

Ask God to show you how to live today.

"Lead me, Lord; help me walk in your light. I place my trust in you, and my hand in yours. Amen."

Tuesday, September 25, 2018

Know that God is present and ready to converse.

"Jesus, you draw close to me now. I want to draw closer to you by reading your Word."

Read the gospel: Luke 8:19–21.

Then Jesus' mother and his brothers came to him, but they could not reach him because of the crowd. And he was told, "Your mother and your brothers are standing outside, wanting to see you." But he said to them, "My mother and my brothers are those who hear the word of God and do it."

Notice what you think and feel as you read the gospel.

Jesus loves his family, but here he extends membership to his family membership to all who hear the Word of God and do it. Our relationship to God and God's Word and our obedience make us members of God's holy family.

Pray as you are led for yourself and others.

"Lord, I hear your Word; let me do it in my thoughts, words, and deeds. I pray now for those who struggle to obey you . . ." (Continue in your own words.)

Listen to Jesus.

This is entry into the kingdom of heaven: to love others not of your own family, to serve others, to work with others to alleviate suffering, to share the Good News of God's complete salvation. What else is Jesus saying to you?

Ask God to show you how to live today.

"Lord, I give myself to all you ask. What shall I do first? Amen."

Wednesday, September 26, 2018

Know that God is present and ready to converse.

"Lord, your Word is a lamp to my feet. Let me walk in your will."

Read the gospel: Luke 9:1–6.

Then Jesus called the twelve together and gave them power and authority over all demons and to cure diseases, and he sent them out to proclaim the kingdom of God and to heal. He said to them, "Take nothing for your journey, no staff, nor bag, nor bread, nor money—not even an extra tunic. Whatever house you enter, stay there, and leave from there. Wherever they do not welcome you, as you are leaving that town shake the dust off your feet as a testimony against them." They departed and went through the villages, bringing the good news and curing diseases everywhere.

Notice what you think and feel as you read the gospel.

Jesus gives power to the apostles to cast out demons, to heal, and to proclaim the kingdom of God. He urges them to go without preparation and to move on when they are not welcomed. As workers for him, they can trust God for everything.

Pray as you are led for yourself and others.

"Lord, I am your servant. I pray I may trust you more each day. I pray for all you send out into the world. Let them trust in you . . ." (Continue in your own words.)

Listen to Jesus.

I know you, dear disciple, and your concerns for yourself and those you care for. It is natural for you to have such concerns. But there are many things you cannot do anything about, many things you cannot prepare for. Will you trust me? What else is Jesus saying to you?

Ask God to show you how to live today.

"Give me the Spirit you gave to your apostles, Lord. Show me where to go and how to go there in your service. Amen."

Thursday, September 27, 2018

Know that God is present and ready to converse.

"Jesus, make yourself known to me by your Word."

Read the gospel: Luke 9:7–9.

Now Herod the ruler heard about all that had taken place, and he was perplexed, because it was said by some that John had been raised from the dead, by some that Elijah had appeared, and by others that one of the ancient prophets had arisen. Herod said, "John I beheaded; but who is this about whom I hear such things?" And he tried to see him.

Notice what you think and feel as you read the gospel.

Herod is perplexed by what he is hearing about Jesus, fearing he is John the Baptist raised from the dead, for Herod had had John killed. Who is this Jesus?

Pray as you are led for yourself and others.

"You are Lord of heaven and earth, Jesus. Let all people know and worship you . . ." (Continue in your own words.)

Listen to Jesus.

People will do what they do, dear disciple. They will come to me if they hear about me—some of them. I am mercy, I am patience, I am the Lamb of God. God's will is being done. What else is Jesus saying to you?

Ask God to show you how to live today.

"I am saddened by those who do not come to you. What can I do to let them know you are calling them? Show me, Lord. Amen."

Friday, September 28, 2018

Know that God is present and ready to converse.

"Jesus you are here to reveal yourself to me through your Word. I thank you."

Read the gospel: Luke 9:18–22.

Once when Jesus was praying alone, with only the disciples near him, he asked them, "Who do the crowds say that I am?" They answered, "John the Baptist; but others, Elijah; and still others, that one of the ancient prophets has arisen." He said to them, "But who do you say that I am?" Peter answered, "The Messiah of God."

He sternly ordered and commanded them not to tell anyone, saying, "The Son of Man must undergo great suffering, and be rejected by the elders, chief priests, and scribes, and be killed, and on the third day be raised."

Notice what you think and feel as you read the gospel.

Jesus asks his disciples who people think he is, and they report the people's confusion. After Peter affirms that Jesus is the Messiah, Jesus tells them of his Passion, Death, and Resurrection.

Pray as you are led for yourself and others.

"You suffered and died for me, Lord. Thank you. Your rising was life and victory for me, too, Lord. Thank you. Let others know your salvation, Savior . . ." (Continue in your own words.)

Listen to Jesus.

I hear your prayers, beloved disciple. I am glad you walk with me. Take time to pray. I will meet you in prayer. I will make myself known to you in prayer. What else is Jesus saying to you?

Ask God to show you how to live today.

"Let me pray as I walk, Lord. Let me spend time alone with you. Amen."

Saturday, September 29, 2018
Saints Michael, Gabriel, and Raphael, Archangels

Know that God is present and ready to converse.

"Lord of hosts, you are with me now. Alleluia."

Read the gospel: John 1:47–51.

When Jesus saw Nathanael coming towards him, he said of him, "Here is truly an Israelite in whom there is no deceit!" Nathanael asked him, "Where did you come to know me?" Jesus answered, "I saw you under the fig tree before Philip called you." Nathanael replied, "Rabbi, you are the Son of God! You are the King of Israel!" Jesus answered, "Do you believe because I told you that I saw you under the fig tree? You will see greater things than these." And he said to him, "Very truly, I tell you, you will see heaven opened and the angels of God ascending and descending upon the Son of Man."

Notice what you think and feel as you read the gospel.

Jesus tells Nathanael he saw him under the fig tree. Nathanael immediately recognizes that Jesus is the Son of God. Jesus tells him that in the future he will see the angels ascending and descending upon him.

Pray as you are led for yourself and others.

"Jesus foretells the end of the age, his second glorious coming. Then all will see and know that he is Lord and King. I pray we are ready . . ." (Continue in your own words.)

Listen to Jesus.

I have tarried, but I will not tarry forever. I am moved by love and would gather all my sheep. You need have no fear. Just love me and trust me. Obey my commandments with all your heart. Live in my mercy. What else is Jesus saying to you?

Ask God to show you how to live today.

"I want to love and trust you every moment of this day, Lord. Fill me with your light. Amen."

Sunday, September 30, 2018
Twenty-Sixth Sunday in Ordinary Time

Know that God is present and ready to converse.

"Jesus, instruct me how I may please you."

Read the gospel: Mark 9:38–43, 45, 47–48.

John said to Jesus, "Teacher, we saw someone casting out demons in your name, and we tried to stop him, because he was not following us." But Jesus said, "Do not stop him; for no one who does a deed of power in my name will be able soon afterwards to speak evil of me. Whoever is not against us is for us. For truly I tell you, whoever gives you a cup of water to drink because you bear the name of Christ will by no means lose the reward.

"If any of you put a stumbling block before one of these little ones who believe in me, it would be better for you if a great millstone were hung around your neck and you were thrown into the sea. If your hand causes you to stumble, cut it off; it is better for you to enter life maimed than to have two hands and to go to hell, to the unquenchable fire. . . . And if your foot causes you to stumble, cut it off; it is better for you to enter life lame than to have two feet and to be thrown into hell. . . . And if your eye causes you to stumble, tear it out; it is better for you to enter the kingdom of God with one eye than to have two eyes and to be thrown into hell, where their worm never dies, and the fire is never quenched."

Notice what you think and feel as you read the gospel.

Jesus emphasizes the importance of removing obstacles to personal holiness, even at great sacrifice. The important thing is to enter the kingdom of God.

Pray as you are led for yourself and others.

"Lord, what hinders my holiness? Help me to relinquish obstacles, especially the ones I hold dear. I pray for all those who face obstacles within themselves . . ." (Continue in your own words.)

Listen to Jesus.

You bear the name of Christ, beloved. You follow me as I lead you, and that is right. Others follow me in different ways, and that is also right. Be at peace about the differences. I know my sheep and they know me. What else is Jesus saying to you?

Ask God to show you how to live today.

"Open my heart to embrace all your children, Lord. Let me welcome them. Amen."

Monday, October 1, 2018

Know that God is present and ready to converse.

"Jesus, let me be your child. I come to you now."

Read the gospel: Luke 9:46–50.

An argument arose among them as to which one of them was the greatest. But Jesus, aware of their inner thoughts, took a little child and put it by his side, and said to them, "Whoever welcomes this child in my name welcomes me, and whoever welcomes me welcomes the one who sent me; for the least among all of you is the greatest."

John answered, "Master, we saw someone casting out demons in your name, and we tried to stop him, because he does not follow with us." But Jesus said to him, "Do not stop him; for whoever is not against you is for you."

Notice what you think and feel as you read the gospel.

Jesus tells his disciples that the greatest among them must be the least among them, like a child.

Pray as you are led for yourself and others.

"Teach me to put aside self-reliance and trust entirely and only in you, Lord, like a child. I pray for all your followers, that they simply trust in you . . ." (Continue in your own words.)

Listen to Jesus.

Faith is the first virtue, dear child. It begins small but grows into complete abandonment to the will of God. It becomes an all-consuming love for God and for others. Trust me. What else is Jesus saying to you?

Ask God to show you how to live today.

"You must hold me, Lord, as we walk, for I cannot trust myself to cling to you. Amen."

Tuesday, October 2, 2018
The Guardian Angels

Know that God is present and ready to converse.

"Lord of glory, here now with me, let your Word change me today into whatever you would have me be."

Read the gospel: Matthew 18:1–5, 10.

At that time the disciples came to Jesus and asked, "Who is the greatest in the kingdom of heaven?" He called a child, whom he put among them, and said, "Truly I tell you, unless you change and become like children, you will never enter the kingdom of heaven. Whoever becomes humble like this child is the greatest in the kingdom of heaven. Whoever welcomes one such child in my name welcomes me.

"Take care that you do not despise one of these little ones; for, I tell you, in heaven their angels continually see the face of my Father in heaven."

Notice what you think and feel as you read the gospel.

As they worry about their greatness, Jesus tells the disciples they must change and be like children to enter the kingdom of heaven. The humble will enter. Love children, for their angels dwell with our Father in heaven.

Pray as you are led for yourself and others.

"I thank you for the angels of the children, Lord. Let them protect all children and lead them to the kingdom of heaven . . ." (Continue in your own words.)

Listen to Jesus.

People measure greatness by power, fame, and wealth. Those things do not confer greatness, even in this world. Faith, hope, and love confer greatness both in this world and in the eternal kingdom of God. What else is Jesus saying to you?

Ask God to show you how to live today.

"Help me to turn away from seeking worldly greatness and to walk humbly with you toward eternity. Amen."

Wednesday, October 3, 2018

Know that God is present and ready to converse.

"Almighty Lord and Savior, give me ears to hear you will as I read your holy Word."

Read the gospel: Luke 9:57–62.

As they were going along the road, someone said to him, "I will follow you wherever you go." And Jesus said to him, "Foxes have holes, and birds of the air have nests; but the Son of Man has nowhere to lay his head." To another he said, "Follow me." But he said, "Lord, first let me go and bury my father." But Jesus said to him, "Let the dead bury their own dead; but as for you, go and proclaim the kingdom of God." Another said, "I will follow you, Lord; but let me first say farewell to those at my home." Jesus said to him, "No one who puts a hand to the plough and looks back is fit for the kingdom of God."

Notice what you think and feel as you read the gospel.

Jesus says "follow me" and receives reasonable excuses in response, but he demands complete and persevering commitment. The reward is the kingdom of God.

Pray as you are led for yourself and others.

"Lord, forgive me my excuses. Help me follow you closely. Help all of us overcome the excuses that hold us back . . ." (Continue in your own words.)

Listen to Jesus.

Following me is an act of the will, the mind, and the heart. Count the cost: you stand to lose much in this life. Search your heart: How much do you love me? I ask you to enter fully into the love of God. You will gain everything, including everlasting life with God. What else is Jesus saying to you?

Ask God to show you how to live today.

"I resolve today to think about my excuses and ask you to remove them one by one. With your help, Lord, I will love you with my whole heart, mind, soul, and strength. Amen."

Thursday, October 4, 2018

Know that God is present and ready to converse.

"You are near me, Lord. Instruct me and give me grace to obey."

Read the gospel: Luke 10:1–12.

After this the Lord appointed seventy others and sent them on ahead of him in pairs to every town and place where he himself intended to go. He said to them, "The harvest is plentiful, but the laborers are few; therefore ask the Lord of the harvest to send out laborers into his harvest. Go on your way. See, I am sending you out like lambs into the midst of wolves. Carry no purse, no bag, no sandals; and greet no one on the road. Whatever house you enter, first say, 'Peace to this house!' And if anyone is there who shares in peace, your peace will rest on that person; but if not, it will return to you. Remain in the same house, eating and drinking whatever they provide, for the laborer deserves to be paid. Do not move about from house to house. Whenever you enter a town and its people welcome you, eat what is set before you; cure the sick who are there, and say to them, 'The kingdom of God has come near to you.' But whenever you enter a town and they do not welcome you, go out into its streets and say, 'Even the dust of your town that clings to our feet, we wipe off in protest against you. Yet know this: the kingdom of God has come near.' I tell you, on that day it will be more tolerable for Sodom than for that town."

Notice what you think and feel as you read the gospel.

Jesus sends out seventy disciples to proclaim the good news in many towns. He says they should act as laborers, harvesting for the Lord. He bids them go like lambs among wolves, traveling light, trusting in the generosity of others and the care of God. Their job is to announce the good news of the kingdom.

Pray as you are led for yourself and others.

"Today there are many ways to spread the good news of the kingdom. Send me, Lord. I pray for those who hear your good news from me . . ." (Continue in your own words.)

Listen to Jesus.

The centuries roll out long since I came to reconcile humanity with God. All this passing of time is for the purpose of gathering in the Lord's harvest of souls. The kingdom of God is still near. Thankfully, many are hearing the good news and drawing near to God. Thank you for being part of that, beloved. What else is Jesus saying to you?

Ask God to show you how to live today.

"So I will go out today with you by my side, Jesus. Give me your words, your actions, that my efforts may bear fruit to the glory of God and the good of others. Amen."

Friday, October 5, 2018

Know that God is present and ready to converse.

"Lord, I am before you as a blank sheet of paper. Inscribe your words on my heart."

Read the gospel: Luke 10:13–16.

Jesus said, "Woe to you, Chorazin! Woe to you, Bethsaida! For if the deeds of power done in you had been done in Tyre and Sidon, they would have repented long ago, sitting in sackcloth and ashes. But at the judgement it will be more tolerable for Tyre and Sidon than for you. And you, Capernaum, will you be exalted to heaven? No, you will be brought down to Hades.

"Whoever listens to you listens to me, and whoever rejects you rejects me, and whoever rejects me rejects the one who sent me."

Notice what you think and feel as you read the gospel.

Jesus pronounces woe on the cities that will neither hear him nor repent.

Pray as you are led for yourself and others.

"Lord, the stakes are high. Let us be a repenting people. I pray for those who resist repenting . . ." (Continue in your own words.)

Listen to Jesus.

Many have rationalized away their sin. Yet they see it in others. They will be judged by their own measure. Those who repent of sin will be given the gift of even deeper repentance, as they learn to see how their thoughts, words, and actions offend the holiness of God. They are on the path to joy and complete union with me. Come to me, dear child. What else is Jesus saying to you?

Ask God to show you how to live today.

"Lord, I am sorry for offending you. Give me deep repentance, as I long for you. Amen."

Saturday, October 6, 2018

Know that God is present and ready to converse.

"Jesus, my Lord and Savior, open my eyes to the treasures of your Word."

Read the gospel: Luke 10:17–24.

The seventy returned with joy, saying, "Lord, in your name even the demons submit to us!" He said to them, "I watched Satan fall from heaven like a flash of lightning. See, I have given you authority to tread on snakes and scorpions, and over all the power of the enemy; and nothing will hurt you. Nevertheless, do not rejoice at this, that the spirits submit to you, but rejoice that your names are written in heaven."

At that same hour Jesus rejoiced in the Holy Spirit and said, "I thank you, Father, Lord of heaven and earth, because you have hidden these things from the wise and the intelligent and have revealed them to infants; yes, Father, for such was your gracious will. All things have been handed over to me by my Father; and no one knows who the Son is except the Father, or who the Father is except the Son and anyone to whom the Son chooses to reveal him."

Then turning to the disciples, Jesus said to them privately, "Blessed are the eyes that see what you see! For I tell you that many prophets and kings desired to see what you see, but did not see it, and to hear what you hear, but did not hear it."

Notice what you think and feel as you read the gospel.

The seventy Jesus had sent out return with joy that Jesus had given them authority to do great works. But he says the proper reason to rejoice is that their names are written in heaven. Jesus prays, thanking his Father that not the wise and intelligent but infants understand the truths of God. To understand the ways of God and to know God are priceless.

Pray as you are led for yourself and others.

"Lord, let me be an infant before you. Let me know the Father, Son, and Holy Spirit. May others also learn the secrets of finding God . . ." (Continue in your own words.)

Listen to Jesus.

Finding and knowing the Father is very simple, beloved. Just desire him and you have already found him. Realize your need of the Father and simply turn to him. He has already enfolded you in his arms. We are here for you. What else is Jesus saying to you?

Ask God to show you how to live today.

"Thank you, loving Lord. Let me simply stay with you today and return your love in everything I do. Amen."

Sunday, October 7, 2018
Twenty-Seventh Sunday in Ordinary Time

Know that God is present and ready to converse.

"Lord, right and wrong can be difficult to discern. Give me, by your Word, the wisdom I need."

Read the gospel: Mark 10:2–16.

Some Pharisees came, and to test him they asked, "Is it lawful for a man to divorce his wife?" He answered them, "What did Moses command you?" They said, "Moses allowed a man to write a certificate of dismissal and to divorce her." But Jesus said to them, "Because of your hardness of heart he wrote this commandment for you. But from the beginning of creation, 'God made them male and female.' 'For this reason a man shall leave his father and mother and be joined to his wife, and the two shall become one flesh.' So they are no longer two, but one flesh. Therefore what God has joined together, let no one separate."

Then in the house the disciples asked him again about this matter. He said to them, "Whoever divorces his wife and marries another commits adultery against her; and if she divorces her husband and marries another, she commits adultery."

People were bringing little children to him in order that he might touch them; and the disciples spoke sternly to them. But when Jesus saw this, he was indignant and said to them, "Let the little children come to me; do not stop them; for it is to such as these that the kingdom of God belongs. Truly I tell you, whoever does not receive the kingdom of God as a little child will never enter it." And he took them up in his arms, laid his hands on them, and blessed them.

Notice what you think and feel as you read the gospel.

Jesus upholds strict standards of marriage, opposing divorce. Then he blesses the children, urging those who are near to receive God's kingdom as little children.

Pray as you are led for yourself and others.

"Lord, give me that childlike innocence and simplicity as I live and follow you. Keep me true to all my promises and let me welcome children . . ." (Continue in your own words.)

Listen to Jesus.

You can know your own motives, dear follower, but you cannot know others'. People do the things they feel they must do or want to do. Do not judge them, for by judging you harm your own soul and bring judgment unto yourself. Mercy, mercy, always mercy. What else is Jesus saying to you?

Ask God to show you how to live today.

"Keep your words of mercy before me, Lord, today, tomorrow, and all my life. I would grow in reflecting the mercy of God. Thank you for your great mercies to me. Amen."

Monday, October 8, 2018

Know that God is present and ready to converse.

"Lord, I long to know and do your will. Let your Word lead me in your way."

Read the gospel: Luke 10:25–37.

Just then a lawyer stood up to test Jesus. "Teacher," he said, "what must I do to inherit eternal life?" He said to him, "What is written in the law? What do you read there?" He answered, "You shall love the Lord your God with all your heart, and with all your soul, and with all your strength, and with all your mind; and your neighbor as yourself." And he said to him, "You have given the right answer; do this, and you will live."

But wanting to justify himself, he asked Jesus, "And who is my neighbor?" Jesus replied, "A man was going down from Jerusalem to Jericho, and fell into the hands of robbers, who stripped him, beat him, and went away, leaving him half dead. Now by chance a priest was going down that road; and when he saw him, he passed by on the other side. So likewise a Levite, when he came to the place and saw him, passed by on the other side. But a Samaritan while travelling came near him; and when he saw him, he was moved with pity. He went to him and bandaged his wounds, having poured oil and wine on them. Then he put him on his own animal, brought him to an inn, and took care of him. The next day he took out two denarii, gave them to the innkeeper, and said, 'Take care of him; and when I come back, I will repay you whatever more you spend.' Which of these three, do you think, was a neighbor to the man who fell into the hands of the robbers?" He said, "The one who showed him mercy." Jesus said to him, "Go and do likewise."

Notice what you think and feel as you read the gospel.

The lawyer is aware of the great commandment to love God and neighbor, but he wants to split hairs and asks whom he should consider to be his neighbor. In response, Jesus tells the parable of the good Samaritan. Those who know the law of charity and have the means to help the wounded man on the roadside pass by. But the Samaritan, deemed by Jews to be outcast and ignorant of the law, is moved with pity, and he takes care of the wounded man at his own expense of time and money. Jesus commends the Samaritan as a keeper of the great commandment.

Pray as you are led for yourself and others.

"I would go and do likewise, Lord. Let my prayers become actions of love for others . . ." (Continue in your own words.)

Listen to Jesus.

Do you sometimes look away from those who suffer? Are you overwhelmed by the needy? Don't be. Let your heart pity them. See them one by one and do what you can. I will give you the ability to do as the good Samaritan did. What else is Jesus saying to you?

Ask God to show you how to live today.

"I depend on your grace every day, Lord. Help me to do as you ask, loving God and neighbor. Amen."

Tuesday, October 9, 2018

Know that God is present and ready to converse.

"You are present with me now, Lord. Let me be present with you."

Read the gospel: Luke 10:38–42.

Now as they went on their way, Jesus entered a certain village, where a woman named Martha welcomed him into her home. She had a sister named Mary, who sat at the Lord's feet and listened to what he was saying. But Martha was distracted by her many tasks; so she came to him and asked, "Lord, do you not care that my sister has left me to do all the work by myself? Tell her then to help me." But the Lord answered her, "Martha, Martha, you are worried and distracted by many things; there is need of only one thing. Mary has chosen the better part, which will not be taken away from her."

Notice what you think and feel as you read the gospel.

When Jesus visits the house of Martha and Mary, Martha is distracted by her many tasks, and she complains to Jesus that Mary is not helping her. Mary was sitting at Jesus' feet and listening carefully to him. Jesus is gentle with Martha, but he defends and praises Mary's choice.

Pray as you are led for yourself and others.

"Lord, stop me when I am too busy for you. Let me listen. I pray for all those who feel too busy to spend time with you . . ." (Continue in your own words.)

Listen to Jesus.

There are times for action, but action becomes fruitful when it is accompanied by prayer. I have much to say to you, beloved, and what I say will change your heart and your approach to all things. Listen to me and love me. What else is Jesus saying to you?

Ask God to show you how to live today.

"So I shall listen and love you today. Direct my actions and the motives of my heart to be pleasing to you. Amen."

Wednesday, October 10, 2018

Know that God is present and ready to converse.

"Lord, teach me to pray."

Read the gospel: Luke 11:1–4.

He was praying in a certain place, and after he had finished, one of his disciples said to him, "Lord, teach us to pray, as John taught his disciples." He said to them, "When you pray, say:

Father, hallowed be your name.
Your kingdom come.
Give us each day our daily bread.
And forgive us our sins,
for we ourselves forgive everyone indebted to us.
And do not bring us to the time of trial."

Notice what you think and feel as you read the gospel.

Jesus teaches his disciples how to pray: we are to approach God as Father, with praise and longing for the kingdom. As we ask for what we need, we ask also for forgiveness and make an effort to forgive those who have hurt us.

Pray as you are led for yourself and others.

"Thank you for allowing me to come before you, Father; I trust that you will take care of me. Help me now to forgive all those who have offended me . . ." (Continue in your own words.)

Listen to Jesus.

Forgiveness is a gift from God. If you want to forgive someone, I will give you the grace to do it. It may not be immediate, but over time, I will wash away all resentment in your heart, and you will be free. Dear disciple, forgive everyone. What else is Jesus saying to you?

Ask God to show you how to live today.

"Let me forgive today, and let me not receive offenses as I might. Surround me with protective grace, Lord. Thank you. Amen."

Thursday, October 11, 2018

Know that God is present and ready to converse.

"My needs are great and many, Lord. You have come to supply my needs."

Read the gospel: Luke 11:5–13.

And Jesus said to them, "Suppose one of you has a friend, and you go to him at midnight and say to him, 'Friend, lend me three loaves of bread; for a friend of mine has arrived, and I have nothing to set before him.' And he answers from within, 'Do not bother me; the door has already been locked, and my children are with me in bed; I cannot get up and give you anything.' I tell you, even though he will not get up and give him anything because he is his friend, at least because of his persistence he will get up and give him whatever he needs.

"So I say to you, Ask, and it will be given to you; search, and you will find; knock, and the door will be opened for you. For everyone who asks receives, and everyone who searches finds, and for everyone who knocks, the door will be opened. Is there anyone among you who, if your child asks for a fish, will give a snake instead of a fish? Or if the child asks for an egg, will give a scorpion? If you then, who are evil, know how to give good gifts to your children, how much more will the heavenly Father give the Holy Spirit to those who ask him!"

Notice what you think and feel as you read the gospel.

With a human illustration, Jesus teaches persistence in prayer. Ask, search, knock, he says, and you will receive what you ask from God. God will give you good things, including the greatest gift, the Holy Spirit.

Pray as you are led for yourself and others.

"I ask for the Holy Spirit today, Lord. Let the Spirit come into me and guide my whole life. Then I will please you in serving others . . ." (Continue in your own words.)

Listen to Jesus.

I myself relied on the gift of the Holy Spirit, who gave me authority, power, love, and guidance. I breathe my Holy Spirit upon you, beloved disciple. Persist in praying. What else is Jesus saying to you?

Ask God to show you how to live today.

"Thank you for your good gifts, Lord. Show me how to use them. Amen."

Friday, October 12, 2018

Know that God is present and ready to converse.

"Lord, you are pure Spirit, the creator and ruler of all spirits. I reject all powers that are not of you."

Read the gospel: Luke 11:15–26.

But some of the crowd said, "He casts out demons by Beelzebul, the ruler of the demons." Others, to test him, kept demanding from him a sign from heaven. But he knew what they were thinking and said to them, "Every kingdom divided against itself becomes a desert, and house falls on house. If Satan also is divided against himself, how will his kingdom stand?—for you say that I cast out the demons by Beelzebul. Now if I cast out the demons by Beelzebul, by whom do your exorcists cast them out? Therefore they will be your judges. But if it is by the finger of God that I cast out the demons, then the kingdom of God has come to you. When a strong man, fully armed, guards his castle, his property is safe. But when one stronger than he attacks him and overpowers him, he takes away his armor in which he trusted and divides his plunder. Whoever is not with me is against me, and whoever does not gather with me scatters.

"When the unclean spirit has gone out of a person, it wanders through waterless regions looking for a resting place, but not finding any, it says, 'I will return to my house from which I came.' When it comes, it finds it swept and put in order. Then it goes and brings seven other spirits more evil than itself, and they enter and live there; and the last state of that person is worse than the first."

Notice what you think and feel as you read the gospel.

Jesus receives criticism that he casts out unclean spirits by the power of Satan. Jesus repudiates that accusation, saying he is God's instrument only. The kingdom of God has come to earth in him. He asks his hearers to gather with him, lest they scatter. He will give protection against the return of unclean spirits.

Pray as you are led for yourself and others.

"I do not know how to discern spirits, Lord, and I do not know how to take authority over them. Let me trust in you. I pray for all souls who are afflicted by unclean spirits . . ." (Continue in your own words.)

Listen to Jesus.

The world of spirits is larger and more deceitful than people know. Many would deny the existence of unclean spirits. I assure you they are still active on earth. Gather with me for protection. I have overcome them. What else is Jesus saying to you?

Ask God to show you how to live today.

"I will have no fear today, Lord, for you are with me. You are my strong shield against all things that would harm me. Amen."

Saturday, October 13, 2018

Know that God is present and ready to converse.

"Lord, I am happy to hear you today."

Read the gospel: Luke 11:27–28.

While Jesus was saying this, a woman in the crowd raised her voice and said to him, "Blessed is the womb that bore you and the breasts that nursed you!" But he said, "Blessed rather are those who hear the word of God and obey it!"

Notice what you think and feel as you read the gospel.

Jesus tells the woman and the crowd how to be happy—hear the Word and obey it. That is all.

Pray as you are led for yourself and others.

"I have heard, Lord, now I seek to obey. I pray for all those who struggle to obey. Give us grace, Lord . . ." (Continue in your own words.)

Listen to Jesus.

The will and desire to obey are an important foundation, my child. They will lead you to all my commandments, as they are all based on love for God and others. Then as you rely on God you will learn obedience and be a witness to me. I will be walking with you all the way. What else is Jesus saying to you?

Ask God to show you how to live today.

"I resolve to do your will, Lord; help me to trust and obey you in all things. Thank you for traveling with me, my Jesus. Amen."

Sunday, October 14, 2018
Twenty-Eighth Sunday in Ordinary Time

Know that God is present and ready to converse.

"Lord, you have blessed me greatly. I seek you before all else."

Read the gospel: Mark 10:17–30.

As Jesus was setting out on a journey, a man ran up and knelt before him, and asked him, "Good Teacher, what must I do to inherit eternal life?" Jesus said to him, "Why do you call me good? No one is good but God alone. You know the commandments: 'You shall not murder; You shall not commit adultery; You shall not steal; You shall not bear false witness; You shall not defraud; Honor your father and mother.'" He said to him, "Teacher, I have kept all these since my youth." Jesus, looking at him, loved him and said, "You lack one thing; go, sell what you own, and give the money to the poor, and you will have treasure in heaven; then come, follow me." When he heard this, he was shocked and went away grieving, for he had many possessions.

Then Jesus looked around and said to his disciples, "How hard it will be for those who have wealth to enter the kingdom of God!" And the disciples were perplexed at these words. But Jesus said to them again, "Children, how hard it is to enter the kingdom of God! It is easier for a camel to go through the eye of a needle than for someone who is rich to enter the kingdom of God." They were greatly astounded and said to one another, "Then who can be saved?" Jesus looked at them and said, "For mortals it is impossible, but not for God; for God all things are possible."

Peter began to say to him, "Look, we have left everything and followed you." Jesus said, "Truly I tell you, there is no one who has left house or brothers or sisters or mother or father or children or fields, for my sake and for the sake of the good news, who will not receive a hundredfold now in this age—houses, brothers and sisters, mothers and children, and fields, with persecutions—and in the age to come eternal life."

Notice what you think and feel as you read the gospel.

The rich man cannot bring himself to obey and follow Jesus. Jesus tells his disciples that it is hard for a rich person to enter the kingdom of God;

only with God is it possible. Then he promises great rewards, now and in eternity, to those who abandon all and follow him.

Pray as you are led for yourself and others.

"Lord, I know I cling to things that make me feel secure. I want to abandon all things in my heart and in my actions, that I may trust you more and draw nearer to you. I pray for all of us who rely on things and money rather than God . . ." (Continue in your own words.)

Listen to Jesus.

Every person who comes to me is different. I understand, dear disciple, your needs, your comings and goings, and the purposes for which you were born. Abandon yourself to me, and I will give you peace and fulfill your destiny in God. What else is Jesus saying to you?

Ask God to show you how to live today.

"Let me have what I have without clutching it. Let me give what I have without counting it a loss. Lord, I will follow you today. Amen."

Monday, October 15, 2018

Know that God is present and ready to converse.

"Jesus, you are the Son of God, the very Word of God. Speak to me now."

Read the gospel: Luke 11:29–32.

When the crowds were increasing, Jesus began to say, "This generation is an evil generation; it asks for a sign, but no sign will be given to it except the sign of Jonah. For just as Jonah became a sign to the people of Nineveh, so the Son of Man will be to this generation. The queen of the South will rise at the judgement with the people of this generation and condemn them, because she came from the ends of the earth to listen to the wisdom of Solomon, and see, something greater than Solomon is here! The people of Nineveh will rise up at the judgement with this generation and condemn it, because they repented at the proclamation of Jonah, and see, something greater than Jonah is here!"

Notice what you think and feel as you read the gospel.

Jesus condemns those who remain skeptical and seek a sign. He says the only sign they will see is the "sign of Jonah." Yet despite many witnesses, people deny that sign as well. God have mercy on those who do not believe.

Pray as you are led for yourself and others.

"Lord, I too want to see evidence that you are working in my life. I let that go and trust you, for you are faithful. I pray for those who falter in their faith . . ." (Continue in your own words.)

Listen to Jesus.

Again and again I put myself forward to draw unbelievers to me. I have drawn people to me by my Spirit throughout the centuries, yet many will not come. Dear disciple, let the good news flow through you. What else is Jesus saying to you?

Ask God to show you how to live today.

"I am willing, Lord. I offer my day, my life, to you. Lead me. Amen."

Tuesday, October 16, 2018

Know that God is present and ready to converse.

"Lord and Master, you look to the inner person, not the outer. Make me clean by the reading of your Word."

Read the gospel: Luke 11:37–41.

While Jesus was speaking, a Pharisee invited him to dine with him; so he went in and took his place at the table. The Pharisee was amazed to see that he did not first wash before dinner. Then the Lord said to him, "Now you Pharisees clean the outside of the cup and of the dish, but inside you are full of greed and wickedness. You fools! Did not the one who made the outside make the inside also? So give for alms those things that are within; and see, everything will be clean for you."

Notice what you think and feel as you read the gospel.

Jesus speaks to the Pharisee and all present about the nature of cleanliness. It is not clean cups and dishes God desires but clean hearts and minds.

Pray as you are led for yourself and others.

"Lord, cleanse me from within. Free me of all greed and wickedness. You alone are the source of holiness . . ." (Continue in your own words.)

Listen to Jesus.

Because you have given yourself to me and asked me to care for you, I make you clean. It pleases me that you seek to be clean and good, for God is good. This is the one thing to strive for in your life. Follow me, beloved. What else is Jesus saying to you?

Ask God to show you how to live today.

"Let me take your words seriously today, Lord. By your grace, I will strive for a clean heart and mind. Amen."

Wednesday, October 17, 2018

Know that God is present and ready to converse.

"Lord of all Truth, light my way. Let the light of your Word dispel the shadows of falsehood and hypocrisy from my heart and life."

Read the gospel: Luke 11:42–46.

Jesus said, "But woe to you Pharisees! For you tithe mint and rue and herbs of all kinds, and neglect justice and the love of God; it is these you ought to have practiced, without neglecting the others. Woe to you Pharisees! For you love to have the seat of honor in the synagogues and to be greeted with respect in the marketplaces. Woe to you! For you are like unmarked graves, and people walk over them without realizing it." One of the lawyers answered him, "Teacher, when you say these things, you insult us too." And he said, "Woe also to you lawyers! For you load people with burdens hard to bear, and you yourselves do not lift a finger to ease them."

Notice what you think and feel as you read the gospel.

Jesus condemns the hypocrisy of the Pharisees and lawyers, for they make rules for others they themselves do not keep. They are more concerned about their prestige.

Pray as you are led for yourself and others.

"I have seen myself pretending to be good when I have no right to do so. Lord, I have confessed my hypocrisy so that you can root it out of my heart. I pray for those trapped by their own hypocrisy . . ." (Continue in your own words.)

Listen to Jesus.

The efforts people go through to look good exceed the efforts they go through to be good. What is goodness—to not get caught, to measure up to some social standards? No, it is to love God with all your being and your neighbor as yourself. Come to me, child, and you will learn what it means to be truly good. What else is Jesus saying to you?

Ask God to show you how to live today.

"You challenge me, Lord Jesus. I place myself in your hands today and open myself to learn what your goodness demands. Thank you for being with me. Amen."

Thursday, October 18, 2018
Saint Luke, the Evangelist

Know that God is present and ready to converse.

"King Jesus Christ, I wish to enter your kingdom. You invite me by your Word."

Read the gospel: Luke 10:1–9.

After this the Lord appointed seventy others and sent them on ahead of him in pairs to every town and place where he himself intended to go. He said to them, "The harvest is plentiful, but the laborers are few; therefore ask the Lord of the harvest to send out laborers into his harvest. Go on your way. See, I am sending you out like lambs into the midst of wolves. Carry no purse, no bag, no sandals; and greet no one on the road. Whatever house you enter, first say, 'Peace to this house!' And if anyone is there who shares in peace, your peace will rest on that person; but if not, it will return to you. Remain in the same house, eating and drinking whatever they provide, for the laborer deserves to be paid. Do not move about from house to house. Whenever you enter a town and its people welcome you, eat what is set before you; cure the sick who are there, and say to them, 'The kingdom of God has come near to you.'"

Notice what you think and feel as you read the gospel.

Jesus instructs the seventy how to proclaim the good news of the kingdom. First he asks them to pray that God will send laborers into his plentiful harvest. Then he bids them to travel without preparation to speak to any who will listen and to offer the Lord's peace. As the disciples trust in God, God will bring in the harvest.

Pray as you are led for yourself and others.

"Let me speak of your peace today, Lord. I pray for all those who reject your peace . . ." (Continue in your own words.)

Listen to Jesus.

I am the Prince of Peace, beloved, and I grant peace the world cannot know. In the midst of war and conflict, I am Peace. I derive my peace from the being of my Father, who has all things in his power and who rules the universe with justice and love. What else is Jesus saying to you?

Ask God to show you how to live today.

"Lord, let me abide within your peace today, despite the tumult of my day. Be my still point in a turning world. Amen."

Friday, October 19, 2018

Know that God is present and ready to converse.

"Lord, you are Lord of small things. I am a small thing, turning to you now."

Read the gospel: Luke 12:1–7.

Meanwhile, when the crowd gathered in thousands, so that they trampled on one another, he began to speak first to his disciples, "Beware of the yeast of the Pharisees, that is, their hypocrisy. Nothing is covered up that will not be uncovered, and nothing secret that will not become known. Therefore whatever you have said in the dark will be heard in the light, and what you have whispered behind closed doors will be proclaimed from the housetops.

"I tell you, my friends, do not fear those who kill the body, and after that can do nothing more. But I will warn you whom to fear: fear him who, after he has killed, has authority to cast into hell. Yes, I tell you, fear him! Are not five sparrows sold for two pennies? Yet not one of them is forgotten in God's sight. But even the hairs of your head are all counted. Do not be afraid; you are of more value than many sparrows."

Notice what you think and feel as you read the gospel.

Jesus teaches that hypocrisy is like keeping dark secrets within your heart. You will be exposed by the truth. We fear people when we should be fearing evil, for evil has the power to damn. Live in truth, and God will care for you, as he cares for the sparrows.

Pray as you are led for yourself and others.

"Lord, I seek your purity. I will trust myself to you today, and I will also entrust to you those you have given me . . ." (Continue in your own words.)

Listen to Jesus.

I come demanding inner purity of people, demanding authenticity that comes from a good heart and an honest mind. You don't need to pretend anything. You can't pretend before God; why pretend before people? Beloved disciple, follow me. What else is Jesus saying to you?

Ask God to show you how to live today.

"Lord, reveal to me the pretenses I hide even from myself and let me abandon them. I praise your holy name. Amen."

Saturday, October 20, 2018

Know that God is present and ready to converse.

"Holy Spirit, Author of the Word of God, teach me."

Read the gospel: Luke 12:8–12.

Jesus said, "And I tell you, everyone who acknowledges me before others, the Son of Man also will acknowledge before the angels of God; but whoever denies me before others will be denied before the angels of God. And everyone who speaks a word against the Son of Man will be forgiven; but whoever blasphemes against the Holy Spirit will not be forgiven. When they bring you before the synagogues, the rulers, and the authorities, do not worry about how you are to defend yourselves or what you are to say; for the Holy Spirit will teach you at that very hour what you ought to say."

Notice what you think and feel as you read the gospel.

To receive Jesus is to acknowledge him to the world. The world may reject us as it rejected him. When we are persecuted for our faith, trust the Holy Spirit to teach us what to say.

Pray as you are led for yourself and others.

"Lord, forgive me the many small ways I have denied you. Give me your Spirit that I might acknowledge you before others, even when I am opposed by them. I pray for those who resist you . . ." (Continue in your own words.)

Listen to Jesus.

To people the world is large and time seems endless. But God exists in eternity far beyond space and time. Here is the kingdom of God, your destiny, beloved. Pursue your destiny. What else is Jesus saying to you?

Ask God to show you how to live today.

"Lord, make me mindful of the kingdom all day. Let your Spirit be upon me as I follow you to glory. Amen."

Sunday, October 21, 2018
Twenty-Ninth Sunday in Ordinary Time

Know that God is present and ready to converse.

"Lord God, I seek your glory. How shall I find it?"

Read the gospel: Mark 10:35–45.

James and John, the sons of Zebedee, came forward to Jesus and said to him, "Teacher, we want you to do for us whatever we ask of you." And he said to them, "What is it you want me to do for you?" And they said to him, "Grant us to sit, one at your right hand and one at your left, in your glory." But Jesus said to them, "You do not know what you are asking. Are you able to drink the cup that I drink, or be baptized with the baptism that I am baptized with?" They replied, "We are able." Then Jesus said to them, "The cup that I drink you will drink; and with the baptism with which I am baptized, you will be baptized; but to sit at my right hand or at my left is not mine to grant, but it is for those for whom it has been prepared."

When the ten heard this, they began to be angry with James and John. So Jesus called them and said to them, "You know that among the Gentiles those whom they recognize as their rulers lord it over them, and their great ones are tyrants over them. But it is not so among you; but whoever wishes to become great among you must be your servant, and whoever wishes to be first among you must be slave of all. For the Son of Man came not to be served but to serve, and to give his life a ransom for many."

Notice what you think and feel as you read the gospel.

The apostles James and John want to be great in the kingdom of heaven, and they ask Jesus directly for this. He answers that they can be great in heaven but all who wish to be great must do two things: suffer as he suffered and serve as he served.

Pray as you are led for yourself and others.

"Lord, if you are with me, I can suffer and I can serve. Grant me the greatness of your love. I pray for these you give me to serve . . ." (Continue in your own words.)

Listen to Jesus.

Suffering and service are not onerous, dear follower, because I have led the way and many have walked that way behind me. You can walk it too, for I am always with you. Give yourself to my way. What else is Jesus saying to you?

Ask God to show you how to live today.

"Lord, I give myself. With you, I rejoice in my suffering and I commit myself to my service of others. Amen."

Monday, October 22, 2018

Know that God is present and ready to converse.

"Jesus, you know me from the inside. Purify my heart by your holy Word."

Read the gospel: Luke 12:13–21.

Someone in the crowd said to Jesus, "Teacher, tell my brother to divide the family inheritance with me." But he said to him, "Friend, who set me to be a judge or arbitrator over you?" And he said to them, "Take care! Be on your guard against all kinds of greed; for one's life does not consist in the abundance of possessions." Then he told them a parable: "The land of a rich man produced abundantly. And he thought to himself, 'What should I do, for I have no place to store my crops?' Then he said, 'I will do this: I will pull down my barns and build larger ones, and there I will store all my grain and my goods. And I will say to my soul, Soul, you have ample goods laid up for many years; relax, eat, drink, be merry.' But God said to him, 'You fool! This very night your life is being demanded of you. And the things you have prepared, whose will they be?' So it is with those who store up treasures for themselves but are not rich towards God.'"

Notice what you think and feel as you read the gospel.

Jesus warns against greed, teaching that life does not consist in possessions. We tend to think it does, like the man who builds bigger barns to store all his grain and goods while he eats, drinks, and is merry. But possessions mean nothing in eternal life, so Jesus teaches the crowd to be rich toward God, instead.

Pray as you are led for yourself and others.

"Direct my eyes to the things of God, Lord, and away from all greed. Be my treasure, Jesus, for your love I can carry with me into the eternal kingdom of heaven. I pray for all who are slaves of greed . . ."

Listen to Jesus.

I know that you need things, child, and I will continue to provide for you. Do not allow things to distract you from me. Do not compare what you have with what others have. Do not judge others. You are mine and are heir to all the treasures of heaven. Follow me. What else is Jesus saying to you?

Ask God to show you how to live today.

"Thank you for taking care of me, Lord. I accept what you do for me and rejoice in you alone. Let me carry you in my heart all day long. Amen."

Tuesday, October 23, 2018

Know that God is present and ready to converse.

"Lord, I watch and wait for your coming. I am ready now."

Read the gospel: Luke 12:35–38.

Jesus said, "Be dressed for action and have your lamps lit; be like those who are waiting for their master to return from the wedding banquet, so that they may open the door for him as soon as he comes and knocks. Blessed are those slaves whom the master finds alert when he comes; truly I tell you, he will fasten his belt and have them sit down to eat, and he will come and serve them. If he comes during the middle of the night, or near dawn, and finds them so, blessed are those slaves."

Notice what you think and feel as you read the gospel.

Jesus bids his disciples to be ready for his return. When he returns, he says, he will have us sit down and will serve us. Blessed are those who are ready.

Pray as you are led for yourself and others.

"Lord, I am ready now. Keep me faithful all my life, every day. I pray for all who have grown impatient in waiting . . ." (Continue in your own words.)

Listen to Jesus.

Your time is short, beloved. In the end your whole life will be compressed into a single moment. Yet while the days stretch before you, look forward to my coming. You will be with me in eternity. What else is Jesus saying to you?

Ask God to show you how to live today.

"This day, this moment, I look to you, Lord. Let your Holy Spirit be my lamp, burning brightly within me to keep me awake and show me your coming. I know you will keep your promises to me. Amen."

Wednesday, October 24, 2018

Know that God is present and ready to converse.

"Lord, you have come. Please return soon and establish justice."

Read the gospel: Luke 12:39–48.

Jesus said, "But know this: if the owner of the house had known at what hour the thief was coming, he would not have let his house be broken into. You also must be ready, for the Son of Man is coming at an unexpected hour."

Peter said, "Lord, are you telling this parable for us or for everyone?" And the Lord said, "Who then is the faithful and prudent manager whom his master will put in charge of his slaves, to give them their allowance of food at the proper time? Blessed is that slave whom his master will find at work when he arrives. Truly I tell you, he will put that one in charge of all his possessions. But if that slave says to himself, 'My master is delayed in coming,' and if he begins to beat the other slaves, men and women, and to eat and drink and get drunk, the master of that slave will come on a day when he does not expect him and at an hour that he does not know, and will cut him in pieces, and put him with the unfaithful. That slave who knew what his master wanted, but did not prepare himself or do what was wanted, will receive a severe beating. But one who did not know and did what deserved a beating will receive a light beating. From everyone to whom much has been given, much will be required; and from one to whom much has been entrusted, even more will be demanded."

Notice what you think and feel as you read the gospel.

Jesus predicts his coming at an unexpected hour. He asks us to be faithful and prudent until he returns.

Pray as you are led for yourself and others.

"Lord, I have not been as faithful and prudent as you would like. Forgive me. By your grace I will do better. Help me to know your will, that I may do it and may help others to do so also . . ." (Continue in your own words.)

Listen to Jesus.

Beloved, I speak to you. You listen. You know what I ask of you, that you take care of what I have given you. I also ask you to look beyond to see what else needs doing. I will reward your efforts to act in love for the good of those in need. What else is Jesus saying to you?

Ask God to show you how to live today.

"Open my eyes to the needs of others, Lord, the needs I would not see on my own, and let me act, manifesting your love. Amen."

Thursday, October 25, 2018

Know that God is present and ready to converse.

"Lord, be my peace now, for the world is often violent."

Read the gospel: Luke 12:49–53.

Jesus said, "I came to bring fire to the earth, and how I wish it were already kindled! I have a baptism with which to be baptized, and what stress I am under until it is completed! Do you think that I have come to bring peace to the earth? No, I tell you, but rather division! From now on, five in one household will be divided, three against two and two against three; they will be divided: father against son and son against father, mother against daughter and daughter against mother, mother-in-law against her daughter-in-law and daughter-in-law against mother-in-law."

Notice what you think and feel as you read the gospel.

Jesus understands that his coming among us will lead to dissension, even within families. He does not lament this because everyone must make a personal decision whether to believe in Jesus.

Pray as you are led for yourself and others.

"Lord, I believe, even in the midst of strife and dissension among those I love. Let me persist in prayer for them . . ." (Continue in your own words.)

Listen to Jesus.

I am pleased by your faith, my child. I know it is not easy. But it is better for you to continue with me by your side than to go forward without me. With me you can do anything. You can pray in genuine hope for those you love. What else is Jesus saying to you?

Ask God to show you how to live today.

"Lord, give me the grace to live in hope, praying even for situations that may seem hopeless. Thank you for this power, Lord. Amen."

Friday, October 26, 2018

Know that God is present and ready to converse.

"Lord, I will search the scriptures for your truth, that I may act in obedience to you."

Read the gospel: Luke 12:54–59.

Jesus also said to the crowds, "When you see a cloud rising in the west, you immediately say, 'It is going to rain'; and so it happens. And when you see the south wind blowing, you say, 'There will be scorching heat'; and it happens. You hypocrites! You know how to interpret the appearance of earth and sky, but why do you not know how to interpret the present time?

"And why do you not judge for yourselves what is right? Thus, when you go with your accuser before a magistrate, on the way make an effort to settle the case, or you may be dragged before the judge, and the judge hand you over to the officer, and the officer throw you in prison. I tell you, you will never get out until you have paid the very last penny."

Notice what you think and feel as you read the gospel.

Jesus tells the crowds that they should recognize that this is the time of salvation, for he is among them. This is the time to get right with God.

Pray as you are led for yourself and others.

"Lord, I hear you say that the situation is urgent. I throw myself upon you, trusting you to save me. I forgive all who have hurt me . . ." (Continue in your own words.)

Listen to Jesus.

In the span of a life, there are many times of urgency. Moments of danger should drive you back to me. I want you to trust me in danger and trust me in tranquility. You will find me faithful at all times. You are dear to me. What else is Jesus saying to you?

Ask God to show you how to live today.

"Lord, in danger or tranquility today, I will trust in you. Amen."

Saturday, October 27, 2018

Know that God is present and ready to converse.

"Lord, I look out at the world and see what I see. I come to your Word to see what you see."

Read the gospel: Luke 13:1–9.

At that very time there were some present who told him about the Galileans whose blood Pilate had mingled with their sacrifices. He asked them, "Do you think that because these Galileans suffered in this way they were worse sinners than all other Galileans? No, I tell you; but unless you repent, you will all perish as they did. Or those eighteen who were killed when the tower of Siloam fell on them—do you think that they were worse offenders than all the others living in Jerusalem? No, I tell you; but unless you repent, you will all perish just as they did."

Then he told this parable: "A man had a fig tree planted in his vineyard; and he came looking for fruit on it and found none. So he said to the gardener, 'See here! For three years I have come looking for fruit on this fig tree, and still I find none. Cut it down! Why should it be wasting the soil?' He replied, 'Sir, let it alone for one more year, until I dig round it and put manure on it. If it bears fruit next year, well and good; but if not, you can cut it down.'"

Notice what you think and feel as you read the gospel.

Jesus says we cannot consider the demise of others as the judgment of God. We are all susceptible to judgment and need to repent. We are all expected to bear fruit for the good of others. The Lord is patient with us, but the time for us to act is now.

Pray as you are led for yourself and others.

"Lord, I want to bear fruit and fulfill my obligation. I want to please you. I pray now for your help and guidance. What do I need to know? . . ." (Continue in your own words.)

Listen to Jesus.

Your desire is my own, beloved. I want to awaken your heart to all I have for you. I want to give you treasure to give to others. Will you receive it? I will tend you, feed you, and prune away your faults, so that you can bear my gifts to the world. Give, and you will receive even more. What else is Jesus saying to you?

Ask God to show you how to live today.

"I will give today not to receive but just to show love. Lord, make me an instrument of your love. Amen."

Sunday, October 28, 2018
Thirtieth Sunday in Ordinary Time

Know that God is present and ready to converse.

"Almighty God, you are mercy. Be merciful to me, a sinner."

Read the gospel: Mark 10:46–52.

They came to Jericho. As Jesus and his disciples and a large crowd were leaving Jericho, Bartimaeus son of Timaeus, a blind beggar, was sitting by the roadside. When he heard that it was Jesus of Nazareth, he began to shout out and say, "Jesus, Son of David, have mercy on me!" Many sternly ordered him to be quiet, but he cried out even more loudly, "Son of David, have mercy on me!" Jesus stood still and said, "Call him here." And they called the blind man, saying to him, "Take heart; get up, he is calling you." So throwing off his cloak, he sprang up and came to Jesus. Then Jesus said to him, "What do you want me to do for you?" The blind man said to him, "My teacher, let me see again." Jesus said to him, "Go; your faith has made you well." Immediately he regained his sight and followed him on the way.

Notice what you think and feel as you read the gospel.

Jesus heals a blind man, Bartimaeus, on the spot because of his great faith. After that, Bartimaeus follows Jesus.

Pray as you are led for yourself and others.

"Lord, I am in need of your mercy. Heal me. I will follow you. I pray for all who need your mercy . . ." (Continue in your own words.)

Listen to Jesus.

I am the source of all blessing, all goodness, and all mercy, dear child. I am generous with you and all those you present to me. Realize that it is the love and goodness of God that orchestrate the circumstances of life. Give God the glory. What else is Jesus saying to you?

Ask God to show you how to live today.

"I glorify the Lord of Hosts. I am just a person constantly dependent upon God's mercy. Call me to you, Jesus, that I may follow you. Amen."

Monday, October 29, 2018

Know that God is present and ready to converse.

"Jesus, may your Word free me from error and sinful habits of mind."

Read the gospel: Luke 13:10–17.

Now Jesus was teaching in one of the synagogues on the sabbath. And just then there appeared a woman with a spirit that had crippled her for eighteen years. She was bent over and was quite unable to stand up straight. When Jesus saw her, he called her over and said, "Woman, you are set free from your ailment." When he laid his hands on her, immediately she stood up straight and began praising God. But the leader of the synagogue, indignant because Jesus had cured on the sabbath, kept saying to the crowd, "There are six days on which work ought to be done; come on those days and be cured, and not on the sabbath day." But the Lord answered him and said, "You hypocrites! Does not each of you on the sabbath untie his ox or his donkey from the manger, and lead it away to give it water? And ought not this woman, a daughter of Abraham whom Satan bound for eighteen long years, be set free from this bondage on the sabbath day?" When he said this, all his opponents were put to shame; and the entire crowd was rejoicing at all the wonderful things that he was doing.

Notice what you think and feel as you read the gospel.

Jesus heals the crippled woman and is criticized by the leader of the synagogue for doing it on the Sabbath. Jesus puts all his accusers to shame, and the crowd rejoices.

Pray as you are led for yourself and others.

"Forgive me for my own small-mindedness, Lord. Let me rejoice in the good fortune of others. I pray for all those who are critical, that they may receive and be freed by your mercy . . ." (Continue in your own words.)

Listen to Jesus.

People can do what they will, but they don't have control of the day, much less of their lives. All creatures depend upon God to live, and they will die in God's time. Accept that fact with joy and cast yourself on the mercy of God. God is good. What else is Jesus saying to you?

Ask God to show you how to live today.

"Lord, I rejoice at the wonderful things you have done for all your people. When I start to criticize today, help me let go of my own narrow vision and instead look for the good you are doing in every situation. Amen."

Tuesday, October 30, 2018

Know that God is present and ready to converse.

"Lord, I am before you, seeking to grow in understanding and love."

Read the gospel: Luke 13:18–21.

Jesus said therefore, "What is the kingdom of God like? And to what should I compare it? It is like a mustard seed that someone took and sowed in the garden; it grew and became a tree, and the birds of the air made nests in its branches."

And again he said, "To what should I compare the kingdom of God? It is like yeast that a woman took and mixed in with three measures of flour until all of it was leavened."

Notice what you think and feel as you read the gospel.

The kingdom of God is among us, Jesus says. It starts small and grows miraculously. The kingdom grows both within us as individuals and throughout the whole world.

Pray as you are led for yourself and others.

"Lord, grow your kingdom in me and in those you have given me . . ." (Continue in your own words.)

Listen to Jesus.

By the power of the Holy Spirit, the kingdom of God grows among you. It has been growing for thousands of years, and it will not stop. God is among you. I am with you. I shall never depart from you or abandon my Church. What else is Jesus saying to you?

Ask God to show you how to live today.

"Lord, thank you for your faithfulness. I seek to be faithful to you today. Lead me. Amen."

Wednesday, October 31, 2018

Know that God is present and ready to converse.

"Jesus, I want to know you. I want to enter your kingdom."

Read the gospel: Luke 13:22–30.

Jesus went through one town and village after another, teaching as he made his way to Jerusalem. Someone asked him, "Lord, will only a few be saved?" He said to them, "Strive to enter through the narrow door; for many, I tell you, will try to enter and will not be able. When once the owner of the house has got up and shut the door, and you begin to stand outside and to knock at the door, saying, 'Lord, open to us,' then in reply he will say to you, 'I do not know where you come from.' Then you will begin to say, 'We ate and drank with you, and you taught in our streets.' But he will say, 'I do not know where you come from; go away from me, all you evildoers!' There will be weeping and gnashing of teeth when you see Abraham and Isaac and Jacob and all the prophets in the kingdom of God, and you yourselves thrown out. Then people will come from east and west, from north and south, and will eat in the kingdom of God. Indeed, some are last who will be first, and some are first who will be last."

Notice what you think and feel as you read the gospel.

Jesus answers the question about whether only a few will be saved. He says many will not be able to enter. Who cannot? Those who do not know him. He calls them evildoers. Yet many from east, west, north, and south will enter the kingdom of God.

Pray as you are led for yourself and others.

"Let me not take you for granted, Lord. I do not know and love you as much as I should, as much as you ask. I pray for myself and for all who long to love you more . . ." (Continue in your own words.)

Listen to Jesus.

If you spend time loving me, child, you will know me, and I will welcome you into the kingdom of God. Loving me is not something you do once. It is a habit of living. Confide in me, trust me, give me your sorrows and struggles, come to me for cleansing. What else is Jesus saying to you?

Ask God to show you how to live today.

"Lord, a closer walk with you, that's my prayer. What can be more important? Amen."

Thursday, November 1, 2018
All Saints

Know that God is present and ready to converse.

"Lord, call me to yourself. Teach me your blessedness."

Read the gospel: Matthew 5:1–12a.

When Jesus saw the crowds, he went up the mountain; and after he sat down, his disciples came to him. Then he began to speak, and taught them, saying:

"Blessed are the poor in spirit, for theirs is the kingdom of heaven.

"Blessed are those who mourn, for they will be comforted.

"Blessed are the meek, for they will inherit the earth.

"Blessed are those who hunger and thirst for righteousness, for they will be filled.

"Blessed are the merciful, for they will receive mercy.

"Blessed are the pure in heart, for they will see God.

"Blessed are the peacemakers, for they will be called children of God.

"Blessed are those who are persecuted for righteousness' sake, for theirs is the kingdom of heaven.

"Blessed are you when people revile you and persecute you and utter all kinds of evil against you falsely on my account. Rejoice and be glad, for your reward is great in heaven, for in the same way they persecuted the prophets who were before you."

Notice what you think and feel as you read the gospel.

Happiness does not come as we expect, Jesus says, for happiness comes through suffering and want. Not the mighty but the weak and poor will be blessed by God. Those who pursue righteousness and peace and who show mercy will inherit the kingdom of God.

Pray as you are led for yourself and others.

"Lord, am I worthy of suffering for you and your righteousness? I give myself to you now for whatever you would have me do. I pray for any who despise me . . ." (Continue in your own words.)

Listen to Jesus.

I speak to prepare you for whatever comes upon you. I want you to hope in me whatever happens, for your trust in me gives me joy. Your suffering is not a curse but a blessing. Let it bring you closer to me. What else is Jesus saying to you?

Ask God to show you how to live today.

"Lord, let me thank you and rejoice in every difficulty, for your blessed will is being done. Let me learn what I need to learn. Let me trust you in everything. Amen."

Friday, November 2, 2018
The Commemoration of All the Faithful Departed (All Souls)

Know that God is present and ready to converse.

"I come to you in your Word, Lord. Let me hear and obey you."

Read the gospel: John 6:37–40.

Jesus said, "Everything that the Father gives me will come to me, and anyone who comes to me I will never drive away; for I have come down from heaven, not to do my own will, but the will of him who sent me. And this is the will of him who sent me, that I should lose nothing of all that he has given me, but raise it up on the last day. This is indeed the will of my Father, that all who see the Son and believe in him may have eternal life; and I will raise them up on the last day."

Notice what you think and feel as you read the gospel.

Jesus promises resurrection and eternal life for all who believe in him. This is his Father's gift to him.

Pray as you are led for yourself and others.

"Lord, I believe in you, and I look forward to eternal life. How may I live now to please you? I pray for those who do not yet believe in you . . ." (Continue in your own words.)

Listen to Jesus.

Some speak of the mysterious ways of God. God in his fullness is beyond comprehension, yes, but you can know God. Do you know what love is? Have you felt it? All love is God's love. God is love. I love you. What else is Jesus saying to you?

Ask God to show you how to live today.

"Let me walk in your love today, Lord. I love you. Amen."

Saturday, November 3, 2018

Know that God is present and ready to converse.

"Lord, it is I, here before you seeking wisdom, seeking you in your Word."

Read the gospel: Luke 14:1, 7–11.

On one occasion when Jesus was going to the house of a leader of the Pharisees to eat a meal on the sabbath, they were watching him closely. . . .

When he noticed how the guests chose the places of honor, he told them a parable. "When you are invited by someone to a wedding banquet, do not sit down at the place of honor, in case someone more distinguished than you has been invited by your host; and the host who invited both of you may come and say to you, 'Give this person your place,' and then in disgrace you would start to take the lowest place. But when you are invited, go and sit down at the lowest place, so that when your host comes, he may say to you, 'Friend, move up higher'; then you will be honored in the presence of all who sit at the table with you. For all who exalt themselves will be humbled, and those who humble themselves will be exalted."

Notice what you think and feel as you read the gospel.

Jesus knows that people seek honor for themselves, so he teaches them to choose humility. Those who exalt themselves will be humbled; those who humble themselves will be exalted.

Pray as you are led for yourself and others.

"Jesus, you present a paradoxical way to godliness. Help me to humble myself, gladly and from the heart, so that I may please you. I pray for all who seek honor and recognition in this world, that they may find instead your glorious and humble love . . ." (Continue in your own words.)

Listen to Jesus.

Friend, move up higher. Come to me. I am meek and lowly of heart. I am your Lord and Master, but I am also your servant. Follow me. What else is Jesus saying to you?

Ask God to show you how to live today.

"Jesus, there is no one like you. Let me be worthy of you. Help me live in loving service to others, as you lovingly serve me. Amen."

Sunday, November 4, 2018
Thirty-First Sunday in Ordinary Time

Know that God is present and ready to converse.

"Lord, I seek the kingdom of God in your Word. Teach me."

Read the gospel: Mark 12:28b–34.

One of the scribes came near and heard them disputing with one another, and seeing that he answered them well, he asked him, "Which commandment is the first of all?" Jesus answered, "The first is, 'Hear, O Israel: the Lord our God, the Lord is one; you shall love the Lord your God with all your heart, and with all your soul, and with all your mind, and with all your strength.' The second is this, 'You shall love your neighbor as yourself.' There is no other commandment greater than these." Then the scribe said to him, "You are right, Teacher; you have truly said that 'he is one, and besides him there is no other'; and 'to love him with all the heart, and with all the understanding, and with all the strength,' and 'to love one's neighbor as oneself,'—this is much more important than all whole burnt offerings and sacrifices." When Jesus saw that he answered wisely, he said to him, "You are not far from the kingdom of God." After that no one dared to ask him any question.

Notice what you think and feel as you read the gospel.

Jesus teaches the great commandments: love God with all your might and love your neighbor as yourself. Those encompass all our obligations to God and others.

Pray as you are led for yourself and others.

"I have not kept your commandments, Lord. May I ask you to perfect love within me? I will begin with prayer for those I love . . ." (Continue in your own words.)

Listen to Jesus.

Heaven is a world of love, dear disciple. The love you learn here will remain with you there. The love you show hear will be your treasure there. Love is stronger than death. Do you love me? What else is Jesus saying to you?

Ask God to show you how to live today.

"Let me go all in for love today, Jesus. I need you to show me how. I ask you to lead me. Amen."

Monday, November 5, 2018

Know that God is present and ready to converse.

"Lord, I come to you and to your Word because I want to learn how to please you. You are the Lord."

Read the gospel: Luke 14:12–14.

He said also to the one who had invited him, "When you give a luncheon or a dinner, do not invite your friends or your brothers or your relatives or rich neighbors, in case they may invite you in return, and you would be repaid. But when you give a banquet, invite the poor, the crippled, the lame, and the blind. And you will be blessed, because they cannot repay you, for you will be repaid at the resurrection of the righteous."

Notice what you think and feel as you read the gospel.

Jesus teaches that we are rewarded for doing good when we do not seek a reward. When we are generous with the needy, we will be rewarded at the resurrection of the righteous.

Pray as you are led for yourself and others.

"Lord, let me be generous, seeking no reward. I pray now for those in need . . ." (Continue in your own words.)

Listen to Jesus.

My advice is simple, beloved. Just love and give and stop thinking about yourself. God is with you. All shall be well with you. What else is Jesus saying to you?

Ask God to show you how to live today.

"Lord, I will trust in your word today. I will not strive for my own happiness, but I will seek to make someone else happy. Amen."

Tuesday, November 6, 2018

Know that God is present and ready to converse.

"Lord, by your Word compel me to come into your kingdom."

Read the gospel: Luke 14:15–24.

One of the dinner guests, on hearing this, said to him, "Blessed is anyone who will eat bread in the kingdom of God!" Then Jesus said to him, "Someone gave a great dinner and invited many. At the time for the dinner he sent his slave to say to those who had been invited, 'Come; for everything is ready now.' But they all alike began to make excuses. The first said to him, 'I have bought a piece of land, and I must go out and see it; please accept my apologies.' Another said, 'I have bought five yoke of oxen, and I am going to try them out; please accept my apologies.' Another said, 'I have just been married, and therefore I cannot come.' So the slave returned and reported this to his master. Then the owner of the house became angry and said to his slave, 'Go out at once into the streets and lanes of the town and bring in the poor, the crippled, the blind, and the lame.' And the slave said, 'Sir, what you ordered has been done, and there is still room.' Then the master said to the slave, 'Go out into the roads and lanes, and compel people to come in, so that my house may be filled. For I tell you, none of those who were invited will taste my dinner.'"

Notice what you think and feel as you read the gospel.

Jesus agrees that those who come into the kingdom of God are blessed, but his parable speaks of the many excuses people have for not coming to God. They are all too busy living today. How does God respond to that? Like the man serving the banquet. He invites everyone who will come.

Pray as you are led for yourself and others.

"Lord, I will come. Thank you for favoring me. Make me worthy of you. I pray that others come, too . . ." (Continue in your own words.)

Listen to Jesus.

The ways of God are not like the ways of people, beloved. God is patient and kind to all. God does not lose hope that people will come into his kingdom. Look out upon the world with hope. What else is Jesus saying to you?

Ask God to show you how to live today.

"Lord, I will be hopeful today. Let it become a habitual virtue for me. Amen."

Wednesday, November 7, 2018

Know that God is present and ready to converse.

"Lord, you demand much of your disciples. Strengthen me by your Word."

Read the gospel: Luke 14:25–33.

Now large crowds were travelling with Jesus; and he turned and said to them, "Whoever comes to me and does not hate father and mother, wife and children, brothers and sisters, yes, and even life itself, cannot be my disciple. Whoever does not carry the cross and follow me cannot be my disciple. For which of you, intending to build a tower, does not first sit down and estimate the cost, to see whether he has enough to complete it? Otherwise, when he has laid a foundation and is not able to finish, all who see it will begin to ridicule him, saying, 'This fellow began to build and was not able to finish.' Or what king, going out to wage war against another king, will not sit down first and consider whether he is able with ten thousand to oppose the one who comes against him with twenty thousand? If he cannot, then, while the other is still far away, he sends a delegation and asks for the terms of peace. So therefore, none of you can become my disciple if you do not give up all your possessions."

Notice what you think and feel as you read the gospel.

Jesus asks that those who would follow him must repudiate all earthly relationships, putting him before all people and things. We are to become disciples, aware of the cost.

Pray as you are led for yourself and others.

"Lord, I offer you all I have, even those I love. Make me true to you and all shall be well . . ." (Continue in your own words.)

Listen to Jesus.

You are right not to cling to the people and things of your life. I alone can save you from death. I alone can lead you to the Father and the everlasting kingdom he has prepared for you. Let everything else go and trust me. What else is Jesus saying to you?

Ask God to show you how to live today.

"What do I cling to, Lord? Let me put your will before all other things. Amen."

Thursday, November 8, 2018

Know that God is present and ready to converse.

"I come to you, Lord. You have found me."

Read the gospel: Luke 15:1–10.

Now all the tax collectors and sinners were coming near to listen to him. And the Pharisees and the scribes were grumbling and saying, "This fellow welcomes sinners and eats with them."

So he told them this parable: "Which one of you, having a hundred sheep and losing one of them, does not leave the ninety-nine in the wilderness and go after the one that is lost until he finds it? When he has found it, he lays it on his shoulders and rejoices. And when he comes home, he calls together his friends and neighbors, saying to them, 'Rejoice with me, for I have found my sheep that was lost.' Just so, I tell you, there will be more joy in heaven over one sinner who repents than over ninety-nine righteous people who need no repentance.

"Or what woman having ten silver coins, if she loses one of them, does not light a lamp, sweep the house, and search carefully until she finds it? When she has found it, she calls together her friends and neighbors, saying, 'Rejoice with me, for I have found the coin that I had lost.' Just so, I tell you, there is joy in the presence of the angels of God over one sinner who repents."

Notice what you think and feel as you read the gospel.

Jesus makes it clear to the scribes and Pharisees that he came to save sinners, not the righteous—or self-righteous. There is joy in heaven when a sinner repents.

Pray as you are led for yourself and others.

"Lord, thank you for coming for me. I pray for those who need you but have not yet come to you . . ." (Continue in your own words.)

Listen to Jesus.

Beloved disciple, I rejoice in you. I have found you and am preparing you for eternity in heaven. You are mine, and I am yours. Let us grow in our love. What else is Jesus saying to you?

Ask God to show you how to live today.

"Let the joy of the Lord be my strength today, Jesus. Use me as you will. Amen."

Friday, November 9, 2018
The Dedication of the Lateran Basilica in Rome

Know that God is present and ready to converse.

"Lord Jesus Christ, King of Kings, I am before you seeking truth, pardon, and acceptance."

Read the gospel: John 2:13–22.

The Passover of the Jews was near, and Jesus went up to Jerusalem. In the temple he found people selling cattle, sheep, and doves, and the money-changers seated at their tables. Making a whip of cords, he drove all of them out of the temple, both the sheep and the cattle. He also poured out the coins of the money changers and overturned their tables. He told those who were selling the doves, "Take these things out of here! Stop making my Father's house a marketplace!" His disciples remembered that it was written, "Zeal for your house will consume me." The Jews then said to him, "What sign can you show us for doing this?" Jesus answered them, "Destroy this temple, and in three days I will raise it up." The Jews then said, "This temple has been under construction for forty-six years, and will you raise it up in three days?" But he was speaking of the temple of his body. After he was raised from the dead, his disciples remembered that he had said this; and they believed the scripture and the word that Jesus had spoken.

Notice what you think and feel as you read the gospel.

Jesus drives out of the temple the money changers and all those who use the temple as a marketplace. Jesus refers to himself as the temple and prophesies that he will rise on the third day after he is killed. Even his disciples do not understand his meaning at the time.

Pray as you are led for yourself and others.

"Lord, give me righteous zeal for your name, your honor. I pray for those who dishonor you . . ." (Continue in your own words.)

Listen to Jesus.

You are the temple of God, beloved. My Holy Spirit lives and works in you and through you. Allow the Spirit to play a greater role in your life. This is the way to peace, fruitfulness, and joy. What else is Jesus saying to you?

Ask God to show you how to live today.

"I offer all I am to the Holy Spirit today. Lord, abide in me and let me obey you. Amen."

Saturday, November 10, 2018

Know that God is present and ready to converse.

"Jesus, Master, purify my heart in its commitment to you."

Read the gospel: Luke 16:9–15.

Jesus said, "And I tell you, make friends for yourselves by means of dishonest wealth so that when it is gone, they may welcome you into the eternal homes.

"Whoever is faithful in a very little is faithful also in much; and whoever is dishonest in a very little is dishonest also in much. If then you have not been faithful with the dishonest wealth, who will entrust to you the true riches? And if you have not been faithful with what belongs to another, who will give you what is your own? No slave can serve two masters; for a slave will either hate the one and love the other, or be devoted to the one and despise the other. You cannot serve God and wealth."

The Pharisees, who were lovers of money, heard all this, and they ridiculed him. So he said to them, "You are those who justify yourselves in the sight of others; but God knows your hearts; for what is prized by human beings is an abomination in the sight of God."

Notice what you think and feel as you read the gospel.

What is dishonest wealth? Reliance on earthly goods, complacency, pride. What are true riches? Utter surrender to God's love and the eternal life he has created us for. Jesus says a person cannot serve God and wealth both. Only one of them will be the master of that person.

Pray as you are led for yourself and others.

"I choose you, Lord. All I have is yours. Purify my heart, strip away my complacencies, that I may serve only you . . ." (Continue in your own words.)

Listen to Jesus.

People have always sought to gain riches, as if somehow that will help them achieve happiness or even eternal life. They acquire sometimes much more than they can spend in a lifetime, and they keep seeking more. Do not fall victim to greed, beloved. Greed makes you a slave. You are free with me. What else is Jesus saying to you?

Ask God to show you how to live today.

"Let me accept the life and work and income you have given me, Lord, and help me rely on your providence. You are my treasure. Our love endures forever. Amen."

Sunday, November 11, 2018
Thirty-Second Sunday in Ordinary Time

Know that God is present and ready to converse.

"Lord, I have much to learn about you. Thank you for being with me now and teaching me by your Word."

Read the gospel: Mark 12:38–44.

As Jesus taught, he said, "Beware of the scribes, who like to walk around in long robes, and to be greeted with respect in the marketplaces, and to have the best seats in the synagogues and places of honor at banquets! They devour widows' houses and for the sake of appearance say long prayers. They will receive the greater condemnation."

He sat down opposite the treasury, and watched the crowd putting money into the treasury. Many rich people put in large sums. A poor widow came and put in two small copper coins, which are worth a penny. Then he called his disciples and said to them, "Truly I tell you, this poor widow has put in more than all those who are contributing to the treasury. For all of them have contributed out of their abundance; but she out of her poverty has put in everything she had, all she had to live on."

Notice what you think and feel as you read the gospel.

Jesus condemns the hypocrisy of the scribes, who take the houses of widows and then make a show of saying long prayers. But he commends the poor widow who gives just two small coins. Her gift is the greatest.

Pray as you are led for yourself and others.

"Jesus, you teach that my attitude toward and handling of money have spiritual significance. Let me not be greedy or stingy, for everything I have is yours . . ." (Continue in your own words.)

Listen to Jesus.

Money is the downfall of many. It hijacks the soul and the spirit of a person. It worries the mind and the heart of a person. It becomes an obsession. What you possess will possess you, stealing all your freedom and peace. What else is Jesus saying to you?

Ask God to show you how to live today.
"Lord, let me heed your words today and cling only to you. Amen."

Monday, November 12, 2018

Know that God is present and ready to converse.
"Jesus, you know the dangers around me. Save me."

Read the gospel: Luke 17:1–6.
Jesus said to his disciples, "Occasions for stumbling are bound to come, but woe to anyone by whom they come! It would be better for you if a millstone were hung around your neck and you were thrown into the sea than for you to cause one of these little ones to stumble. Be on your guard! If another disciple sins, you must rebuke the offender, and if there is repentance, you must forgive. And if the same person sins against you seven times a day, and turns back to you seven times and says, 'I repent,' you must forgive."

The apostles said to the Lord, "Increase our faith!" The Lord replied, "If you had faith the size of a mustard seed, you could say to this mulberry tree, 'Be uprooted and planted in the sea,' and it would obey you."

Notice what you think and feel as you read the gospel.
Knowing human vulnerability to sin, Jesus still holds up the highest standard of behavior. He tells his disciples to forgive unceasingly and to have faith, because there is power in faith.

Pray as you are led for yourself and others.
"Lord, increase my faith and teach me to practice it wisely, that it may bring others to you . . ." (Continue in your own words.)

Listen to Jesus.
Your faith pleases God, beloved. When you know and love God, faith grows. With faith you can accomplish much for the good of others and the glory of God. Start in prayer. What else is Jesus saying to you?

Ask God to show you how to live today.
"Lord, by your grace I will pray in faith today. I will serve you and others in faith. Amen."

Tuesday, November 13, 2018

Know that God is present and ready to converse.

"Jesus Christ, look upon your servant and teach me obedience."

Read the gospel: Luke 17:7–10.

Jesus said to his disciples, "Who among you would say to your slave who has just come in from ploughing or tending sheep in the field, 'Come here at once and take your place at the table'? Would you not rather say to him, 'Prepare supper for me, put on your apron and serve me while I eat and drink; later you may eat and drink'? Do you thank the slave for doing what was commanded? So you also, when you have done all that you were ordered to do, say, 'We are worthless slaves; we have done only what we ought to have done!'"

Notice what you think and feel as you read the gospel.

Jesus expects his disciples to do what they ought to do without expecting special favors or praise.

Pray as you are led for yourself and others.

"Lord, let me do my work, your work, without pride or expectation of rewards. My work now is to pray for those you have given me . . ." (Continue in your own words.)

Listen to Jesus.

Simplicity and humility are royal garments in the kingdom of God, my child, beloved servant. No one can steal your simplicity and humility. Your work will bear much fruit. What else is Jesus saying to you?

Ask God to show you how to live today.

"Lord, I will do my duty today without expectation of reward. I will glory in the greatness of God today. Amen."

Wednesday, November 14, 2018

Know that God is present and ready to converse.

"I come before you today, Lord, to learn from you, to be near you, to please you."

Read the gospel: Luke 17:11–19.

On the way to Jerusalem Jesus was going through the region between Samaria and Galilee. As he entered a village, ten lepers approached him. Keeping their distance, they called out, saying, "Jesus, Master, have mercy on us!" When he saw them, he said to them, "Go and show yourselves to the priests." And as they went, they were made clean. Then one of them, when he saw that he was healed, turned back, praising God with a loud voice. He prostrated himself at Jesus' feet and thanked him. And he was a Samaritan. Then Jesus asked, "Were not ten made clean? But the other nine, where are they? Was none of them found to return and give praise to God except this foreigner?" Then he said to him, "Get up and go on your way; your faith has made you well."

Notice what you think and feel as you read the gospel.

Jesus heals ten lepers, but only one returns to thank him.

Pray as you are led for yourself and others.

"Lord, make me truly thankful for what you have done for me and continue to do for me. I thank you also for these people for whom I pray . . ." (Continue in your own words.)

Listen to Jesus.

Let thankfulness be a large part of your conversation with God, beloved. All good things come to you as free gifts from God. Your life, your loved ones, and all you have come from our Father who loves you. What else is Jesus saying to you?

Ask God to show you how to live today.

"Thank you, Father. I will walk in gratitude today. Thank you. Amen."

Thursday, November 15, 2018

Know that God is present and ready to converse.

"Lord, give me eyes to see and understand the truth of your Word."

Read the gospel: Luke 17:20–25.

Once Jesus was asked by the Pharisees when the kingdom of God was coming, and he answered, "The kingdom of God is not coming with things that can be observed; nor will they say, 'Look, here it is!' or 'There it is!' For, in fact, the kingdom of God is among you."

Then he said to the disciples, "The days are coming when you will long to see one of the days of the Son of Man, and you will not see it.

They will say to you, 'Look there!' or 'Look here!' Do not go, do not set off in pursuit. For as the lightning flashes and lights up the sky from one side to the other, so will the Son of Man be in his day. But first he must endure much suffering and be rejected by this generation."

Notice what you think and feel as you read the gospel.

Jesus says the coming of the kingdom cannot be observed, but is already among us. And when the Son of Man returns it will not be in secret but as observable as lightning flashing in the sky.

Pray as you are led for yourself and others.

"I long for your return, Lord, but until then I will rejoice in your kingdom, present with me even now. I pray for others to come in . . ." (Continue in your own words.)

Listen to Jesus.

The things that are not seen are the true treasures of God. The love between us, dear one, is not visible, but it is real and priceless. Faith, hope, love, peace, thankfulness, joy—these are the invisible treasures of God. I give them to you. What else is Jesus saying to you?

Ask God to show you how to live today.

"Let me love the invisible things of God today, Lord. I am blessed beyond all imagining. Thank you. Amen."

Friday, November 16, 2018

Know that God is present and ready to converse.

"Jesus, you live and you speak to me. I will hear you now."

Read the gospel: Luke 17:26–37.

Jesus said to the disciples, "Just as it was in the days of Noah, so too it will be in the days of the Son of Man. They were eating and drinking, and marrying and being given in marriage, until the day Noah entered the ark, and the flood came and destroyed all of them. Likewise, just as it was in the days of Lot: they were eating and drinking, buying and selling, planting and building, but on the day that Lot left Sodom, it rained fire and sulphur from heaven and destroyed all of them—it will be like that on the day that the Son of Man is revealed. On that day, anyone on the housetop who has belongings in the house must not come down to take them away; and likewise anyone in the field must not turn back.

Remember Lot's wife. Those who try to make their life secure will lose it, but those who lose their life will keep it. I tell you, on that night there will be two in one bed; one will be taken and the other left. There will be two women grinding meal together; one will be taken and the other left." Then they asked him, "Where, Lord?" He said to them, "Where the corpse is, there the vultures will gather."

Notice what you think and feel as you read the gospel.

Jesus speaks of his return at the end of our age. His return will be sudden and unexpected. Those who try to save themselves will lose their lives; those who lose their lives will save them.

Pray as you are led for yourself and others.

"Lord, teach me how to lose my life as you teach. I offer my life and all I am and have for the good of those you have given me . . ." (Continue in your own words.)

Listen to Jesus.

You live in the day to day, but the great day of my return will be like no other. I am coming to gather my own. Watch and pray, servant. What else is Jesus saying to you?

Ask God to show you how to live today.

"I resolve to watch and pray today, ready to let go of my own life so that I may be among those you gather to yourself. Amen."

Saturday, November 17, 2018

Know that God is present and ready to converse.

"Let my prayer come before you, Lord, and let me hear your Word."

Read the gospel: Luke 18:1–8.

Then Jesus told them a parable about their need to pray always and not to lose heart. He said, "In a certain city there was a judge who neither feared God nor had respect for people. In that city there was a widow who kept coming to him and saying, 'Grant me justice against my opponent.' For a while he refused; but later he said to himself, 'Though I have no fear of God and no respect for anyone, yet because this widow keeps bothering me, I will grant her justice, so that she may not wear me out by continually coming.'" And the Lord said, "Listen to what the unjust judge says. And will not God grant justice to his chosen ones who cry to him day and night? Will he delay long in helping them? I tell you, he will quickly grant justice to them. And yet, when the Son of Man comes, will he find faith on earth?"

Notice what you think and feel as you read the gospel.

Jesus teaches persistence in prayer, likening God to a judge and his chosen ones to a widow who continues to appeal to the judge for justice against her opponent. The judge eventually gives in to her just to be free of her. How much more will God grant justice to his chosen ones who cry to him day and night?

Pray as you are led for yourself and others.

"Lord, you are coming to establish justice. I pray that you will find faith on earth when you come . . ." (Continue in your own words.)

Listen to Jesus.

Seeing the great injustices that continue in every community everywhere, you can get discouraged. You can look past injustice and refuse to acknowledge them because of your own helplessness to set them right. Don't give up on justice. Cry to God day and night. I am the just Judge of all, and justice will be done! What else is Jesus saying to you?

Ask God to show you how to live today.

"Lord, how may I work for justice in my own community? Open my eyes, Lord, and show me what to do. Amen."

Sunday, November 18, 2018
Thirty-Third Sunday in Ordinary Time

Know that God is present and ready to converse.

"Lord, you are here with me now. Make me ready to welcome your coming in great power and glory."

Read the gospel: Mark 13:24–32.

Jesus said, "But in those days, after that suffering,

the sun will be darkened,
and the moon will not give its light,
and the stars will be falling from heaven,
and the powers in the heavens will be shaken.

Then they will see 'the Son of Man coming in clouds' with great power and glory. Then he will send out the angels, and gather his elect from the four winds, from the ends of the earth to the ends of heaven.

"From the fig tree learn its lesson: as soon as its branch becomes tender and puts forth its leaves, you know that summer is near. So also, when you see these things taking place, you know that he is near, at the very gates. Truly I tell you, this generation will not pass away until all these things have taken place. Heaven and earth will pass away, but my words will not pass away.

"But about that day or hour no one knows, neither the angels in heaven, nor the Son, but only the Father."

Notice what you think and feel as you read the gospel.

Jesus prophesies his great coming in the clouds to gather the elect. The event will be cosmic with great power and glory. No one knows when this will happen, but there are signs. He has given his word about this, and his word will not pass away. These things will take place.

Pray as you are led for yourself and others.

"Who can be ready for that day, Lord? Prepare us to meet you with joy . . ." (Continue in your own words.)

Listen to Jesus.

Time and history are not an infinite loop, beloved. They begin and end, and all time is in the power of eternal God. Heaven and earth are passing away, but my words will never pass away. Pray for the coming of the kingdom of heaven. What else is Jesus saying to you?

Ask God to show you how to live today.

"Let me live in serious expectation of your coming soon, Lord. What shall I do differently? Amen."

Monday, November 19, 2018

Know that God is present and ready to converse.

"Let my cry come to you, Lord, that you may heal me by your Word."

Read the gospel: Luke 18:35–43.

As Jesus approached Jericho, a blind man was sitting by the roadside begging. When he heard a crowd going by, he asked what was happening. They told him, "Jesus of Nazareth is passing by." Then he shouted,

"Jesus, Son of David, have mercy on me!" Those who were in front sternly ordered him to be quiet; but he shouted even more loudly, "Son of David, have mercy on me!" Jesus stood still and ordered the man to be brought to him; and when he came near, he asked him, "What do you want me to do for you?" He said, "Lord, let me see again." Jesus said to him, "Receive your sight; your faith has saved you." Immediately he regained his sight and followed him, glorifying God; and all the people, when they saw it, praised God.

Notice what you think and feel as you read the gospel.

Jesus hears the cry of the blind beggar, and he heals him. The man immediately follows Jesus, glorifying God. All who see it praise God.

Pray as you are led for yourself and others.

"Jesus, you have particular love for each of us. Let us cry to you in all our needs . . ." (Continue in your own words.)

Listen to Jesus.

How many times have I said, "Your faith has saved you"? Pray in faith, beloved, and I will grant your prayer. Persist in faith and it shall be done for you. Give God the glory. What else is Jesus saying to you?

Ask God to show you how to live today.

"Lord, my faith is often weak. Forgive me. Help me to pray and walk in faith. Amen."

Tuesday, November 20, 2018

Know that God is present and ready to converse.

"I have come seeking you, Lord, and you are already here. Thank you."

Read the gospel: Luke 19:1–10.

Jesus entered Jericho and was passing through it. A man was there named Zacchaeus; he was a chief tax collector and was rich. He was trying to see who Jesus was, but on account of the crowd he could not, because he was short in stature. So he ran ahead and climbed a sycamore tree to see him, because he was going to pass that way. When Jesus came to the place, he looked up and said to him, "Zacchaeus, hurry and come down; for I must stay at your house today." So he hurried down and was happy to welcome him. All who saw it began to grumble and said, "He has gone to be the guest of one who is a sinner." Zacchaeus stood there and said to the Lord, "Look, half of my possessions, Lord, I will give to the poor; and if I have defrauded anyone of anything, I will pay back four times as much." Then Jesus said to him, "Today salvation has come to this house, because he too is a son of Abraham. For the Son of Man came to seek out and to save the lost."

Notice what you think and feel as you read the gospel.

Zacchaeus, a tax collector, tries to see Jesus. Jesus finds him in a tree and invites himself to Zacchaeus's house. Jesus says that salvation has come to that house today, for Zacchaeus was lost in greed, but Jesus comes to seek out and save the lost.

Pray as you are led for yourself and others.

"Lord, let me be changed by you as Zacchaeus is changed. I give myself to you for conversion and salvation. Also these . . ." (Continue in your own words.)

Listen to Jesus.

By my Spirit I am still present to seek and to save the lost. Sinners still repent and make amends. The sick are healed. The redeemed do great acts of love. All acts of love are great. Welcome me into your heart, beloved. What else is Jesus saying to you?

Ask God to show you how to live today.

"I praise you, Lord Jesus, my Savior. Seek me out and stay with me today, every day, all my life. Amen."

Wednesday, November 21, 2018

Know that God is present and ready to converse.

"Lord of Hosts, touch my heart as I encounter you in the Word of God."

Read the gospel: Luke 19:11–28.

As they were listening to this, Jesus went on to tell a parable, because he was near Jerusalem, and because they supposed that the kingdom of God was to appear immediately. So he said, "A nobleman went to a distant country to get royal power for himself and then return. He summoned ten of his slaves, and gave them ten pounds, and said to them, 'Do business with these until I come back.' But the citizens of his country hated him and sent a delegation after him, saying, 'We do not want this man to rule over us.' When he returned, having received royal power, he ordered these slaves, to whom he had given the money, to be summoned so that he might find out what they had gained by trading. The first came forward and said, 'Lord, your pound has made ten more pounds.' He said to him, 'Well done, good slave! Because you have been trustworthy in a very small thing, take charge of ten cities.' Then the second came, saying, 'Lord, your pound has made five pounds.' He said to him, 'And you, rule over five cities.' Then the other came, saying, 'Lord, here is your pound. I wrapped it up in a piece of cloth, for I was afraid of you, because you are a harsh man; you take what you did not deposit, and reap what you did not sow.' He said to him, 'I will judge you by your own words, you wicked slave! You knew, did you, that I was a harsh man, taking what I did not deposit and reaping what I did not sow? Why then did you not put my money into the bank? Then when I returned, I could have collected it with interest.' He said to the bystanders, 'Take the pound from him and give it to the one who has ten pounds.' (And they said to him, 'Lord, he has ten pounds!') 'I tell you, to all those who have, more will be given; but from those who have nothing, even what they have will be taken away. But as for these enemies of mine who did not want me to be king over them—bring them here and slaughter them in my presence.'"

After he had said this, he went on ahead, going up to Jerusalem.

Notice what you think and feel as you read the gospel.

Jesus tells the parable of the ten servants to whom a nobleman gives ten pounds. They are supposed to increase the money through trading. When the man returns, he asks the ten to give an accounting of their gains. Those who have made money receive praise and reward. But one servant hid his pound for fear of the master's harshness. The master rebukes him and gives his pound to the one who has ten.

Pray as you are led for yourself and others.

"Lord, you have given gifts to me. Let me not hold them in fear, but let me use them for the glory of God and the good of others . . ." (Continue in your own words.)

Listen to Jesus.

Do not be afraid, beloved. I love you and care for you. I rejoice when you are brave in my service. Stay close to me and you will do good things. What else is Jesus saying to you?

Ask God to show you how to live today.

"What would you have me do, Lord? How may I use what you have given me for the good of others? Amen."

Thursday, November 22, 2018

Know that God is present and ready to converse.

"Jesus, do not pass me by. I call to you."

Read the gospel: Luke 19:41–44.

As Jesus came near and saw Jerusalem, he wept over it, saying, "If you, even you, had only recognized on this day the things that make for peace! But now they are hidden from your eyes. Indeed, the days will come upon you, when your enemies will set up ramparts around you and surround you, and hem you in on every side. They will crush you to the ground, you and your children within you, and they will not leave within you one stone upon another; because you did not recognize the time of your visitation from God."

Notice what you think and feel as you read the gospel.

Jesus prophesies the destruction of Jerusalem and laments that those who hear him do not recognize that he is the Messiah.

Pray as you are led for yourself and others.

"Jesus, you mourned over Jerusalem, over unbelievers—you want to save everyone, but not everyone will recognize your peace; and to those without peace, destruction will inevitably come. Mercy, Lord, have mercy! Send us your peace . . ." (Continue in your own words.)

Listen to Jesus.

Seek mercy. Seek peace. Bring my peace to the world. I am with you. What else is Jesus saying to you?

Ask God to show you how to live today.

"Jesus, show me the things that make for peace, and let me share them with all I encounter today. Let all I do and say give glory to God. Amen."

Friday, November 23, 2018

Know that God is present and ready to converse.

"Jesus, teach me. Let me love your Word, for it is a lamp to my feet."

Read the gospel: Luke 19:45–48.

Then Jesus entered the temple and began to drive out those who were selling things there; and he said, "It is written,

'My house shall be a house of prayer';
but you have made it a den of robbers."

Every day he was teaching in the temple. The chief priests, the scribes, and the leaders of the people kept looking for a way to kill him; but they did not find anything they could do, for all the people were spellbound by what they heard.

Notice what you think and feel as you read the gospel.

Jesus drives the sellers out of the temple, calling them robbers. He teaches every day in the temple, and though the leaders are looking for a way to kill him, they cannot, because the people are spellbound by Jesus' words.

Pray as you are led for yourself and others.

"I, too, love to hear you, Lord Jesus Christ. You have the words of truth and salvation. Let your Word go forth by the power of your Spirit . . ." (Continue in your own words.)

Listen to Jesus.

Search the scriptures, beloved, and find the riches of God's Word within. These promises are for you. If you want to be happy and good, meditate upon my Word. Listen to me speak through it. Grow in faith, hope, and love. What else is Jesus saying to you?

Ask God to show you how to live today.

"Let my mind be filled with your words, Lord, and let my heart sing for joy that you are with me. Amen."

Saturday, November 24, 2018

Know that God is present and ready to converse.

"Jesus, speak to me and let me receive your truth."

Read the gospel: Luke 20:27–40.

Some Sadducees, those who say there is no resurrection, came to Jesus and asked him a question, "Teacher, Moses wrote for us that if a man's brother dies, leaving a wife but no children, the man shall marry the widow and raise up children for his brother. Now there were seven brothers; the first married, and died childless; then the second and the third married her, and so in the same way all seven died childless. Finally the woman also died. In the resurrection, therefore, whose wife will the woman be? For the seven had married her."

Jesus said to them, "Those who belong to this age marry and are given in marriage; but those who are considered worthy of a place in that age and in the resurrection from the dead neither marry nor are given in marriage. Indeed they cannot die anymore, because they are like angels and are children of God, being children of the resurrection. And the fact that the dead are raised Moses himself showed, in the story about the bush, where he speaks of the Lord as the God of Abraham, the God of Isaac, and the God of Jacob. Now he is God not of the dead, but of the living; for to him all of them are alive." Then some of the scribes answered, "Teacher, you have spoken well." For they no longer dared to ask him another question.

Notice what you think and feel as you read the gospel.

The Sadducees try to trick Jesus into supporting their belief that there is no resurrection of the dead. Jesus sets them straight, saying that the resurrection is not as they imagine. Those in heaven are like angels; they are the children of God, for God is the God of the living, not the dead.

Pray as you are led for yourself and others.

"Lord, let faith in the resurrection of the dead attend me in all I do and think. Let the reality of it sink into me, drawing me closer to you and more faithful in service . . ." (Continue in your own words.)

Listen to Jesus.

I speak often of the kingdom of heaven, but I cannot describe the wonder that awaits you there. I cannot describe it because you cannot receive it or conceive it in your mind. I have promised you eternal life with God, and I will keep that promise. What else is Jesus saying to you?

Ask God to show you how to live today.

"Thank you for your promises, Lord. You are the Way, the Truth, and the Life. I cannot see heaven, but show me how to bring about your kingdom on earth. Amen."

Sunday, November 25, 2018
Christ the King

Know that God is present and ready to converse.

"Jesus, King of Kings, I bow to you. I listen to your voice."

Read the gospel: John 18:33b–37.

Then Pilate entered the headquarters again, summoned Jesus, and asked him, "Are you the King of the Jews?" Jesus answered, "Do you ask this on your own, or did others tell you about me?" Pilate replied, "I am not a Jew, am I? Your own nation and the chief priests have handed you over to me. What have you done?" Jesus answered, "My kingdom is not from this world. If my kingdom were from this world, my followers would be fighting to keep me from being handed over to the Jews. But as it is, my kingdom is not from here." Pilate asked him, "So you are a king?" Jesus answered, "You say that I am a king. For this I was born, and for this I came into the world, to testify to the truth. Everyone who belongs to the truth listens to my voice."

Notice what you think and feel as you read the gospel.

Pilate asks Jesus if he is king of the Jews. Jesus replies by questioning Pilate's motives, and then he goes on to say his kingdom is not of this world. He was born to be king, to testify to the truth. Those who love truth listen to him.

Pray as you are led for yourself and others.

"I ask you to be Lord of my life, Jesus, and Lord of all those I pray for . . ." (Continue in your own words.)

Listen to Jesus.

I spoke the truth, and many would not hear it. I was not rewarded for speaking the truth but tortured and killed. My reward was pleasing my Father. My cross became my glory because it revealed the mercy of God to those who would receive it. What else is Jesus saying to you?

Ask God to show you how to live today.

"Jesus, you reign in glory at the right hand of your Father. Just Judge of all, come quickly. Amen."

Monday, November 26, 2018

Know that God is present and ready to converse.

"How shall I live, Lord? Teach me by your Word."

Read the gospel: Luke 21:1–4.

Jesus looked up and saw rich people putting their gifts into the treasury; he also saw a poor widow put in two small copper coins. He said, "Truly I tell you, this poor widow has put in more than all of them; for all of them have contributed out of their abundance, but she out of her poverty has put in all she had to live on."

Notice what you think and feel as you read the gospel.

When Jesus sees the poor widow put two small copper coins into the treasury, he uses her as an example of true generosity. It's not how much a person gives but the sacrifice the giving entails. By giving even what she has to live on, she shows her trust in God.

Pray as you are led for yourself and others.

"Lord, let me please you by sacrificial generosity. Let me give out of love for others . . ." (Continue in your own words.)

Listen to Jesus.

Your sacrifices can involve many things—your money, your possessions, your time, your work, and your words. You can make your sacrifices in secret, known by God alone. Do it for love, my dear disciple. What else is Jesus saying to you?

Ask God to show you how to live today.

"Let me be bold in faith and trust, Lord, and I will give of myself today. Make it a habit in my life. Thank you. Amen."

Tuesday, November 27, 2018

Know that God is present and ready to converse.

"Teacher, help me understand your purposes for me in my life."

Read the gospel: Luke 21:5–11.

When some were speaking about the temple, how it was adorned with beautiful stones and gifts dedicated to God, Jesus said, "As for these things that you see, the days will come when not one stone will be left upon another; all will be thrown down."

They asked him, "Teacher, when will this be, and what will be the sign that this is about to take place?" And he said, "Beware that you are not led astray; for many will come in my name and say, 'I am he!' and, 'The time is near!' Do not go after them.

"When you hear of wars and insurrections, do not be terrified; for these things must take place first, but the end will not follow immediately." Then he said to them, "Nation will rise against nation, and kingdom against kingdom; there will be great earthquakes, and in various places famines and plagues; and there will be dreadful portents and great signs from heaven."

Notice what you think and feel as you read the gospel.

Jesus speaks of the future destruction of the temple. He warns of false messiahs. Wars and insurrections, earthquakes, famines, and plagues will come before the end. Do not be afraid.

Pray as you are led for yourself and others.

"Lord, terrifying things have come, but the end has not yet come. Let your children be brave and wise, ready for your coming . . ." (Continue in your own words.)

Listen to Jesus.

My own will recognize the signs from heaven. You, my beloved, are safe in me, but pray you will not have to endure the final test. Do not be afraid. What else is Jesus saying to you?

Ask God to show you how to live today.

"Lord, let me soberly watch and pray, for the day is coming, perhaps soon, perhaps not. Keep me in your way. Amen."

Wednesday, November 28, 2018

Know that God is present and ready to converse.

"Lord, prepare me for the end."

Read the gospel: Luke 21:12–19.

Jesus said, "But before all this occurs, they will arrest you and persecute you; they will hand you over to synagogues and prisons, and you will be brought before kings and governors because of my name. This will give you an opportunity to testify. So make up your minds not to prepare your defense in advance; for I will give you words and a wisdom that none of your opponents will be able to withstand or contradict. You will be betrayed even by parents and brothers, by relatives and friends; and they will put some of you to death. You will be hated by all because of my name. But not a hair of your head will perish. By your endurance you will gain your souls."

Notice what you think and feel as you read the gospel.

Jesus speaks of the violence his disciples will experience before the end: persecutions, betrayals, hatred, and death. He will give his followers words and wisdom in their defense. Though they will suffer, by their endurance they will gain their souls.

Pray as you are led for yourself and others.

"Jesus, you yourself endured hatred, betrayal, torture, and death. I offer all to you and ask you to make me worthy of you. I offer what I endure for the good of those you have given me . . ." (Continue in your own words.)

Listen to Jesus.

I will give you power to endure all your suffering, beloved, and through me it will be redemptive. You join in my great salvation, and you increase the numbers in the kingdom of heaven. We share that noble purpose. I am with you. What else is Jesus saying to you?

Ask God to show you how to live today.

"Thank you for your constant companionship, Lord Jesus, Redeemer and King. Whom shall I fear? Amen."

Thursday, November 29, 2018

Know that God is present and ready to converse.

"Lord, I raise my eyes to you. You are my redemption."

Read the gospel: Luke 21:20–28.

Jesus said, "When you see Jerusalem surrounded by armies, then know that its desolation has come near. Then those in Judea must flee to the mountains, and those inside the city must leave it, and those out in the country must not enter it; for these are days of vengeance, as a fulfilment of all that is written. Woe to those who are pregnant and to those who are nursing infants in those days! For there will be great distress on the earth and wrath against this people; they will fall by the edge of the sword and be taken away as captives among all nations; and Jerusalem will be trampled on by the Gentiles, until the times of the Gentiles are fulfilled.

"There will be signs in the sun, the moon, and the stars, and on the earth distress among nations confused by the roaring of the sea and the waves. People will faint from fear and foreboding of what is coming upon the world, for the powers of the heavens will be shaken. Then they will see 'the Son of Man coming in a cloud' with power and great glory. Now when these things begin to take place, stand up and raise your heads, because your redemption is drawing near."

Notice what you think and feel as you read the gospel.

Jesus describes the terror of the final desolation. Violence among people, displacement, war, disruption in the heavens and in the seas. Then we will see the Son of Man coming in a cloud, our Redeemer.

Pray as you are led for yourself and others.

"Lord, you have arranged a happy ending for your children. I pray for those who suffer and who will suffer . . ." (Continue in your own words.)

Listen to Jesus.

The people of the earth have always believed they could save themselves. The progress of humanity is toward self-destruction. I and all the prophets have spoken the truth about the final devastation. I call out to everyone to turn to God now before the terrible days. What else is Jesus saying to you?

Ask God to show you how to live today.

"I come to you, Lord. I will not fear. Let me not falter as I follow you. Amen."

Friday, November 30, 2018
Saint Andrew, Apostle

Know that God is present and ready to converse.

"Jesus, you call. I hear you and follow you."

Read the gospel: Matthew 4:18–22.

As he walked by the Sea of Galilee, he saw two brothers, Simon, who is called Peter, and Andrew his brother, casting a net into the lake—for they were fishermen. And he said to them, "Follow me, and I will make you fish for people." Immediately they left their nets and followed him. As he went from there, he saw two other brothers, James son of Zebedee and his brother John, in the boat with their father Zebedee, mending their nets, and he called them. Immediately they left the boat and their father, and followed him.

Notice what you think and feel as you read the gospel.

Jesus calls two pairs of brothers from their fishing to follow him. They do so immediately. What drew them?

Pray as you are led for yourself and others.

"What draws me to you, Jesus? How may I obey you and follow you closely? . . ." (Continue in your own words.)

Listen to Jesus.

You follow me well because you love me well. I am the Holy One of God, and I make you a child of my Father. I speak to you the truth. I give you the power and joy of my Holy Spirit. Follow me and fish for people. What else is Jesus saying to you?

Ask God to show you how to live today.

"Lord, I would love to be used by you to draw people into your kingdom. Work with me today. Amen."

Saturday, December 1, 2018

Know that God is present and ready to converse.

"Lord, I seek to be alert to you. I will hear your Word."

Read the gospel: Luke 21:34–36.

Jesus said, "Be on guard so that your hearts are not weighed down with dissipation and drunkenness and the worries of this life, and that day does not catch you unexpectedly, like a trap. For it will come upon all who live on the face of the whole earth. Be alert at all times, praying that you may have the strength to escape all these things that will take place, and to stand before the Son of Man."

Notice what you think and feel as you read the gospel.

Jesus warns his followers of dissipation, drunkenness, and the worries of this life. He urges readiness for the end and prayer, for we will all stand before the Son of Man.

Pray as you are led for yourself and others.

"Lord, help me to grasp the dangers of the judgment. I pray for myself and for all those you have given me; help us to stand before you . . ." (Continue in your own words.)

Listen to Jesus.

People bring judgment and condemnation upon themselves. They choose what they receive. I bring life and salvation. Choose me. I am the Good Shepherd. What else is Jesus saying to you?

Ask God to show you how to live today.

"Lord, I choose you today. Let me follow you faithfully all my life. Amen."

The SACRED READING Series

Inspired by the traditions of Ignatian spirituality, the Sacred Reading series by the Apostleship of Prayer—an international Jesuit prayer ministry—is a unique guide to the use of lectio divinia through a simple, six-step process that provides a prayerful and imaginative exploration of the daily gospel readings and helps readers look for application in their own lives.

Ignatian Spirituality for Every Season

Find next year's editions wherever books and eBooks are sold.
For more information, **visit avemariapress.com.**

The Apostleship of Prayer (The Pope's Worldwide Prayer Network) is an international pontifical prayer ministry served by the Jesuits that reaches more than 35 million members worldwide through its popular website, ApostleshipofPrayer.org, and through talks, conferences, publications, and retreats. The Apostleship's mission is to encourage Christians to make a daily offering of themselves to God in union with the Sacred Heart of Jesus.

Douglas Leonard, who compiles Sacred Reading, served as the executive director of the Apostleship of Prayer in the United States from 2006 to 2016. He earned a bachelor's degree in English in 1976, a master's degree in English in 1977, and a PhD in English in 1981, all from the University of Wisconsin–Madison. Leonard also has served in higher education, professional development, publishing, and instructional design as an executive, writer, editor, educator, and consultant.